GAY POLITICS, URBAN POLITICS

D1506614

POWER, CONFLICT, AND DEMOCRACY:
AMERICAN POLITICS INTO THE TWENTY-FIRST CENTURY
ROBERT Y. SHAPIRO, EDITOR

Power, Conflict, and Democracy:
American Politics into the Twenty-first Century
Robert Y. Shapiro, Editor

This series focuses on how the will of the people and the public interest are promoted, encouraged, or thwarted. It aims to question not only the direction American politics will take as it enters the twenty-first century but also the direction American politics has already taken.

The series addresses the role of interest groups and social and political movements; openness in American politics; important developments in institutions such as the executive, legislative, and judicial branches at all levels of government as well as the bureaucracies thus created; the changing behavior of politicians and political parties; the role of public opinion; and the functioning of mass media. Because problems drive politics, the series also examines important policy issues in both domestic and foreign affairs.

The series welcomes all theoretical perspectives, methodologies, and types of evidence that answer important questions about trends in American politics.

JOHN G. GEER, *From Tea Leaves to Opinion Polls: A Theory of Democratic Leadership*

KIM FRIDKIN KAHN, *The Political Consequences of Being a Woman: How Stereotypes Influence the Conduct and Consequences of Political Campaigns*

KELLY D. PATTERSON, *Political Parties and the Maintenance of Liberal Democracy*

DONA COOPER HAMILTON AND CHARLES V. HAMILTON, *The Dual Agenda: Race and Social Welfare Policies of Civil Rights Organizations*

HANES WALTON, JR., *African-American Power and Politics: The Political Context Variable*

AMY FRIED, *Muffled Echoes: Oliver North and the Politics of Public Opinion*

RONALD T. LIBBY, *ECO-WARS: Political Campaigns and Social Movements*

GAY POLITICS, URBAN POLITICS

Identity and Economics in the Urban Setting

Robert W. Bailey

COLUMBIA UNIVERSITY PRESS

NEW YORK

Columbia University Press
Publishers Since 1893
New York   Chichester, West Sussex

Copyright © 1999 Columbia University Press
All rights reserved

Library of Congress Cataloging-in-Publication Data
Bailey, Robert W., 1957–
Gay politics, urban politics : identity and economics in the urban
setting / Robert W. Bailey
p.   cm. — (Power, conflict, and democracy)
Includes bibliographical references and index.
ISBN 0-231-09662-3 (alk. paper). — ISBN 0-231-09663-1 (alk. paper)
1. Gays—United States—Political activity. 2. Gays—United
States—Identity. 3. Municipal government—United States. 4. Group
identity—Political aspects—United States. I. Title. II. Series.
HQ76.3.U5B35   1998
305.38'664—dc21   98-22051

Casebound editions of Columbia University Press books are
printed on permanent and durable acid-free paper.
Printed in the United States of America
c 10 9 8 7 6 5 4 3 2 1
p 10 9 8 7 6 5 4 3 2 1

Contents

Preface

This book has three purposes. First, it assesses the social and political impact of lesbians and gay men on urban America, a subject that has largely been ignored by political scientists. The struggle toward self-empowerment by lesbians and gay men has been one of the most compelling stories in American urban politics over the past three decades. It has contributed to change in the political language of our cities, influenced electoral coalitions, altered public policy, and introduced its values and vocabulary into the social organization of urban governance. Although these effects have been most conspicuous in New York and San Francisco, they now are evident in most large and medium-size cities of the United States.

Second, this book attempts, as older empiricists might have said, to "operationalize identity." What are the specific characteristics of the category "identity," and how does this category differ from the interest groups or pure economic models that now dominate discussions of public policy-making in our cities? Some political scientists have explored many of these issues in the framework of comparative politics, but few American urbanists have explored identity in our cities. Anyone who has ever driven up Shankhill Road in Belfast or walked through the streets of Old Jerusalem or from the French to the Anglo sections of Montreal knows implicitly that identity politics is a factor—in some cases the dominant factor—in urban politics. Americans have often tried either to subsume identity under the category of "ethnic politics" or to equate it with racial politics. But the women's movement, the gay rights movement, and, increasingly, American Islam no longer allow us to relegate the complexity of urban politics to euphemisms of the past. It may be true that no American city will ever reach the point of a divided and then reunited Jerusalem, but the analogy differs only in degree, not type.

Third, I use an identity approach to urban politics, but my intent is not to trivialize or dismiss economic arguments for explaining urban political phenomena. Although the underlying precepts of urban economism clash with the underpinnings of identity theory—differences that go to the heart of why the economic approach has relegated identity politics to a minor role in its view of the urban polity—I do not see them as mutually exclusive. Indeed, economism has helped explain much in regard to urban fiscal and development policy. Accordingly, I see the category identity as a bounding axiom on the utility of economism to explain urban political phenomena, and economics as a bounding axiom on the usefulness of identity to explain urban political phenomena. My task is thus to find metaphors—modes of comprehending phenomena—in which identity and economics complement each other.

Toward these goals I have used a multimethod approach that combines theory, the analysis of aggregate data, and the exploration of specific case studies of policymaking. In the descriptive chapters, largely chapters 4 to 10, I have used theory to illuminate specific issues. It is in the three introductory and the final two chapters that I sacrifice the integrity of case and data analysis to more formal theoretical structuring.

A Note on Aggregate Data

The analysis in chapters 4 through 6 rely on aggregate data, most of which are from nontraditional sources. They include professional marketing data, commercial exit-poll data, and information compiled by local political activists and consultants from around the country. The most important data sources are the national and local exit polls conducted by Voter Research and Surveys/Voter News Service—the consortium organization of the major television networks and the Associated Press—as well as data from the exit polls of the *Los Angeles Times* and from David Binder, Research of San Francisco. In reporting analyses of these data, I will often present results in a form that includes tenths of a percent. This reporting is meant to reflect simple "snapshots" of one data set at one time and should not lead the reader to impute a degree of accuracy beyond the standard margins of error associated with the number of cases available in each analysis. In most situations, the "n" is noted either as a footnote or in the text and should be taken into acount when assessing the reliability of results. In addition, I used the national "community mailing list" of Strubco, Inc., a direct-marketing firm based in New York City. Because these data are from various sources and their authors used different methods in obtaining them, there have been some minor problems in making them compatible. Still, this is an advance over our present knowledge, since there are no data from the more traditional sources in academic political science.

A Note on Policy Cases

Fieldwork was another important source of information for this book. All the policy case studies are based on interviews, documents, newspaper files, and the academic literature on policymaking in those cities and on the specific policy subject chosen for analysis. The four cases were not chosen for easy comparative analysis but, rather, for the specific subjects of politics and policymaking. Thus the social organization of identity for political effect, the interaction of identity theory and representation theory, and regime theory and identity theory are the actual subjects of the chapters. These are not meant to be comparative but instead have two other purposes: first, to explore the category identity within the urban setting and, second, to discover the degree to which sexual identity has altered the discourses, processes, and social organization of governance in specific cities. The result is not a set of firm conclusions based on tightly drawn comparative cases but, rather, a picture of how sexual identity has challenged several cities' traditional governance patterns.

Acknowledgments

Writing this book has been a protracted effort in which I incurred many debts along the way. I could not have completed the task without the assistance of dozens, even scores, of others. I am grateful to all the activists, journalists, and scholars with whom I have talked over the past seven years about gay politics, urban politics, and the overlap of the two. I was given a great deal of access to movement groups around the country, had informal conversations with many writers for lesbian and gay newspapers and journals, and informally discussed the role of identity politics in American cities with colleagues at universities around the country. Although I cannot list everyone who has made some unknowing contribution to this volume, I shall try to acknowledge some of them.

First, I'd like to thank members of the Lesbian, Gay and Bisexual Caucus of the American Political Science Association. Many parts of this book were presented in several papers at venues established by the caucus. The criticism and, most important, the support offered by caucus members were invaluable in formulating approaches and conclusions and in sustaining technical accuracy when dealing with new data sources. I would especially like to thank the members of the caucus primarily identified as theorists: Mark Blasius, Shane Phelan, Martha Ackelsburg, Joan Tronto, Michael Melody, and Jackie Stevens. One of the truly positive aspects of the caucus is that people inclined toward empirical and behavioral work have been able to have an open discourse with sympathetic theorists. The result has been an opportunity to reexamine the assumptions underlying the methodologies of voting and policy studies through the work of identity and queer theory. The result, I think, is a more credible approach to empirical material.

The analysis of data would have been impossible without the cooperation of many people. For over a decade, Murray Edelman of Voter News

Service (VNS) has been a consistent source of data, criticism, support, and suggestions. First at CBS News, Voter Research and Surveys, and now VNS, Edelman has been the prime mover in including gay and lesbian self-identifiers on national and local exit polls. A generation of political scientists and sociologists will use these data sets to examine voting patterns and political attitudes among lesbians and gay men. In addition, the assistance offered by the staff at VNS, especially LeeC Shapiro, has been invaluable. The late John Brennan, first at ABC News and later at the *Los Angeles Times*, created a valuable second series of data sets containing lesbian and gay identifiers. He, too, is an unsung hero of the study of lesbian and gay political attitudes. Doug Muzzio, a frequent elections consultant to ABC News and a friend, made data available from ABC in the early stages of this project, and I am grateful to him. The staff of the *Los Angeles Times* poll offered occasional but important assistance in interpreting and documenting their exit-poll results. In addition, I would also like to thank Gregory Haley, director of the EDS Lab at Columbia University, and Scott Bilder, of Rutgers University Computer Services, for their assistance in securing other data sets and documentation.

Data of a different kind were made available by Sean Strub. In 1990, Sean and Daniel Baker of Strubco allowed a complete run of their community mailing list for New York City to be analyzed. Strub later supplied a complete run of his national list, broken out by ZIP code, which we then merged with extract files from the 1990 census and reformatted for GIS systems compatibility. Chapter 4 would not have been possible without the assistance of Sean Strub, Dan Baker, and the Strubco staff. Russ Campbell, a research assistant at Rutgers and now working at Chilton, conducted much of the reformatting work necessary to make the Strubco data usable for GIS. Thomas Mills, M.D., consultant to the University of California, San Francisco, Community AIDS Prevention program, shared the results of CAP's effort to map HIV transmission episodes among men who have sex with men in urban America. The work of CAP was a valuable corroboration of and check on the results offered here. In addition, Jerry Lee Kramer of the University of Minnesota shared his work mapping the residential patterns of gay men and lesbians in the Twin Cities. It was used as a check on the reliability of the dimensions used here.

At various stages, the central quantitative chapters were reviewed by several persons who offered constructive comments. Lawrence Knopp and Karen Murphy saw early drafts of chapter 4 and challenged some of the assumptions underlying them. Kenneth Sherrill commented on a paper drawn from chapter 5, and Kathy Frankovich and Michael Della Carpini offered important criticisms of chapters 5 and 6. Della Carpini and Sherrill were especially helpful in forcing me to reexamine the role of generational cohorts and ideology on the formation of political identity among lesbians and gay men. Frankovich warned against reading too much into one exit-poll data set.

In the case chapters also, many people were critical to obtaining data, offering background information, or sitting for interviews. Professor Genie Stowers first suggested looking into how gay men and lesbians sustained their community in Birmingham, Alabama. It was a wise suggestion. Professor Steven Haeberle of the University of Alabama, Birmingham, helped me set up interviews and guided me through the politics of Birmingham. Several individuals spent long periods with me, including Allen Francis, Dennis Luft, Rick Adams, Patrick Cather, David White, June Holloway, and Bob Burns, as well as several women from the Tuscaloosa Lesbian Coalition (TLC). Professor Edward LaMonte of Birmingham-Southern University, who had also served as a senior adviser to Mayor Richard Arrington, was especially helpful on the history of electoral politics and governmental reform in Birmingham. I am grateful also to Patricia Todd, who made available her master's thesis on Birmingham AIDS Outreach, and to the staff of the Birmingham Public Library, who assisted in obtaining voting records and newspaper files.

For the chapter on districting in New York City, I had the advantage of being a participant-observer in the creation of the first "post-*Morris*" City Council districting plan. I'd like to thank the entire staff of the New York City Districting Commission who were open to my inquiries at the time and especially to Alan Gartner, executive director of the staff, who made available to me his own history of decision making at the commission. In addition, members of the Gay and Lesbian Independent Democrats (Manhattan) and Lambda Independent Democrats (Brooklyn) offered information and assistance, as did the staffs of FAIRPAC/Empire State Pride Agenda, especially Candida Scott Piel and Lisa Parrish. Frank Macchiarola, chair of the commission, and Professor Joseph Viteritti offered valuable suggestions on the text of the chapter. Similarly, many people in Philadelphia assisted in providing documents, perspectives, and background information on the development of police reform and police–gay community relations in Philadelphia. I am especially grateful to Thomas Gibbons Jr., Rita Addessa, Larry Gross, Mark Segal, Susan Vasbinder, Tommi Avicolla-Mecca, Stephen Presser, and Jack Greene, who sat for interviews and/or provided documents and background information. Edward Harris of the Municipal Police Academy, Montgomery County Community College, arranged for me to conduct one of the diversity sessions at the Philadelphia Police Academy—an experience that allowed for a personal assessment of recruits' responses to curricular materials. I'd especially like to thank Lieutenant Donald Jirak of the New York Police Department, who guided me through many of the issues of police training, especially as it relates to lesbians and gay men.

In San Francisco, David Binder made a critical contribution to the analysis of gay and lesbian voting in referenda by making available some of his own data from exit polls and several phone polls conducted in the late 1980s and early 1990s. This material would not generally be available through ICPSR or the Roper Center, and I am grateful to him for his help. In addition, Richard DeLeon made available to me raw data from the State of the City poll conducted at the San Francisco State University Social Science lab. David Kirp was especially helpful in conceptualizing the chapter as a whole and the education and domestic partnership sections in particular. Both David Thomas and Lincoln Mitchell were valuable academic guides to the politics of San Francisco. Corey Busch, Melinda Paras, Larry Bush, T. J. Anthony, Dick Pabich, the former mayor Art Agnos, Myra Kopf, Tom Ammiano, Kevin Gogin, and Wayne Friday sat for interviews (in Ammiano's case, by phone), and I am thankful to each.

For several years now, Bob Shapiro of Columbia University has been a source of academic and moral support. He reviewed and commented on early drafts of the theoretical and quantitative chapters and surely made the book a better one as a whole. More important, early on he recognized the potential value of this project, and I am grateful to him for that. Hank Savitch and especially Paul Kantor were present at both the beginning and the end. Kantor's comments on a late draft were especially helpful. I also had the advantage of relying on the (as yet) unpublished work of several graduate students. Mark Stein's dissertation "City of Brotherly and Sisterly Love" was used as a critical source of background for the chapter on Philadelphia. His thesis in revised format is to be published by the University of Chicago Press. Similarly, the work of historian John Howard was valuable in obtaining insights into the history of lesbians and gay men in the urban South—including Birmingham, Alabama. When his project is completed,

Howard will have made a major contribution to American gay studies. I also had the benefit of many discussions of quantitative analysis as it relates to sexual identity issues with Doug Strand of the University of California, Berkeley, Ph.D. program in political science and Alan Yang of the Columbia University program, and Dalton Conley, now on the faculty of Yale University. In addition, I received important suggestions and moral support from the Gay/Lesbian Study Group on working-class issues, organized by Alan Berube through the Center for Gay and Lesbian Studies at the CUNY Graduate Center.

Needless to say, even though all these people helped in this effort, none is responsible for errors in fact or analysis. I claim those for myself.

Throughout my writing, John Michel of Columbia University Press has been a patient and supportive editor. It was through his encouragement that I went down this road—a more troubled road than I imagine he expected. My colleagues at the Graduate Public Policy faculty at Rutgers University, Camden, were encouraging throughout the ordeal, as was Robert Crain of Teachers College. Many friends—especially Gerry Robinson, Laura Morrison, and Phil Ryan, among others—helped ease the way. On a quite personal note, I'd also like to thank Daniel Jennings and Stephen Weiss of New York University and Dr. Mitchell Kahn for their support. Finally, Brian O'Dell, my companion of a decade or so, sat endlessly waiting for the completion of this project. It is now done.

⋮⋮⋮

In Memoriam

This book was written in memory of friends lost to happenstance and indifference, each of whom suffered from some sort of neglect from those whom life usually binds to an obligation of assistance and each of whom found a measure of courage that even society's designated defenders do not routinely display these days.

On this day, I remember Jeff Dunn, Philip Gregory, Ralph Artino, T. R. Witomski, Frank Kelly, Ronald Fox, and Patrick Regan . . . and many, many others.

RWB, October 1998, New York City

What is the real condition of this group of human beings?
Of whom is it composed, what sub-groups and classes exist,
what sort of individuals are being considered?
. . . the student must clearly recognize that a complete
study must not confine itself to the group, but must specially
notice the environment; the physical environment of the city,
sections and houses, the far mightier social environment—
the surrounding world of custom, wish, whim and thought
which envelops this group and powerfully influences its
social development.

W. E. B. DuBois, *The Philadelphia Negro*

PART I

⁘

Sexual Identity and Urban Politics

⁖

CHAPTER I

Lesbian and Gay Politics in the Urban Setting

Despite the important legal and legislative changes made at the national and state levels, the lesbian and gay rights movement has made its most dramatic political impact in the cities. Although the debates over homosexuality in family law or in the military may have the broadest social effect as the various challenges and appeals now pending move through the federal court system will have taken effect, it is in the cities where change is most evident. The evolution of state case law on employee protections, the status of sodomy laws, and the regulation of sexuality through public health codes also are critical, as is the legal battle over state referenda barring the passage of local ordinances offering gay men and lesbians protections in housing and employment. The transformation in cultural expression by writers, filmmakers, and other artists has also helped change the language of social and political discourse.

But the change most apparent to people who are neither lesbian nor gay is the open presence of communities identified by sexual identity in the urban setting. Among those groups replacing the white middle class as it moved to the suburbs of America were gay men and lesbians. They helped revitalize many central city neighborhoods and sometimes came into conflict with urban groups—blacks and Latinos especially—who were left behind in the exodus of the 1960s and 1970s. Gay men and lesbians regarded these neighborhoods as safe spaces to affirm their emerging identity and eventually as bases for political mobilization and influence.

Lesbians and gay men, like many others, moved into the city partly because new opportunities were being created by the changing urban economies and partly because their skills had become more valued in this new economy. The impact of their identity movement centered on same-sex sex-

uality reaches beyond economic factors, however. Rather than purely economic gain, these urban residents sought both an affirmation of their identity and a sense of community.[1]

That the gay communities of the United States have affected local politics and public policy seems irrefutable. More than 135 cities or counties
have passed local ordinances that provide some sanction against those who
discriminate on the basis of sexual orientation, and the number of such ordinances is growing.[2] Openly gay mayors and members of city and county councils have been elected in urban regions from Melbourne, Iowa, to
Dallas, Texas. Openly lesbian and gay school board members have been
elected or appointed. Urban districts have sent openly gay representatives
to state legislatures, and more and more states have passed legal prohibi-
tions against discrimination based on sexual orientation. Indeed, the gay
rights movement has had a sustained impact on every aspect of American
city government.

The dominant school of urban politics since the mid-1970s, sometimes
referred to as *urban economism*,[3] has little to say about the political effects
of sexual identity—indeed, most identity movements—because the underlying assumptions of the economism approach to urban political phenomena minimize noneconomic motivations in politics. But the political mobilization of urban gay men and lesbians is not predicated solely on market
criteria or the kind of resource distribution that dominates much of interest-group politics. The goals of identity politics also cannot be reduced to
the kind of mini–max solution of a preference–payoff calculus associated
with rational-choice theory, since identity politics does not assume the single rational actor that choice theorists posit as a given. Instead, more than
economic gain or even rational calculation, affirmation is the centerpiece of
identity politics. That is, the *deep agenda* for the movement is the *affirmation* of its *identity*, both collectively and individually.

The central task of this book is to assess the political impact of the lesbian
and gay movement on urban politics in the United States. Like those of past
social movements, its effects are both multifaceted and tentative, with conflict evident on many fronts.

The second goal is to explore the usefulness of the category "identity"
in urban political studies. Can identity explain certain effects or set limits on the dominant organizing themes of contemporary urban political
science?

The Status of Sexual Identity in American Political Studies

The political study of gay men and lesbians did not start in mainstream political science but at the political peripheries of psychoanalysis, sociology, and historiography. In these other disciplines, "politics" was usually seen as conflict over the redefinition and reorganization of important analytical categories. In psychology and psychoanalysis, politics was implicitly identified with conflict over the sexual and identity overtones of the central psychoanalytic metaphors. Critiquing those categories and eventually withdrawing professional authority from the medicalization of homosexual behavior were the final outcomes of this collective and professional self-reflection. Sociologists drew on the intellectual strength of the critical tradition and of social constructionism, sometimes combining the two and viewing the emergence of lesbian and gay social movements as outgrowths of larger forces of social change.[4] Historians relied on techniques of social history, social construction theory, or both to trace the cultural expression of homosexual men and women over time.[5] Much of this work was therefore less about politics than about being political: it was an attempt to integrate a previously marginalized group of men and women into social analysis by reorganizing the categories of the social and psychological professions.

Outside academia, there have been advances in the study of gay and lesbian politics by practitioner demographers and social analysts. In the analysis of voting behavior, in residential and development patterns, in the districting of city councils, and in marketing research, the category "sexual orientation" is typically defined in the most economical and usable ways available to those conducting the surveys. Only a few are randomly generated samples, and many are required to rely on clusters of surrogate variables rather than direct measures of behavior.

It is not surprising, then, that when political scientists did begin incorporating differences in sexuality into their analysis, they did so through the most mainstream of methods: interest-group analysis and voting behavior. More recently, sexual identity and the gay rights movement have been housed in the "new social movements" literature or as an expression of the "values shift" evident in postindustrial (postmaterial?) societies.

Interest-Group Analysis

Looking at the gay communities as a set of interest groups is attractive, for in many ways, the techniques of organization—such as political action

committees, national and state lobbying organizations, electoral campaigns, and voter registration programs—are similar to those of other interest groups. Indeed, when political science began to address gay or lesbian
concerns, interest-group formation and confrontational motifs dominated
the analysis.[6] John D'Emilio's history of the gay rights movement could
thus be the history of nearly any other group's struggle over identity and
self-confidence, organizational sophistication, and political effectiveness—
interest-group formation as bildungsroman. Australian political scientist
Dennis Altman saw the growing network of community-based gay organizations as preparatory to the formation of more effective HIV-related
groups and organizations that followed in the mid-1980s and that could be
seen as interest groups. Altman argued that public policy regarding HIV is
directly related to the advancement of the gay rights position:

> The point has often been made that the epidemiology of AIDS would have
> been very different in most western countries had it not been for the expansion
> of gay sexual networks in the 1970s. Equally, the response of governments would
> have been very different—and almost certainly slower and more repressive—had
> not this expansion also been accompanied by the growth of gay political organi-
> zations which provided a basis for the development of community-based groups
> in response to the epidemic.[7]

Altman's use of the most centrist modes of process analysis focused on
the effect of an emerging interest group. By the mid-1980s, the lesbian and
gay community was an important (and legitimated) influence in policymaking regarding HIV and HIV-spectrum diseases in most major American cities. Leaders of ACT-UP were dealing directly with policymakers at
the Food and Drug Administration and the Centers for Disease Control.

Common as interest-group analysis is to American political science, especially to urban politics, its application to the study of sexual identity is
limited. Group analysts understand the economic and social dynamics of
interest-group formation but remain weak on its psychological aspects, frequently forcing researchers to rely on the groups' own definitions.

Maybe unintentionally, many writers began to use "ethnic-group" methods to study lesbian and gay coalition activity, since they seemed to mimic
ethnic-group strategies, especially at the urban level. But an identity group's
social and economic grounding is not always clear to "outside" researchers
relying on purely analytical means to define its boundaries. Even when this
method is applied to gay politics, the social scientist's definition of the

group(s) cannot escape the issues of formation of the identity itself. In the wide range of identity politics, therefore, interest-group analysis needs to be expanded and tempered—maybe replaced—by the cultural and psychological aspects of identity.

The Variable "Gay and Lesbian" in Public Opinion and Voting Studies

A second major area in which the category "gay and lesbian" has begun to be incorporated into behavioral political studies is in voting behavior and public opinion. Although changes are being made, the category gay and lesbian has not yet been incorporated into the fundamental data streams generated by professional political science. Even in the late 1980s, neither the American National Election Study (NES) data sets at the University of Michigan nor the General Social Survey at the National Opinion Research Center (NORC) collected many usable data to examine lesbians' and gay men's actual political behavior and opinion. Rather, in the NES surveys, most indicators referring to gays or lesbians pertained to the public's attitudes toward gay men and lesbians (or, more accurately, toward homosexuality); toward them as citizens, individuals, and organizations; and toward their policy positions or political actions, sexual acts, and influence as a collective. In addition, using data from public opinion and survey research methods, a number of scholars have looked at the political impact of lesbian and gay mobilization as well as the resulting opposition of religiously affiliated social conservative movements.

Not until 1988 did NORC include indicators that could be used to identify a gay and lesbian sample within the General Social Survey. The indicator was included in part to generate information for a national survey (conducted through the University of Chicago) on sexual practices, and it has been less useful in linking political activity with sexual behavior or identity. The U.S. Census Bureau is also not a useful alternative, as it did not ask the sexual identity of citizens in its decennial census, although this is also true of other important sociopolitical indicators such as religious tradition or identity. In fact, until 1990, most gay men, lesbians, or bisexuals might have preferred not to answer such questions in any official government survey, with the current relative openness itself an indication of social change. The 1990 housing survey portions of the census does give some indirect indication of committed same-sex couple households, but the sample was small and did not include lesbians and gay men living with parents, non-couple roommates, and, most important, single-person households, the category, according to other surveys, in which gay men and lesbians are disproportionately represented.

Political analysts of electoral projections have fared better. In 1981, working for WCBS-TV in New York, the CBS News polling unit included as an experiment a reference to sexual orientation on its New York City Mayoral Democratic Primary exit-poll data collection sheets. In 1984, CBS again introduced a gay and lesbian measure into its "grab bag" list of miscellaneous demographics for the national election process, but only in the New York and California state Democratic primaries. The number of respondents was quite low, however, and the sexual identity variable did not significantly help explain voter choices. In 1988, both ABC and CBS included a gay and lesbian self-identifier on some of its Democratic presidential primary exit polls. Again, n was small but sufficient for some analysis.[8] By 1990, for the first time, CBS and Voter Research and Surveys—the consortium of CBS, NBC, ABC, and CNN—included a gay and lesbian indicator on the national congressional elections data sheet. These data sets have been an important source of information for some analysts, and the urban samples from these exit polls are used extensively in chapters 5 and 6.

Social Theory, "Culture Shifts," and the New Social Movements (NSMs)

Social theorists in North America and Europe have struggled to give meaning and structure to the emergence of what have come to be called the *new social movements* (NSMs). Writers variously refer to them as including the gays rights movement, the "Greens," regional movements (Scots, Basques, etc.), worker movements that demand participatory management, feminism, and European Islam. The movements are new in that they do not fit easily into the more traditional political borders of European class politics. Nevertheless, in Western Europe and North America, their occurrence is associated with developments in late capitalism, preceded by the emergence of postindustrial economic forms and paralleling the development of postmodern political theory. All these shifts preceded or accompanied the movements for liberalization in Eastern Europe and the eventual dissolution of the Soviet Union and its dominance in Central and Eastern Europe.

Marxists saw the emergence of the "new" social movements as a new moment in Marxist thought. The de-centering of the class-based struggle for liberation and its devolution into splinter movements advancing the seemingly fragmented consequences of capitalism's political dominance—pollution, sexism, sexual repression, state dominance of minority interests and identities, and so forth—are challenging the more traditional European Marxist ideas of the immediate post–World War II period. To these Marxist writers, the NSMs are diversions from the main goal of seizing state power or even from the dream of class solidarity.

Those writing in a more Weberian tradition see the new social movements as an outgrowth explained largely (though not exclusively) through modernization. Schmitt-Beck categorizes the explanations for the emergence of the NSMs as a political expression of a "crisis in modernity." He offers four explanations for the German context: the resistance of individuals to the expansion of the public realm into private life; the increasing risks of technology development: the nuclear industries, including nuclear weapons, specialty chemicals, and the pollution tied to them; the rise of the new middle class linked to advanced business services, personal services, and the "intellectuals of the humanities and social scientists"; and, finally, the need of new groups to use alternative techniques of participation—protest, media events, direct mail—as state and private bureaucracies are dominated by the "iron triangle" of older interest groups.[9]

In France, the theoretical background is more semiologic, poststructural, and postmodern, drawing much of its inspiration from the new left and from the tradition of French social thought from Rousseau through Sorel, de Saussure, Barthes, de Beauvoir, and Lyontard. Attention is focused on language, symbols, psychoanalytic categories, and culture in general. The deconstruction of those theoretical constructs most closely associated with power and legitimacy in the West—medicine, family, state, behavioral science, and science itself—became the center of a new stage of understanding. Bourdieu and Foucault, of course, have been the principal figures, with Foucault especially important to the analysis of sex, its regulation by the state, and the formation of sexual identity.[10]

These traditions are considerably weaker in the American context. Here, analysts have concentrated on more organizational approaches to the new social movements, seeing them less as questions of identity than of networks of communication, organizational competencies, and the mobilization of resources. Where the new social movements have influenced American social science is in the reinvigoration of values and culture as important influences on politics.

Some of the NSMs' achievements are ascribed to a lowered concern for material matters, since abundance has removed a major driving force in social relations. The new economic forms have led, in turn, to greater attention to the psychological and social aspects of society and politics. Ronald Inglehart led this trend in his analysis of a culture shift in the postindustrial and the postmaterialist societies throughout the West and elsewhere. In his *Culture Shift*, Ingelhart speaks of homosexual men and women as being more "tolerated" by a new generation more involved with personal freedom and affirmation of diversity.[11] Even after taking into account life cycles and the assumption that the young of every generation are more tolerant, he and Abramson concluded that the young of today are much more tolerant than were the young of yesterday, proving that the shift in cultural values has had a positive effect on attitudes toward homosexuals.[12]

Little of the literature on the new social movements deals directly with the lesbian and gay rights movement. Except for those scholars familiar with "queer culture" and the debates within the gay community over tactics as aspects of postmodern social expression, the new social movement literature reads as if the gay rights movement were almost an afterthought. Nor does the "culture shift" argument really address the dynamics of the movement, although certainly the "resource mobilization" perspective on the NSMs is useful. In short, in political science, the formal study of a lesbian and gay sexual identity movement has only just begun.

Identity and Economics in the City

Throughout this book, I contrast identity theory and urban economism partly to highlight the differences in theory and partly because they conflict in the real politics of everyday life. Although identity theory has a strong and controversial tradition in women's studies and has heavily influenced the study of comparative and international politics, its application to urban politics has been limited.[13] Here I am using "identity" as described in comparative politics, postmodern political theory, and social organization theory as an alternative narrative to the political–economic "metaphor" common in urban political analysis today.[14]

As a category for use in politics, a more appropriate subject is not "identity" as such but the "problematic of identity"—the ongoing dialogue between the changing individual (or self) and the continuity of the collective identity known by its name as a signifier of social meaning. Neither the identity as signifier—with its meanings resonant in history and language—nor the individual—with his or her political development—is static. The dynamic among the developing individual, the meaning of the collective identity, and the social meaning associated with that identity embedded in language limits the options available to the individual. The (temporary) outcome of this problematic of identity—the ongoing dialogue—is a constructed identity.

Clashes over identities, values, and cultural attributes have taken center stage on the urban agenda. Candidates for the mayoralty of large cities must now address issues of, for example, multicultural curricula in schools, their support of or opposition to government regulation of abortion, the extent of environmental controls, bi- and multilanguage policies for municipal courts and official records, and the subtleties of racial identity and social construction as they affect the criminal justice system. These conflicts are not replacements for the distributional and service issues that have always been part of urban politics but are additions to them.

This approach to understanding urban politics is far removed from the view of urban economism, which tends to see broad, national—even international—economic change as driving the political agenda in local policymaking. The transformation of cities from industrial to postindustrial and the decline of those cities that failed to make the transition are regarded as part of the globalization of economic activity. Flowing from this change is a recycling of urban land from industrial uses to postindustrial residence, specialized service spaces, and the broad patterns associated with gentrification.

The rise of economism as a school of thought had its roots in the physical transformation of the cities between 1960 and 1990; in the near bankruptcy of Cleveland, New York City, Philadelphia, and Washington, D.C.; and in the rise of cities in the Sun Belt—three trends occurring concurrently. This emphasis on economic concepts in the study of urban politics and policymaking clarified some central notions in political analysis and added a greater sense of discipline to the study of urban affairs. But there were drawbacks as well to economism. Its assumptions necessarily underestimated noneconomic motivations in politics, and the utility of cultural and psychological links as a basis for political identity and mobilization perspectives was devalued in the face of economically defined processes and groups. If cultural or psychological categories were used at all, they were incorporated through an expansion of the basic economism model, bringing economics into territory usually ceded to psychology and cultural anthropology.

The fundamental academic argument in this book is that the emphasis on the systematic political effects of economic change has made even political scientists look at urban politics as a mere reflection of broader economic change. Moreover, because the rational, calculating individual that underlies the economic model is conceptualized as static and "unitary," the model sees the political system as changing but the individual as constant. The alternative metaphor presented here is based on the postmodern and social organization theory notion of "identity" merged with another concept from that tradition—"field" or "network." This alternative metaphor can explain how and why gay men and lesbians have a distinctive voting pattern that cannot be predicted by their income, gender, or race; why, even though in many cities gay men and lesbians take advantage of economic change to obtain jobs, they are not reliable partners for either progrowth or antigrowth politics; why, even though many gay men and lesbians relocated to postindustrial cities partly because of the recycling of older housing stock, economic change cannot explain the emergence of residential clusters defined primarily by household variables and by sexual identity; and why sexual identity can explain mobilization in regard to demand's being incorporated into the ground rules of urban legislative districting.

Most important, political action can change the meanings invested in language by society as a whole. Identity politics is not simply a veneer over distributional politics; instead, distributional politics takes on both real and symbolic overtones as a result of identity politics. To emphasize this point: the argument is not that economic factors are unimportant to political motivation and behavior but that the hegemony that economics has claimed for urban politics has gone too far. Even though it can explain much about development policy and fiscal policy, the model is not powerful enough to relegate all other political phenomena—whether tied directly to economic change or completely separate from it—to a catchall category of last resort: "postindustrial politics." Identity is not at the periphery but at the core of urban life, and lesbian and gay politics is a central example.

Interest Groups Versus Identity Groups: A Deep Agenda

Urban economism was a refinement of the latent economic models underlying the inter-interest-group-bargaining formulations of the 1960s and early 1970s. The theorizing of the 1970s and 1980s pushed the application of rational, microeconomic metaphors up to the next level of analysis—from intracity competition among groups to intercity competition among urban economies. Both approaches brought with them corollaries from microeconomics, especially in regard to political motivation. Politics pertained to an isolated, individual, psychologically unified actor, rationally calculating and working (1) individually through the political market or (2) through common-interest-group associations that were themselves rational if collective actors in the political market. Since these urban policy games were discrete—separate from city to city—they were driven by changes in each city's political and economic ecology.[15] Changes in economic payoffs, economic structure, or demographics drove political action, not changes in political identity, cultural affinity, or sense of self.

The nature of identity politics reveals an agenda deeper than interest-group analysis might indicate. Interest-group politics is largely about coming together to advance collective economic, budgetary, or regulatory interests that, when dealing with public policy in an economic framework, are usually for economic gain or protection. In identity politics, the individual "identifies" with the group primarily for psychological or cultural reasons. Socially, the characteristics ascribed to the identity by the enveloping social matrix become one focus of conflict. The other focus is the self-organization of the identity among those self-identifying. Politically, the identity becomes important to social action, and the source of meaning for the identity is one point of contention.

Interest-group analysis looks toward rational policy gains, rationally pursued as its agenda, which is why some of its leading foundation theorists have been economists. It is not that the individual issues pursued by an identity group are irrelevant but that they are manifestations of something deeper than the economic gains of other definitions of groupings. That is, the *deep agenda* is the affirmation of the identity.

How can identity politics work together with a policy approach to urban politics? An initial reaction might be that identity, centered as it has been on cultural analysis, would not be very useful in explaining the sources of public policies. But combining concepts from interest analysis and the symbolic aspects of identity-associated politics offers advantages not immediately expected.

To be at least as useful as interest-group analysis in the policy approach, identity politics must, first, be described as a movement or grouping whose binding criteria and rationale are not solely economic interest. This does not preclude economic interest from being a part of the "paste" holding the group together, but economic interest must not exhaust the group's rationale. An identity movement must show that it has something binding it together other than economic gain; that is, it must have a "deep agenda."

Second, an identity movement must show that in the process of creating public policy, broad noneconomic factors are brought together through identity to have a substantive policy effect. But identity politics also means that these effects need not be only changes in resource allocation patterns. Changes in status, access, and the distribution of affirming symbols would also be considered an important policy effect.

Third, such a movement must show that it has importance in more than one policy arena. Because identity and deep agendas are intimately linked and both cut across what organizationally focused social scientists term *functionally based issue arenas*—education, health care, criminal justice, economic development, and so on—the older separation among issue arenas is moot. Since the social organization of the modern public sector resisted centralized authority, policy politics largely concentrate on specific issues— health, education, criminal justice, social welfare, and the other policy arenas usually associated with the urban public sector—whereas identity politics cuts across them. The test for identities as actors also includes their impact on policy, but it can be an uneven impact in several different policy arenas at one time. That is, it need not be limited to one arena but should be demonstrated to some degree in several.

In a broad sense, the very nature of identity politics also changes the definition of its effect on policy. Changes in purely symbolic issues or in the range of political discourse can therefore be seen as real policy effects—the real test is a change in the framing of the policy discourse and a real effect on some policy decisions.

PART II

▦

Methods, Models, and Metaphors of Identity in Urban Politics

···

CHAPTER 2

Identity, Sexual Identity, and Political Behavior

What is identity, and how can it be used in the study of politics?

From the start, lesbian and gay politics has been labeled *identity politics*. In most cases, this was meant to be derisive, as indeed it still is to some degree today among liberal and conservative commentators alike, the initial criticism coming from social movement politics.[1] The lesbian and gay movement was grounded in the politics of the social movements of the 1960s, even though the founding members of the Gay Liberation Front viewed a social movement centered solely on gender or sexual orientation as abandoning the potential for social transformation through a broad-based, nonviolent, youth-oriented movement of the left.[2]

In the 1960s, the word *identity* was applied to those movements organized around gender or sexual orientation and not aligned with what should have been class-based political movements of the left. This label properly described the assertive nature of a "gay alliance," as opposed to one in which a gay "identity" was submerged in the race-, class-, and "other-ly" centered urban movements.

The establishment of a gay liberation movement led primarily by white males in the large cities was itself challenged, first by women-identified women[3] and then by African Americans, Latinos, and other people of color. "Identity" immediately lost its universalist assertion within sexual identity, especially its implied claim that all lesbians and all "gay" men of color fit easily into a single "gay" identity. Thus the current debate in gay and lesbian discourse concerns the extent to which sexual identity brings together a wide range of differing identities under one category.

Identity and Its Uses

Identity should be distinguished from *interest.* Identity speaks to cultural, psychological, and other nonmarket valuations, whereas interest primarily concerns economic interests, assessed in a rational manner from a unified individual perspective. Identity is not new to the social sciences or even to political science but can be traced to behavioral politics, cultural anthropology, and, more recently, women's studies and postcolonialist studies.

Identity and Identification in Behavioral Political Science

In American politics, the traditional question asked of identity was, With whom does the object of study identify? This strictly behavioral perspective on identity, seen as a categorization scheme created by social scientists and imposed on the objects of research, was useful to the underlying agenda of positivist political scientists. Two classic works in American political science show how identity was used by the first generation of behavioral social scientists and subjected to their cruder behaviorism: Campbell and colleagues' *The American Voter* and Almond and Verba's *The Civic Culture.*

In voting behavior, researchers saw identities as "predictors" of voting behavior. Race, gender, religious affiliation, geographic affinity, and the like all are vessels of accumulated experiences, vocabulary, assumptions, memories, and fears that influence the way a person votes. In *The American Voter,* for example, Campbell, Converse, Miller, and Stokes wrote about party "identification," although they were less interested in party identification itself than in its underlying structures, development, and deviation across time. Thus during periods of normal politics, parental party identification was a good predictor of a voter's party identification: Republicans beget Republicans; Democrats, Democrats. What events might change such patterns in the aggregate? For Campbell and his colleagues, changes produced by "personal forces" and those introduced by "social forces" can alter the underlying structures of political identification. Sometimes, as in war and economic dislocation, these come together: "An event of extraordinary intensity can arouse any significant part of the electorate to the point that its established political loyalties are shaken.... The political upheaval associated with the Civil War imposed a regional dimension on the partisan attachments of the American electorate."[4]

The slow accumulation of broad social changes can also have this effect.

For instance, the regionalism in American voting that Campbell and his colleagues described and that lasted for more than a century has been changing. Accordingly, by the 1992 presidential elections, "gender" and "urbanization" better explained voting behavior than regionalism did. The economic modernization and urbanization of America, the homogenizing effects of the mass media on the country, the emergence of the women's movement, and the internal migration of African Americans before and after the civil rights movement all altered primary political identities in voting behavior.

That Campbell and his colleagues use the word *identification* rather than *identity* in *The American Voter* indicates their greater interest in the effects of identity on behavior than in the development of the "self" or the self-constitution of that identity. Because the outcome of this development process is a sociopolitical outcome, not a personal or self-reflective one, explaining the process of party identification is a process of political socialization rather than psychosocial development. Nevertheless, one intent of *The American Voter* was to study the development of political identity as an aspect of voter behavior, but because of the emphasis on observable correlates, the authors of *The American Voter* chose *identification* as their term.

Similarly, Almond and Verba's *Civic Culture* is an exercise in political sociology or, more accurately, political anthropology. In establishing the themes of their five-nation survey of political culture, they adapted concepts from the noneconomic social sciences to explain why democracy works (or does not work). Again, identity as the emergence of self is not their main topic of interest; rather, it is the manner in which the surrounding culture structures and influences political identifications:

> We speak of..."political socialization" rather than child development or child rearing in general terms, not because we reject the psychological and anthropological theories that relate political attitudes to other components of personality, or because we reject those theories which stress the relationship between child development in general terms and induction of the child into his adult political roles and attitudes.... Here we can only stress that we employ the concept of culture in only one of its many meanings: that of the *psychological orientation toward social objects*. When we speak of the political culture of a society, we refer to the political system as internalized in the cognition, feelings, and evaluation of its population.[5]

Almond and Verba see the political system as internalized and expressed through the cognition and feelings of the population. They do not say that other factors are not important to the development of "cognition and feelings" but that these other factors are not part of their research agenda. Moreover, they see the self as passive, as a vehicle of mediation through which the society's tensions are expressed. Their intent is to study the variation in cultures as reflected in the understanding of politics—what they call *political cognitive maps*.[6]

Almond and Verba also draw inferences from anthropological metaphors, concluding, "Conflicts of political culture have much in common with other culture conflicts, and political acculturative processes are more understandable if we view them in the light of resistances and the fusional and incorporative tendencies of cultural change in general."[7] What divides Almond and Verba from identity writers today is their strict behavioral perspective: to understand the political acculturative process, they tried to build metaphors as expressed through a passive self.

Again, as with *The American Voter*, identification for Almond and Verba is less an issue of self than of behavioral manifestations of political socialization. Do the citizens of any one nation "identify with" their governments? Yes, but to varying degrees—which is itself an aspect of political culture.[8] More generally, the transference of identification from tribe or group to crown or state is seen by writers in this political development tradition of the 1960s as a first step toward a "stable democracy." That is, the *personal* reflection of this change in identification *follows* the political development process rather than leads it.

These two references to identification politics in classic texts of political science are meant as illustrations. Because both deal with the psychology of identification, they reflect behavioral and experimental psychology and thus are concerned with identification and not identity per se. Neither text, of course, discusses sexual identity. For Almond and Verba and for Campbell and his colleagues, "identification" is behavioral and can be estimated, formulated by the environment. As it is evolving in theory today, "identity" represents a richer approach through identity formation, in which the self is active.

Identity, Ethnic Identity, and the Danger of Reification in Field-Based Anthropology

To resolve the problems of using identity in fieldwork, ethnographers have devised several approaches. Assessing a sense of identity among ethnic groups requires both technical development in defining indicators of an identity appropriate to each group and an overarching theoretical approach to identity. Sometimes using the word *identity* interchangeably with *ethnicity* or jointly, as in *ethnic identity*, cultural anthropologists have already confronted some of the problems that political science is facing in integrating "identity" into its set of analytical tools. Three broad approaches have been developed: (1) a contextual approach, (2) a "core" (or essentialist) approach, and (3) a social constructivist approach.

THE CONTEXTUAL APPROACH

The contextual approach to ethnic or religious identity is a purely positivist formulation. The ethnographer generates a catalog of defining characteristics that can be used to compare and contrast groups. Describing these characteristics as "ascriptive endowments," David Busby Edwards further defines them as "a ready made set of endowments and identifications which every individual [in the group] shares with others from the moment of birth by chance."[9] Such "endowments and identifications" are necessarily seen in a context, or are situational, and are best understood through a comparative field method. For the cultural anthropologist, understanding these "ascriptive endowments" of a group is easier as more cases become available. Differences among the cases create a broader categorization typology. One implication of this approach is that ethnicity (ethnic identity) is clearest at the boundaries of the group, where interaction with other groups (or identities) makes the defining characteristics of each group more observable to group members as well as to anthropologists. The group's "sense of identity" is thus heightened in multi-identity contexts.

One disadvantage of this approach is that the ethnographers impose the taxonomy on the group rather than allowing the group to define itself. Thus, even the most reserved and professional field anthropologists who attempt to minimize the effect of their work on social processes in the end dominate the group's identity by controlling its definition in anthropology. The analogy in the study of sexual identity would be that social scientists, not the individuals or the movement itself, determine the dimensions of a "gay" or "lesbian" identity.

THE "CORE" (OR ESSENTIALIST) APPROACH

A second method is to obtain through direct observation a group's defining core and deep social characteristics—in a sense, the group's defining structural characteristics. This "core" approach has the advantage of respecting the group's uniqueness but the disadvantage of making the ethnographers the interpreters of such deep social structures. Unlike the contextual approach, in which the identification is intensified at the edges of the group, in the core approach, the group's identity is greatest at the center of its institutions: the social processes, languages, and rituals that "define" it. Context is not unimportant, but it does not define the group's identity. It also is clear, however, that a core approach (or even a structural approach specific to a single group) invites a reification—taking the category advanced as a tool to understand reality as reality—of the group's identity over that of the individuals within it. The analogy in lesbian and gay studies is called *essentialism*, that is, subsuming all diversity within the group under its overriding sexual characteristic, thereby denying gender, race, or other factors also important to those individuals defining themselves. The lesson here is that reification is a latent threat in all essentialist methods.

THE "SOCIAL CONSTRUCTIVIST" APPROACH

The third approach could be termed *constructivist*, as social identity is "constructed" in a dynamic between the group and the social—-political context. This approach grows out of the observation by field-based anthropologists that a group maintains its identity in new contexts by adjusting to that context. For example, the imposition of "state" administrative and regulatory schemes alters the identity of traditional groups. A new "identity" grounded in tradition grows in response to the imposed regulatory schema and the associated mix of imposed and indigenous understanding of the group and the characteristics of its identity.

Identity Politics as Liberation

Much of the current work on identity politics is the polar opposite of the behavioral tradition of American political science that led to identity's being equated with identification. That is, more recent theorists have provided a language and a set of categories to structure the experience of the feminist movement, ethnic-identity movements, and the uneven experience with decolonization in the non-Western world. Largely as a defense against the dominant cultures, identity politics in these contexts has been a force for change in many places. In those nations that have deep Islamic roots, for example, and that were colonized by the French or British civil service, the need to reexamine, reexplore, and rearticulate their Islamic tradition is seen as a political act—not just a cultural or theological act. The revival of Islam as a transnational movement can thus be seen as a struggle for a culturally and religiously based identity in the face of Western "modernism."[10] In fact, the very term *moderate Muslims* juxtaposed with *Islamic fundamentalism* is viewed as a continuum referring solely to Western interests.[11]

National, ethnic, or religious identities in diaspora are especially pressed to nurture and defend (or remember) aspects of their traditions as aspects of political and cultural resistance to oppression and a sign of the community's continuity. Western and Central Africans in America, Jews in eastern Europe and the Russian Federation, and South Asians in Britain and America, among others, have experienced the intellectual and political struggles to define an "identity in diaspora."[12] The political—-cultural task of transformation is removing the layers of adulteration imposed by the dominant culture and to seek the initial group identity as it was in its "purest form" before colonization or the scattering of a people.

One problem with identity politics as cultural reclamation is its implied "idealism." The switch of political focus toward recapturing poorly defined cultural expressions (often myths) contains the danger of re-*constructing* such past identities out of fragments drawn from present-day politics. The political goals of this analytical method necessarily emphasize the collective aspects of a group's (identity's) history in the common experience of colonization by the "other." The boundaries are drawn without forethought, and diversities within the identity are submerged. This is the issue that women face when an Islamic identity is valued higher than a feminist identity in a Muslim political movement or—more pertinent to this book—an African American gay identity is subsumed in one place under a gay identity and in another under a black identity. That is, the possibility of multiple political identities is minimized.

The initial attribute separating a sexual-identity social movement from the class-based, cross-gender, cross-race movement of the 1960s new left is itself challenged by diversities within the identity. Thus for lesbian and gay studies, a "politics of difference" approach brings with it both strategic and methodological problems.

What separates "identity politics" in gay and gender studies from identity politics as an aspect of the decolonization process is its emphasis on the psychological and constructionist aspects of political conflict and a deep resistance in gay and lesbian studies to the reification of any category. There is no attempt to recapture cultures long gone but instead to search for and critique deep structures and processes in the present-day culture. The psychosexual aspects of gay and lesbian identity go to the core of ego and identity integration and thus methodologically weigh more heavily in social meaning as embedded in language and symbols than in categorical continuity in history. The political situation of sexual identity—cutting across other identities constructed around gender, race, class, religion, and so forth—may also require that the categories gay or lesbian be seen as temporary constructs.

Identity in Political Action

If identity is to be used as a coordinating category for the writing of politics, we must understand how an identity-motivated political actor model differs from a rational actor model in not only formal theory but also the bargaining models of interest-group politics. The identity actor model is developmental, cultural, and psychological and operates in a political context defined by structuring roles, signs, and languages. The rational actor model, however, sees the actor as singular, self-contained, and given—that is, without change—making calculations in an environment of preference payoffs.

If behavioral political scientists see the issue of identity as an outgrowth of political socialization mediated by a "passive" self, and more recent social theory sees "identity" as the battleground for ongoing decolonization and cultural wars, contemporary political analysis needs to find an intermediate way to use the concept to describe behavioral expression. In response to the question "Who am I?" a contemporary perspective on identity politics can assign the answer to neither the domain of psychology and psychoanalysis nor the imposition on the subject of empirically manipulatable taxonomies. Rather, identity politics should assume a special domain for politics, including an active role for the individual in defining himself or herself. Political scientists should study the political action associated with the identity, understanding that language and identities also are changing through that action.

To explore this viewpoint, we borrow metaphors from social organization theory,[13] which today largely builds on, but also differs from, Erving Goffman. Writing in the early 1960s, Goffman examined the issues in the representation of the self through his or her social role, finding a conscious difference between "identity" and the "presentation of identity" to the outside world.[14] This difference was the result of the increasing specialization of social "roles"—like that of parent, police officer, "celebrity," civil servant—that limits a person's ability to define his or her own identity. The presentation of self in everyday life thus requires an accumulation of skills appropriate to the role that the person is playing. To the degree that the skillful presentation of the self associated with an assigned social role differs from the individual's "actual" self-identity, that person becomes vulnerable to anxiety.

Although the language has changed since the 1960s, Goffman's insights still are relevant to present-day identity theory. The social role today is seen as a social construction, and the specific role each person plays is—in part, at least—a choice of that individual. Understanding how a person manages the problems associated with the anticipated tension between the self and the expectations linked to a social role was one of Goffman's goals. His analysis of role implied a permanent discontinuity between the "self" and its presentation. In some ways, the distinction between "sense of self" and "presentation of self" minimized the developmental aspect of the self in identity. Or to put it in another way, it made impossible a politics of authenticity.

In present-day social organization theory, identity is dynamic and associated with action and conflict. Rather than growing out of the social role, as Goffman saw it, it is based on contingencies; that is, it cannot necessarily be presumed. These life contingencies may be as uninteresting as getting up each morning or as eventful as a civil war or, in the case of gays and lesbians, the occasion of first apprehending their attraction to others of the same sex. In any case, these contingencies are presented by everyday life and give rise to what Harrison White calls *contentions*. Contentions are conflicts among identities which, in political science, are political contentions with other identities. In seeking to manage or obtain protection from contingencies that might affect them negatively, individuals (or a group) seek control of their environment. In a social dynamic, their actions may create further contentions for other identities. If these other identities, in turn, choose to act, the process will be further refined through the response.[15]

Identities are seen as continuous (in an everyday sense) by other social observers who invest in them meaning and signification. Although identities are continuous, they are not static roles as Goffman may have envisioned them in his work. The continuity in present-day theory is not in the stability of a social role but in the consistency of the *name*. That is, the role itself may change fundamentally—as that of "homosexual" has modulated over the past twenty years from social deviant to social activist—but the name changes more slowly.

Accepting an identity or, more accurately, agreeing to participate in a dialogue with the identity in process is the subject's act of self-identification. In contemporary social organization theory, acceptance of an identity opens a dialogue with the social meaning of the "name." For Goffman, the tension between a social role and an individual's sense of self creates a series of issues that need to be managed. This need for management was especially urgent for what he termed *spoiled identities*—such as that of the homosexual.[16] A more dynamic notion of identity, however, requires a constant reevaluation of identities, and each action creates contentions that in reaction may further define other identities.

When social organization and social action are political, political scientists can translate identity, action, and contention into a broad range of political language. For our analysis, five aspects of identity are politically important: identity as a *self*, as a *name*, as a *group*, as an *action*, and, finally, as part of a *matrix of differences*. We now apply these characteristics to the study of gay and lesbian politics.

IDENTITY IS DEVELOPMENTAL: THE SELF

Identity grows in action and emerges in increasing detail and commitment as it confronts and challenges attempts to define itself socially. The self-reflective aspects of this commitment and refinement are developmental. This characteristic of identity is especially relevant to gay and lesbian identity. From the beginning, gay politics has been identity politics but has not been conceptualized solely as a self-calculating and rationally acting interest group.[17] Rather, it has been a conflict over roles and meanings (in addition to civil liberties and economic gain). Indeed, it is in psychology and psychiatry where the "politics of self," particularly as it relates to gender and issues of sexual orientation, is clearest. In the words of psychiatrist Robert Stoller and anthropologist Gilbert Herdt:

> By *preference* we imply a commitment and therefore a complex of organized motives, beliefs, and behaviors that can be summarized in words such as *character structure, personality, self, or identity*. It is our hypothesis—one that all [psycho] analysts probably share—that such a homoerotic commitment is not simply a product of chance encounters at susceptible moments.[18]

Such inferences are key to understanding why the "self" is a battleground for gender and gay and lesbian politics, with the "self" active in this analysis.

Accepting an identity is the starting point, not the end point, of identifying with the association (or the identity). It leads to a dialogue between the individual and the name (in this case, lesbian or gay), which is the carrier of social meaning. The struggle is to tailor the name to the various aspects of the subject. As Shane Phelan wrote, "Coming out is partially a process of revealing something kept hidden but it is more than that. It is a process of fashioning a self—a lesbian or gay self—that did not exist before coming out."[19] There is no excavation of an adulterated identity here—in this case, the clearing away of layers of sexist and heterosexist scripting—to find the "genuine self." Rather, it is a set of choices along a developmental route, predisposed by a sexual affinity, that expose the person to experiences associated with the identity.

IDENTITY IS A SIGNIFIER WITH SOCIAL MEANING: A NAME

A politics of identity is also a politics of social meaning. That is, because identity is a name, it is a signifier of social meaning.

Goffman saw the social role as a limiting factor creating tension between the presentation of the self and the social definition of a role. In present-day theory, it is less the role that offers this tension than the meanings that rest in language: The name is the mechanism through which the social construction of meaning influences self-identity, since it is the name—in this case, gay and lesbian—that signifies identity and is invested with meaning by society as a whole. Within the social contours of the identity and by means of the accumulated history of behavior by and toward those individuals who choose or who have the "name" identified with them, these people come to terms with and try to alter the social meaning of the name.

Investing in the dialogue of "what it means to be 'Irish,'" for example, is a choice, in part predisposed by history and family and in part an outgrowth of self-reflection and choice. The choice is to expose oneself to Irish and Celtic myths and stories, religious texts, music, literature, history, and language(s), that is, to invest in the identity. The social meaning invested in the name presents a contingency that the individual likely feels a need to fight or tailor to his or her own sense of self. In this framework, one might say that the individual is predisposed to identify himself or herself as Irish but also chooses to become Irish.

Maybe a better example is the identity of police officer as a social identity. To say that one is a "police officer" and to wear the signs of the office (uniform and badge) is both to identify with the role internally and to invite the application to oneself of all the various meanings that others associate with the name "police officer." In the social matrix of meaning, a police officer can be seen as anything ranging from helpful citizen to cruel oppressor, depending on the memories and meanings that one's own identity associates with police officer. These subtle meanings often conflict, and thus a police officer struggles to assert her "real" identity against the language and meanings assigned to the name. For the new police officer to accept the name and struggle to change its meaning to meet her needs is thus to accept the identity and to engage in identity politics.

IDENTITY IS A COLLECTIVE WITH A COMMON SENSE: A GROUP

If identity did not lead to collective political action, it would not be of interest in politics. That various political identities are in fact active and effective in many arenas—from South Asia to the Middle East to San Francisco—shows that they are a basis for collective action.

The issue of collective identity as a basis for political action may be the most difficult aspect of using identity in political science. Simply because there is a common interest, as interest-group theorists might say, or a common "sense," as we might say here, does not mean that the group will in fact materialize. Although homosexual behavior and even same-sex "safe spaces" have long histories, the current political movement based on sexual identity is a product of our own epoch. Why does identity progress from individual struggles to a collective struggle?

The economic model might indicate that it should not. The preliberation strategy to deal with same-sex affinities—at least among middle-class homosexuals—was to keep it from public inspection, to not jeopardize career or family ties, or to move into professions in which homosexuality would more likely be accepted. These usually were occupations that had little power or that allowed for the individual application of personal or professional skills.[20] When compared with the uncertain and general gains associated with social change, the certain and specific losses to established individuals should have precluded the collective identity from political action, but it did not.

One response, well documented by historians of the beginning of the movement for lesbian and gay identity, was that the early struggle was centered not in the middle class but in the working class. Because working-class people had less to lose professionally, they were the first to resist the state regulation of their sexual lives. Or we might say that the psychological costs of personal isolation came to outweigh the uncertain possibilities of professional gain. But because psychological benefits are the most difficult to assess in rational models, we will not pursue further their role in political action.

We will, however, challenge the economic model of groups, in at least three ways. The first concerns the cost/benefit analysis of participating in the formation of groups for social or political activity. Mancur Olson argued that in small groups, in which costs and benefits are easily identified, the anticipated collective gain as a result of acting may outweigh the individual costs assessed in time and resources.[21] Assuming the distribution of benefits is equal, this small-group payoff may establish a context in which rational actors have an incentive to act collectively. In large groups, however, the marginal gain for each individual is probably outweighed by the personal costs of the initial actors, and thus to avoid free-rider problems, larger groups must enforce adherence. This surely was the case in labor organizing.

For Olson, the payoff is more on the gain side of the equation. If an individual can gain just as much on his own, why should he join a specific group that insists on his loyalty? The reason that gay men and lesbians act together is less for the benefits they might gain from joining than for the removal of costs that might be incurred by not taking collective action. The nature and breadth of these costs are not calculated as easily for the rational actor who does not see the costs of inaction measured in language, options denied, and the arbitrary limits imposed by social structures.

Second, although Olson did acknowledge that his economic rationale can encompass status and community respect as a potential gain, he sees it as an individual concern. Since the perspective of the economic model is the individual as such, status issues in Olson's framework discourage collective action. "The existence of these social incentives to group-oriented action does not, however, contradict or weaken the analysis of this study. If anything, it strengthens it, *for social status and social acceptance are individual and non-collective goods.*"[22] But as in the case of many identity movements, the struggle for acceptability and social status is, by definition, a collective achievement, since it is the category, to use Goffman's phrase, that is "stigmatized." The difficulty is in changing the stigma by altering the social meaning invested in the name. Olson's framework would not predict this, however, since he never considered that status, as a variable, could have a negative value.

Third (and this is an insight from both postmodern theorists and the previous generation of existential social theory), some aspects of the minority identity are in fact created by the majority. Olson asked why individuals would act together when the gains are uncertain and the costs are specific. Left implicit was his assumption of looking toward the formation of "new" groups, especially those that are economically focused (labor, class, business). But in the case of gay men and lesbians, the group as name has long been known during this century, in theology, the law, and the group's medicalization. Furthermore, the group was not created sui generis but has always existed and has been defined in most of society's regulatory agencies. Therefore, the more that social structures and language stigmatized the category "homosexual" or the identities "gay" and "lesbian," the more that gay men and lesbians were pushed into collective action.

IDENTITY IS PHENOMENOLOGICAL: AN ACTION

Since identities arise from contentions in our framework, it is action that defines identities, both socially and personally. Identity grows out of any action of choice (i.e., those other than simple biological or physiological needs) into which the actor or others can read meaning. In the world of "gay politics," this is easily translated. To act politically on own's sexual orientation is a social (political) action into which others are invited to read meaning. "Identities emerge from action and counteraction."[23] Political identities emerge from political acts—current or past. For example, one can engage in same-sex sexual behavior and yet not identify oneself as "gay" or "lesbian." There may appear to be a discontinuity here, but only if one defines the identity "gay or lesbian" in terms of sexual acts. If, however, one is observing the political effects of an identity movement, the definition of the identity must be more specific than, in this case, sexual acts—for even some who engage in such acts do not in fact consider themselves gay. Although this may come as a surprise to many, lesbians and gay men know this implicitly.

The point is that as social scientists (and not psychoanalysts), we need a theory of identity grounded in social and political action that allows for an "observable" assessment of the impact of identity on politics. To encompass not only lesbian and gay politics but also identity politics in general, the theory must also take into account the more subtle and developmental aspects of identity.

IDENTITY IS COMPLEX: A MATRIX OF DIFFERENCES

In addition to being developmental, associated with meanings through its name, defined through action, and grouped politically, identity is complex. That is, it is not singular or isolated but exists among other self-identities, other differences within the category.

These multiple identities are both internal (an aspect of self) and "out there" (in political space). They occasionally conflict and create psychological tension and political cross pressures. As Michel Maffesoli notes:

The notion of a sexual identity is too narrow, for the ego is constituted of at least a plurality of personalities, if not an infinity. The successive identifications which can be observed empirically express such a "multipersonality," whose characteristics are more or less crystallized in each individual, but which are, nonetheless, a sign of the times, in general and for everyone.[24]

The proliferation of contemporary social forms as bases for political identity and as linkages for political mobilization has provided more choices and created multiple arenas of political action. But it also means multiple identities. What we might call *identity multiplexing* is the layering and ranking by individuals of their different identities in different arenas. The voting behavior tradition adds theoretical insight here: By collapsing identity into identification in voting behavior, political scientists specializing in election behavior saw the key to voting as less the actual vote than the resolution of the underlying cross pressures among the various identifications of the individual voter. Thus, if gender explained nothing, the category could be eliminated from the analysis without imposing a specific meaning of, for example, "woman" on all political activity.

In politics internal to the gay and lesbian community, diversity is especially strong. Leaders spend a large portion of their time mediating differences among the gender, race, religious, urban/rural, and class distinctions that frequently threaten to shatter the cohesion of the group identity defined according to sexual orientation. And yet the words *lesbian* or *gay* as signifiers of a category emphasize the community's commonality, sometimes to an inappropriate extreme. The ideal of community, as Iris Young says, "privileges unity over difference."[25] The danger is that the identity "gay" may impose attributes rather than liberate individuals and expand their life options.

Conclusion

Although identity politics is a new phenomenon, identity as such is not new to behavioral political science. In the past, the concept was largely drawn from sociology and anthropology but was used in political science in a purely positivist manner. The category was thus less "identity" than "identification." Political development was limited to early family or cultural influences; the self was passive in the identification process; and identity was formulated through either political socialization or an acculturative process.

Our task of conceptualizing a richer notion of identity for the study of politics could take some guidance from cultural anthropology. From field-based ethnography, we can see the effect of the interaction of context, construct, and core characteristics on group identity. Although informative, the peculiar psychosexual aspects of gay and lesbian identity in political analysis preclude a direct transference of identity from field-based ethnography to gay studies. We also know that we must be sensitive to language and social meaning and their construction and transformations. Accordingly, the two most important insights we can draw from ethnography are those that comparative and international politics also have found useful: (1) Identities are important actors in politics, and (2) they are primarily defined by non-market characteristics.

With its themes of social action, contingency, and contention and a better understanding of identity formation, social organization theory is a particularly attractive setting for identity as a category of analysis transferable to political science. This theory assumes an active self but places the burden of analysis on observable political actions and their effect. This formulation of identity as a category for analysis does not preclude the appropriation of other categories to the study of its effects—and thus can work well with some traditional and newer categories in political science. The main focus, however, is social action with a political effect. Since identity is also a name and the name itself is a matter of change and contention, the influence of social construction on meaning is presumed.

Analyzing urban politics by studying the social action of individual and group identities offers a greater understanding of political action than does analyzing interest groups. It invests the actor with agency while at the same time recognizing social structuring in institutions, signs, and languages. But this sort of analysis does introduce a problem. An advantage of interest-group analysis is that the boundaries of such groups can easily be defined, through an "objective" understanding of whose economic interests are truly engaged. Those persons whose interests are engaged fall inside the group's boundaries, whereas those whose interests are not engaged fall outside them.

But because we recognize politics as occurring in an environment of multiple individual and group identities, we must replace the hard lines of economic interest with the softer borders of identities. These softer borders do not require policing or enforcement, as the boundaries of interest groups sometimes do; instead, they trail off into other identities. The analytical threat to understanding urban politics through an identity metaphor is thus its fragmentation at the edges, threatening to break down in a process of ever more specific identities and numerically smaller and smaller identity groupings. The humanism and inclusionary impulses that drive identity as a politics or as a method also jeopardize the coherence of the group and force the analyst at times to pursue a method that Irigary might call a strategy of tactical (and temporary) essentialism.

⣿

CHAPTER 3

Economism and Identity in Urban Politics

A politics of identity understood as both interest association and cultural expression contradicts the dominant organizing metaphors from economics as they are currently applied to the study of urban politics and policymaking. The urban economism viewpoint sees broad, national, even international economic change as driving the political agenda in local policymaking. When economism reached the status of a full-blown public philosophy, it was translated into a single message: that economic development is (should be?) the primary goal of urban public policy.

The economism perspective has also produced a new perspective on urban politics, generally organized around two poles. The first pole is urban regimes, progrowth coalitions, or other descriptors of coalitions of economic and social interests that encourage economic change and would gain from it. The other pole is community-based interests, neighborhood organizations, and those at the margin of the older economy (frequently racial minorities)—all that would lose in this reorganization of the urban economy. Since these urban policy games differ from city to city, they are driven by changes in each city's social and economic ecology. Changes in economic payoffs, economic structure, or demographics—not changes in political identity, cultural affinity, or sense of self—drive political action. In economism, politics has become the medium—and a limited one—in which larger economic forces operate.

Firms, Regimes, and Identities

At its base, urban economism envisions cities as separate "firms" competing with others in a marketplace. The microeconomic models applied to urban politics are clearly ahistorical and, in some cases, prescriptive as well as explanatory. In this tradition, the interactive dynamic imposed on urban politics and planning was seen as a political agenda defined by economic criteria.[1] Paul Peterson crystallized this confluence of thought by modifying Charles Tiebout's public-choice (pareto-optimizing) model of a pure theory of public expenditures and applying it to cities (i.e., firms) operating in a larger, competitive political economy. Peterson used the hypothesis that given these economic constraints, cities would tend to direct their scarce resources toward development and that politics in the traditional group-dynamic sense would be limited to the distribution of municipal services. Then, using aggregate data on local expenditure patterns, Peterson presented inferential evidence supporting his hypothesis.[2]

Although Peterson relied heavily on Tiebout to formulate his transcendent "interest of the city," it may be more relevant to this book to look at the use of the microeconomics literature in urban politics in the work of Albert Breton.[3] Breton also recognizes Tiebout's contribution in relating the microeconomic literature to urban and regional finances (actually, Tiebout was writing on the optimal size of cities, a question of some interest to urban economists and sociologists in the 1950s), but applies the "theory of the firm" to urban finance. By integrating the two literatures and creating a calculus of debt limits, Breton, too, creates a transcendent "city interest" much as Peterson does, but more explicitly through microeconomics and the theory of the firm.

Applying the theory of the firm to urban economics and, ultimately, policy gives us a clue to how microeconomics as an organizing theme of urban development policy can be critiqued, that is, by using the modes developed in response to pure theories of the firm in microeconomics and the literature of business organization. Although the literature from business and organizational science used to be largely behavioral and case and process oriented (Herbert Simon, Alfred Chandler, etc.), it has been influenced more recently by network theory and the theory of "weak ties" in sociology. Similarly, the case literature of urban transformation reveals behavioral nuances that the pure theories of economism cannot fully predict. And despite the inferences or outright statements by urban writers heavily influenced by microeconomics and public-choice theory (Tiebout, Breton, Forrester, Peterson, etc.), the case literature also shows that urban transformation creates new tensions, not a transcendent "city interest."

Traditional urban politics emphasizes ethnic and interest-group politics in the distribution of urban services. The politics of urban transformation creates a different conflict, between a new class of transients—those who control mobile capital and human resources—and entrenched residents—those who continue to reside in changing cities. Neither has a transcendent "city interest." In short, as political scientists have focused on economic variables to determine public policy, their case studies have shown how, even in the narrative of economism, the elegance of economic theory must be tempered by the vagaries of political conflict.

Regime Theory as a Critique of Economism

The most effective schools critiquing economism models—the "urban transformation" literature and the "regime" literature—have roots in both economics and (though less so) history.

The urban transformation literature focuses on the negative aspects of economic change and how these might create coalitions to temper the agenda of "progrowth coalitions." But here, too, economic structures and spillover effects and not cultural, identity, or other noneconomic sources of mobilization are at the center of the analysis.

Largely growing out of the transformation literature of urban affairs, regime theory has been identified with the interaction of markets, private actors, and the local state—especially as these relate to issues of economic development. The regime coalition uses the sustained, informal overlap of economic resources and public instrumentalities to form its strategic economic perspective. Although there typically is no central and coordinating arena—formal or informal—in which policies and broad strategies are determined, there is a matrix of relationships through which leaders of the regime's differing component elites come to feel comfortable with one another and generate the regime's perspective.

Regime theory critiques economism by looking at the formation and interaction of sets of groups during extended periods of economic structuring and restructuring. Regime change is associated with the economy's underlying transformation but is more dynamic than microeconomic models. Regime theorists show how federal urban renewal monies are used in different cities to create new spaces for progrowth development agendas and how potentially resistant groups are incorporated into the urban economic transformation process. As such, regime theory has the great advantage of incorporating into the model the dynamics of interest-group analysis, the structural dimensions of urban transformation literature, and a historical perspective that allows analysts to incorporate class and ethnic identity.

But regime theory also has disadvantages. First is the "softness" of the concept, with issues of periodization and comparability a principal concern for some critics. Can those of us working in an urban regime framework even agree on the time frames of different regimes in a single city or even on how many there have been? And if we cannot agree on such things in one city, how can we build a framework to compare all cities?

Regime theorists generally believe that regimes are sustained over an extended but limited period of time, that they are "an ongoing accomplishment." Transitional periods of breakup and reconsolidation set the time bounds on the definition and coherence of urban regimes. Thus Stephen Elkin can see broad defining periods in which the burden of responsibility for governance is borne unequally by public and private actors in a market republic. The periods of "regimes are...subject to historical variation, in which internal and external forces trigger a reordering of alliance patterns among local politicians, land interests, city bureaucracies and electoral interests."[4] The boundaries of these time periods, however, have not been well drawn.

Second, regime theorists do not agree on the extent of or limitation on regime power. Some emphasize the potential for change available to regime opponents or to local policymakers who might wish to cushion the effects of economic change on their weakest constituents. Others try to identify areas of political liquidity in the process of urban transformation.[5] Still others study strategies for effective community mobilization in the face of progrowth coalitions.[6] Richard DeLeon shows how Mayor Moscone first, and Agnos second, used San Francisco's resources to advance neighborhood economic and identity interests for Asians, gays, Latinos, and blacks.[7] John Mollenkopf outlines the opposite in the case of Mayor Ed Koch in New York City.[8] Koch pressed for additional progrowth policies in the central business core and supported services for the city's middle class, not the displaced. Implicitly, however, all three mayors emphasized the vitality of the local governing regimes, walking the tight rope between existing political systems with a wide range of options and a deterministic, economically structured commonality.

An important aspect of regime theory has been its ability to stress the capacity and dynamics of local regimes without minimizing the influences of economic structure. While understanding the pressures that push local coalitions toward development politics, regime scholars still see room for diversity among regimes in different cities. This "power to do" reasserts politics not so much as an autonomous domain as a link between market context and the city as polity. Policies imposed on local governance from the economic context still require local officials to be elected and government to have the organizational capacity to implement the policies. Local systems with stable tax bases and growing economies have more resources to deal with such issues, whereas those desperately seeking investment have fewer options. Nonetheless, having these options does not necessarily ensure that scarce resources will be used to remedy the social and local effects of economic change.

In this later dynamic context of regime theory, some thought has been given to "identity," but it has been limited. In the case of Atlanta, for example, Clarence Stone regards racial identity as an aspect of regime governance, although he is interested in identity as it is associated with economic exchange (especially as it involves Atlanta's black middle class).[9] The allocative outcomes of electoral behavior thus do not exhaust all aspects of black voting.

What unites all regime theorists is the conception of regime as a sustained, informal coalescence bonded by a common vision and the ability to work through both private and public channels to achieve its goals. Viewing regimes as actors tends to focus on the dynamics of urban politics rather than on the contextual issues that primarily concern scholars of urban transformation and economism. The contribution of regime theory is that it allows for both structure and process, for economics and history, without devaluing politics.

Economism and Identity Theory

Despite the debates within economism generally, using regime theory as a basis for critiquing it, most students of urban politics still seem to focus on cities as economic enterprises or economic arenas, not as habitats or settings for identity politics. Economism may explain some of the intersection points of economic change with the rise of lesbian and gay rights movement, although it cannot explain much about motivation, strategies, target

TABLE 3.1
Understanding Urban Politics

Through the Unified Economic "Model"	*Through an Identity "Metaphor"*
Cities as Competing Firms Operating in a Market Matrix	Cities as Locales in Networks of Aligned Political Forces
Cities in a Hierarchy of Specialized Functions and Domains	Cities on a Common Plane, Each a Setting for Differing Political Expressions of a "Deep Agenda"
Urban Space Used Primarily for an Economic Function	Space Used for Identity Development and Community Bonding
The Primacy of Economics over Politics	The Primacy of Identity Expressed through Economics and Politics
"Unwalled" Cities: Open Economies/ Discrete Politics	Fully "Unwalled" Cities: Open Economies/Open Politics

issues, symbol manipulation, emotional vesting, and other aspects of identity movements as expressed in urban politics.

The core argument here is that identity-based movements, such as the gay and lesbian rights movement, are bounding cases to the comprehensiveness of the economism model of urban politics. Alternatives—or a broader perspective—are needed to understand the dynamics of these movements and to ensure that the academic study of politics does not unwittingly contribute to their social denial. The alternative metaphor presented here is based on the social organization theory notion of "identity" merged with another concept from that tradition—"field" (or "network") (see table 3-1 for an outline of and differences between the two models). The following are five themes of an identity metaphor of urban politics, which illustrate its differences from a "unified economic" model.

Cities Suspended in Fields of Aligned Political Identities

The political-economy model sees cities as firms competing for the available investment, human skills, and potential tax revenue in a changing market. Because people (especially those with a high income potential) and capital (especially investment capital) are mobile, the rational policymaker pursues progrowth policies. Like firms competing in a consumer market, cities also are competing. At its best, such competition creates incentives to eliminate waste in service delivery and enhance public-sector productivity. In the end, however, the city is seen as a discrete game, a separate firm, seeking to optimize its position in a shifting market.

Identities, however, are not parcels of land or specific locations whose value is tied to value-added capacity. Nor do they need local reaffirmation and support as a precondition for political action in a time of mass media and rapid personal communications. Rather, they emerge and are defined in contention with other identities, necessarily moving across borders as symbols, communications, and transportation bring people together or pull them apart. Harrison White notes that this "network" aspect of a field model has its roots in political science.[10]

The attraction of identity and network theory in this current analysis is that it allows for interest-group mobilization but also takes into account residual and unmobilized (latent?) interests through identity. Furthermore, this theory has shown substantial utility in comprehending social patterns that may never reach the institutional stage but that endure beyond temporary convenience. The theory has been used, for example, to describe emerging corporate forms and the management of debt capacity in urban development policy. Regardless of its sophistication in application, the common assumption of network theory is the informality of its horizontal links, which move through and across hierarchies, institutions, organizations, and, we might add, cities.

Cities as a Setting for Political Action

Identities are not products of urban politics so much as phenomena that form and find expression in an urban setting. They "present themselves" through individual and group activity supported by identity fields. This idea differs from a second theme constant in urban political economy: cities as a hierarchy of specialized nodes of economic activity, that is, cities divided into "world cities," "national centers," "regional capitals," and so on, with the sector specialization increasing as the domain contracts.[11]

The incorporation of trade and location theory brings export and production into the model.[12] Location theory draws the attention of policymakers to the factors of production—labor, transportation facilities, human skills, capital, access to markets—to seek strategies that maximize economic advantage. The end result is that in seeking to take the greatest advantage of location and production factors, cities come to specialize largely as a result of location or economic history. For example, Houston has become a center of oil and energy production, its finance, and the manufacture of support products. Chicago is the center of North America's internal market, and so its rail facilities and agricultural-finance businesses dominate its culture.

Identity politics, however, offers no such specialization. Although each city's politics is based on its own, locally specific policy agenda, it also contains a deep agenda that is the same in every city. Accordingly, "gay politics" in one urban area may concentrate on AIDS prevention and social support; in another, on school curricula; in another, on women's shelters; and in still another, on attempts to create "lesbian/gay" electoral districts. It is the deep agenda of identity politics that affirms the particular identity and offers some control of the space for its expression.

Seen in this light, cities are "nodes" in identity fields, or maybe more accurately, the expressions of a gay and lesbian identity through issues and groups are nodes in the identity field. It is the identity that drives the politics. One way to conceptualize this notion is to think of it as a topological map in which the contours of an identity rise and fall across the political plane. Hills and mountains could represent various intensities of expression and different "geologies" of issues. We could also contrast this topology with the bounded and separated group game prevailing in much contemporary urban political analysis.

Urban Space as an Arena for Identity Development and Affirmation

The economism model of cities sees urban space mainly for its economic value—space arranged for production or consumption—ultimately defined in its relation to the city's economic function and specialization. As cities assume specialized functions in a competitive environment, spaces (regions) in cities also assume specific functions; the spaces become an ecology of functionally specific areas defined by economics. The relationship of residential space (initially defined by class and race), production space, consumption space, and transportation space is significant and changes over time.

The first theoreticians of urban space as an ecology of economic function saw "rings" around a central business district. This was the Chicago school's notion of urban space as function. The effects of transformation (or economic restructuring) "leapfrog" from the first ring to the third, leaving the second to decline, its support manufacturing, transportation, warehousing, and shipping function having been bypassed.[13]

Some sociologists and many urban political geographers disagree with this conceptualization of urban space. Those scholars who view political geography through a social constructionist lens have attempted to reconceptualize urban space as a historically specific idea that changes over time. Still others see the same regions of urban space as differing among different groups, since each group attributes a different meaning to the space and its contents.[14]

Some of the first works on gay and lesbian history and politics discussed cities as "safe havens" for sexual minorities.[15] Whether or not this is true, urban space does have a bearing on gay politics, particularly in voting behavior and social services. Identity certainly finds greater refinement in an urban space, if only for its population density. Not surprisingly, lesbians and gay men tend either to live in or to feel more comfortable in self-identifying urban areas.

The Primacy of Identity and Politics over Economics

One outcome of the economic model's hegemony in urban politics was the ensuing debate over political autonomy (or political liquidity) in the dynamics of local politics. Although this debate slowed the rush to economic determinism in urban politics, those writers using regime analysis who had tried to broaden the economic framework by combining interest-group analysis with historical analysis still saw economic function as the pole around which politics occurred.

Identity politics has a different if varied relationship between politics and economics. Although the expression of some social movements has an economic base in postindustrial politics or a focus on economic patterns that has a social effect, none uses economics as the primary motivator in politics. In particular, identity politics sees deeper motivations in politics.

Open Economy/Open Politics

The ultimate issue for students of urban political movements is whether cities are isolated political systems or arenas in which larger social forces express their political agenda. In short, the economic model draws its fundamental themes from the open nature of the urban economy. But it makes no similar assumption regarding an open political system. Links *among* cities or, more precisely, *among groups among cities* are manifested in cities pursuing different strategies.

The economic model has always underestimated the political interaction of urban life, as it must, since it assumes the preeminence of microeconomics and the separateness of cities as competing "firms." But it was never true that the Afro-nationalist movements in Chicago and Atlanta, Detroit and Oakland, New York and Montgomery were separate. And today it is not true that the political effects of the lesbian and gay rights movement are limited to San Francisco and New York. Likewise, other identity movements—for instance, those pursuing an Asian or Latino agenda or even a Christian fundamentalist agenda—are not separate from city to city.

The economism model assumed and is based on an open-economy model of urban politics, but it uses a discrete and isolated model of urban political behavior. There may be commonalities in the politics of Chicago and Houston, Rochester and Seattle, or even Paris and New York, but today these are largely considered as aspects of economic function and change. Concessions are made to history, patterns of emigration, and intergovernmental relations, but individual events are unique. The end point of the economism model is a city open economically but closed politically, whereas the identity field (or network) model outlined here assumes both an open economy and an open political system. It does not preclude neighborhood- and community-based politics challenging the effects of larger economic trends on localities but sees urban politics as going beyond such phenomena.

Conclusion: Complementary Metaphors of Politics in the Urban Setting

In the past two decades, although political economists and regime theorists have made important contributions to the study of urban politics, both have also presented problems.

The refinement of the economic model leaves little room to explain political phenomena that are not economically motivated, as economism's language, categories, and assumptions cannot structure or illuminate experience motivated by nonmarket rationales. Indeed, the success of advocates of microeconomic analogies in urban politics can be measured by the degree to which their vocabulary is now embedded in our own discourse about urban politics—and how distant it is from cultural anthropology and social theory.

The main argument here is that the political effects of the gay and lesbian social movement on urban politics cannot be comprehended by this dominant political-economy model of urban politics and policy. At best, the political-economy model can devalue the gay and lesbian movement as well as other urban social movements by assigning them to a catchall category of "postindustrial politics."

Key insights that an identity approach can suggest to the study of urban politics is that both the individual and the political system change; that involvement in politics changes the way that the individual sees politics; that the individual not only can change strategies but can also change his or her approach to experiencing political phenomena. Moreover, an identity approach can also explain why relatively minor allocative issues can suddenly become lightning rods for intense conflict. Most important, political action can change meanings—the meanings invested in language and social roles by society as a whole. Again, identity politics is not simply a veneer over distributional politics; rather, distributional politics acquires both real and symbolic overtones as a result of identity politics.

Regime theory offers more promise than does economism for incorporating identity-based movements into its metaphors, but it has limits, too. As used in economic development policy, a regime is a coalition that can maintain an electoral base sufficient to be elected for an extended period of time and to accommodate enough potential opponents that the regime's goals will not be jeopardized. It must have a broad "vision" for the city, one that serves as the base of consensus among the regime coalition. The regime also must have enough governing skills, resources, and organizational capacity to implement its vision. This vision, an elite vision, serves as a guide for the independent actions of the regime's members. While regime theorists focus on a postindustrial vision among elites, alternative visions associated with other identities are relegated to the sidelines of the modern city.

The contribution of postmodern and identity theory to regime theory is that it understands how "visions" are embedded in the languages and structures of politics at their deepest levels and how politics ultimately becomes a clash of identities, signs, and languages. But postmodern and identity theory can succeed only if regime theory returns to its roots in comparative politics and social organization theory and expands its framework.

Like mobile capital, identity movements test the boundaries of governmental jurisdiction because they involve cultural change, conceptions of self, and the construction of identities across legal boundaries. Identity politics is not "city politics" in the classic sense but uses cities as a stage or setting for the drama of politics. Identity fields cross city lines—they have no "city limits"—but are expressed principally in urban settings. In this narrative, there is no city politics of identity, only identity politics in an urban setting.

PART III

⁛

The Spaces, Values, and Votes of Urban Lesbians and Gay Men

⁙

CHAPTER 4

Identity, Urban Space, and Political Action

How do we make sense of what a pair of pedestrians walking through Philadelphia's Center City would see on an early evening? They might start at Independence Mall where the park is crossed by Market Street. Looking west, down Market, one of the grandest of America's city halls stands amid the office buildings and retail shops on either side of Broad and Market. The office towers and bank buildings that define the city's new skyline are a testament to the boom in Philadelphia in the early 1980s.

Looking south across the mall, Independence Hall frames the park. To the east, in the twenty-block area between Independence Mall and the Delaware River, stand the buildings that housed the First and Second Banks of the United States, the United States Mint and the Federal Reserve Bank of Philadelphia, and the homes of Benjamin Franklin and Betsy Ross. On Walnut Street, near the river is the City Tavern, the hostelry from which John Dickinson, author of the *Letters from a Farmer in Pennsylvania*, maintained the network of colonial correspondents. It was at City Tavern also that the delegates to the First Continental Congress met for discussions after their more formal meetings at Independence Hall recessed. Some of the debates begun in City Tavern found final expression in the themes of the Declaration of Independence and the Constitution. West of Independence Mall is Washington Park where the remains of the unknown soldier of the American Revolution were interred when Philadelphia served as the nation's second capital.

Just past Washington Park, on Ninth Street, our strollers encounter their first street dispenser of *PGN*—the *Philadelphia Gay News*—one of the oldest and most respected news weeklies serving lesbians and gay men in the United States. Farther west, before Twelfth Street, is Quince, a portal into older Philadelphia. Down Quince, south of Pine, and across Lombard, through small alleys and cul-de-sacs are the row houses of one of the oldest sections of Philadelphia. These are some of the loveliest streets in all of urban America. Now converted, these back alleys once housed working immigrants and African freedmen and -women of nineteenth-century Philadelphia. They lived and worked in the Trinity houses and carriage houses that are now quiet urban residences. The inlaid-granite carriageway tracks remain in many of these streets, and the hitching posts for the carriage horses have been restored on many blocks. The houses here fly American flags of the Revolutionary period, the thirteen-star flag of the 1976 bicentennial celebration, and the rainbow flag of lesbian and gay identity.

This area of old Philadelphia, now the gay-identified portion of Center City, bounded by south Eighth Street and Juniper on the east and west and Walnut and South Street on the north and south, was the core of the nineteenth-century Seventh Ward, the subject of W. E. B. Dubois's study *The Philadelphia Negro*. Dubois chose this area not only for its concentration of Africans but also for its diversity among Africans. Many of the homes of Philadelphia's nineteenth-century black professional and business classes are now occupied by urban gentrifiers, both gay and straight.

Neighborhoods in recycled and abandoned urban space such as Philadelphia's Center City where gay men and lesbians have homes can be found in nearly all the older cities of the United States. These urban domains of sexual identity are the most conspicuous expressions of the change brought by the cultural and political movement of city-dwelling lesbians and gay men. They are much like other urban spaces defined by cultural or ethnic affinities, with small merchants offering specialized services for the community, entertainment establishments, community service organizations, and even religious and customized government services. Many of these urban spaces include community centers that offer services for lesbians and gay men that were not provided in a comfortable way in other public or private venues. They are bounded by identity signifiers: "rainbow flags" along Santa Monica Boulevard in West Hollywood or North Clark Street in Chicago; billboards advertising same-sex vacation packages on Sheridan Square in New York; street fairs during June celebrating "Pride Day" and the events at Stonewall in 1969 in most cities; or even homeless gay men and youth on Market Street in San Francisco. The boundaries are subtle and not well defined, but the careful eye will catch them. What is the theoretical meaning of these territories, and what is their political significance?

From Private Spaces to Urban Sexual Domains

Since the initial studies of urban sexual domains,[1] the recovery of the identities of lesbians and gay men in the larger cities has been an important theme. Private "safe spaces" for lesbians and gay men predated the emergence of the cities' present-day sexual territories, but they were more limited in scale and function.

In his history of the commercialization of sex in New York City, Timothy Gilfoyle found that in the mid-nineteenth century, New York was relatively tolerant of prostitution, abortion, and homosexuality. The city's rapid industrialization as well as the cosmopolitanism associated with its Atlantic shipping traffic allowed for more liberal attitudes. Gilfoyle notes even the emergence of a "small but noticeable" gay male subculture in New York in the 1840s. The "sporting press" reported that young men attired in signifying clothing and of "feminine appearance and manners" cruised Broadway, City Hall Park, and farther south toward Cedar Lane.[2] In addition to these open spaces, heterosexual brothels provided an additional venue for same-sex sexual contact. "Boys" were available in many of the lower Manhattan brothels that catered primarily to heterosexual men, and in many cases, these "boys" were of African descent.

The dominant mercantile class that ran mid-nineteenth-century New York[3] regarded homosexuality as one of the costs associated with New York's emerging international status. Maybe more important was the fact that same-sex sexual behavior was not then viewed as a threat to "families." Forty years before the term *homosexual* was introduced into English, the perceived threat of same-sex sexuality was not to family and religion, but its "foreign nature" and "effeminacy." In short, to the city's commercial elite, tolerating homosexuals was an acceptable cost in the effort to make New York a major manufacturing and trade center.

The Emergence of "Bachelor Landscapes" and "Women's Spaces"

In the early part of the twentieth century, protected social spaces for men could be found in the big cities, such as men's private and public baths, drag balls, and gay-friendly bars and cruise areas. By the 1920s, at least in New York, a number of these areas were sufficiently defined that they were known as areas of male homosexual activity.

George Chauncey identified four such areas of early twentieth-century New York: Greenwich Village; the entertainment strips of Harlem;[4] the Bowery (and later Times Square as New York's entertainment center moved from the one to the other); and Brooklyn Heights, especially around the St. George Hotel.[5] Chauncey explains the identification with gay culture less in terms of the entertainment strips in these locales than the availability of single male and transient "bachelor housing." Similar clusters of women's housing in Greenwich Village and Harlem led to these as being identified as lesbian locales.[6]

These clusters of commercial sex establishments and friendly entertainment venues coexisted with gay boarding houses defining "gay space" in major cities, whereas small, informal groups were the focus of socializing outside these urban centers. In any case, open displays of affection were rare, except in the most protected spaces. Even in closed spaces, gay men and women were hesitant about revealing too much and usually exchanged only first names. The social barriers and spatial boundaries of sexual identity were frequently just the space between two people.

Although there were no female equivalents of "bachelor domains" in the major cities in the 1930s, there were "women's spaces," many of which were women's identified bars and social clubs. Such clubs existed in New York, Cleveland, and Oakland among other places. Faderman identified some women's bars in San Francisco and Chicago as having a specific working-class character.[7] In addition, women's "tea shops" catering to lesbians on the near North Side of Chicago and elsewhere also showed the emergence of "women's spaces." But none of these spaces were ever completely safe.

Upstate New York offered fewer options in the 1930s than did New York City, San Francisco, or Chicago, though Kennedy and Davis identified several lesbian-friendly spaces in Buffalo, including bars which became more open during the war years.[8] House parties, frequently racially mixed, gave many women who either were not welcomed or who did not feel comfortable in such bars a greater sense of identity and social affirmation. For black lesbians race, gender and class all worked against inclusion even in some local women's community making less formal spaces even more attractive. Kennedy and Davis show how African-American lesbians tended to rely on these house parties for socializing in pre-war industrial Buffalo.[9] The diversity of Buffalo's lesbian community in terms of class, race and "butch/femme" roles found expression in those supportive venues. In rural areas, informal groups and clubs were the sustained arenas for socializing with other lesbians.

World War II left an archipelago of new lesbian- and gay-identified spaces, especially on the West Coast. Many gay men and lesbians who had never been to a large city found new opportunities in the training centers and staging ports for the war. It was not uncommon for lesbians to find social spaces in gay male bars in the bigger cities. In the segregated black sections of some major cities, the tradition of the "drag ball" continued through the war years, with gays welcome, although gay blacks were still often excluded from "white-only" establishments and hotel lounges that were the sexual cruising sites in the South, Washington, D.C., Chicago, and (in fact) in most other parts of the country.[10]

The war's relocation effects created or expanded what are now some of the most vibrant lesbian and gay urban spaces. Although the location of gay and lesbian safe spaces in these cities were determined by the dynamics of the local urban landscape, their existence was not an expression of economic change effected by the emergence of the postindustrial urban complex or the new social movements of postmaterial politics. Instead, their existence predated the economic restructuring of postindustrial cities and took root in spaces previously identified as bohemian, minority, or some other identification not associated with middle-class values.

From Identity to Identi-*ties*

An increased interest in diversity within the contemporary urban sexual domains is also evident in the recent switch from the study of sexual "identity" to that of identi-*ties*. This work, largely conducted in the 1980s and early 1990s, emphasizes race and gender (and, in some cases, class), thus stretching the category "community" to encompass more diversity.[11] Historians and urban geographers have been at the forefront of this effort. The demographic components of urban gay communities (their own gender, racial, and class identities) have become the social basis of conflicting individual identities constructed across class, race, and gender.

Diversity in regard to race, especially in American cities, has been an important theme. African American and Latina feminists, regardless of their sexual orientation, have pointed to the problematics of a "gay identity" constructed as primarily white, male, well educated, and middle class. The demographic data, however, reveal much more diversity than this construct does and include even differences in identity formation. Stephen Murray, for example, offers an interesting analysis of diversity in identity formation in San Francisco's gay community, showing a wide variation not only in race and gender but also in education level, willingness to engage in political activism, and economic status. Trying to find common ground for political mobilization among all these identities has become one of the most difficult tasks of what has come to be called the gay rights movement.

The emphasis on the urban characteristic of sexual identity—particularly its focus in the United States on New York City, Los Angeles, New Orleans, and San Francisco, in Britain on London, and in Canada on Toronto, Montreal, and Vancouver—presents a somewhat false picture of gay and lesbian culture. New York, Los Angeles, and San Francisco are seen almost as exceptions to the way that lesbians and gay men living outside these cities conduct their everyday lives, and indeed, in many ways, they are.

Both the increased interest in diversity among gay men and lesbians and the historical reconstruction of sexual identity in urban settings beg the question of the assumed relationship between cities and gay identity in America. Yet with all the variance and diversity among men and women who identify with queer politics, the effect of this politics remains greatest in the urban setting.

The Urban Dimension of Present-day Sexual Identity

Three studies offering surrogate variables for gay and lesbian identity and which also offer urbanization scales indicate that despite the wide variance, sexual identity and urbanization are in fact linked. Whether this is because cities offer a "safe haven" for sexual identity and thus encourage in-migration or whether the presence of so many gay men and lesbians find sufficient support in urban areas to reach a fully gay/lesbian political identity cannot be ascertained from these data. Nevertheless, the association seems clear. The data sets are the 1988–1994 University of Chicago Survey of Sexual Behavior in the United States, the 1992 national presidential exit poll conducted by the Voter Research and Surveys (now the Voter News Service), the consortium of television networks that administers the national exit polls, and residential patterns derived from one of the nation's largest mailing lists of gay and lesbian contributors, activists, magazine subscribers, and others.

Urban Lesbian and Gay Presence: The NORC Data

In studies by the National Opinion Research Center for the University of Chicago's survey on sexuality, *The Social Organization of Sexuality*, a merged data set from several years of the annual General Social Survey, shows a strong association between urbanization and gay identity.[12] After distinguishing among same-sex sexual *behavior*, same-sex erotic *appeal*, and a declared gay, lesbian, or bisexual *identity*, the Chicago team examined several aspects of these three dimensions of being "gay." The differences in responses among those living in the twelve largest American cities, the next eighty-eight cities (thus one hundred cities in all), as well as those living in suburbs and nonurban areas affirm the strong relationship between urbanization and sexual identity (see table 4-1).

In the two most important categories, same-sex sexual behavior and self-identification as gay, lesbian, or bisexual, the percentages of positive reporting increase with urbanization. In one merged data set, the average percentage of the sample indicating at least one occasion of same-sex sexual contact since their eighteenth year in the twelve largest Metropolitan Statistical Areas (MSAs) was 16.2 percent for men and 6.2 percent for women. The results of the NORC self-administered and confidential questionnaire for the National Health and Social Life Survey (NHSLS), which also was used in the NORC's analysis, indicate similar same-sex sexual behavior: in the core cities of the twelve largest MSAs, this was 14.2 percent for men and 6.5 percent for

TABLE 4.1

Urbanization and Percentage of Gay/Lesbian/Bisexual Identity

Place of Residence:	Men	Women
Top 12 Central Cities (CCs):	9.2	2.6
Next 88 CCs:	3.5	1.6
Suburbs of Top 12 CCs:	4.2	1.9
Suburbs Next 88 CCs:	1.3	1.6
Other Urban Areas:	1.9	1.1
Rural Areas:	1.3	0.0

Source: National Opinion Research Center, as reported in Edward O. Laumann, John H. Gagnon, Robert T. Michael, and Stuart Michaels, *The Social Organization of Sexuality: Sexual Practices in the United States* (Chicago: University of Chicago Press, 1994), tables 8.1 and 8.2, pp. 303–5.

Note: Total (all sexual orientations), n = 8,125.

women. The reported rate of same-sex sexual behavior declined with the degree of urbanization of the interviewee's residence, with the lowest in rural
areas: about 2.5 percent from men and 2.0 percent for women.[13]

For our purposes, "gay/lesbian" identity—self-knowledge of and willingness to affirm one's sexuality—is a more important dimension. For both men
and women, the percentage of gay, lesbian, and bisexual self-identification of
residents in the central (core) cities of metropolitan areas increases as the
MSA's population size increases. Men in rural areas and suburbs show smaller rates of self-identity on the survey, and women in all categories show a lesser rate of identification than men do. The range on the NHSLS questionnaire
was 9.2 percent for men and 2.6 percent for women in the twelve largest central cities (see table 4-1). Again, there is a decline in gay/lesbian identity as
urban becomes rural. Other, less exhaustive surveys on sexual behavior conducted since the HIV epidemic have shown similar results.[14]

The National Exit-Poll Data

The national samples of self-identified gay men, lesbians, and bisexuals
from both the 1990 and 1992 Voter Research and Surveys exit polls show a
residential patterning of gay men and lesbians toward cities. The 1990 and
1992 national exit polls provided a data collection box for gay and lesbian
(these polls are described in more detail in chapter 5). In addition, the entire data set was geocoded to analyze voting patterns in regions of different
populations. Six categories were offered: (1) cities of more than 500,000 in
population, (2) cities of 250,000 to 500,000, (3) cities from 50,000 to
250,000, (4) suburbs (not further defined), (5) small towns (5,000 to
25,000), and (6) rural areas. These geocategories display the results of representative precincts chosen by VRS sampling selected on a nationwide
basis and do not represent any specific city or region. U.S. Census Bureau–defined MSAs provided the urbanization scale.

When self-identification rates are linked to the relative population of the
jurisdiction in which the selected precincts were located, patterns immediately emerge. As table 4-2 indicates, the larger cities tend to have overall
greater percentages of self-identification. In medium-size cities with populations of 250,000 to 500,000, the identification rate is as high as 8.2 percent, equal for men and women. The highest general rates are in these cities.
The sample precincts chosen from the very largest cities, more than
500,000 in population, do not indicate as consistent a pattern between the

TABLE 4.2

Urbanization and Percentage of Gay/Lesbian/Bisexual Voter Identification

Locale of Sample Precinct:	Men	Women
Large Cities (above 500,000):	8.1	3.3
Medium Cities (250,000–500,000):	8.3	8.4
Smaller Cities (50,000–250,000):	3.5	2.0
Suburbs:	2.5	2.1
Small Towns (5,000–10,000):	1.3	1.2
Rural Areas:	2.3	1.5

Source: VRS 1992 national presidential exit poll, November 1992.

Note: Data weighted by VRS formulas for analysis. Gay/lesbian/bisexual sample: n = 420, total sample: 15,490 unweighted.

genders as the other levels of urbanization do but still provide a comparatively high rate.[15] Women in large cities are not as likely to self-identify as lesbian or bisexual as men are to self-identify as gay. Smaller cities and rural areas provide the lowest rates of self-identification.

Some regional and large-city exit polls also began to offer a gay/lesbian self-identifier on their data collection sheets. First in New York and then in San Francisco and Los Angeles, sexual orientation is now an ongoing part of exit-poll data collection sheets. In each city's exit polls, rates much higher than the national self-identification rates are indicated: In Los Angeles (not including West Hollywood), the rate was 5 percent in the 1993 mayoral runoff and 4 percent in the 1997 general election. In San Francisco, the rate was between 13 and 16 percent (when bisexuals were included as a separate category), and in New York City, the rate was as high as 7.9 percent in the November 1993 general election. Of course, all these indicators, whether national, state, or large city, are percentages of voters, not of the general population. As is discussed in Chapter 5, it is not known whether gay voters tend to "overvote" or "undervote" as a percentage of all voters. In any case, since the first inclusion of gay/lesbian self-identifiers, exit polls have shown higher rates of sexual identity in cities than nationwide, with the rates higher among men than among women.

Gay/Lesbian Organizational Mailing List Data

Another indicator of urban concentration of lesbian and gay identity can be found in the gay community. An analysis of the nation's largest mailing list of donors, subscribers, activists, and participants in social and political events in the gay community reveals the same patterns as in the NORC sexual identity and VRS voter self-identification data. The list of more than 500,000 was merged with raw (unweighted) data from the decennial census aggregated at the zip code level, also showing a general tendency toward urban concentration. On a per capita basis, the raw data from the list and the zip code area data from the census indicated a weak but positive and certain correlation with the percentage of residents living in cities and a mild negative correlation with the percentage of suburban, rural, and farm residents (see table 4-3). When the data were reorganized and referenced against a national mean for the concentration of list households by zip code, the urban association was even stronger.

These were simple correlations. But when the same data were tested for possible curvilinear relationships, a more complicated pattern emerged: 131

TABLE 4.3
Gay and Lesbian Activists/Subscribers/Donors in Cities

Per Capita Rate of Addressees by Zip Code

Census Bureau Categories	Correlate of Addressees per Capita[a]
Urban, Central Cities:	.1702
Urban Suburbs:	−.0333
Nonurban:	−.1374
Rural, on Farms:	−.0904[b]

Zip Code Concentration of Gay/Lesbian Households

Census Bureau Categories	Correlate of Residential Concentration
Urban, Central Cities:	.2110
Urban Suburbs:	−.0213
Nonurban:	−.1886
Rural, on Farms:	−.0863[b]

Sources: Strubco, Inc., and U.S. Census Bureau.

[a]Simple correlation coefficients (r). All correlations are significant at less than .001. To eliminate office complexes with their own zip codes and federal government business zip codes, zip code areas with populations of less than 150 were eliminated from the base. In all, 28,294 zip codes were subjected to the analysis. The business zip codes eliminated were overwhelmingly in urban areas (per capita correlation with urban was $r = .3543$).

[b]The Census Bureau defines a rural area as not in an urbanized area and not in a town of 2,500 or more population. The definition of a farm is complex but includes sales of agricultural products of at least $1,000 in 1989.

zip codes were found in which at least 2.5 percent of the total population of the zip code area was gay, lesbian, or bisexual residents (with the base representing all demographic groups, including children and senior citizens). Nearly all were in major urban centers, college communities, or vacation communities that traditionally have a strong lesbian and gay presence (such as Provincetown, Massachusetts; Guerneville, California; Key West, Florida). In sixty-one zip code areas, at least 5 percent of the total population was gay, lesbian, or bisexual residents. Again, all were in major urban areas or vacation communities. Penetration rates as high as 2.5 percent and 5 percent are extraordinarily high for such mailing lists, especially for a population that is probably less than 10 percent of the total. The pattern here resembles more a hyperbolic than a linear association, with levels of per capita residents in each zip code increasing dramatically with proximity to gay- and lesbian-identified urban neighborhoods.

Although all these data sources imply an association of gay and lesbian identity with cities, many lesbians and gay men do not live in cities, and even those who do live in cities do not necessarily, or even primarily, live in the centers of gay/lesbian concentration. But whatever the curve of the chart or the nuances of the measures, it is clear that sexual identity, at least as expressed in politics, is related to urbanization in the United States.

Mapping the Urban Domains of Sexual Identity

The urban characteristic of gay identity is not a new finding, however; it just is now better defined empirically. We can identify urban space as a primary locus of gay identity, but what about the differences within those spaces, especially outside Manhattan, West Hollywood, and San Francisco? What do these urban spaces mean for lesbians and gay men and also for the cities themselves?

Early Attempts at Mapping Sexual Identity

The first sophisticated studies of spacial patterning by sexual identity were conducted in San Francisco. Manual Castells, working with Don Lee and Karen A. Murphy, examined what he came to call the *gay territory* of San Francisco and its role as a base for a social and political movement built on sexuality. Castells and Murphy used five dimensions to classify and map sexual domains in San Francisco.[16] None of the measures was used to the exclusion of others, and in the end, Castells relied on a judgmental assessment of the overlapped maps of spaces identified by these five indicators.[17] The method could not, however, reveal lower-income lesbian and gay San Franciscans living in the older Polk Valley area or more wealthy ones (largely gay men) living in Buena Vista, on the east side of Twin Peaks.

Having defined these areas as gay territories (and others as nongay territories), Castells further analyzed them according to twelve census variables.[18] He concluded that the gay territories did in fact have identifiable social roots. Most important, he found that the percentage of the population under age eighteen was a strong descriptor of gay versus nongay territories. This he termed a *family space* variable.

A second variable distinguishing between gay and nongay territories was what Castells called *property*, the census dimension referring to the percentage of housing units that were owner occupied. He found no other relationship in the measures tested and concluded that gay (male) territory was culturally rather than economically based. Castells also described property and family values as "major walls protecting the 'straight universe' against gay influence."[19]

Using other techniques, Castells added *higher rent* and *education* dimensions to explain more differences in the two territories.[20] He found that although gay territory was rental, it did not encompass the highest rental spaces in the city. Higher rents would add a third barrier to expansion of gay territory in San Francisco.

Fifteen years later, much is still true about Castells's, Murphy's, and Lee's analysis. Gay territory is still concentrated in the Castro district, where men outnumber women and whose residents have a higher rate of educational achievement than that of the general population. But by the 1990s, other trends were evident as well. The expansion of gay territory was not limited by higher rents, as Castells and Murphy had expected, but by "family territory." There has been gay and lesbian in-migration to the higher-rent, higher-value Pacific Heights area but no in-migration into the higher-income St. Francis Woods area, a domain of upper-middle-class family housing. There has been some expansion onto the avenues west of Twin Peaks, but conflict between gay entrepreneurs and Latino activists at the perimeter between the Castro and the Mission districts has limited expansion in that direction.

Despite these relatively minor problems in their analysis, the most controversial aspect of his study was how Castells defined lesbians out of the analysis. San Francisco's lesbians may have been less visible in the late 1970s then were gay men, though they certainly were present. By the 1990s, there were identifiable women's areas in the general MSA that overlapped with the Castro at Bernal Heights and Noe Valley but also included neighborhoods in Berkeley and Oakland across the bay, as well as in the South Bay areas of San Jose. In addition, whereas gay men such as Harvey Milk, Jim Foster, and Harry Britt once dominated lesbian and gay politics in San Francisco, the combined effect of women's assertiveness and the HIV epidemic has been the rise of women as the principal leaders of the city's sexual minority, including Roberta Achtenberg, former supervisor and assistant secretary of housing and urban development who ran for mayor in 1995; Carol Migden, a member of the Board of Supervisors; and Melinda Paras, a former health commissioner who was made executive director of the National Gay and Lesbian Task Force in 1995.

One problem with Castells and Murphy's analysis was its inferring from the apparent lack of women's neighborhood spaces that lesbians were not territorial because they were women. Castells and Murphy's generalization about women may be the result of a negative approach to gay space; that is, they see space as defensive, as opposed to other social forms and constructions. But by stating that women are less territorial because they could not find such spaces, Castells and Murphy relegated to a secondary status the issues of income, race, and space in regard to lesbians. This conclusion also ascribes to women universal characteristics that may in fact be socially constructed. Readers familiar with recent debates in gay studies will immediately see this as an essentialist conclusion.

Maybe the most important problem with Castells and Murphy's conclusions, at least for urban studies, was that even though their work was confined to San Francisco, many scholars were tempted to generalize it to other cities. As a result, the gentrifying role of gays and the rehabilitation of older Victorian houses in the city are now established in the urban development literature. But San Francisco is only one case and hardly the typical case, for either the political and economic processes that surround urban transformation or the politics of lesbians and gay men.

Finding the Urban Domains of Sexual Identity

To compare lesbian and gay territories, we need a way to view the specific characteristics of different cities. The first step is to establish a surrogate indicator for the concentration of lesbian and gay residents, as Castells and Murphy did. The second is to study these identified urban spaces in the context of a data set that permits comparison.

As noted earlier, the decennial census provides a surrogate indicator for dedicated same-sex households.[21] These data are available at the PUMS (public-use microdata sample) level and can be used for a limited analysis of gay and lesbian households. The sample from the 1990s survey was small, however. The Census Bureau estimated a total of 3.187 million households with unmarried partners—both same sex and opposite sex. Of these, the bureau estimated that only about 145,000 were same sex. The advantage of these census PUMS data is that they can define specific households. But the exclusion from the data set of single, non-co-resident-partnered gay men and lesbians and those living in other arrangements introduces a bias that cannot be overcome through weighting. An additional problem is that in its most useful format—the PUMS 1 percent and 5 percent samples—the data are linked to geographic areas that are far larger than bloc groups, census tracts, or even zip codes, the other potential geostatistical boundaries that can be used with census data. For example, the PUMS area for Rochester, New York, covers the entire city.

This book uses an alternative method, albeit with problems as well. The primary data set used in this chapter to identify gay/lesbian residential concentration is not the decennial census but a direct-mail list created from nearly one hundred smaller regional lists and a smaller number of national lists. Because the data set identifies more than 525,000 households by merging regional lists, this "master" list is the largest of its kind in the country pertaining to lesbians and gay men. It is a "merge and purge" list that covers all fifty states, the District of Columbia, Puerto Rico, and several Canadian provinces. Equally important is that the list is not aimed at direct marketing but at political networking. It includes both small and large donors to gay candidates for local office, subscribers to lesbian and gay newspapers and magazines, and contributors to national gay organizations.[22]

From this source two indicators of residential concentration were constructed. The first is an index of residential concentration that refers to a mean within each Metropolitan Statistical Area (MSA). That is, the zip codes in the U.S. Census Bureau–defined MSA became the base of an analysis of regional concentration. After a mean across the region was established, each zip code was compared with this regional average. If gay and lesbian households were randomly distributed throughout a metropolitan region, the index would be 1.0 in all zip codes. Not surprisingly, no MSA exhibited such a pattern. Those areas containing an unusually large number of lesbian or gay male households scored high on an index of regional concentration. Zip codes with an index of 2 or more also were noted. In some cities, the highest level of concentration was as high as 27 or even 35. The West Village in New York, for example, scored 27 when compared with the 625 zip codes in all the New York State counties in and around New York City.

The second dimension was a simple per capita ratio of gay/lesbian households on the list to the total population in each zip code as reported by Census Bureau for 1990. In some unusual zip code areas, the per capita ratio was as high or higher than 10 or 20 percent. In zip code 94114 in San Francisco, the ratio was 22.5 percent, and in zip code 10014 in New York's West Village, it was 11.6 percent. In Houston, this index was highest, 2 percent, in the city's Montrose section, in zip code 77006. A ratio of 2 percent shows a substantial degree of penetration, and in fact, Montrose is the center of Houston's gay residential neighborhood.

A per capita index can also reveal the difference in degree of concentration in different cities. Chicago, for example, has an extraordinarily compact pattern of gay and lesbian residents, whereas the Tampa/St. Petersburg area has a diffuse pattern.

But relying on these figures can also be misleading, especially in regard to larger cities' downtowns. In Chicago, for example, the 60606 zip code had a greater than 50 percent ratio of names on the list to total population. This figure is highly misleading, however, because this Downtown Loop zip code area contains few real residents; in fact, the total census count was fewer than one hundred individuals. The geographic center of gay identity in Chicago is more accurately found using the other index showing that the greatest concentration of gay residents is farther north in New Town, in the areas covered by zip code 60657. Similarly, New York's Wall Street area (zip code 10005) and nearby Trinity Station (zip code 10006) have per capita rates of more than 12 percent, even though each contains fewer than 150 residents. Outside Manhattan, New York's highest-ranking zip code on a per capita basis is 11371—La Guardia Airport. In each of these Chicago and New York cases, business addresses, not households, dominate.

Nevertheless, this "master" list is obviously not a randomly generated data set. Although its very size ensures that every conceivable subsidiary demographic category is covered, it is unlikely that each category reflects its percentage of the total population. Even though it is not a direct-merchandising list in the usual sense (i.e., heavily geared toward higher-income groups), it does eliminate the lowest economic groups in the gay community. We can also assume that this list is biased toward men rather than women (although all self-identification indicators show that more men identify as gay than women do as lesbian—about 60 percent to 40 percent) and is more representative of whites than minorities.[23] For example, in New York and Chicago, blacks are underrepresented, and in the lower San Francisco Bay Area, Latinos are underrepresented. Thus, in all circumstances, the biases of these data must be taken into account.

Again, these measures are used to identify space, not persons or households. We are seeking the common and differing characteristics of gay neighborhoods defined as concentrations of lesbians and gay men, not those characteristics of households or individuals. That is, the indicators are nothing more then identifiers of "domains of sexual identity."

To check further the reliability of the instrument as an effective indicator of spaces, we compared the indicators with other methods of estimating lesbian and gay geographic concentrations in specific MSAs. In New York, we compared them with a Census Bureau sample of same-sex households; in San Francisco, with electoral precincts that local political consultants consider prime concentrations of lesbian and gay voters; in Minneapolis, with a local analysis of a mailing list conducted independently by the Minneapolis Gay and Lesbian Community Center; and in all forty MSAs studied, with census-tract concentrations of nonfamily household structures. In all four cases, the geographic regions identified by extracts from the mailing list matched areas identified by other means: the census-defined regions of high concentrations of same-sex households, voter concentrations in San Francisco, local mailing lists at the census-tract level, and percentage of nonfamily households nationwide. Nonetheless, we still caution on possible bias. To ascertain the reliability of geographical concentrations generated by MSA residential concentrations on a mailing list, we cross-checked them with standard entertainment and commercial guides produced nationally and locally. In addition, in many cases, we asked local knowledgeable residents to check for errors. Finally, remember that we used the method and data sets solely to identify zip code areas that contain higher-than-average concentrations of gay and lesbian residents—nothing more.

Social and Demographic Correlates of Gay and Lesbian Neighborhoods

The defining characteristics of urban domains of sexual identity are primarily social and demographic, not economic. Although economic variables play differing roles in the cities examined, they display no universal influences. The nature of the cities themselves, almost by region, add a third dimension to the kinds of neighborhoods to which men and women identified as gay and lesbian gravitate. Our analysis of forty MSAs affirms one of Castells and Murphy's initial findings but casts doubt on many others.

Our findings are the result of correlation analysis of a merged file of the surrogate indicators of residential concentration of gay men and lesbians described earlier, with more than two hundred frequently asked variables from the standard extraction files of the 1990 decennial census. We analyzed more than forty MSAs, essentially all those with sufficient data to show patterns. The analysis was conducted metropolitan area by metropolitan area at the zip code level of aggregation.

Simple Demographics

By far the most consistent themes in neighborhoods identified by concentrations of gay residents were age and household structure:

GAY AND LESBIAN URBAN ENCLAVES TEND TO BE YOUNG

In nearly all urban spaces that can be identified as having a strong gay and lesbian presence, the typical resident is young, and the household is small in size. In most of the forty MSAs studied, concentrations of gay and lesbian residents correlated positively and significantly with U.S. Census Bureau–defined 24- to 35-year-old age groupings. Three (Austin, Albany, and St. Louis) of the thirteen MSAs in which the 25- to 35-year-old category did not correlate with the concentration of gay residents contained large student populations. In these cities, the 18- to 24-year-old category correlated with the lesbian and gay presence. In addition, several of the cities showed strong relationships with both of the younger adult age categories (Birmingham, Milwaukee, Philadelphia, Boston, Cincinnati, and Buffalo.) Again, lesbian and gay residential clusters near university communities were important. When the younger adult age categories were collapsed to one 20- to 40-year-old indicator, nearly all the forty cities showed strong correlations with the presence of gay men and lesbians. The exceptions were smaller farm belt cities (such as Omaha) or cities with a large portion of older or retired residents (such as Miami/Fort Lauderdale, Tampa/St. Petersburg, and Las Vegas). An analysis of the middle-age categories reinforces the profile of younger urban gay territories. In most of the cities we studied, there is a negative correlation in the middle-age brackets. The results vary from city to city, but it is clear that lesbian and gay residents tend to live with, or are themselves, younger urbanites.

PRESENCE OF SENIORS

One surprising finding of our analysis was the degree to which lesbians and gay men live alongside senior citizens. Although this was true in cities known as having a high proportion of retirees—Honolulu, San Diego, Miami/Fort Lauderdale, and Tampa/St. Petersburg—it was also true in some of the older cities of the Midwest and South: Chicago (especially in zip code areas with 50 percent or more African American residents), Minneapolis/St. Paul, Milwaukee, New Orleans, Atlanta, Omaha, Rochester, St. Louis, Cincinnati, and Cleveland all showed positive and significant correlations between the presence of gay men and lesbians, and senior citizens. The copresence of gay men, lesbians, and seniors in the same neighborhood in these older cities is probably a manifestation of changing neighborhoods. As we will see later, "gay neighborhoods" are typically older neighborhoods, and so the presence of senior citizens who have remained in changing ethnic neighborhoods is not surprising. In some larger cities, this process has been termed *naturally aging neighborhoods*: urban enclaves whose population is aging and in need of new services, whose neighbors are young people usually requiring few services. Among these younger residents are lesbians and gay men.

HOUSEHOLD SIZE AND STRUCTURE

Aside from age, the two other significant correlates associated with urban spaces of high concentrations of lesbian and gay residents are household size and household structure. "Gay territories" are dominated by single households or couple households without children. In all the cities we studied, the presence of gay and lesbians residents correlated negatively with average household size (the range of correlation coefficients was a low of $r = -.2212$ in the San Francisco Bay Area to a high of $r = -.7036$ in Cincinnati, all at statistically significant levels). It was universally true also that neighborhoods with a strong gay and lesbian presence correlated positively with the percentage of single households and the percentage of people living alone (coefficients ranged from $r = .41$ to $r = .72$). Households in these urban spaces were less likely to be headed by married couples or to be composed of married couples and children. To state it differently, it was universally true in the forty MSAs that those neighborhoods with a strong lesbian and gay presence were dominated by nonfamily households (the range was from $r = .46$ to .76).

THE COPRESENCE OF FEMALE-HEADED HOUSEHOLDS AND GAY AND LESBIAN RESIDENTS

The presence of female-headed households in these spaces adds another dimension to the profile. A substantial body of urban literature has shown that urban space is being "genderized" and that this has important social and economic implications.[24] Many of the cities we studied had a large number of female-headed households residing side by side with gay or lesbian households. The relationship ranges from statistically insignificant to a substantial positive relationship (Baltimore was the highest, at $r = .6628$). In no city or MSA we studied did the presence of lesbian and gay residents correlate negatively with the presence of female-headed households. When we correlated the presence of gay and lesbian residents with the percentage of female-headed households with children, we found a positive and significant correlation in most of the older northeastern and midwestern metropolitan regions: Chicago, Baltimore, Milwaukee, Philadelphia, Washington, Cleveland, Albany, the Quad Cities, the Twin Cities, Buffalo, Boston, Indianapolis, and New Orleans. In fact, in the Northeast, only New York City showed no such relationship. Although this pattern was common in the Northeast, it was also found in other cities around the country, including some of the Sun Belt cities, such as Phoenix, Denver, Sacramento, and Tampa/St. Petersburg. The overlap of gender space and spaces associated with sexual identity seems certain.

The absence of children is also a strong and expected correlate, although it is not a universal aspect of neighborhoods identified by a gay and lesbian presence. Whereas most of the age categories of children correlated negatively with the presence of gay and lesbian residents, in medium-size cities we found very young children (up to four years old) in neighborhoods with a strong identity as gay and lesbian. In the largest cities, however (New York, San Francisco Bay Area, Chicago, Denver/Boulder, and Philadelphia), this was not true.

Thus, our first analysis of lesbian and gay urban spaces shows that age and household structure are two of the most important defining factors. In many cities, the presence of seniors, young nongay couples, female-headed households, and, often, female-headed households with children, reveals the diversity of urban spaces with a strong gay and lesbian presence. The image that emerges is less of "gay spaces"—although from a semiotic perspective, they are—but of spaces dominated by nontraditional families. In fact, it is only in the larger Castro district of San Francisco or portions of West Hollywood or maybe small sections of lower Manhattan where "gay space" may actually apply to 50 percent of residents identifying as lesbians or gay men. It seems that the definition of these urban spaces is not necessarily what is present but what is absent: married couples with children, and their associated family household structures.

Sexual Identity and Racial Patterning of Urban Space

The relationship of race to lesbian and gay urban space is more complicated than to age and household structure.

The initial image of the "gay ghetto" was that it was male, white, and middle class. The "whiteness" of gay communities become a subject of debate, first by African American gay men and lesbians, then Latinos, and, most recently, Asians. As late as the 1980s, some gay bars in New York wanted to project a young, male, collegiate look and so discriminated against black gay men. In San Francisco, the expansion of gay territory into the Western Addition and toward the Haight put lesbian and gay immigrants to the city in conflict with black residents and toward the South of Market areas, with both blacks and Latinos.

In much of urban America, the profile of the educated gay white male as the dominant one of the gay movement conflicted with the economic aspirations of urban African Americans. In some cities, the combination of real economic issues, the traditional affiliation of African Americans with American Baptists and Methodists, and, later, a refocus on Afro-centrism, which viewed homosexuality as a set of behaviors outside African traditions, placed the two communities at loggerheads.

Has the creation of neighborhoods with high concentrations of lesbians and or gay men also been the creation of white, male spaces in urban America? The reality is that in almost all the cities we studied, gay and lesbian territories tend to be more integrated than the urban and suburban areas of the surrounding metropolitan regions. In most MSAs, gay men and lesbians live in the central city, and thus almost by definition, these neighborhoods are more integrated, especially in older center cities. In Philadelphia, Pittsburgh, Baltimore, New Orleans, Washington, Hartford, Sacramento, Albany, the Quad and Twin Cities, Buffalo, Cincinnati, Boston, and Indianapolis, the presence of gay men or lesbians correlates negatively and significantly with the percentage of whites in the region. Nearly all these cities are in the older industrial belt of the East and Midwest. In no MSA we examined did the presence of lesbian and gay residents according to zip code correlate positively with the percentage of white residents.

Nevertheless, in some cities, different patterns specific to those cities are discernible.

CHICAGO

In the Chicago MSA, gay areas on the city's north side contain large enough numbers of Asians, Latinos, and even Native Americans to correlate significantly and positively with the presence of lesbians and gay men. But those areas of the Chicago MSA that have a strong lesbian and gay presence do not show a similar and significant presence of African Americans. The Chicago region as a whole has consistently demonstrated a division by race in housing, economics, and voting patterns.[25] When we examined the city of Chicago apart from its two-state MSA, the racial pattern was even more apparent. Although we could not find any specific patterns of sexual identity in regard to Latinos in the city of Chicago, we did observe two statistically significant trends: a positive correlation of people identifying as Native American and, most important given Chicago's history, an actual negative relationship with black residents ($r = -.3108$). This was unusual in the analysis of the forty case cities; most had a greater mix of Anglo/white and African Americans in gay areas or at least were better integrated when viewed from the MSA's perspective, if not in the core central city. But Chicago's black/white housing patterns, a legacy of the Illinois Jim Crow laws and a policy of the older Democratic machine, were also evident in "gay neighborhoods." Moreover, when we looked at the city's fourteen predominantly black zip code areas, the only statistically significant correlation with gay presence we found was the presence of Asians (probably in part owing to the presence of the University of Chicago and the residential patterns of the Hyde Park area). The presence of lesbians and gays in predominantly black zip code areas were again along the lake, but on the south side of Chicago.

DALLAS/HOUSTON/ATLANTA/NEW ORLEANS

Despite the large black populations in all southern and some Sun Belt cities, there is no marked overlap between lesbian and gay residential spaces and those of African Americans. In Dallas, Birmingham, Houston, and Atlanta, there is no suggestion that zip code areas with a higher-than-average number of gay and lesbian residents are more integrated than other neighborhoods in the same MSA region. In almost all metropolitan areas of the Northeast corridor and the Midwest, gay space is more likely to be integrated (i.e., significantly and negatively correlated with the presence of whites), whereas there is no such finding at either the MSA or the city level in the larger southern urban areas we analyzed. In fact, Houston showed a negative correlation between the presence of gay men and lesbians and that of African Americans. In Atlanta, the presence of gay men and lesbians in zip code areas is also correlated negatively with presence of African Americans ($r = -.4087$) and positively with whites and Latinos. In the city of Dallas, independent of the greater Dallas/Fort Worth area, the presence of gay and lesbian residents again is correlated negatively with presence of African Americans ($r = -.3038$).

New Orleans, however, with its strong tradition of lesbian and gay culture, showed a different pattern. When analyzed simply as a city (and not an MSA region), New Orleans has statistically almost perfect racial segregation in housing (the correlation coefficient between the percentages of whites and blacks in New Orleans's seventeen zip codes is $r = -.9365$). But in the zip code areas with a large gay presence, there is no statistically significant relationship between the percentages of white and black residents. In short, in the city of New Orleans, those neighborhoods with a large gay and lesbian presence are less likely to be segregated than is the surrounding city. These findings are especially important, since both Houston and Atlanta are seen as the new centers of lesbian and gay life in the South. That the housing patterns in these two new centers of gay presence are racially the most separate says much about the structural differences and growth patterns in these cities as they affect the development of "gay neighborhoods." It also demonstrates why the image of the white, male, middle-class gay neighborhood is often credible.

THE LOS ANGELES BASIN

Los Angeles, the second largest gay center in the country, also shows a mixed racial pattern in relation to sexual identity. The greater Los Angeles/Long Beach/Riverside MSA demonstrates no statistically significant regional relationship between racial categories and measures of lesbian and gay presence at the zip code level. If the analysis ended here, however, it would be highly misleading. When Los Angeles County was examined independent of the overall Los Angeles/Long Beach/Riverside MSA, (so as to include Santa Monica, Pasadena, and West Hollywood but exclude Riverside County), racially defined housing patterns against sexual identity did emerge. This is actually a mildly positive but statistically significant correlation between the presence of gay men and lesbians and the presence of Anglos/whites ($r = .2093$). Again, this is a pattern very different from those observed in the Northeast and Midwest.

In fact, when Los Angeles is examined alone (and thus excluding West Hollywood), the degree of racial patterning is even stronger. Those zip code areas in Los Angeles City with a defined presence of gay men and lesbians have a strong positive correlation with the percentage of white residents ($r = .5426$) and a strong negative relationship with the percentage of black residents ($r = -.4225$). This is also the pattern of Houston, Atlanta, and Dallas.

THE SAN FRANCISCO BAY AREA

The San Francisco Bay area displays no regional correlation between gay and lesbian residential concentration and race. None. Thus the question is a local one, essentially of the cities of San Francisco, San Jose, and the East Bay communities. In San Francisco itself, no correlation met the minimal significance threshold used in this section of the study ($p = .01$).[26] In the East Bay counties of Alameda and Contra Costa, which include the cities of Oakland, Berkeley, and Richmond, no statistically significant relationships were found. In Alameda County alone, the only relationship identified is weak and negative regarding Latinos. In Santa Clara County, the county containing San Jose, no statistically significant evidence was found regarding possible overlaps in the patterns of gay and racial housing. Nor was anything statistically significant found in the city of San Jose, although "gay" space and Latino areas seem to overlap somewhat. Thus a small amount of gay white separation can be found in San Francisco proper, but the East Bay communities of Alameda, Berkeley, and Oakland, typically identified as women's space by the Bay Area's gay community, show no appreciable sign of racial separation at the zip code level.

THE BOROUGHS OF NEW YORK CITY

The New York City metropolitan area also displays a wide variety of results. In the five counties of New York as a unit, racial patterning, though evident, is not nearly as strong as it is in Los Angeles. The city's 165 zip code areas have a mild negative correlation with the presence of African Americans citywide ($r = -.2302$) and a mild positive correlation with the presence of whites ($r = .2674$).

This racial pattern is more apparent in Manhattan. When we removed Manhattan from the calculations and examined just the four outer boroughs (Queens, the Bronx, Brooklyn, and Staten Island), we found no statistically significant correlations with race. In Manhattan itself, the zip codes with a high concentration of lesbian and gay residents correlate significantly with the percentage of white residents ($r = .5768$) and negatively with the percentage of black residents ($r = -.4507$). Manhattan's overall housing patterns also are reflected in gay territories. Even the rapid growth of the gay and lesbian population in the East Village near the Lower East Side and in the northern portions of the Upper West Side adjacent to Harlem do not compensate for the fact that in Manhattan, blacks and the self-identified lesbians and gay men affiliated with some sort of community organization do not live side by side in large numbers.

The situation in Brooklyn is different. We discovered no significant results when we correlated the concentration of lesbian and gay residents with the racial categories of Brooklyn's thirty-seven zip codes. This finding reinforces anecdotal information that Brooklyn's lesbian and gay residential clusters reflect the city's overall racial makeup better than Manhattan does or that at least they are located in closer proximity to black- and Latino-identified areas.

In middle-class Queens, the overlap of a large Latino population with lesbian and gay residents in Jackson Heights (as well as a strong Latino gay community itself) is clearly observable, as are overlapping clusters of lesbian and gay residents and Korean, Chinese, and South Asian residents in the Jackson Heights and Kew Gardens/Forest Hills areas of central Queens. There are strong and significant positive correlations between the gay presence and the Latino presence in Queens ($r = .4961$; $p = .000$) and with Asians ($r = .4378$; $p = .001$). But as in Manhattan, there is a clear separation between clusters of gay residents and the middle-class African American neighborhoods of southeast Queens ($r = -.3537$; $p = .006$).

Lesbians and gay men tend to live in more integrated neighborhoods than straight people do, largely because they choose to live in center cities, which almost by definition are more integrated. Nevertheless, in many of the cities we studied, housing still displays a racial pattern, much of which is related to household income.

In addition, across the country, "gay neighborhoods" are more likely to be integrated by Latinos and Asians than by African Americans. The reason may be greater mobility among newer immigrants, the historic legal discrimination against blacks in cities of the South, Washington, and Chicago, or economic factors. These patterns are different in the Sun Belt cities where separation is strong. The patterns of Los Angeles, Houston, and Atlanta may reflect their spatial growth and economic change, which has exacerbated racial patterning in housing.

Nevertheless, we found a wide variation in the degree to which lesbian- and gay-identified space is "race-neutral" space. On balance, these neighborhoods are more integrated than most of their surrounding urban spaces, even in the central cities. But it is clear that sexual identity is not so strong that it can overcome the historical patterns of housing separation in America, a fact that creates a series of flash points in many cities between gay identity and African American identity in school policies, development policy, and policies regarding HIV and AIDS.

Gender, Sexual Identity, and Urban Space

As a counterpoint to the essentialism of Castells and Murphy—that men are more "territorial" than women—several researchers have tried to show that women's communities add an important spatial dimension to women's and lesbians' identity. The principal focus of these studies are areas known in the women's community as having a large lesbian presence—East San Francisco Bay; greater Park Slope in Brooklyn; Northampton, Massachusetts; Santa Fe; and some medium-size and smaller cities not usually identified with sexual spaces.

The study of these lesbian "identity spaces" has been added to the larger body of research on the genderization of urban space, largely conducted by scholars interested in the interaction of social welfare policy and women's studies. Some urban spaces are identified by gender primarily because of changes in urban household structures, especially the dramatic increase in female-headed households. In the past, the usual gender identification of urban (and nonurban) spaces pertained to the percentage of senior citizens. That is, the percentage of older women was much higher in older ethnic neighborhoods and retirement communities, owing to the differences in the sexes' life expectancies.

To add to this body of research, we attempted to identify differences in urban residential patterns between lesbians and gay men. Again, given the method used here, the sample pool is made up of those individuals who are sufficiently engaged in a gay or lesbian political or social activity to be on the network mailing list. Note that most names/households on the list were not identified by gender (except in New York City and the San Francisco Bay Area), but despite these limitations, some residence patterns of gay men and lesbians can be determined.

Several MSAs were broken out by sex. The six communities analyzed were Atlanta, Birmingham, Brooklyn, Albuquerque/Santa-Fe, Baltimore, and the San Francisco Bay Area (including the cities of San Francisco and San Jose and the counties of the South Bay and the East Bay). In each of the six samples, the pattern in the female-coded households is not surprising, but in some cases, the results are important.[27] Three themes are significant.

MORE OVERLAP THAN EXPECTED

There was more overlap in residential patterns among gay men and lesbians than expected. In the San Francisco Bay Area, for example, in which the East Bay communities of Berkeley and Oakland are typically identified as "women's communities," the greatest concentration of resident lesbians in the Bay Area is actually in San Francisco. The zip code with the highest per capita rate of women on the mailing list is thirty times greater than the regional mean, whereas for men, the same measure is fifty-three times greater than the regional mean. Yet the highest concentration is in the same neighborhood—the Castro/Eureka Valley area. In Atlanta also, there is not as much difference between the geographic patterning among gay men and lesbians as expected—and certainly not as dramatic a contrast as the sexual determinism of Castells and Murphy would suggest. The areas of highest concentration among men and women in Atlanta are the same: those zip codes areas of central-northeast Atlanta between downtown and Piedmont Park; north, especially Ansley Park; east to Little Five Points; and southeast of midtown into the Grant Park area.

Similarly, in Albuquerque, the overlap of men's and women's residential patterns is quite strong ($r = .9399$; $p = < .001$). There are very few significant correlations with other social-demographic indicators that differ for either gay men or women (although the higher number of seniors in areas where lesbians concentrate in Albuquerque is statistically significant).

In Baltimore, gay men and lesbians do not live together as closely as in some other cities. The correlation coefficient between the presence of gay men and presence of lesbians at the zip code level is only .6861, one of the lowest of the six regions examined here. Thus at least some differences between the residential patterns of gay men and lesbians could be expected.

Brooklyn may demonstrate the pattern best. Greater Park Slope has been known for many years as a strong women's community and, in fact, is home to many lesbian-focused resources. But women and men overlap. The main theme of the greater number of gender-coded households on the list (which itself covers 45,000 homes in New York City) is similarity between the sexes, although there are some differences. In Brooklyn, the core of the gay community for both men and women is in western Brooklyn, between Olmstead's Prospect Park and the East River. At its starkest, two poles can be identified: one, an older, largely gay male neighborhood in Brooklyn Heights (and Cobble Hill immediately to its south), and the other, a women's community in Park Slope and Boerum Hill. North of Prospect Park, in Prospect Heights into Fort Green, neighborhoods well integrated or predominantly black also contain both gay male and lesbian residents. Despite these gender identifications (largely by word of mouth), there are overlaps between all these neighborhoods. Indeed, Brooklyn's residential patterns actually do not reveal many differences in the spaces associated with gay men and lesbians. At the zip code level, the overlap between the sexual identity indexes of the two sexes correlates substantially ($r = .8134$; $p = < .001$, one-tailed). As a result, the correlations between the sociodemographic and economic variables examined and the indexes of gay men and lesbians are overall much the same, although in many cases the correlations for women are weaker. In sum, then, there is more similarity than Castells and Murphy would ever have imagined, but some differences anticipated by profiles of "women's communities" are correct in understanding this as a matter of degree.

WOMEN LESS "GHETTOIZED" THAN MEN

The second theme is that there does not appear to be as concentrated a residential pattern among women as among men. That is, although the peak concentrations of gay men and lesbians do overlap, at the margins women

are more dispersed. In pure statistical terms, gay men have higher per capita rates (when assessed against a mean established among men) than do lesbians. The lesbian communities stretching across Oakland and Berkeley, for
example, are clearly observable, as is that in the Noe Valley area, at the border between the Castro and Mission districts, and even in the avenues west
of Twin Peaks in San Francisco proper. As in the other cities we examined,
women identifying with lesbian and gay organizations are more dispersed
than are gay men in the Bay Area, or maybe a better way of putting it is that
gay men are more concentrated than women.

Santa Fe has a strong concentration of both lesbians and gay men on the
north side of the city, but the entire Santa Fe/Albuquerque region has a
stronger residential pattern for women than for men in outlying areas. Atlanta contains identifiable, though comparatively smaller, clusters of
women in some outlying areas: Sandy Springs and a portion of southwest
Atlanta. Although Atlanta has some identifiable concentrations of
women—especially around Grant Park, Little Five Points below Emory
University, and south of Fort McPherson—overall, women there seem to
be less "ghettoized" than men.

WOMEN BETTER ASSIMILATED IN "NONGAY" NEIGHBORHOODS

This dispersion of women at the edges of lesbian and gay clusters adds a
third theme.

The data from Atlanta, for example, show that those neighborhoods
with a comparatively strong lesbian presence are slightly less likely to be upscale and more likely to be in zip code areas with a large number of female-
headed households. Since these two categories have been identified as nearly universal characteristics of "sexual identity" space, the fact that women's
presence does not correlate as strongly as men's does reinforces the previous
conclusions that women are less "ghettoized"—or, stated more positively,
although the peak concentrations of gay men and women overlap, women
are more likely to be integrated into a broader range of neighborhoods in
the city.

In the Bay Area, women are slightly more likely to live in areas with mar-
ried-couple households and senior citizens and with slightly lower incomes
and housing valuation. On a regional basis, women in the Bay Area are
slightly more likely to live in integrated white and African American neighborhoods, clearly reflecting the strength of the lesbian presence in Oakland

(the correlation between the lesbian index and the percentage of blacks in the East Bay is $r = .2081$; $p = .032$) and strongly correlating with Latinos in San Francisco, an obvious reflection of the overlap of Noe Valley and the Mission district.[28]

In Brooklyn, women are slightly less likely to live in childless neighborhoods and less likely to live in neighborhoods with single households. In those neighborhoods in which men tend to reside, their per capita incomes correlate more strongly in Brooklyn than women's do, but both are relatively strong (men: $r = .7269$; women: $r = .6047$; $p < .001$, one-tailed). But men are more likely to live in neighborhoods with a large number of senior citizens. For both gay men and lesbians, no statistically significant relationship for housing tenancy was found.

In Baltimore, the presence of both gay men and lesbians correlates negatively with the presence of whites (at over $r = -.4495$), but the negative correlation for women is not as strong ($r = -.3867$; $p = .012$). Men are more likely to overlap with African Americans, women with Asians, and both with Latinos. The presence of U.S. Census Bureau–defined very poor people also is noticeable, as are the higher rates of unemployment in zip code areas containing a large number of lesbians. Women are also more likely than men to live in neighborhoods with large numbers of seniors.

Most of these findings raise more questions about gender, sexual identity, and urban space than they answer, but they do have some implications for urban politics and the role of sexual identity. Much of the scholarship critiquing Castells—that is, seeking to find women's spaces so as to show that spatially defined lesbian communities do exist—has underestimated the presence and role of women, both individually and as a spatially defined community, among the concentrations of sexual-identified residents in urban areas dominated by gay men. These "gay ghettos" or identity spaces are quite complicated, certainly more complicated than Castells and Murphy thought. At their peak concentration, two coterminous, sexually defined communities exist, overlap, and interact almost literally in the same urban spaces, more separated socially than outsiders might expect but more closely linked politically than some insiders might perceive. There is a lattice of ties—social and political, loose and strong—linking two struggling identities defined by sex and sexuality who experience and make use of that space differently, all operating within a larger political identity.

Economic Correlates of Gay and Lesbian Neighborhoods

There is a general perception that gay men and lesbians have high incomes[29]—and if this were true, the natural corollary would be that gay neighborhoods in the standard metropolitan areas are richer than others. But as in the case of race, there is a wide variation in the relative economic status of urban spaces in which lesbian and gay men tend to cluster.

Household Income

Most of the forty metropolitan areas we studied show little correlation between the dimensions of household income and the measures of gay and lesbian residential concentration. In fact, if there is a general relationship at all, it is a slightly negative one. In metropolitan areas such as Baltimore, Las Vegas, New Orleans, Chicago, Washington, Denver/Boulder, Milwaukee, the Twin Cities, Detroit, St Louis, Austin, and Boston, the household incomes of zip code areas in which gay male and lesbian residents are concentrated correlates positively with the lower- to lower-to-moderate-income brackets or negatively with the upper-income categories. In no MSA does the presence of lesbian and gay men correlate positively with household incomes of $50,000 to $75,000 or $75,000 to $99,000. Only in Atlanta, Los Angeles/Riverside, and Manhattan does their presence correlate with household incomes of more than $100,000. In the aggregate, then, except in these three locations, the notion that gay neighborhoods are relatively well off is not true.

Measures of Community Economic Status

A slightly different picture emerges, however, when the income dimensions are switched from household to community income characteristics. When per capita income is considered—thus taking into account the size of the household as well as the total household income—a different set of correlation coefficients emerges. Among the nearly forty MSAs we studied, although generally there are no statistically significant relationships, either positive or negative, between per capita income and the presence of lesbian and gay residents, there are some exceptions. In greater Los Angeles, Seattle/Tacoma, Birmingham, Houston, New York City, and Atlanta, the presence of gay men and lesbians in a zip code area does correlate positively with per capita income in their respective urban regions. In Atlanta—not New York or Los Angeles—this relationship is strongest.

We also found signs of economic distress in some gay and lesbian communities. Baltimore, for example, has a negative relationship between a gay presence and per capita income—the only MSA of the forty to display such a relationship. Also in Baltimore, the percentage of U.S. Census Bureau–defined "poor" and "very poor" households correlates significantly with the concentration of lesbian and gay residents in the same general urban spaces. These areas are also below the median family income for the region, have a significantly higher percentage of the population unemployed, and have a high percentage of female-headed households with children. This is not the profile of an upscale community.

A third pattern emerged in greater Detroit and Pittsburgh. In both, the neighborhoods in the center city where lesbians and gay men tend to converge are poorer than the surrounding regions. Even at the county level—Allegheny for Pittsburgh and Wayne for Detroit—gay neighborhoods still have an urban center city profile. But when the analysis was restricted to the borders of Pittsburgh or Detroit, the results were different. In both cities, individuals tend to live in more economically prosperous neighborhoods compared with the rest of the city. This rough, reverse "doughnut" pattern is most extreme in Detroit, where the gay presence correlates positively with both median cash rent and per capita income in the central city.

In the largest metropolitan areas, which tend to have multiple centers of gay and/or residential concentrations, there again is a wide variation. In New York City, on balance, indicators of neighborhoods' relative economic prosperity correlate with a substantial lesbian and gay presence. Citywide, there is a positive correlation with neighborhood per capita income and mean household income. In Manhattan alone, a gay presence correlates with all the middle- and upper-income brackets and none of the lower-income brackets. The concentration of gay and lesbian residents in Brooklyn correlates with neighborhoods with even higher household incomes and, in fact, strongly correlates with per capita income and the higher household incomes. It seems to be the most bifurcated of the boroughs, with gay men and lesbians living in the more affluent sections of western Brooklyn but also in less affluent neighborhoods in north Brooklyn and elsewhere in the borough. In Queens, where a strong gay presence is found in the Jackson Heights and Kew Gardens/Forest Hills sections of the borough, a third profile emerges for New York. Not surprisingly, the strongest correlation in Queens is in the middle-income brackets of $25,000 to $35,000, with negative correlations for the upper-income brackets.

In San Francisco, no significant correlations between lesbian and gay concentrations and indicators of household income or per capita income were found. Across the bay, however, the lesbian and gay presence in the eighty zip codes of Contra Costa and Alameda Counties do correlate with the lower-income brackets ($10,000 to $15,000 and $15,000 to $25,000) as well as with the percentage of U.S. Census Bureau–defined very poor residents. The economic status of Oakland and Berkeley's lesbian and gay residential concentrations appears less affluent than that in San Francisco proper. Yet even in the city of Oakland, "lesbian and gay space" has a higher economic status than do many other portions of the city.

In greater Los Angeles also, there are differences among the several clusters of gay residential concentrations. The Los Angeles/Long Beach/Riverside MSA shows little correlation generally, but some specific relationships did emerge in separate regions of the Los Angeles Basin. Los Angeles County seems to resemble most gay neighborhood profiles in regard to income. Whereas household income tends to correlate toward the middle-to lower-middle range of per capita income, the correlation with the middle to high brackets is positive. In the city of Los Angeles, as in Brooklyn, gay neighborhoods display both a correlation with the percentage of poor and very poor and with the income bracket of $50,000 to $75,000.

The New York region (including Hudson and Bergen Counties in New Jersey), the San Francisco Bay Area, and the Los Angeles Basin are so extensive geographically and economically that there are several or sexual identity spaces, each with slightly different racial, gender, and income profiles. There is no one national economic profile of urban spaces of sexual identity—or even one profile in certain cities.

Housing Stock, Gentrification, and Sexual "Enclaves"

The interest of urban specialists in the emergence of gay and lesbian identity enclaves has coincided with the economic and spacial restructuring of postindustrial cities. Many of the references to gay men and lesbians in the literature on urban affairs concern their relation to the gentrification process. In turn, much of the literature refers to the initial work by Castells and Murphy and to Castells alone, who pointed to the gay community as a potential source of political transformation. Castells properly observed that homosexuals were among the gentrifiers of the older ethnic neighborhoods of San Francisco, especially the old Irish working-class communities of San Francisco in Eureka Valley and in the northwestern portion of the Mission district. It is clear that gay men and lesbians have rehabilitated older sections of some cities to the advantage of both the city and the gay community. South Beach in Miami, Capital Hill in Seattle, portions of northwest Washington, downtown Tampa, the brownstone belts of Brooklyn and Jersey City, and the Marigny district of New Orleans are the examples most often cited.

Other scholars have attributed the apparent coemergence of gentrification and urban sexual domains not just to an economic rationale but also (or instead) to changes in family structure and economics.[30] Lesbians and gay men are among a group of rapidly growing household forms—unmarried and attached cohabitants, young unmarried couples, roommates, and single and coupled lesbians and gay men—who are changing the residential patterns of center cities. The question is whether in doing so they have displaced other city residents.

The analysis of neighborhoods defined by zip codes with a strong gay and lesbian presence found several common factors in their housing markets.

LESBIAN AND GAY NEIGHBORHOODS HAVE PREDOMINANTLY MULTIPLE-UNIT, RENTAL HOUSING

In all but the smallest cities (Des Moines and the Quad Cities), the presence of lesbian and gay men correlates strongly and significantly with multiple-unit housing. This is true of the more sprawling modern cities of the Sun Belt as well as the older industrial cities of the Northeast and Midwest. In addition, in nearly all cities (Honolulu and Des Moines are the only exceptions), the presence of gays and lesbians correlates either positively with the percentage of "renters" or negatively with the percentage of "owners" or, more likely, both. Thus, multiple-unit, rental housing dominates these sexual domains.

GAY NEIGHBORHOODS HAVE A HIGH PROPORTION OF OLDER HOUSING STOCK

Gay enclaves are consistently in the older sections of cities in the Northeast and Midwest and also in the newer, rapidly growing cities of the Sun Belt. This is somewhat surprising. In Tampa/St. Petersburg, Houston, San Diego, Atlanta, and Miami/Fort Lauderdale, gays tend to live in neighborhoods with a high percentage of housing units built before World War II. In only one county we studied does the presence of lesbian and gay residents in zip code areas correlate positively with the percentage of housing units built since 1985: Hudson County, New Jersey. Hudson County contains three cities with observable gay and lesbian populations: Union City and especially Hoboken and Jersey City. These cities grew substantially in the 1980s as housing prices in lower Manhattan pushed many younger professionals across the Hudson River into New Jersey. Waterfront development in Jersey City especially has been extensive, causing the costs of gentrification to become the primary political issue in Jersey City for more than a decade.

The choice of older, multiple-unit dwellings and rental neighborhoods by many lesbians and gay men presents additional questions associated with the process of center city in-migration and "gentrification," the displacement of one group or class by another in older neighborhoods. Does the location of gay men and lesbians in inner-city, older rental neighborhoods necessarily mean that they have displaced other residents? Or does this influx revive deteriorating neighborhoods and sustain the value of older housing markets? Using aggregate data, we may be able to clarify some of these issues and identify those metropolitan housing markets where sexual identity has had a role in displacing older residents.

Assuming that a strong positive correlation between gay presence and vacancy rates means little or no displacement by gay in-migration, we correlated vacancy rates and sexual identity indexes in all the metropolitan areas we studied.

The results are interesting. In most MSAs, there is no statistically significant relationship at the macro level between vacancy rates and a gay presence. In some metropolitan areas—such as Philadelphia, Chicago, Cincinnati, Indianapolis, Washington, D.C., the Quad Cities, and Denver—the vacancy rates and presence of gay residents actually correlate positively. That is, any lesbian or gay in-migration was to city areas whose housing stock was underutilized. Obviously in cities whose vacancy rates are low—like New York City—changes in any individual's or group's housing choices at the aggregate level has an effect on the market. But overall, there is no specific reason to believe that a gay presence caused either more or less pressure on the housing market in these metropolitan areas.

Only in Albany/Troy/Schenectady and the Hartford, Connecticut, MSAs are the vacancy rates and presence of gay and lesbian residents correlated negatively; that is, in-migration by gay men and lesbians might push up rental prices. Eventually this could displace residents at the edges of gay domains. That both Hartford and Albany are state capitals and university towns is telling.

At a more micro level, important relations in some center cities gave rise to more questions. In Brooklyn, for example, a lesbian and gay presence correlates strongly with a neighborhood's median valuation of housing, per capita income, and household income, so it is not surprising that median rents also correlate positively. Interestingly, the dimensions of owner, renter, and gay presence do not display a significant relationship, nor do the measures for single- and multiple-unit housing. We can speculate that there are probably several lesbian and gay owners, renters, and investors. The vacancy rate also relates positively, indicating that the expansion of these sexual domains—part of the general gentrification of western and south Brooklyn (sometimes referred to as the "Brownstone Belt")—can continue before exhausting underutilized housing stock and causing extensive dislocation.

The tristate Cincinnati region is representative of a second way in which sexual identity affects urban housing markets, as housing vacancy rates correlate positively with the presence of gay and lesbian residents both regionwide and citywide. But unlike Brooklyn, housing values and median rents and the presence of gays do not correlate. In the region, gay residents do not seem to have had a disproportionate effect on the housing market. In the city of Cincinnati, one of the strongest statistical correlations is between a gay presence and the percentage of group housing—which may be student housing—but no correlation with median rents or vacancy rates was found. Thus in Cincinnati, the gay presence has had little or no effect on housing.

A third and mixed profile emerges in the East Bay communities around San Francisco Bay. In zip code areas with a strong lesbian and gay presence, some of the income variables and median rents correlate negatively in Alameda and Contra Costa Counties. But again, the dynamic is more complicated. The twelve zip code areas of Oakland show a very strong correlation between a lesbian and gay presence and per capita income ($r = .8268$; $p = .001$). Compared with the rest of the Bay Area, median rents in gay neighborhoods in Oakland are low, but in Oakland, no relationship could be found between a gay presence and median rents. The vacancy rates in Oakland neighborhoods with a comparatively strong gay presence are statistically no higher or lower than those of the surrounding areas (the center of gay residence has a vacancy rate in 1990 of 7 percent). The situation in Oakland seems to be in balance. Yet the comparatively high per capita income in neighborhoods with a strong gay presence is one indication that this balance could be offset, especially if the kind of dramatic changes in San Francisco's housing market that occurred in the 1970s and 1980s force across the bay additional waves of black middle-class families and middle-income lesbians and gay men of all colors.

The impact of lesbian and gay men on local housing markets obviously depends more on the local housing market itself than on sexual identity. Ultimately, however, it is not sexual identity that describes dislocation but the interaction of the local housing market with the in-migration of many groups, including gay men and lesbians. There is no reason to believe that except in some rare circumstances, the assertion of sexual identity over urban spaces as part of a broader gentrification movement has led to a widespread displacement of poorer residents. San Francisco may be the only real exception on a citywide basis. Parts of Brooklyn, Jersey City, and Philadelphia show a similar though weaker trend. What seems more likely is that in cities like Cincinnati, Detroit, Indianapolis, Albany, Washington, D.C., Baltimore, Chicago, and Oakland, the lesbian and gay presence is sustaining local housing markets that otherwise might experience further disinvestment.

The Primacy of Social over Economic Variables in Urban Sexual Terrain

Castells and Murray found two overriding factors in San Francisco that describe some of the differences between "gay territory" and "nongay territory": (1) the proportion of owner-occupied housing and (2) the proportion of resident population under eighteen years old. In both cases, these two factors are more closely associated with census tracts identified by Castells and Murphy as being "nongay" spaces, that is, not having a large gay population. In addition, a gay presence correlated negatively with high rents and positively with higher educational achievement among all residents in the census tract. In addition, Castells and Murphy also applied several other variables that did not help explain the difference between gay territories and nongay territories in San Francisco: percentage of the population engaged in blue-collar occupations, median housing value, and median family income. From these data, Castells and Murphy concluded that there was an invisible economic and cultural wall between "gay space" and "nongay space."

Our analysis affirms two of Castells and Murphy's most important findings as generalizable to most of the forty MSAs we studied. First, "gay territory" is largely rental. Second, whereas Castells and Murphy used the lack of children in the 1970 census as a definition of nonfamily space (and, by inference, a "gay space"), we used the census factor called *nonfamily households*, which confirms their finding. In all the cities studied there is a strong correlation among the measures of sexual identity, the percentage of nonfamily households, and the percentage of persons living alone.

But here our agreement with Castells and Murphy ends. Whereas they found that based on 1970 data, a "high-rent" barrier in San Francisco was keeping gay men out of some neighborhoods, we found that based on 1990 census data, such barriers were weaker or nonexistent. Stated in another way, today, in the late 1990s, in the greater San Francisco area, one can find higher-rent lesbian or gay neighborhoods (Pacific Heights and Buena Vista), middle-class neighborhoods (the Castro and portions of Diamond Heights), and lower-middle- and middle-income neighborhoods (portions of Noe Valley and, across the bay, of Oakland).

Beyond the San Francisco Bay Area, there is little or no evidence that rents themselves, as opposed to owner occupancy, have had an effect on lesbian and gay residential concentrations in the forty MSAs. No consistent pattern was found between median rental prices and a concentration of lesbian and gay residents across the cities we studied. In cities such as Baltimore and Indianapolis, low rents are common. In cities such as Atlanta, Houston, and Los Angeles, there is no statistically significant difference. In short, and contrary to Castells and Murphy's findings, high rents and housing values are not an unsurmountable barrier to establishing a gay/lesbian presence.

In addition, these sexual domains demonstrate a wide range in economic status, and in the larger metropolitan areas (New York, the Los Angeles Basin, and the San Francisco Bay Area), differing economic statuses (read classes) can be identified among different clusters of lesbian and gay residents.

Not all these conclusions are a surprise, and in some ways, their intuitive nature suggests additional faith in the indicators and methods of analysis used here. Smaller-than-median household size is an obvious correlate of fewer children per capita, but it also may be the older housing stock. In fact, in some cities, its age links the expansion of gay territories with the movement toward "gentrification." The presence of senior citizens is expected in older neighborhoods. The relative youth of gay residents living side by side with senior citizens and the absence of married couples with children shows a pattern of out-migration of soon-to-be-middle-aged couples with or plan-

ning on children. In many of the cities we studied, children are more likely to be present in households with unmarried female heads than they are
in some other areas of the MSAs.

Gay neighborhoods are defined demographically by the relatively few
households that are owner occupied, and headed by a married couple with
children in residence—an exact description of the suburbs of most of these
center cities. The picture, then, is not just of gay spaces as negative spaces
and defensive spaces, set in a binary juxtaposition with family space, as
Castells conceptualized it, but as domains in central cities open to many
identifications but particularly sexual identity. In fact, the lasting impression is not that sexual identity spaces are closed off but that the homoge-
nized space, the one that sets its own identity limits and defines its own barriers, is "family space."

Functional, Postindustrial, and Postmodern Urban Space

The finding that social demography and household structure are more likely than economic factors to define urban spaces of high gay and lesbian residential concentration is only half the story, however, as it overlooks the serious economic argument that economic functions, not simply
microeconomic measures, define urban spaces. In addition, the method we
used here—correlating objectified dimensions of sexual identity with census measures—tends to devalue the individual and complex characteristics
and actions of those who identify as gay or lesbian. In words common to
contemporary gay studies, the method *essentializes* the categories "gay" or
"lesbian" to the detriment of other diversities within the same identity. To
appreciate these distinctions, we now must switch from finding spaces associated with sexual identity to understanding the conflicting meanings of
urban space in larger social science narratives.

Sexual Spaces and Urban Functionalism

In the end, Castells's assessment of gay territory in San Francisco is acceptable to those urban geographers and sociologists who regard urban space as
primarily an expression of its surface function. His emphasis was on social
and progressive movements within what contemporary postmodern geographers call *Cartesian space*. These urban social movements were triggered

by the localization of class and other interests and by the overall pattern of space utilization in contemporary social and economic processes.

The functionalist approach that dominated human geography and much of American urban sociology in the first half of the century saw the meaning of urban space as contingent on the development of technologies and the "objective" process of industrialization and urbanization in what urban geographer Edward Soja termed the *descriptive generalities*.[31] The driving force behind these changes was not class conflict but technology—technological innovation in transportation, production processes, and communities. New transportation technologies altered spatial arrangements, and new production processes (such as from vertical center city building in the old garment industry to horizontal production processes or even piecemeal work separated by distance) changed land valuations and how industrial locations were linked.

In sociology, the masters of this functional/human ecology approach to urban space investigated the cultural patterns of "urban subcultures" to find replications of larger social and urban functions in these subsystems. They operated from a worldview that saw the individual meaning of different urban spaces as derived from the overall arrangement of urban space. "Ghetto" enclaves were a measure of urban dysfunction, although time was seen as on the side of functionality. The interaction of ghetto residents with other ethnic groups in the context of the overall urban society generated additional common experiences as the groups related to one another in the framework of a city's overriding function. They had an implicit faith in the acculturation of ethnic groups and the eventual dissolution of "dysfunctional" ethnic enclaves (ghettos).

Studies of urban ethnic communities were the more celebrated products of this approach, usually associated in the 1920s and 1930s with the University of Chicago. A portion of the Chicago school was fascinated with marginal social subsets. They sought out "deviant" subcultures peripheral to city life, looking less at their contribution to the sense of the city than to the effect of the city on their production (and reproduction). "Street people," hoboes, shoe-shine boys, taxi dancers, billiard players, and the like all were objects of study. The dysfunctions of the city, owing to the mix of urban subcultures, made for a "safe haven" for many of these social subgroups. Although there was little study of homosexual spaces by the Chicago scholars, one inference they made from their functionalist perspective on urban space, one implied by Castells and drawn more explicitly by other sociologists, was that the "dysfunction" of cities created "safer" spaces for homosexual men and women, not because the urban social dynamic created tolerance for differing ways of living, but because cities were appropriate ecologies for deviance from subtly enforced social codes. It was the surface chaos of cities that afforded some measure of refuge for homosexual men and women, not an invisible hand tending toward functionality in space utilization and social interaction that eventually would include gay and lesbian self-identity.

Intended or not, Castells's notion of gay territory as negative space, defensive space, a geography in which public space would be invested with the symbols and meanings of lesbian and gay identity was consistent with these older ethnographic conceptualizations of ghettos. These new "gay ghettos" were bounded by symbols, juxtaposed with "family space" as ethnic spaces had been juxtaposed with one another a generation earlier. The scholarly search for woman's (lesbian) spaces had similar underlying precepts.

The Postindustrial City and the "Queer Gentry"

The themes of urban functionalism in geography have continued during the current debates over the restructuring of urban space in postindustrial cities. As many (but not all) cities moved from primarily industrial production functions to administrative and service functions, urban space is being recycled. Warehouses have become residential apartments and retail or entertainment spaces; offices were created out of industrial space for the new "cottage industries" of the service era—small publishing, law, design, public relations, and xerography among many others. Production processes are no longer the routinized system of the large-scale manufacturing model based on Henry Ford's assembly line but are now based on smaller-scale niche manufacturing, addressing highly specialized markets with large investments in capital, telecommunications, computerization, and human skills.[32]

This recycling of buildings and the associated reinvestment (and disinvestment) in postindustrial patterns of space utilization reversed land-pricing structures in some cases, changed status values in nearly all, and altered the dynamics among differing segments of urban space. Prestige housing was no longer seen as broad expanses distant from the filth of industrial cities, but housing of proximity in either high-rise modern towers or older, refurbished, classic buildings.

Geographers, planners, and urbanologists again sought "objective rules" for the process of the postindustrial city. The themes now were different:

Alterations in space utilization, density ratios, the effects of technology (especially telecommunications and transportation) on the postindustrial city, and the "gentrification" and "back to the city" movements all were linked. The industrial ring that bounded the older central business districts of the manufacturing city were allowed to deteriorate through disinvestment and depreciation. New investment in the transformation of the central business district and in corporate campuses in the third (and, in some cases, fourth) ring was now the "objective rule" of the postindustrial city.[33]

It was in this context that urban spaces of sexual identity came to be regarded as middle-class domains. To the extent that these new "gay spaces" were examined by scholars of urban transformation in the 1970s and 1980s, they were linked with the "back to the city" and gentrification movements of urban transformation. Thus the cliché of gay men buying and restoring Victorian homes in what once were San Francisco's ethnic neighborhoods became a template applied to many other cities, but the clusters of lesbian and gay residents in cities that had not maneuvered as successfully through the economic changes of the 1970s and 1980s were overlooked.

The role of political economy in the growth of gay enclaves was given more attention by the early students of the gay rights movement. Dennis Altman and Barry Adam were influenced by both the political-economic description of the reorganization of urban space for consumption rather than production and the advocacy of lesbian and gay rights.

Altman came to see the open sexuality among men in New York and San Francisco's gay urban domains not only as a facet of identity and sexual experimentation but also as a representation of American capitalist consumerism—filtered through a lens of sexual liberation and sexual identity.[34] This theme of Altman's early work brings together identity politics with one of Ira Katznelson's important insights from his study of the history and political economy of northern Manhattan: The separation of work and residence dramatically changed the nature of progressive politics.[35] Altman feared that the compartmentalization of sexual identity in residential or even commercial spaces would also compartmentalize identity, confining the struggle to affirm identity to only residential neighborhoods or commercial sex establishments, neither of which could seriously challenge established heterosexist power.

It is true that the emergence of postindustrial cities has altered price structures, destroyed older patterns of space utilization, created new opportunities for many groups (including gay men and lesbians), and displaced those at the margins of the housing and labor markets (including gay men and lesbians). It is probably also true that the administrative society and information culture of the emerging service industries has placed a higher value on personal skills, thus giving many gay men and lesbians as individuals more bargaining power for their labor than an individual industrial worker might have had in the past. But the collective construction of lesbian and gay spaces was not ensured by the changes caused by patterns of postindustrial spatial utilization, nor was urban transformation a prerequisite for the construction of zones of sexual identity. As we have seen, areas of lesbian and gay identity existed before the emergence of the large-scale neighborhoods of gay men and lesbians in present-day postindustrial cities.

Identity, Space, and Social Action

Disagreeing with the functionalist school, both political economists and urban geographers interested in social action have presented alternative views of the meaning of urban space. Before David Harvey adopted a fuller postmodern perspective, he had already questioned the meaning of space, since space itself had become problematic in Marxist political economics.

In his attempt to integrate themes from political economy and geography while also preserving personal agency for the occupants of various spaces, Harvey noted the enormous range of human behavior in which space is a factor or product—from street gangs' battles over turf to the wide variety of markets—and warned against falling into "spatial fetishism":

> It would be all too easy in the face of such diversity to succumb to that "spatial fetishism" that equalizes all phenomena *sub specie spatii* and treats the geometric properties of spatial patterns as fundamental. The opposite danger is to see spatial organization as a mere reflection of the processes of accumulation and class reproduction.[36]

Harvey, who began his exploration of space from a Marxist perspective, reserves the political-economic dimension of spatial analysis (the will to profit and the accumulation of capital are the motivating forces of urban spatial organization, regardless of the contemporary technology) but also allows for personal actions and agency in constructing urban spaces and reproducing the social classes—what he calls the *active moment*.

Going a step further than Harvey, those interested in identity politics see space as deriving its meaning less from a dominant class, an emergent political economy, or the technical-functional arrangements of cities than through the investment of meaning by individuals as mediators and agents of collectively (and individually) constructed cultural identities. The Swiss geographer Benno Werlin, for example, advances the critique of the functionalist school by radically subjectivizing the meaning of space in general and urban space in particular. He argues for an action-oriented theory of space and reemphasizes the subject in a geographic dialogue, thus critiquing the determinism in both the functional and the political-economic approaches to geography.

Werlin's theory gives us two insights we can use in an identity theory of space for urban politics. First, he sees meaning as being invested in space by the actions and intentions of individual actors and groups understood through their particular frames of reference. In this analysis, the meaning(s) of urban space does not rest in the juxtaposition of territories to one another in the overall political-economic or functional process. Instead, it rests in the purposeful actions of agents occupying the space. Or more to the point, it is a battleground for conflicting constructs—in our context, one an expression of a same-sex ethos and the other a social deposition toward the regulation of sexual activity. The actual location of action is less important than the multiple meanings of action and the frames of reference that give meaning to action. It is these that invest individual meaning in space.[37]

Second, space as points on a globe can have multiple meanings, that is, different meanings as different frameworks of significance are applied. Thus, the meanings of a territory change as the scale of observation changes or time changes. In the case of the scale of observation, residential spaces can have meaning within a broad, functional perspective of the entire city. On the street level, the meanings have different overtones, heavily influenced by identity and social action. In fact, the same geographic point at the same time of day may have two or more different meanings to two different people. At 3:00 A.M., for example, in New York City's Fourteenth Street meat market area, truckers and meat packers work side by side while younger gay men congregate in and around bars and sex clubs in the same section of urban space. The range of meanings of this jointly occupied space derive not from the overall patterning of space by the political economy but from each actor's different frame of reference for this space. In terms of time, meaning based on the cycle of the day or the week also changes as action or identities change, as each invests meaning in "space."

For our purposes, we need not go so far as Werlin's fragmenting of urban geography to grasp the importance of intentionality and the real action of individuals within their frames of reference. The point is to move the sources of meaning away from an exclusive "metanarrative" explanation of the meanings of space. We can agree that just as objects have different meanings in different languages and arrays of signifiers, space also has differing meanings. The domains of same-sex erotic identity in the 1920s might have meant "drag balls" in New Orleans or Turkish baths in New York, but today they mean more open residential enclaves in large metropolitan areas. What has changed is the social regulation of sexual activity and also the expectations of lesbians and gay men for a fuller life. These expectations derive from an identity that is formed through individual agency in the context of contemporaneous social and economic structures. There also is a continuity in the identity that is neither defined by economics nor secure from the effects of interaction with other identities.

Two additional themes can be drawn from this sense of space and identity. First, we need not think of lesbian or gay territories as bounded spaces in this framework—as Castells, Martin Levine, and others may have done—but as one of many shifting and overlapping fields of meaning in the urban setting. Lesbian space or gay (male) space (or queer space), to the extent that they are points on a map (or surfaces on a globe), are not only or even primarily defensive enclaves but are better considered as nodes in networks of ties of identity that radiate from these points of gathering. In a sense, a subject need not physically inhabit such an identity space to be in its field, to know that it exists, or to be influenced by it.

Second, it follows from this view that "space" is not fixed because identity is not fixed. Instead, it acquires subtle overtones of new meaning as the actors' actions and intentions invest newer meanings into space. One implication of looking at identity as a developmental process—as we did earlier—is that it alters our view of urban space. Since we have defined identity as developmental, the textures of identity space are partly contingent on the formation of identity.

But it is the reverse process that is more important politically, how the existence of these identity spaces influences the construction of individual political identity among those who use such spaces. Ester Newton's history of Cherry Grove, the traditional women's space on Fire Island, New York, is an example. It has no year-round residents, and yet it illustrates how even temporary occupation of space can influence identity and how the construction of collective identity is influenced by it. The confluence of the effects of the intentional actor(s) on identity space and the effect of meaning-*full* identity space(s) on individual identity formation presents a set of cross-current processes.

The beginnings of gay or lesbian spaces, gay neighborhoods, or networks of identity are not an example of economic development but an assertive and self-conscious construction of identity in the context of economic change and social regulation. The traditional appropriation of a portion of urban space for sexual entertainment also resulted in some of the first centers of same-sex identity: Covent Garden and the Moorfields area of eighteenth-century London; the Tuilleries in eighteenth-century Paris; lower Broadway and the Front Street areas of early-nineteenth-century New York; and the Bowery, Harlem, and Greenwich Village in New York, the Tenderloin in San Francisco, and the French Quarter in New Orleans earlier in this century.

Although the location of these areas was surely determined by the dynamics of the local urban landscape and its economy, their existence was not an expression of economic change effected by the emergence of the postindustrial urban complex. Instead, their existence predated the economic (and spatial) restructuring of the postindustrial cities. Same-sex erotic identity spaces held sway through mercantile economic formations, industrial formations, and postindustrial formations. But they were shaped by the social and economic structures of their time. That any of these spaces would become middle-class neighborhoods is what would have surprised the "gay people" of the nineteenth century, not their existence.

Conclusion

What, then, is the meaning of those domains of sexual identity to our two strollers in Center City Philadelphia? In some ways, it depends on whether either or both have a gay or lesbian identity. If they do, they will see signifiers of meaning that others may not see. If they do not, they may see other signifiers of meaning, of American identity, of antiques and early American fixtures, or of the history of American medicine.

But such a postmodern perspective can be carried too far. Empirical analysis does show some commonalities of gay domains but also differences that tend to undermine economic explanations for these spaces. The dominant characteristics for these zip code–defined gay and lesbian spaces in all forty cities we studied are associated with demographic, social, and household structures and housing variables. The single most common factor in nearly all the cities is the relative absence of white, owner-occupied households of married couples with children. Economic factors, however—including average household income, association with income bracket, median rent and vacancy rates, and per capita household income—vary widely from MSA to MSA. There are few if any economic influences on the micro level of analysis of these domains. If there are any, they tend to be broad and citywide, such as the differences between the older cities of the Northeast and Midwest and the cities of the new South and Sun Belt. Our conclusion is that these factors influence some of the characteristics of gay space rather than determine their very existence.

In fact, economic diversity seems to be the dominant theme when comparisons of the larger MSAs are possible. In New York City, for example, a white, middle- to upper-middle-income neighborhood describes the areas of residential concentration of lesbians and gay men in Manhattan, but not in Queens. There, the less upscale neighborhood of Jackson Heights, with its heavy Latino presence (gay and nongay) stands in relief to Manhattan's Chelsea and Greenwich Village. In Brooklyn, a third economic profile leans toward the extremes of economic status. Similarly, if San Francisco and Oakland are examined in the context of the overall Bay Area MSA, the spatial reproduction of class divisions in the gay community (associated with race and gender) also are evident.

By emphasizing these spaces as the boundaries of an enclosed gay ghetto, modeled on the older ethnographic analysis of ghettos, those few urban specialists who noted spaces of sexual identity missed several features. First, they underestimated the importance of such spaces in the formation of the personal and collective political identity of those who do not actually reside in these physical spaces. Second, as Castells did, they focused on the spatial expanse of such domains, not on their internal identity transformations over time. Finally, they transformed characteristics that may be only transitory and descriptive into general themes—essentializing them, if you will—and thus lost some of the diversity that exists in gay or women's space. Even in those gay neighborhoods that may have middle-class overtones, for example, some inhabitants have more economic options, and others, fewer.

This analysis offers two conclusions: First, that the presence of same-sex identity spaces existed well before the transformation of city economies from industrial to postindustrial, from urban space organized primarily around efficiency in production to efficiency in consumption. Second, identity space is less a location than a process, a dialogue between the intention of actors to create and exist in that space and the effect of those spaces on the individual and collective development of identity. Viewed in this way, identity space is less a location than a field, a field through which the agents move, taking and giving meanings, meanings that are contingent on and give form to the identity.

CHAPTER 5

:::

Identity Formation and the Urban Gay and Lesbian Vote

Just as the residential clusters of lesbians and gay men in cities have a geographic pattern, their sexual identity in electoral behavior also has a pattern. The litmus test for a lesbian and gay identity grouping as an object of study in voting behavior and identity formation should be much the same as for other voting blocs organized around an identity. Showing that issues are linked to a gay or lesbian identity is not enough; an actual voting pattern associated with the cohort also must be present. A set of policy preferences and a general attitude toward ideology and party linked to sexual identity should be evident as well. Together, these factors should indicate not just a pattern of voting behavior but also a sense of common identity and a common political consciousness that forms the framework for processing political information.

A coherent vote organized around sexual identity can be discerned in both the urban setting and the nation. It has a sociodemographic profile, an agenda of specific policy priorities, and a set of predispositions toward party, ideology, and government. Accordingly, as a voting group displaying common characteristics, electoral predispositions, and considerable cohesiveness, the gay communities of the United States have had an impact on electoral outcomes in several major cities.

This chapter explores the aggregate characteristics and significance of lesbian and gay identity as an aspect of voting behavior in the urban setting. It suggests that understanding the descriptors of lesbian or gay male self-identification as they pertain to voting behavior adds to and takes theoretical insight from a postfamilial developmental and constructivist perspective on identity formation, as opposed to the stark behavioral perspective of early models of political socialization. Thus, rather than viewing it as a tidy demographic category, we use lesbian or gay (or bisexual) self-identification here as a marker for a group constructing an individual and collective polit-ical identity organized around sexuality. In statistical terms, we use *identity* as both an independent and a dependent variable. Our analysis relies primarily on news media election-day exit polls with national samples and extracted urban subsamples, as well as large city and, in some cases, state samples.[1]

Self-identification as a Marker of Identity in Formation

How should a gay or lesbian identity be used in voting studies? Should it be defined primarily in terms of sexual behavior, and if so, does such be-havior need to be continuous over a lifetime or are shorter periods of same-sex sexual activity adequate for such an identification? Should the category be applied only to those who consciously link sexual identity with their po-litical values or behavior, and if so, should it be the social scientist who de-termines the nature of that link?

Researchers who equate sexual identity with sexual behavior immediate-ly encounter problems. Despite the examples of survey research in which reports of sexual behavior have been used for political research, it would be impractical at this point to conduct a survey on the scale necessary to pro-duce a large enough sample for a complete profile of the interaction of same-sex practices and politics. Besides, for our purposes, actual sexual practice is less important than sexual identity.

The second option, obtaining a sample of those who consciously link their sexual identity to their political behavior, may be begging the ques-tion: What about those who identify as bisexual or gay or lesbian but who do not want these identities politicized or have resisted their politicization by their social context? Surely, in any sample of lesbians and gay men, there are such individuals. We cannot assume that sexual behavior or identity can be universally translated into a political identity.

An intermediate approach is to use a voter's acknowledgment of a gay or lesbian identity as a marker of an undefined but sexually linked political identity. Without imposing on the voter the traits of a sexually associated political identity—except in the broadest terms—he or she is left to self-de-fine as well as to self-identify. This route is not free of danger, however, since it is the analyst that offers the single-identity choice, without really know-ing to what the respondent is attesting by accepting the label gay, lesbian, or bisexual.

The category gay (or lesbian or bisexual) may appear on a data collection sheet, but it is fraught with nuances. For survey researchers, however the fact of nuance in a category is not unique to sexual identity. It is also present in, say, "religion" or "race." Should Mormons choose "Protestant" as their religious category, even though it does not really fit their theological tradition, or should Afro-Caribbeans chose Latino, their language-group affinity, or black, referring to their continent of origin, as their self-identified racial category? An advantage of this approach to sexual identity is that the individual chooses to have the identity (or the name) associated with him or her, without specifically defining the understanding or experience of his or her being a gay man or a lesbian. The researcher can then use the marker "gay" or "lesbian" to tease out, through standard statistical techniques, the common general social and political dimensions of the identity grouping, that is, to find, by empirical means, the "sameness" in the identity grouping.

To the pure empiricist, this concern about the fluidity of "identities" may seem to be a serpentine route to understanding voting behavior. After all, the experience accumulated in the voting models of both the commercial and academic worlds has relied on discrete and mutually exclusive categories, and these models and the categories on which they were built were useful in the past. But if such work is to be taken seriously by those in gay, lesbian, women's, or postcolonial studies—a scholarly community that has developed a sophisticated critique of the solidity of categories—this concern must be investigated. As a product of social interaction, however, identity involves the individual and the group, both seeking areas of control (assertion) of that identity. The individual is not conceived as passive, nor is the collective identity static; both are constantly being renegotiated, even reformulated, as new experiences and new information are incorporated.

Similarly, although an individual can chose the marker "gay" or "lesbian" as an identity, it would be foolhardy to assume that all his or her voting behavior could be explained by a single self-identification. And although a pattern of political attitudes or voting behavior associated with the sexual identity category can (and, to some extent, will be) established through statistical techniques, it, as a norm, cannot in turn be projected back in each case onto the individuals who accepted the marker of the identity grouping.

These constraints must be kept in mind when dealing with the actual data. The markers "gay" or "lesbian" or "bisexual" are a way to distinguish those engaged in the discourse over what a sexual identity means, not those who have arrived at a fixed point and not a box labeled "gay." Even though the identity "gay" (or "lesbian") may be simply affirmed by checking a box, without the social scientist's having to define its meaning, each identifier may have many possible meanings.

The Lesbian and Gay Identity Grouping as a Sociopolitical Cluster

To see whether the experience of lesbian and gay voters adds anything to the discussion of urban politics—or to the discussion of political social-ization and identity formation in political science more generally—it first is necessary to define the groupings as a whole. In the absence of panel data of the type used by Jennings and Jennings and Niemi, many of the kinds of questions that political science would find useful in regard to sexual identity cannot be fully answered. The only reliable data on lesbians' and gay men's voting behavior and political attitudes are from the various elec-tion-day exit polls conducted by the commercial media in the United States. These data are aggregate data, and so again, they are useful only to the extent that they can answer our questions. Nevertheless, the data do define a grouping—demographically, politically, and in voter behavior—whose characteristics tend to undermine much of the early political so-cialization model.

Underlying Social Descriptors of Gay and Lesbian Self-identification

A search for sociodemographic patterns of gay and lesbian self-identifiers in several different exit-poll samples reveals that many of the social character-istics of self-identifiers are the same, even though the location, election, sampling techniques, and data collection methods are different. These pro-files of the gay and lesbian self-identifiers are also a partial profile of those whose social structures, life experiences, resources, "language," and social action interact to construct a political identity. These profiles are a set of factors that collectively provide the social and temporal context for assert-ing a "gay (lesbian)" identity. It is not surprising, then, that the three fac-tors most important to identity development overall also explain much of the difference between the self-identified gay and lesbian voters and the general sample. These factors are age (viewed as both a historical cohort and a biological age), gender, and education.

AGE OF RESPONDENTS AND LESBIAN/GAY IDENTIFICATION

Age has been a consistent descriptor of gay/lesbian self-identification in the exit-poll data. A generational shift in values and the influence of the women's movement, the civil rights movement, the gay rights movement, and the political effects of HIV and its associated diseases may have contributed to the relationship between age and self-identification. The data show that younger men and women are more likely to identify as gay or lesbian than older men and women are. The effect of the "post-Stonewall" and the later "queer" generations are clearly observable in these sample profiles.

In the 1988 New York City Democratic presidential primary sample (ABC), for example, 45 percent of the total (though small) gay and lesbian sample group was 30 to 39 years old. Only 7 percent of the gay sample was 50 to 59 years old, and only 7 percent was 60 years or older. Almost the exact pattern was found in the ABC News California Democratic presidential primary sample from that same year: 46 percent of the sample fell between 30 and 39 years of age, with only 15 percent of the total in the 40-years-and-older cohort.

Taking into account the different voting patterns among age cohorts (seniors tend to "outvote" their younger counterparts), there still are important differences between age and self-identification among gays and lesbians. Both the 1992 Voter Research and Surveys national exit poll and the *Los Angeles Times* 1992 exit poll show the gay/lesbian/bisexual samples to be concentrated in the below-40-years-old cohort and underrepresented in those older than 40 years of age.[2] This is consistent with the 1993 New York City and Los Angeles mayoral samples, although there are some minor differences (see figure 5-1). In both cities, the lesbian and gay samples cluster around the 30- to 40-year-old classification, although the national sample is somewhat younger than the Los Angeles or New York City samples. Despite these variations, the self-identification rates of all three samples are highest among 25- to 45-year-olds. A history of same-sex sexual activity should in fact grow with age among homosexuals, but the exact opposite is evident in the political self-identification profiles. Self-identification peaks between the age associated with waning family influence and that of establishing oneself as a thriving adult. Obviously, social context as well as sexual affinity is at work in forming this cohort's political identity.

The association of self-identification as gay or lesbian with the younger age categories raises the question of whether the political values and voting behavior associated with a gay and lesbian self-identification are fully linked

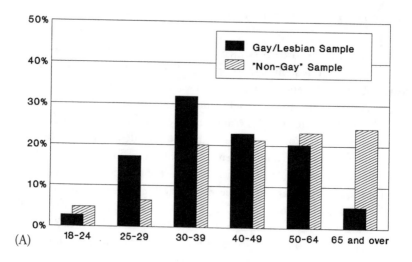

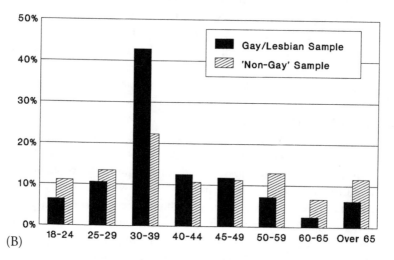

FIGURE 5.1
GLB self-identifiers tend to be younger than the rest of urban voters.
(A) Los Angeles, mayoral runoff, June 1993. (Source: *Los Angeles Times* Exit Poll.)
(B) New York City mayor general election, November 1993. (Source:
Voter News Service exit poll.)

to sexual identity or are only a partial expression of a generational shift in values. This could be a "culture shift," as Inglehart might have called it, pertaining to both material security and the new values associated with a world of "postmaterial" politics.

A substantial body of literature has studied the combination of forces that drive generational change as expressed in political ideology and party affiliation.[3] Greater political independence and a strong skepticism of government characterized the generation that came to age not only during Stonewall but also during the civil rights era, the rebirth of feminism, the Vietnam War, and the assertion of a youth culture in places as far apart as Paris, Berkeley, Prague, Morningside Heights/Harlem in New York, Mexico City, and Kent State University in Ohio, all this culminating in the Watergate scandals of the mid-1970s.

The cumulative influence of these events on the gay rights movement has been well documented by historians (indeed, the 1992 VRS data set indicates that self-identified gay men and lesbians were slightly more likely to have participated in anti–Vietnam War protests than was the nongay sample in all age cohorts but especially in the 40-to-49-year-old age cohort), but generational change does not completely explain the gay and lesbian association with party and ideology. When examining the data further and controlling for age, gay men and lesbians are still a discrete cluster. In the Los Angeles sample, self-identified lesbians and gay men were more liberal than the nongay sample in every single age cohort. In regard to party registration, the gay sample was far more likely to be registered as Democrats, up to the 50-year-old category. In all age categories, gays were much less likely to be registered as Republicans. The New York City samples show much the same figures.

The total VRS 1992 sample broken down by six age categories shows that in the youngest two categories—18 to 24 years old and 24 to 30 years old—the gay sample was substantially more liberal than the remainder of their age cohort, with many fewer respondents labeling themselves as conservative. The label of moderate, however, shows no statistically significant difference regarding sexual orientation. The immediate post-Stonewall cohort—the 30-to-40-year-old gay/lesbian grouping—was very liberal, with only 5.6 percent labeling themselves as conservative and only 37.4 percent as moderate. The remaining half or more self-assessed their ideological predisposition as liberal. But the 40-to-49-year-old gay cohort, the actual 1960s/early 1970s/ Vietnam War generation, was even more liberal compared with their nongay generational colleagues, and those 50 to 59 years old were more liberal still, with only 3 percent of a small sample saying that they were conservative while 32 percent of their nongay counterparts said that they were conservative. Only at 60 years old did the gay sample begin to balance off at moderate, at which point the entire sample moves quickly to conservative. That is, throughout the age cohorts of the 1992 national VRS sample, the ideological predispositions evident in Los Angeles and New York are the same, although the degree may differ. All the samples demonstrate that even when controlled for age, self-identified gay men and lesbians see themselves as much more liberal than the nongay/lesbian samples do.

It also seems certain that a portion of the upswing in the exit polls' gay/lesbian/bisexual self-identification rates is a result of the aging of the lesbian and gay cohort: the first set of self-identifiers who were willing to accept the name "gay" or "lesbian" in the mid-to-late 1980s is now approaching middle age in the late 1990s. Behind them are more and younger self-identifiers for whom this identification is a less frightening leap. Indeed, identification rates among voters under 40 years of age were as high as 5 percent in the 1996 VNS national sample. We can, in fact, expect this gradual increase in gay/lesbian self-identification to be sustained as the older cohorts, who have the lowest self-identification rates, are slowly replaced by the younger, post-Stonewall, and queer-generation age cohorts.

RESPONDENTS' EDUCATION AND SELF-IDENTIFICATION

Self-identified gay, lesbian, and bisexual samples are typically better educated than the general-population samples from which they were drawn (see figure 5-2). The difference is greatest at the upper levels of educational achievement, with a larger portion of self-identifiers having a graduate education or having completed graduate degrees than the samples as a whole. Because there are strong correlations between education level and voter turnout—the more educated the sample is, the more likely they are to be engaged in political activity—it is likely also that the sample's political consciousness is greater. Indeed, some measures from the 1992 VRS sample show that in suburbs, rural areas, and medium-size cities, the gay and lesbian sample is more likely to wear buttons of support for their candidates than is the general sample. In all sizes of cities, they are substantially more likely to do volunteer work for a candidate.

Since the gay and lesbian self-identification samples are typically younger then the general-population samples from which they are drawn,

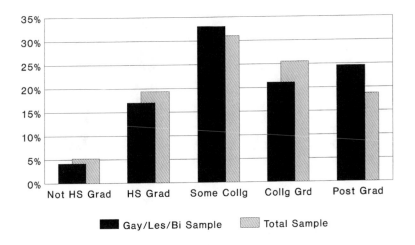

FIGURE 5.2

Gay/lesbian urban sample and education (self-IDs better educated than total).
VRS 1992 National Election Sample Subsample from cities over 50,000, *n* = 2,242;
GLB sample, *n* = 112.

the availability and expectations for education should be higher than for previous generations. But again, when age was controlled for in the 1992 VRS nationwide exit poll, the gay and lesbian sample still was better educated than the overall sample of 15,488. Since the gay and lesbian sample in the VRS nationwide sample was heavily urban and urban dwellers usually have higher education rates, this aspect of the profile might also be misleading. Yet again, in cities of 50,000 or more, the gay and lesbian sample was better educated, especially in the percentage of high school graduates and the number of postgraduates. In small towns and rural areas, the trend was even stronger. Interestingly, it was only in the suburbs that the gay sample either matched or fell below the education levels of the nongay sample, but the suburban gay sample also was more likely to have attended graduate or professional school. Overall, the pattern of education levels in the national urban sample is evident also in the 1993 Los Angeles and New York City mayoral samples (see figure 5-3).

GENDER, SEXUAL IDENTITY, AND SELF-IDENTIFICATION RATES

Perhaps the most interesting descriptor of self-identification in these samples is gender, or, rather, the interaction of gender, its construction, and the

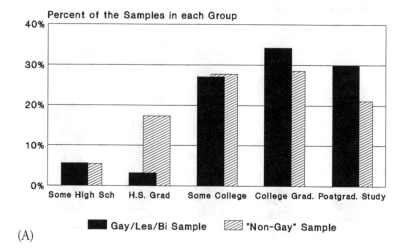

(A)

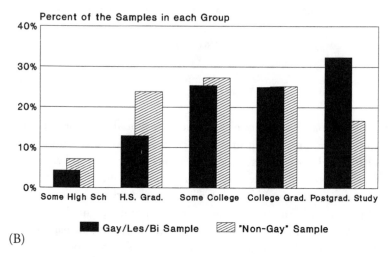

(B)

FIGURE 5.3
Education and gay/lesbian identity. (A) Los Angeles, 1993.
(Source: *Los Angeles Times* mayoral exit poll. June, 1993.) (B) New York City, 1993.
(Source: NYC General mayor election [weighted]. Voter News Service,
November 1993.)

data collection instruments themselves. The initial profile of self-identifiers from the first exit-poll samples generated in the late 1980s was of a white middle-class male in his thirties, well educated, and earning a higher income than the sample as a whole. Males initially composed a much larger portion of the self-identified gay and lesbian samples than females did. For example, in the ABC 1988 California Democratic presidential primary sample, with an overall self-identification rate of 3 percent, men made up more than two-thirds of the total. In the 1988 ABC Democratic presidential primary extract from New York City, the gender differential was even greater: 81 percent of those self-identifying were male, and only 19 percent were female (with a self-identification rate of 4 percent statewide).[4] In the 1989 ABC New York City mayoral/general election, with a self-identification rate of 3.2 percent, men composed 60 percent of the sample ($n = 84$). In all these cases, however, the gay and lesbian sample was quite low. In more recent samples, the sample sizes were greater in terms of both cases and percentage of the total sample, and the difference between the sexes was not as large. By 1993, the New York City general election gay/lesbian/bisexual sample was 58 percent male and 42 female (with a self-identification rate of about 8 percent and an n of 111).[5] There also was a change in the gender ratio between 1990 and 1992 and between 1992 and 1994 in the VRS/VNS national exit-poll samples. In the smaller 1990 sample, women represented 45.1 percent of the total (in the entire sample, women represented 51.7 percent). In 1992, women composed 47.0 percent of the sample ($n = 420$).[6] In the smaller 1994 sample, this fell to 41 percent.[7] But in the 1996 national sample, there was virtually no difference between the sexes in their self-identification rates.

Although a small portion of these traditional differences in self-identification rates between men and women may be explained by differences in turnout by men and women, there still appears to be some reason that men tend to self-identify as gay at greater rates than women do as lesbians. The first and most obvious possible explanation is that same-sex behavior and the political identity that comes with it are less prevalent among women than among men. The second is that women might feel less secure financially or socially in revealing their sexuality, even in the relative protection of anonymous exit-poll questionnaires. This factor likely works in combination with other factors in a subtle interaction, such as a double sense of possible discrimination against lesbians as both women and "queers" or the combination of fewer life options and differing development patterns in lesbians and gay men in the process of psychological self-identification.[8]

A third explanation is that the interaction of gender, the construction of identity, and differences in social power between the sexes is more complex in women than in men. This is an important theme among those writing about lesbian ethics. From this perspective, women who exercise their full moral agency frequently threaten the permanence of the simple dichotomized gender identity of male and female. By creating their own lives, both inside and outside the constructions presented by time and place, women (particularly lesbians) press the limits of gender identity. Sarah Hoagland's lesbian ethics, for example, describes the challenge to the dichotomous categories of male/female or heterosexist/homosexist and offers instead a broader range of sexual identity for women.[9] French psychiatrist and theorist Luce Irigaray has taken a middle course on these issues, allowing the presentation of a well-defined category "woman," for tactical reasons but recognizing its wide variation.[10] The paths that women must navigate—the structuring forces of family and society—are influenced by (and influence) both gender and sexual identity. Thus lesbians might need to separate from men in order to create their own identities and lives, whereas for men—gay or not—such conversations would be disingenuous at best.

Building on Hoagland, Elizabeth Daumer sees bisexuality as expanding the range of moral agency that separates women from heterosexism, resisting both the general social as well as gay male pressures to reduce sexual identity to only two categories: straight and gay, in which "gay" is really "gay male."[11] When this broader range of sociosexual expression is linked to politics, the agent woman's channels of expression (or identi-*ties*) are also broader than men's.

Interestingly, not only is Daumer's argument representative of much contemporary feminist and lesbian theory, but it also finds support in the data available on self-identification rates. Some survey researchers discovered that the self-identification rate of nonheterosexuals increased when the category available for self-identification was altered from "gay and lesbian" to "gay/lesbian/bisexual" or—more to the point—when a check box for "bisexual" was added to the options (see figure 5.4).[12] In analyzing the results of a self-administered questionnaire for lesbian- and bisexual-identified women ($n = 365$), sociologist Paula Rust found that the category "bisexual" was stable for many women, and a sizable portion of her sample did indeed choose bisexual, as opposed to lesbian, as their identity and de-

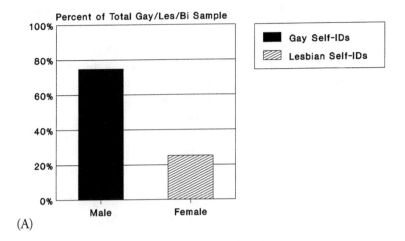

(A)

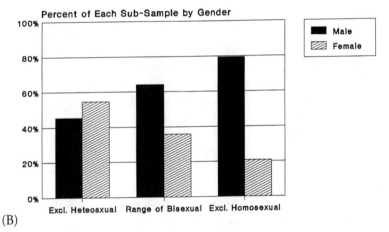

(B)

FIGURE 5.4

(A) Gay/lesbian self ID by gender (when not offered the option *bisexual* the sample is dominated by men).

(Source: NYS 1990 64th A.D. exit poll.)

(B) "Bisexual" and female response (when offered the option *bisexual,* female self-ID rate increases).

(Source: NYS 1990 64th A.D. exit poll.)

scriptor, despite some prejudice in the gay and lesbian community and even in women-identified women communities against accepting a bisexual identity. Rust sees this resistance as culturally and historically specific, a reaction to the dichotomies of male/female, heterosexual/homosexual, presented by contemporary culture. She recognizes that *bi*sexual responses to these poles create a tactical problem for many lesbian (and, we could add, gay male) activists, who see a bisexual identity as undermining the full strength of a strong, individual "lesbian" identity to counter the socially constructed heterosexual identities offered to women by the present-day culture. Although Rust was dealing with sexual attraction and identity in her work, and not necessarily politics and identity, women's acceptance of the category "bisexual" is important here.[13]

The effects of viewing sexual orientation as a range rather than as a dichotomous indicator can be analyzed empirically using an exit-poll study conducted in the Sixty-fourth Assembly District of the Lower West Side of Manhattan (referred to throughout this book and elsewhere as the Glick study).[14] In addition to the standard question (offering only a "gay/lesbian" check box), a modified Kinsey scale for self-assessment of sexual behavior was included at the end of the data collection sheets: "Which best describes your sexual orientation? (1) Exclusively Heterosexual; (2) Mostly Heterosexual; (3) Bisexual; (4) Mostly Homosexual; (5) Exclusively Homosexual." When offered only a dichotomized gay/lesbian, nongay/nonlesbian choice, the sample of self-identifiers was 75 percent men and only 25 percent women (total $n = 87$). When the categories Exclusively Homosexual, Mostly Homosexual, and Bisexual were merged into one category, the sample increased in terms of weighted percentages (from 16.9 to 23.3 percent). More to the point, the reorganization of categories increased the percentage of women in the gay and lesbian (and now also bisexual) pool from 25 percent to 31 percent in the same overall sample. It is clear that this was a result of the higher rate of self-identification among women when a range of bisexual identification was offered. Although we can determine nothing definitive from this group of 124 who identified as bisexual or gay, it is a tantalizing indication of the differences between the sexual identity of women and men in what is called "the gay community."

RACE AND SELF-IDENTIFICATION

Age, education, and sex explained most of the differences between the pool of gay and lesbian self-identifiers and the remaining exit-poll samples. Race, income, and religion did not. Race is the most contentious of these dimensions. Since the earliest data containing a gay and lesbian identifier—before the press began to report on a "gay vote" in anything but the most general terms—there was concern that racial minorities were being underrepresented in the samples, beyond even their historically low turnout rates. The New York City 1989 Democratic mayoral primary samples, for example, had a low self-identification rate among African Americans, even though in anticipation of electing the city's first black mayor, the turnout among African American New Yorkers was the highest it had ever been.

More recent data, however, show less skewing toward or away from any one racial grouping. Samples of gay and lesbian African Americans—

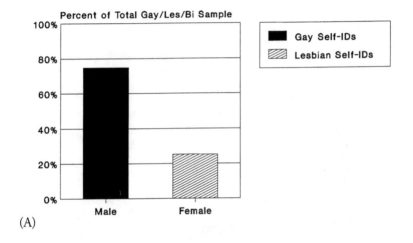

(A)

FIGURE 5.5

(A) Race and sexual ID. National urban sample (1992),
drawn from all cities over 50,000.
(Source: VRS 1992 National Exit Poll. Urban extract total n = 4,306;gay/les/bi n = 199.
Data weighted by VRS formula.)
(B) Los Angeles, 1993.
(Source: *Los Angeles Times* mayoral runoff exit poll (June). Total n = 2,829;
gay/lesbian n = 162. Data weighted by *Los Angeles Times* formulas.)
(C) New York, 1993.
(Source: 1993 VNS NYC General Election Exit Poll. total n = 1,267;
gay/les/bi n = 110. Data weighted by VNS formulas.)

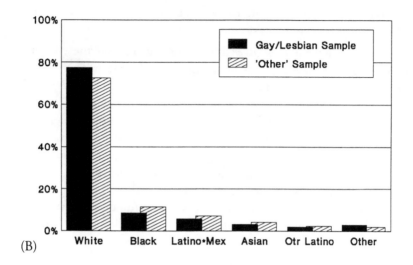

(B)

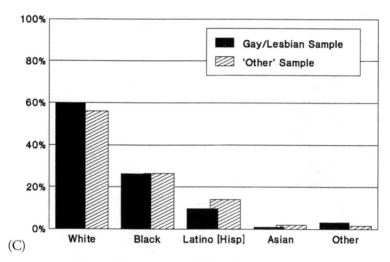

(C)

at least in medium-size and large cities—have approached their proportional numbers in the overall samples (see figure 5-5). These urban samples, drawn from the 1992 VRS exit polls (from sample precincts in cities of 50,000 or more) indicated a self-identified gay and lesbian subsample of 17.3 percent African Americans—not very different from the 16.2 percent African American representation of the entire sample. (But in both the 1990 and 1994 urban samples, African Americans were the only racial group significantly underrepresented in the gay and lesbian sample of self-identifiers.) Similarly, in 1992, the Latino/Mexican samples were 5.1

percent and 5.6 percent, respectively (the respective n's were proportionately low). As in the case of women, changes in the data instruments as well as the social context have brought the gay sample among people of color closer to their proportion in exit-poll samples (which is not to say that they approached the proportion in general demographics or even registration rates).

In New York and Los Angeles, an approximation of racial representativeness is also evident in the sample; it is certainly more representative than age, gender, or education.[15] Nonetheless, the 1993 New York City Voter News Service mayoral sample is more representative of the overall New York voting population in regard to race than is the *Los Angeles Times* gay and lesbian sample of voters in Los Angeles (but in neither city does race meet the test of statistical significance in explaining the differences between the gay and nongay subsamples). As in the case of gender, the influence of racial constructions on self-identification as gay or lesbian complicates the nuances of both sexual and racial identity. The construction of "gay" as white and male, especially to African Americans, surely has made women and men of color hesitant to use the name "gay" as their primary political identity.

The "Civic Culture" of Sexual Identity: Attitudes, Party, and Policy Preferences

Recognizing a separate if (at this point) only general sociodemographic profile for gay men and lesbians is a first step toward determining whether political values and voting behavior do differ among this identity grouping. The influence of age and education variables show the impact of generational clustering and changing social context. When we examine political values, party association, policy interests, and specific issues, we find discernible differences between gay and lesbian self-identifiers and nonidentifiers in both the national and urban exit-poll samples. In general, these differences tend to fall into one of three categories: (1) intensity of personal reactions to the candidates and identifiable attitudes toward the role of government, (2) specific association with party and/or ideological position, and (3) specific opinions about substantive issues pertinent to lesbians and gay men, such as education and health care.

Personal Attitudes Toward Politicians and Government

The personal nature of sexual identity is reflected in the reaction of gay men and lesbians to political candidates. In 1992, for example, gay men and lesbians responding to the VRS exit poll tended to be more trusting of Bill Clinton's explanation of his past personal problems than of George Bush's explanation of the country's economic performance and his own role in the Iran–contra affair. It was not so much on which side of these issues lesbians and gay men stood (though they were clearly more pro-Democratic than Republican) but that they differed from the overall sample in their intensity of reaction to the candidate's personal reputation. The 1992 *Los Angeles Times* national exit poll showed that when asked what characteristic of their candidate most influenced their decision, 40.1 percent of gay and lesbian respondents said their candidate—overwhelming Bill Clinton—"cares about people like me." Only 21.1 percent of nongays offered such a response about their vote.[16] Nongays responded that "experience" was the characteristic of their candidate most influencing their vote. It seems clear that gay men and lesbians were more emotionally involved in the 1992 race than were their non-"queer" neighbors.

In the 1994 VNS congressional election sample, despite the general perception in the gay community that the president had failed to end discrimination in the armed forces, their support for President Clinton continued. Under strong pressure from social conservatives and the rising Republican prospects for victory in many open House districts, the general attitude of self-identified gay men and lesbians toward (a then Democratic) Congress, Clinton, and the country became more positive. Unlike the nongay majority, the sexual identity voting bloc thought the nation was "going in the right direction" (about 54 percent) and found value in the experience of incumbent House members. Among those who explained why they voted for a particular congressional candidate, the gay sample indicated that they wanted to support President Clinton. The nongay sample had the opposite—but not nearly as strong—reaction.[17] Interestingly, the 1994 self-identified gay and lesbian sample lived in congressional districts held by Democratic House incumbents at a rate of more than two to one, and they voted more than two to one for incumbent members.[18]

This intensity and cohesion have not been true of gay and lesbian attitudes toward economic policy, however. In their economic perceptions and general assessment of the economy's performance, the attitudes of gay voters going to the polls in 1990 were virtually identical to those of nongay voters. In the urban extract from the 1992 sample, gay and lesbian voters also held views similar to those of the general urban voter. If there was a difference, the 1992 national sample showed that gay voters were slightly more pessimistic in their assessment of the economy, tended to see the nation's economic problems as more structural than temporary (but at only a slightly higher margin). But their expectations for the effects of foreign trade on American employment (a question related to the North American Free Trade Agreement) and their general resistance to higher taxes were identical to those of the nongay sample. The gay and lesbian sample did, however, judge former President George Bush more harshly in his handling of the economy.

Although the economic perceptions of the gay and lesbian and nongay and lesbian samples were similar, there were some differences in their attitudes toward government intervention in the economy. The lesbian and gay sample from the 1992 presidential election, for example, was more supportive of government intervention in economic matters than was the overall national sample (gay/lesbian/bisexual: 66.5 percent, nongay: 54.3 percent)—but some of this difference could be attributed to the general liberalism of the gay sample. Being urban may be as much a distinguishing factor as being lesbian or gay (nationwide, 49.6 percent identified as liberal, as opposed to only 20.6 percent in the nongay sample).

Not surprisingly, opinions about social issues between gay and nongay samples differed much more than those about economic matters. Because they view the state more as a mediator of secular culture than as an administrator of traditional values, self-identifying lesbian and gay voters in 1992 preferred government intervention in civil discourse to encourage "tolerance" rather than "traditional family values" (see table 5-1). The sample also exhibited significant differences from the nongay sample of voters in their unwillingness to blame the nation's problems on a "breakdown in family values" rather than on the government's neglect of domestic problems. Nationwide, lesbians and gay men faulted government neglect of domestic policy, not "family breakdown," for the social problems facing families and the nation as a whole (the gay/lesbian/bisexual sample was 68.5 percent to 31.5 percent for others). The nongay sample, however, was equally divided between the two positions. When looking only at cities of 250,000 or more,

TABLE 5.1

Responses from Gay/Lesbian and Nongay/Lesbian Samples on Social Values

Is It More Important for the Government to...

	National Sample (%)[a]		Urban Sample (%)[c]	
	GLB[b]	NONGAY	GLB[d]	NONGAY
Encourage Traditional Values?	30.8	75.0	12.8	66.1
Encourage Tolerance of Nontraditional Values?	69.2	25.0	87.2	33.9

The Country's Social Problems Are Caused by...

	National Sample (%)[a]		Urban Sample (%)[c]	
	GLB[b]	NONGAY	GLB[d]	NONGAY
Breakdown of Family	31.5	51.6	34.0	47.8
Government Neglect of Domestic Policy	68.5	48.4	66.0	52.2

Source: VRS national exit poll.

Note: Data weighted by VRS formulas for analysis.

[a]Unweighted sample = 3,866.

[b]Unweighted gay/lesbian/bisexual sample = 113.

[c]Unweighted sample from all sample precincts in cities with a population greater than 50,000 = 1,071.

[d]Unweighted gay/lesbian/bisexual subsample = 52.

the percentages of gay and nongay remained about the same, 48.8 percent to 51.2 percent. But within this gay and urban sample, the difference became even clearer: only 19.5 percent of the lesbian and gay male sample saw the "breakdown of the traditional family" as a primary source of the nation's social problems.

On a deeper level, the attitudes toward government overall show a surprising lack of difference, defined by sexual identity, in voters' trust in the federal government. Both the 1990 and 1994 national exit polls asked, "How often do you trust government?" The possible responses were "Just about always," "Most of the time," "Only some of the time," and "Never." In neither year did differences in the responses by self-identified gay men and lesbians and the general sample diverge in a statistically significant way: the modal category in both 1990 and 1994 was "Only some of the time," at a rate of approximately 60 percent. Thus, at least in terms of trust, gay men and lesbians seem no more alienated from the federal government than does the sample as a whole. In fact, for all the distrust that gay and lesbian voters exhibited toward politicians, gay voters were generally more supportive of a positive state than was the overall 1992 VRS sample of 15,490, except in areas pertaining to privacy (if we can use abortion as a surrogate indicator). This is a surprising statement of faith in government, given the catalog of grievances the mobilized gay community offers as evidence of state repression.

Affiliation with Party and Ideological Self-Assessment

As with class, union background, and race, sexual identity is associated with a party identification. As a grouping, self-identifying gay men and lesbians are two and a half times more likely to be registered as Democrats than as Republicans—49.7 percent to 18.4 percent (VRS data; the *Los Angeles Times* national exit poll indicated an even stronger difference, 67.2 percent to 17.2 percent)—far more than would be expected, given other social characteristics such as income, gender, and education. Only African Americans (75.2 percent), Jewish voters (65.3 percent), and those at the bottom of the income and education scales had higher Democratic identification rates in 1992. The Democratic identification rates of gay men and lesbians were roughly equal to those of union members (49.2 percent) and Latinos (50.5 percent).[19]

In urban areas, as expected, the Democratic identification rate was even higher (see table 5-2). The exit poll from the 1993 New York City mayoral election indicated that 70 percent of gay men and lesbians considered themselves Democrats, whereas the remainder of the nongay sample identified as Democrats at a lower, 57.8 percent, rate.[20] In Los Angeles, 77.9 percent of

TABLE 5.2

Percentage of Gay versus Nongay Party Identification by Urbanization

		Democratic	Republican	Independent
Urban	Gay/Lesbian	58.3	13.5	28.2
	Non-GLB	43.9	30.4	25.7
Suburban	Gay/Lesbian	48.5	17.9	33.6
	Non-GLB	34.6	38.3	27.0
Small Town/Rural	Gay/Lesbian	35.7	28.7	35.6
	Non-GLB	36.9	34.5	28.7

Source: VRS 1992 national exit poll. Data weighted by VRS formulas.

the gay and lesbian population were registered Democrats, and 61.6 percent of the nongay sample were Democrats. The nongay Republican registration rate was 31.5 percent, twice that of the gay Republican registration.[21]

Although both gay-identified and nongay-identified large-city voters tend to identity themselves as Democrats, when we compared the sample with the size of the city (or non-center-city areas), the results were different. That is, in the 1992 VRS data, there was no statistically significant difference between the registration patterns of gays and nongays in cities of more than 500,000.[22] The gay and lesbian sample (n = 92) in the smaller 1994 VNS national congressional exit poll showed similar results. But in medium-size cities and in the suburbs, there was a statistically significant difference in the patterns of party identification along the dimension of sexual orientation—but in an unusual way. Although there was a higher rate of Republican registration among nongays in suburbs and medium-size cities, for self-identified gay men and lesbians, "independent," not Republican, was the second reported choice of party identification. Thus, the differences in party identification in medium-size and smaller cities as well as suburbs between the gay and nongay sample cannot be explained solely by the fact that gays in these jurisdictions tend to register as Democrats at higher rates than the does whole sample, and also at higher rates as independents. It is the low rate of Republican identification that really defines lesbian and gay party affiliation in the cities and suburbs. In rural areas, party registration again converges, as both gays and nongays tend to identify as Democratic.

Given their more liberal positions on social issues and their general support for an interventionist state, it is not surprising that gay men and lesbians are much more likely to choose liberal or moderate, rather than conservative, as their ideological designation. In fact, about half the total VRS 1992 gay and lesbian sample (n = 420) nationwide identified as liberal, with another 42 percent as moderate and only 8 percent as conservative. In cities of 50,000 or more, about 43 percent identify as liberal and half as moderate, and only 26 percent of nongays so identify (although in cities of 250,000 or more, the difference between the gay and lesbian sample and the nongay sample identifying as liberal is negligible; both are at about 25 percent).

Identity Groups' Attitudes Toward Substantive Policy Issues

The gay and lesbian samples from 1992, in both urban areas and nationally, do differ from the nongay sample on some fiscal and budget priorities. They were less likely to support cuts in federal programs when confronted with a choice between programs and higher taxes. But in this, gays and lesbians tended to resemble urban voters in general, sexual orientation being only one part of the description of difference. The lesbian and gay sample was significantly less likely to support higher taxes if they were to be used to reduce the federal deficit. Gay and lesbian voters did tend to support higher taxes for job training, a possible reflection of the sample's age and its generally more proeducation profile, and they supported environmental concerns over economic development, but only slightly more than the national sample did. In accordance with the entire sample, the economy and jobs were of paramount importance. In this regard, the gay and nongay samples did not differ.

Not surprisingly, the gay and lesbian sample does differ from the nongay sample in their concern for health care. The 1992 presidential exit poll showed health care to be the top policy priority among lesbian and gay voters across the country. This was true in the suburbs but less so in the urban areas, where it was the second most important issue (table 5-3). The gay and lesbian sample also approved of increased taxes for health care. Only jobs and economic issues competed with health policy as a strong issue for gay men and lesbians. In the 1994 VNS congressional exit poll, the gay and lesbian sample again ranked health care as their top policy priority among the choices provided. When the national gay sample was controlled for age, the gay sample's concern for health care even rose, and the difference between the gay and nongay sample increased. All other issues remained the same. Given the relative youth of the group, this concern for health issues is certainly a result of the disproportionate effect of AIDS and HIV-spectrum diseases on gay men (to say nothing of their cultural impact on all lesbians and gay men). In fact, in most other exit polls that include this option, from differing levels of government and regions of the country, health care has been a major issue of concern for self-identified gay men and lesbians.[23] These attitudes carry over throughout the range of populations—from urban to suburban to rural—although they are strongest in urban areas. According to the 1993 New York City and Los Angeles mayoral exit polls, the nongay sample held different priorities—nationally it was usually taxes and in the cities, crime.

Although one position in the gay community can be associated with a conservative and libertarian position—with Marvin Liebman as its main theoretician, Barry Goldwater its principal nongay political supporter, and others on the left who took their initial inspiration from the organization-

TABLE 5.3
Gay Men's and Lesbians' Concerns—1992 National Election

Which Issues Most Mattered to You in Making Your Choice Today?

	National Sample (%)[a]		Urban Sample (%)[c]	
NOVEMBER 1992	GLB[B]	NONGAY	GLB[D]	NONGAY
Health Care[e]	34.4	15.6	23.0	15.5
Federal Deficit	7.1	14.5	8.9	12.7
Abortion	8.2	7.4	13.2	8.2
Education	5.5	6.9	4.1	8.6
Economy/Jobs	27.5	26.8	30.7	29.0
Environment	3.3	3.2	4.4	4.4
Taxes	5.4	8.9	4.8	8.2
Foreign Affairs	1.6	5.1	1.9	4.5
Family Values	7.0	11.5	9.0	8.9

[a]Unweighted sample = 7,287.
[b]Unweighted gay/lesbian/bisexual subsample = 209.
[c]Unweighted sample = 2,000.
[d]Unweighted gay/lesbian/bisexual subsample = 102.
[e]First mention from VRS list. Data weighted by VRS formulas for analysis.

al accomplishments of labor and the left—these two perspectives do not describe the current tendencies toward consensus among self-identifying lesbians and gay men in the exit-poll samples. The current profile in the sample is a combination of strong concern for privacy, support for regulating
and advancing a liberal culture but seeking state intervention in broad economic matters and specific policy matters of interest—health matters being
the most pronounced.

Social Values and Economic Values in Cities and Suburbs

The gay and lesbian self-identification rate in the suburbs was lower than
in the cities (only 1.2 percent of the total VRS-defined suburban sample in
1992), and the pool was slightly more conservative on economic and fiscal
issues than were its urban gay counterparts. Many in the VRS 1992 suburban sample were first-time voters. In terms of simple demographics, the
sample of suburban lesbian and gay self-identifiers was older, more female,
more disparate in income, and less liberal in economic and fiscal matters—

although certainly not conservative—than their urban counterparts. What the data may be showing is a double cluster of younger lesbians and gay men still living with their parents, balanced by a much larger and older group, more tempered in their politics and less politicized by the gay rights movement (see table 5-4 and figure 5-6).

The greatest differences between the suburban gay and lesbian sample and the nongay and lesbian sample are in those dimensions that could be termed *social values*. On abortion, for example, the gay sample and nongay samples diverge significantly nationwide. But on the urban level, sexual identity explains only some of the differences in attitudes toward abortion (see table 5-5). This disparity between the national gay sample and the urban gay sample is due more to the urban nongay sample's greater support for a "right to choose" position than to less commitment by the lesbian and gay sample to a "choice" position.

Gay and lesbian city dwellers differ most from suburban and rural lesbians and gay men in economic and fiscal matters. On economic questions, the attitudes of gay urbanites in the 1992 VRS sample were much more liberal (or more urban?) than those of their suburban counterparts. The urban gay sample was more apt to support government intervention (76.5 percent) than was the suburban sample (48 percent). Suburban residents were quite similar, regardless of sexual orientation. Support for government intervention in the economy was almost even between the suburban gay and nongay sample (48 percent to 53 percent).

Unlike urban dwellers, however, suburban gay and lesbian voters do not resemble their nongay neighbors on social values, being twice as likely to want government to encourage tolerance of nontraditional lifestyles (gay suburban sample: 52.7 percent, nongay: 25.6 percent). And in questions about abortion, for example, nonurban lesbians and gay men are significantly more prochoice than their suburban nongay neighbors.

TABLE 5.4

Percentage of Age Differential of 1992 VRS Gay/Lesbian Sample by Urbanization

	18–24	25–29	30–39	40–49	50–59	>60	Total	n
Urban	19.2	15.8	35.5	16.2	6.6	6.6	40.9	202
Suburban	9.8	15.1	33.9	13.1	13.5	14.6	38.3	125
Small Town/Rural	10.5	13.9	25.0	25.4	13.3	11.8	20.8	90

Source: VRS 1992 national exit poll.

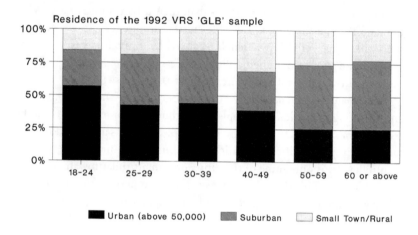

FIGURE 5.6

Younger GLBs tend to live in cities; middle-aged and seniors in suburbs
(percent of each age group by residence).
(Source: 1992 VRS national exit poll [unweighted].
Urban, suburban, and rural extracts GLB subsample—420 [unweighted].)

One conclusion we can draw at this point is that self-identification
among lesbians or gay men is strongly related to urbanization and that in
the aggregate, the political difference between gay and nongay city residents
on social values is not as great as in the suburbs. Whether the impact of gay
voters in the suburbs is as strong as it is distinct remains an open question.
At this stage of the analysis, it appears that suburban lesbians and gay men
stand out more on social issues but are fewer in number. Both their small
number and their political values (being largely liberal in a territory dominated by a conservative politics) put them at a disadvantage for building
coalitions, influencing electoral outcomes, and affecting policy.

On economic issues, however, suburban gay men and lesbians tend to be
more similar to their nongay suburban neighbors than to urban gay men
and lesbians. There is little need, therefore, to organize economic values according to sexually identified organizations or to have sexual identity organizations mediate intergroup relations. The concern of such organizations
in the suburbs is almost exclusively "identity" issues such as discrimination,
anti–lesbian and gay violence, domestic partnership benefits administered
by local government, shelters for women, HIV prevention and support ser-

TABLE 5.5
Nongay Support for Abortion

Which Comes Closest to Your Position on Abortion?

	National Sample (%)[a]		Urban Sample (%)[c]	
NOVEMBER 1992	GLB[b]	NONGAY	GLB[d]	NONGAY
Legal in All Cases:	54.9	34.9	58.0	42.1
Legal in Most Cases:	31.4	30.8	30.1	30.1
Illegal in Most Cases:	9.1	24.8	8.6	20.9
Illegal in All Cases:	4.7	9.5	3.4	6.9

Note: Overall *n* = 420. Data weighted by VRS formulas for analysis.
Note: Data weighted by VRS formulas for analysis.
[a]Unweighted sample = 7,646.
[b]Unweighted gay/lesbian/bisexual sample = 209.
[c]Unweighted sample from all sample precincts in cities with a population greater than 50,000 = 2,108.
[d]Unweighted gay/lesbian/bisexual subsample = 111.

vices, adoption rights, and affirmative school curricula. These organizations offer few bridges to nongay suburbanites, and economic matters do not particularly divide them from their neighbors.

The fairly small number of suburban gay men and lesbians, the age of many of them, and their relatively satisfied economic condition may discourage them from mobilizing to incorporate their sexual identity concerns into local policies. Or stated in the reverse, because urban lesbians and gays are greater in number and closer to the policy and party predispositions of all urban voters, the possibilities for coalition building in cities are much stronger than in the suburbs.

Political Socialization Versus Identity Formation: The "Story Sets" of Sexual Identity

These differences in ideological and party predisposition, attitudes toward government, and specific policy priorities raise questions about identity formation, as opposed to the more traditional literature on political socialization. In the "behavioral revolution" of the 1950s and 1960s, political socialization was the centerpiece of the new, crudely positivist approach to politics. The actual results of such research were not as valuable, however, as the questions that the research raised. By the early 1980s, the assumption that families served as the cauldron of political valuation seemed problematic, as more extended frameworks of political learning provided new insights into the political socialization process. Moreover, as the critique of crudely positivist political science proceeded, it created questions of its own about voters' presumed passivity.

But the current data on lesbian and gay voters—at least those in cities—suggest other dynamics in identity formation and its influences on voting behavior. The descriptors of lesbian or gay male self-identification as they pertain to voting behavior add to and take theoretical insight from a postfamilial developmental and constructivist perspective on identity formation, as opposed to the behavioral perspective of early models of political socialization.

Theories of Political Socialization

In the behaviorism of the political science of the 1960s and early 1970s, "identity" was essentially "identification with." One came to identify with a religion or racial group or, most important, a political party. In this working model, the individual was not an active participant, an agent, in his or her own identity formation but passive onlooker, a "tabula rasa," as Timothy Cook suggests, open to scripting by the socializing structures of family, community, and the mass media.[24] Seeking predictors of latent political identification—usually defined as party identification or partisanship—University of Michigan analysts looked back to the party identification of the voter's parents and then to religious traditions in upbringing, ethnic/racial identity, educational achievement of the parents and the voter, and similar formative influences to explain party and partisan identification.[25] Although a transformative event or series of events could alter political identity, the cumulative childhood and adolescent civic training and experience went far in explaining party identification as it was associated with political identity, and this affected voting behavior for much of the voter's life.

While still working in the Michigan paradigm, Nie, Verba, and Petrocik expanded this model from the initial Michigan system of voter socialization. They noted that the growth of the state was involving people in ever more politicized lives: "perhaps more important than the changing substance of political issues is the fact that they have come to have a more direct impact on daily life."[26] This chipping away at the liberal distinction between the public and the private might well have meant that formerly private issues—in this case, sexuality—could become the basis for political identity and mobilization. The increased role of gender, sexuality, and cultural identity as predictors of voting behavior find theoretical support here. Although Nie, Verba, and Petrocik pointed the way past the influences of family and the community defined by family, they never fully explored nonfamily influences.

Four major research themes emerged from the critiques of the 1960s Michigan model of political socialization. The first was inspired by developmental psychology. A missing and intervening variable in the childhood learning process as understood by political scientists was cognitive development, so researchers studied the relative utility of competing psychological models of cognitive development. The work of Piaget, Kohlberg, and Vygotsky as well as psychoanalytic theory held the most interest in the study of political learning, especially in regard to childhood and early adolescence.

A second research tradition centered on those social structures outside the family that were most influential during the adolescence, such as class identification, the construction of racial identities, gender roles, and postsecondary education.[27] This second stage comes later in youth, when social structures replace family structures as the primary referent of values and as life experience may contradict the socialization to politics offered by the family in childhood. Gary Marks described this distinction as between *intrafamilial* and *extrafamilial* portions of political socialization. Marks, using the political socialization model, saw three primary influences on political socialization: (1) intrafamily socialization, (2) extrafamily (socially structuring) forces, and (3) base issues.[28] Expanding the framework even further than adolescence, Niemi and Jennings organized their research around the twin themes of *persistence* and *change* in political values, finding three models: (1) a life-cycle model, (2) a generational-identity model, and (3) a "lifelong openness" model. These three models of change were in addition to the implied lifelong persistence model embedded in the assumptions of the early political socialization research.[29]

A third line of research critiquing the initial Michigan model, based on the role of issues in voting, focused on the "malleability" of party identification. The political socialization model assumed nearly lifetime stability in the voter's party identification. Any temporary deviance from the party of preference would be overcome by the base forces of party identification honed by early political socialization. The alternative model presented in the early 1980s was one of "retrospective" or "prospective voting," the idea that rational voters saw their interests not through the eyes of childhood and adolescent influences but in the context of a moving multiyear assessment of personal needs, candidates, and party policy offerings. Many data were marshaled to support the perspective.[30] Later refinements resulted in a merged model in which the family did indeed have some initial influence over political identity, which waned as personal issue preferences came into greater prominence as the voter matured.[31] This model combined atavistic socialization with retrospective voting behavior.

The fourth kind of research examined voting according to group identities, that is, individual voting behavior mediated by cultural or "identity groups" that helped formulate individual responses to political information. In this case, political socialization does not look to generational or "youthful" socialization but to the political learning of women/girls, African Americans, Latinos, men/boys, and so forth in a group-specific political discourse. At the same time, others looked into how groups become referents for other voters as a way of identifying their own voting priorities in either support or opposition.[32] It is in this tradition that much of feminist and some African American identity politics has been integrated into voting studies.

Ethel Klein traced the emergence of feminism to the development of a women's consciousness through the suffragette movement and postwar changes in economic and household structure in the 1960s: "The shaky foundations for women's lives collapsed when fertility rates dropped precipitously in the 1960s. Motherhood, the linchpin of femaleness throughout the century, became less central to women's lives."[33] But even the changes in consciousness among women did not necessarily express themselves in voting behavior substantially different from that of men. Feminist issues and maybe voting were important in the 1972 and 1976 elections, according to Klein, but not until 1980 did voting behavior begin to diverge between the sexes in regard to women's rights. Although men were sympathetic to women's rights issues, they were not a contributing factor in their voting. The concern with feminist issues was more central to women, and thus their voting patterns were more heavily influenced by them. Sue Rinehart took the issue one step further to emphasize gender consciousness as it "directs and constrains policy preferences."[34] In short, gender consciousness is an organizing platform for processing political information and action.

Identity Formation Versus Political Socialization

The examination of these self-determined samples—what we have termed a cohort of voters who accept the marker "gay," "lesbian," or "bisexual" as an assemblage (network?) of voters participating in a discourse about sexual identity—shows that some of this cohort's social characteristics are the same, even though the sampling and data collection methods differ.

A gay/lesbian/bisexual political identity—or at least the willingness to express it—was associated with age, gender, and education, three factors of particular importance to earlier students of political socialization. This impression was confirmed by further multiple regression analysis of the three most scientifically sound data sets containing a gay and lesbian self-identifier: the 1992 national VRS data set, the November 1993 New York City Voter News Service general election data set, and the June 1993 *Los Angeles Times* mayoral runoff exit poll. As expected, when these three exit poll samples were subjected to logit regression, the key variables describing the differences between the gay and lesbian cohort and the non-self-identifiers were age, education, and gender—in that order of potency. Thus, the data constructs of self-identity from these three exit polls suggest that the self-identifier samples are not completely separate from their social contexts, that extrafamilial influences on political identity are at work, and that these influences seem to be working not just on individuals but on and through an identity grouping.

Data from a study of California gay and lesbian activists reinforce this tentative conclusion. In analyzing a phone survey of 525 self-identified gay and lesbian activists in California, H. Eric Schockman and Nadine Koch concluded that "gays and lesbians appear to be socialized differently to politics than evidenced in the general population discussed in the literature." The influence of friends, linked in networks of gay and lesbian communication, tended to outweigh the influence of family in the formation of political views.[35] Furthermore, the effect of church and school on the political identity formation of gay men and lesbian activists was largely the result of negative experiences.

From another perspective, the aggregate exit-poll data provide additional hints of a nonfamilial understanding of identity formation. According to the more traditional models of political socialization, it was the family that transmitted the predispositions toward party identification, interest in politics, religious identity, and religiosity. As noted earlier, since the 1970s, most of the theoretical and empirical developments in voter behavior studies have refined (or even undermined) these central conclusions of the first generation of scholars of political socialization.

The data available on the effects of sexual identity on political values and voter behavior reinforce these later findings. The interaction of other identity categories—racial identity, political ideology, party identification, religious identity—were examined in conjunction with sexual identity to obtain some indication of the influences of each on the others as they together influence voters' choices. The first issue was to ensure that the influence of sexual orientation on voter behavior was not simply a surrogate for political ideology; that is, whereas sexual identity and the experience of being a member of a sexual minority may contribute to political ideology, sexual identity still had an independent effect on voter preferences. The second issue was the degree to which family-transmitted identities (race, religion, and, traditionally, party identification) outweighed, or were outweighed by, nonfamilial identities—essentially (here) sexual identity and political ideology.

The first issue is the independent influence of sexual identity on voting behavior. Is the influence of sexual orientation and identity expressed *through* ideology and party identification, or is its influence independent? In a series of procedures using three aggregate exit-poll data sets, voters' candidate preferences were subjected to two competing explanatory non-linear regression models—one including ideology and one not. The elections examined were the 1992 House of Representatives results and the 1992 presidential results from the VRS national exit poll. The 1993 mayoral runoff exit poll conducted by the *Los Angeles Times* was the third data set examined. In all three cases, voters' candidate preferences were set as the dependent variables, and these were subjected to logit models of independent variables typical of voting studies. The results for each of the three elections were run twice—once with political ideology included as a potential explanatory variable and once without it. On all three exit polls, ideology was self-assessed and had three available categories from which the voter could choose: liberal, moderate, and conservative.

Not surprisingly, in all three cases, political ideology was a powerful explanatory variable. In both the 1992 presidential race and the House races, it ranked second to party identification. In the Los Angeles mayoral runoff, ideology ranked second to race in potency, with party identification a close third.

When political ideology was removed from the models to see how it interacted with the other identity variables' explanatory power, the change was readily apparent. In the three elections examined, the explanatory power of party identification increased measurably when ideology was removed (in the Los Angeles mayoral runoff, it had the greatest change), but in two of the three cases, sexual identity increased even more. In addition, in all three elections, the explanatory power of religious identity increased measurably, but—again—sexual identity increased either equally or more so. In two of the three cases, sexual orientation demonstrated the greatest change in potency of all the model's variables. (It was in the national data set on the 1992 House races that the differences were the greatest.)

These results have important implications for our first question. They indicate that sexual identity does indeed work, in at least two ways, on ballot preferences. Since sexual identity was statistically significant in all three logit models—even when ideology was included—it also must directly affect voter preferences. But sexual identity also has indirect effects operating through the formulation of a voter's political ideology. In all the data sets examined here, the self-assessment by lesbians, gay men, and, when data were available, bisexuals showed that they disproportionately accepted the label liberal and disproportionately rejected the label conservative. The independence of sexual identity voting appears certain.

Our second issue is the degree to which family-transmitted identities outweighed nonfamilial identities—especially (here) sexual identity—in the overall formation of political identity, ideology, and candidate choices. In the absence of panel data, nothing definitive can be concluded with certainty. Nevertheless, the data from the three exit-poll data sets do show that the influence of sexual identity on the formulation of political ideology is strong.

Again, when comparing competing logit models designed to examine the relative influence of various factors on the formation of self-assessed political ideology, sexual identity was found to be more significant in establishing ideological predispositions than religious identity was. Similarly, when compared with party identification—an identity that students of voting behavior usually ascribe to family factors (even though the "retrospective voter" model modified this assumption)—sexual identity influenced self-assessed political ideology in approximately equal measure. Nevertheless, party identification and ideology remained the strongest explanatory variables in the 1992 House and presidential races. The fact that sexual identity (a political identity usually associated with extrafamilial influences) was more significant in explaining ideological predispositions than was religious or party identity (identities usually thought to be transmitted primarily through family) has important implications for future research on political socialization.

These results suggest a complicated process of intra- and extrafamilial influences on political identity formation. Although party identification and religious identity (as well as racial identity) obviously continue to exert the residual influences of early childhood political socialization, the demographic and attitude descriptors of lesbian or gay male self-identifiers as they pertain to voting behavior tend to support a postfamilial, time-extended perspective on identity formation, as opposed to the behavioral perspective of early models of political socialization. The results lend weight not so much to a life-cycle explanation of socialization as to more open-ended, extended political learning models, up to and past puberty and into early adulthood as sexual identity develops more fully.

Increases in Gay and Lesbian Self-Identification Rates

The influence of social context on political identity formation is observable from another perspective. There is a clear increase in the willingness of voters caught in exit poll surveys to self-identify, to take on the names *gay*, *lesbian*, or *bisexual* over time.[36] Even taking into account issues of sampling, since the first experiments with exit poll self-identifiers in 1981 to the 1993 New York and Los Angeles mayoral samples used here, there is an uneven, slow, but consistent growth over time in self-identification rates on exit poll questionnaires. The peak in New York was 7.0 percent in November 1993; in Los Angeles in 1993 it was 5 percent. In the national presidential exit poll in 1996, the self-identified gay/lesbian/bisexual cohort was approximately 4 percent—as large as those who self-identify as Jewish and higher than the Asian cohort.

This trend in increased self-identification is most observable when the national exit poll data sets from the four congressional elections between 1990 and 1996 are compared. Between 1990 and 1996, the rate went from 1.3 percent to 5 percent of all voters.[37] Although part of this change is probably related to sampling issues and turn-out rates,[38] the underlying trend of increased self- identification is a real social phenomena itself influenced by other social factors. The first is the construction of lesbian and gay identity in the context of other political influences. A portion of this increase in gay/lesbian self-identification can be attributed to the success of the social movement associated with sexual identity. In bringing sexual identity issues to the political agenda—and precipitating the resistance to those policy initiatives by social conservatives—the 'lesbian and gay rights movement' has created an interactive process of politicization that influences individual identity formation as well as the social discourse. Another possible cause is increased attention paid to the "gay vote" both in the regional gay and lesbian press in the late 1980s and to a lesser extent to reporting by the general press in the early 1990s. Some voters may have become more familiar with the exit-polling process or less fearful of identifying as gay or lesbian on the confidential exit poll data collection sheets. In fact, it appears that as the general political discourse became more resonant to issues of sexual identity, the actual rates of self-identification as lesbian, gay or bisexual have increased.[39] A third factor is the aging nature of the initial lesbian and gay cohort. Indeed, self- identification rates among voters under 40 years of age were as high as 4 percent nationally in 1992 and 6 percent in 1996. What is certain is that combined they have contributed to the gradual increase in self identification rates among lesbian and gay citizens on urban and national exit polls. Finally there is the success of professional survey researchers in finding the proper mechanisms to elicit reliable responses. Although each of these influences has had different effects at different times, it is difficult to assess the relative influence of each or their influence in the aggregate. But the pattern of increased self-identification seems certain.

"Loose Ties," "Networks," and "Story-Sets"

The patterning of lesbians' and gay men's self-identification rates suggests an interaction among the individual active in his or her own identity formation; the change in social meanings transmitted through political discourse, language, and images; and a group of persons undergoing similar though not identical experiences. The total dynamic is probably quite complicated, encompassing identity construction, structuring social forces, the signs and languages of political discourse, simple age demographics, and the technical instruments of measurement.

Nevertheless, there is sufficient difference between these general characteristics of the new, self-consciously constructed gay and lesbian political identity and the more traditional explanations of political socialization to take a different approach to understanding political identity formation. That is, political identity formation regarding sexuality tells a "story," if quite a different "story" from that understood by most others to whom same-sex affinities are not important. As used here, *stories* are personal narratives (and a composite of many is a *story-set*) that describe past struggles for assertion and attempts at control, as well as successful (and unsuccessful) attempts at forming an identity. Harrison White writes that stories "are the essential vehicles for elaborating networks, so as to become the base for further formations"—political formations in our case.[40] Stories give meaning to and animate ties and networks.

For lesbians and gay men, their story might start with their initial political socialization—family, school, and church—each offering little support to adolescents with same-sex affinities. Unable to secure a domain for their emergent identity, they learn the social appropriateness of expressing affection. Their first flirtatious relationship is problematic, whereas those of their heterosexual friends are not. Later, when they come to understand the real legal limitations on their ability to extend extrafamilial relationships that have erotic content, new issues arise: Such relationships are trivialized by the overarching culture and its economic supports, followed by the ironic association of negative behaviors that result from such trivialization of the (sexual) identity, not of the socially constructed stigma associated with the identity.

This is not a tale of political structures being transmitted generation to generation through the scripting of youth but the creation of a subculture, formed from the most intimate of experiences in which as an agent in his or her own development the lesbian or gay man seeks communication and affirmation in subterranean social ties, finding a new "civic culture" in networks that have familiar plotlines and stories and are told in a language finally understood. This is a familiar experience to lesbians and gay men in American cities. These stories accumulate, are combined in a network of sexual identity, and eventually create a common narrative. The result is that lesbian and gay youth are not socialized (in the positive sense); instead, they are unintentionally undersocialized and self-reconstituted through their own social action and agency into a different identity.

What makes the Stonewall generation different from the sixties generation—both in roughly the same age cohort—is this different identity story.

It infuses a different and maybe more intense measure of meaning into actual events: the revolt at Stonewall, the success and failures of the women's movement, the assassination of Harvey Milk, the sexual experimentation of the 1970s, the struggle of lesbians for their place in both the women's and the gay rights movements, the rise of social conservatives who target gay men and lesbians for specific menacing, and the initial indifference toward the personal and life-threatening experience of HIV, which in the gay community is not just a disease but a common reference point of lesbian and gay culture. These events were in addition to the experiences of the Vietnam War era, the student movement, Watergate, and other alienating political events.

The Overall Significance of the Urban Lesbian and Gay Vote

Aggregate and comparative data might answer another question: In what area does the combination of numbers, party, policy preferences, and voter coherence give lesbians and gay men their greatest potential for political leverage when sought through electoral behavior? Or putting it another way, if the lesbian and gay vote is most pronounced at the urban level and most distinct in its social values in the suburbs, what is its overall impact on elections—if any?

The general argument here is that gay politics has had its greatest effect on urban politics, that sexual identity has a geographic contour with political consequences, and that objects of identity politics include but also go beyond the allocative politics of "normal" state and local politics. This proposition dovetails with other assessments of voting behavior, concluding that domestic policy issues best define a voting group organized around sexual identity.[41]

An obvious corollary to these propositions is that it is at local levels—the municipal level and in concisely bounded, single-member legislative districts—that the lesbian and gay vote would be most salient. In our case, this means that in local government and state and federal legislative seats, the combination of raw numbers and voter coherence in election patterns should provide greater salience for sexual identity voting in urban areas. In fact, the national exit-poll data bear out these expectations. Regardless of whether the vote is for House member, senator, or president, the voter's choices among the self-identified gay and lesbian sample are most pronounced in large and medium-size cities—cities larger than 50,000. In the suburbs, the gay and lesbian vote is still identifiable but not as strongly as it is in the cities. Only in small towns and rural areas does the efficacy of the gay vote break down. The lower rates of self-identification in these areas add to local lesbian and gay activists' difficulty in substantively influencing public policy.[42] The data show that in House races (and thus likely also in state legislative districts), the sexual identity vote has some potency, especially where there are strong geographic concentrations of lesbian and gay voters. At the state level, for U.S. senator, the effect of the gay vote again is less strong. In small towns and rural areas, where party identification between the gay and nongay samples is more similar and the number of gays is smaller, the difference between gay and nongay samples of voter choices was statistically insignificant in the House and Senate races of 1992.

The only electoral area where the location of residence of gay men or lesbians did not affect the definition of the vote was at the presidential level—at least in 1992, the first presidential election year for which data exist. Since the vote outside the cities—the suburban and rural gay vote—is dispersed, the aggregative nature of the national election vote for president makes it easier to identify the "gay vote." This identification is especially important to lesbians who appear to be incorporated in more and differing kinds of towns and neighborhoods than are self-identified gay men. In the presidential election, the very scale of the race allows for the aggregation of such dispersed interests. When mobilized by symbol and substance, the "gay" vote is defined collectively, regardless of geographic bounds. Indeed, the presidential vote is the most pronounced of all the races—even the House races, as the urban and nonurban gay vote come together through the simple symbols of affirmation.

As a symbol, the 1992 presidential election was an important milestone for lesbians and gay men. After twelve years of cool reaction to their seeking affirmation of their gay and lesbian identity and a general perception that the Reagan and Bush administrations had done little to control AIDS/HIV—and certainly had not offered any symbolic signs of empathy—lesbian and gay men were waiting eagerly for an extended hand. Especially after the 1992 National Republican Convention, in which not just substantive issues but also the acceptability of lesbians' and gay men's lives came under attack, the symbolism and cultural affinity of identity politics became apparent.

Conclusion

This chapter was based primarily on exit-poll data from multiple sources to explore the questions of sexual identity in the current debates on urban voting behavior and political socialization in the aggregate. There is a greater variance in each of the samples analyzed here (1992 VRS urban extract, 1992 national *Los Angeles Times* data set, 1993 *Los Angeles Times* Los Angeles sample, and 1993 Voter News Service New York City sample) than across them. The consistency of the structures of these data sets in age, gender, and education says much about the nature of gay and lesbian self-identification but, more generally, further undermines cruder models of political socialization. In a positivist sense, we looked at patterns of self-identification as both an independent and a dependent variable—as both a data set to be studied and an indicator of the collective formation of a political identity, that is, as an expression or effect understood as a "story-set" in a network of social ties.

By shifting the focus of personal political development from political socialization to identity formation, we have made a number of assumptions. First, from the beginning, we used a longer-term perspective on the development of political identity. The political socialization model of early childhood was rather static, so we used an identity formation model, which is closer to Niemi and Jennings's lifelong openness model.

Second, the overall social context, not just family dynamics, is a critical aspect of identity formation for lesbians and gay men. The social construction of identities and the confrontation of such social identities by those who may assume their name were combined in the dialogue of a dynamic process of identity formation. In the case of sexual identity, it is not just family or church, not just mainstream media or peer group social forces, but also networks of marginalized identities with which the individual may come in contact that are important. In this sense, the individual is the protagonist in her (or his) own identity formation, since she exposes herself to experiences that advance the development of a particular identity.

Third is the clear affinity between identity formation as "gay" or "lesbian" and a group-referent approach. The existence of most group identities predates the development of individual identities. In Goffmann's sense, the labels "lesbian" or "gay" continue to signify stigmatized identities. There also can be a rather sharp dissonance between the "socialization" by established institutional influences and the stigmatized (marginalized) group discourse. An individual, linear path of political socialization is challenged here by a different model that can create a personal identity conflict and a discontinuity in identity formation. These characteristics of gay and lesbian self-identification beg for an interactive model of identity formation and extrafamilial influences on identity.

More empirically, what can we say about the broad voting patterns of gay men and lesbians in urban politics? Their residential concentration and participation patterns in urban areas give them an arena of political vitality where they can exert some influence and advance their identity and budgetary interests through negotiation with other groups in the area. But it is not just numbers and concentration working on their behalf; it is also the reality that the social values of gay voters more closely resemble those of urbanites in general than those of nongays living in suburbs, small towns, or rural areas. The differences between urban gay men and lesbians and their nongay neighbors is not so much in policy predispositions as in intensity or degree of advocacy. When the policy predisposition of gay suburbanites and nongay suburbanites is the same—on economic and some fiscal matters, for example—there is no need for coalition building to be mediated by identity-centered organizations. Standing coalitions defined by party or other surrogate organizations for socioeconomic and class interests are sufficient. One result, however, of separating gay men's and lesbians' fiscal and budgetary priorities from their identity issues is that sexual identity issues in suburbs are isolated from the larger political discourse of suburban and small town life. In fact, many of these lesbians and gay men often come to see their economic interests as conflicting with their identity interests, at least more so than do urban dwellers in the sexual identity cohort.

It may be a simplification of a rather complicated matter, but we might say that the gay vote is mobilized by a sense of identity and difference and that gay voters are effective because they are so similar to their urban neighbors.

CHAPTER 6

⣿

Sexual Identity Voting in Mayoral Coalitions in Chicago,
Los Angeles, and New York

The balancing acts that mayors must endure to be elected and to effectively govern American cities have become more elaborate with each passing
decade. The equilibrium sought was once only among the different ethnic
groups then streaming through the port cities of the Northeast's emerging
industrial economy. The class- and ethnic-based tensions of the urban industrial culture largely replaced the mercantile culture and politics that proceeded it. Industrialization came to define the nature of urban politics for
most of the second half of the nineteenth century and most of this century. Then after World War II, when the residential patterns of American
cities were again changing, race became the defining force of urban politics
in both northern cities and southern cities, in turn compounding the tensions of the industrial culture.

In the past two decades, new identities have been seeking participation
in politics and influence in the governance of American cities. These identities include new ethnic identities, young (but aging) professionals associated with many cities' emerging informational and administrative cultures,
environmentalists, and the gender-based movements.

In the case of sexual identity, the rising expectations of lesbians and gay
men had become a practical problem for urban political systems still linked
to older governing styles. Many cities' traditional political organizations
have had to deal with the demands of lesbian and gay voting constituencies
for affirmation and participation in governance. Incorporating these new
identities into governing regimes has not been easy, and indeed, in many
cases gays' demands were dismissed and their growing base of influence was
ignored. But the reality of their presence eventually led even recalcitrant
mayors and party organizations to acknowledge them.

From what we have seen so far, three factors contributed to sexual identity's becoming an effective political presence in cities: (1) the comparative concentration of lesbian and gay male self-identifiers in cities; (2) the cohesiveness of a gay vote in cities defined in terms of party, ideology, and issue concerns; and (3) the similarity of urban gay and nongay residents in some policy preferences and party identification. The first factor pertains to raw numbers, meaning that certainly in close elections, but practically in all citywide elections, lesbian and gay preferences and turnout can affect electoral outcomes. The second factor reinforces the first: the gay vote is cohesive in urban areas and more cohesive than in suburbs, small towns, and rural areas. The third factor—the similarity of urban voters in many of their policy preferences, regardless of sexual identity—draws our attention to the promise of electoral coalition building based on policy substance, political ideology, and issue preferences.

What we have seen in the aggregate now needs to be tested in more concrete settings. Accordingly, this chapter examines gay and lesbian voting behavior in the three largest U.S. cities. We analyzed exit-poll data from Los Angeles and New York City, as well as results from key wards in Chicago, to see where lesbians and gay men fall in the broad coalitions that compete for the authority to govern these cities. The data reveal that along with race, party identification, ideology, and, in some cases, religion, sexual identity independently explains a portion of the electoral outcomes. Overall and as a voting group, our analysis shows that self-identified gay men and lesbians have an identifiable voting pattern that adds nuance and cross pressures to current and competing electoral coalitions in large cities.

Methods of Estimating Sexual Identity Voting

In the absence of formal and sustained data on lesbian and gay voting of a kind usually used by political science to assess the disposition and coherence of voting blocs, social scientists interested in the effect of sexual identity on urban political processes have generated alternative data or methods. Three methods have been used to estimate the gay vote and its effect: (1) an inferential approach, (2) a "key-ward or EDs" approach, and (3) commercial exit polls.

The first, what we can call an *inferential approach*, uses geographic concentrations of lesbian and gay residents as an indicator that can be linked to results from electoral wards or districts. The assumption is that the voting behavior of lesbians and gay men citywide can be inferred from the statistical analysis of these geographic concentrations of gay voters. Correlation or regression between group concentrations and voting results is the actual statistical technique. This method is similar to other inferential approaches to voter behavior common among campaign practitioners and experts in districting, especially those looking for specific voter blocs, such as African Americans or Italian Americans who happen to live in residential concentration.[1]

The main limitation in using this method to analyze gay voting groups, as opposed to racial, ethnic, or language groups, is that we have accurate demographic and census information on the latter cases. As noted in chapter 4, even though the household survey data of the 1990 U.S. Census does provide some measures of lesbian and gay households, the number of such households captured by the census is small and, when disaggregated, is not yet fully useful for an application of inferential techniques in most localities. As an approximate but by no means fully acceptable substitute, concentrations of residents revealed on direct mailing lists (a standard technique used in marketing, campaign techniques, and urban districting) have been used in some cities.[2] Another problem is that unlike race or some ethnic identities, it is rare (in fact, almost impossible) for a census tract to have more than 50 percent of its residents self-identifying as lesbian or gay. We should again emphasize that the use of mailing list data is intended to find and describe urban spaces, not individuals or households.

A second method, essentially an *analysis of key EDs*, is also taken from ethnic and racial voting analysis. The historical accumulation of voting behavior in precincts or wards associated with a particular group can provide a profile of how all voters from that class of voters—whether in one location or dispersed throughout a city—has voted or is likely to vote. Urban political scientists rely on this method for much racial and ethnic analysis. The method is similar to the manner in which sample precincts are selected for the model building associated with television network election projections. Key or representative precincts for gay voting have been used most successfully in San Francisco, where a number of private consultants have laid out the development and location of clusters of gay and lesbian voters. Richard DeLeon used a key ED method in creating the dummy variable for lesbian and gay voting in his analysis of the "three lefts" in San Francisco. DeLeon followed San Francisco political consultant David Binder's method of identifying key election districts on census tracts that are at least 30 percent male single households and that also have 15 percent more male residents than females in the 25- to 44-year-old age group.[3] Although the method has been quite helpful in looking at gays and lesbians in citywide elections and referenda, a fundamental problem is that it does not permit analysis of differences of voting within sexual identity groups.

A third method, used extensively in the previous chapter to assess political values and the sociodemographics of sexual identity voting, is *exit polling with a gay and lesbian self-identifier.* This method assumes professional sampling techniques but includes on data collection sheets what has come to be called the *gay and lesbian and sometimes bisexual self-identifier.* If sampling and weighting result in a representative overall sample, and thus also a smaller but representative gay and lesbian subsample, the gay vote can be determined more precisely. But even though these data are likely the best reflection of lesbian and gay voting behavior, this method has limitations also, as self-identification rates vary widely from place to place and election to election. Nevertheless, these data are the most effective in assessing the lesbian and gay vote in cities.

These three methods are not mutually exclusive, nor do they preempt the development of other methods and data sources. In fact, in the absence of broader exit polling in the local or census data on alternative households, these methods are best used as reinforcing tools that work together to explain how the "gay vote" fits into the makeup of urban electoral coalitions.

Chicago and the "Lakefront Liberals"

In many American cities, the effects of the lesbian and gay vote rests on the dynamic of sexual identity and race. In the case of Chicago, lesbian and gay voters (of all races) seek political effect in the context of a racially polarized electorate. Using key-ward analysis (combined with inferential techniques in studying residential patterns), we can show that those wards identified with lesbian and gay voters gave hesitant but eventual support to Harold Washington's 1983 and 1987 victories against the Cook County Democratic organization.

The Emergence of Washington's Biracial Coalition

At one time, writers on urban politics admired Chicago's model of party governance. Through an informal network of governmental and political communication, the Cook County Democratic machine could control Chicago's and Cook County's fragmented public sector. The machine had the further advantage of managing intergroup conflict, at least among white ethnic groups and between downtown business and organized labor. Whether it was the trade-off in votes for governmental services and jobs that held the machine together, the simple organizational capacity, or the ability to define minority aspirations as "unrealistic" and thus not needing to be addressed, the pragmatic nature of Chicago politics was the opposite of the symbolic tone of affirmation more commonly associated with identity politics.

But any discussion of politics in Chicago eventually turns to race. The city's segregated housing and employment patterns began early in the century as the Jim Crow laws of the South were adapted to Chicago's in-migrating black population.[4] Federally subsidized public housing thickened the wall between black and white residences in Chicago, and the local administration of public housing during the 1940s and 1950s made Chicago the most segregated of the major northern cities.[5] But while blacks and whites lived separately, an established black middle class and the poor lived side by side in the South Side before and immediately after World War II.

It was on the South Side that Chicago's African Americans achieved the little political influence they did have. Although their leaders had some control in the African American wards, the black community as a whole never achieved the political status in Chicago or Cook County politics that its numbers or economic contribution might otherwise indicate. This was especially true on Chicago's West Side where the so-called plantation wards were located. Throughout the 1950s, the Chicago organization resisted the wishes of the city's African Americans. Even in the 1960s, with the intercession of Mayor Richard Daley Sr., the flow of federal funds into Chicago's African American community during President Lyndon Johnson's Great Society period largely went to the black middle class.[6] The historical indifference to the problems of Chicago's black population and the failure to deal with the aspirations of Chicago's African Americans eventually undermined the usefulness of the older machine model when measured against its own criteria for success: It was no longer effective in either containing the black community or incorporating it into the city's government.

Gregory Squire and his colleagues described the three principal forces that undermined the machine's effectiveness in the 1970s.[7] One force, and maybe the most important one, was the continued and growing disaffection of Chicago's blacks, especially those not linked to the machine through patronage agreements. For all their loyalty to Democratic party politics, blacks achieved few gains in resources or symbols, in neighborhood development, or in positions in the upper levels of the civil service.

The second force was the rise of independent and reform politicians, largely activists turned office seekers, usually but not exclusively from the lakefront wards or the Fifth Ward, Hyde Park, and the areas around the University of Chicago. For these reformers, it was not just opposition to machine politics that propelled them but also a new criterion of municipal decision making: quality of service.[8] Although they were white, many of these grassroots, reformist candidates aligned themselves with African Americans for community control of education, integration of housing, and the funding of community development programs.

The third force undermining the Chicago organization was the rise of both white and black community-based and neighborhood organizations that resisted the negative effects of downtown economic development on local neighborhoods.

The confluence of these trends plus a generational change in the black community—more aggressive and with higher expectations for the empowerment of African Americans—set the stage for the 1983 election of Harold Washington. Together these factors resulted in a fundamental shift in mayoral election coalitions. Washington's victory was a turning point in postwar Chicago politics, a victory built on a base of disaffected blacks, many Latinos, and those liberal whites who had served as the core of the Chicago's weak reform tradition. Increased black registration also was a key to Washington's victory. By 1982, registered black voters accounted for 86 percent of the total African American voting-age population.[9]

In light of this high black registration, Washington could build a new voter alliance around the "outs" of city government.[10] Manning Marable describes Washington's winning coalition as drawing its "deepest strength from black civic reformists, black nationalists and labor unions. Along with these core constituencies, Washington's candidacy was also favored by black entrepreneurs, a majority of Latino activists and a minority of black clergy and white liberals."[11]

Washington also built his coalition on the emerging cross-racial group alliance of neighborhood and community groups that felt threatened by the downtown development. As a member of Congress, he made a special effort to reach out to these groups, and they rewarded him in the mayoral primary of 1983. But despite Washington's outreach to white voters, only 2 percent of his 1983 primary vote came from white Chicagoans, and most of them came from the lakefront wards on Chicago's North Side.

In the 1983 general campaign, the Republican candidate, Bernard Epton, with strong if covert support from many machine loyalists, attracted the white, anti-Washington base in the Democratic organization. (Four years later this same base propelled Democratic council leader Edward Vrdolyak in his challenge to Mayor Washington.) A coalition of Republicans and white Democrats alienated from Washington carried the lakefront area for Epton in 1983, but with an average margin of only 4,300 votes per ward, well below the margins in the city's other "white" wards. It was clear from the 1983 vote that the "lakefront liberals" were ambivalent toward Washington's election and also ambivalent toward abandoning their liberal roots. They were willing to participate in a biracial coalition but not to be dominated by it.

Finding Chicago's Lesbian and Gay Vote

Most of Chicago's white, liberal, and reform voters live in the traditionally liberal wards along the lake coast north of the Loop—hence the name "lakefront (or lakeview) liberals." Like many other voters in the new urban classes, they voted reform, even liberal, in a city polarized between race and class. The wards covering the area include the Forty-second, Forty-third, Forty-fourth, Forty-sixth, and Forty-eighth (and sometimes the Forty-ninth). In addition to encompassing the well-educated and upper-income groups living directly on Lake Shore Drive, these wards are also the heart of Chicago's white lesbian and gay community, containing many of its social service, commercial, and political centers.[12] An analysis of mailing lists to politically and culturally active lesbians and gay men living in Chicago show that their residential patterns tend to overlap with the near North Side, New Town, Lincoln Park, portions of "Wrigleyville," Lakeview, and Uptown. More than 62 percent of households on a 1989 mailing list of

Chicago activists and contributors to gay political, social, religious, and health organizations lived in zip codes roughly covering these wards.[13] Although this is only a surrogate indicator of population concentrations— and is certainly skewed toward those who have enough money to make political contributions to or be otherwise engaged in gay or lesbian social activities—the fact of concentration is telling.

As noted in chapter 4, the residential patterns of lesbians and gay men in Chicago reflect much of the race segregation in the city's overall housing patterns. The correlation analysis of zip code–defined concentrations of gay and lesbian residential concentrations and standard census variables shows that even though no specific residential patterns can be found in regard to gays, lesbians, and Latinos in Chicago, two statistically significant trends were observed: a positive correlation of people identifying as having a Native American heritage and, more important given Chicago's history, an actual negative relationship with black residents ($r = -.3108$). Most cities have a greater mix of African Americans and Anglos in "gay domains," or at least when viewed from the MSA's perspective if not in the core central city. But Chicago's black/white housing patterns, a legacy of decades of discrimination in the public-housing policies of the Cook County machine and in the private market, are also evident in gay neighborhoods. Thus, in addition to the lakefront wards' being liberal, reform, and white, they are also gay and largely white.

The Flirtation Between Washington and the North Side's Gay Community

It is generally agreed that few white lesbians and gay men supported Washington in the 1983 Democratic primary.[14] The Chicago Gay and Lesbian Democrats, the city's principal political club for gays at that time, endorsed Jane Byrne in the primary after she promised to support some of the gay community's agenda.[15] Washington does appear to have fared better among lesbian and gay voters in the April general election, however. He picked up a substantial portion of Byrne's and Richard Daley Jr.'s primary votes in the Forty-fourth, Forty-sixth, and Forty-eighth Wards, especially in the Forty-fourth. He was within 6 percent of defeating Epton in the Forty-sixth—a ward that was 53 percent white but contains a large portion of zip code 60657, the postal code with the greatest concentration of gay residents. Nonetheless, gay support for Washington was tentative in the 1983 general election.

The situation was different in 1987, however. William Grimshaw noted that one of the voting areas that increased its electoral support for Washington from the 1983 to the 1987 election was the five, white liberal lakefront wards (the other was in the Latino wards). In 1987, Washington carried three of the five lakefront wards, the only predominantly white section of Chicago in which Washington broke even in 1987.

Increased support for Washington among lesbian and gay voters in both the primary and general elections of 1987 was partly a result of his policies. During the same period that Washington was pushing a traditional reform agenda for white liberals, an affirmative action and black nationalist agenda for his African American base, and a series of community process changes to deal with concerns about development issues, he also courted lesbian and gay men in the lakefront wards. He appointed openly gay men and lesbians from community advocacy groups and spoke against homophobia. And in 1986, Washington participated in the annual Gay and Lesbian Pride events on the North Side—all of which added to gay support for Washington in his 1987 reelection campaign. Most important, he supported passage of a local ordinance to protect lesbians and gay men in public employment and certain categories of private employment. As in other cities, the principal opposition to the ordinance came from the Roman Catholic archdiocese. The bill was defeated in 1986 but passed in 1987 after the "Council wars" were settled.

Although there are no precise exit-poll data from the 1987 mayoral primary and general elections, it seems clear that Washington fared much better among Chicago's gay and lesbian voters in 1987 than he had in 1983. He ran less strongly in the predominantly white Forty-third Ward in the 1987 general election, but he carried one of the three wards most closely identified with the white gay vote (Forty-eighth Ward) and ran strongly in two others (Forty-fourth and Forty-sixth Wards) (see figure 6-1). What seems certain, however, is that Washington's outreach to the North Side's gay men and lesbians paid off in expanding his biracial base to sexual identity voters.

Los Angeles and the Passing of the Bradley Coalition

In Los Angeles, for which exit-poll data with a gay and lesbian identifier are available, at least for the 1993 and 1997 mayoral elections, the effect of sexual identity voting can be directly observed. As late as 1989, the votes of gay

FIGURE 6.1

men and lesbians had been subsumed as part of (then) Mayor Thomas Bradley's biracial coalition (as had the votes of most liberal voters). But when that coalition collapsed after the 1992 post–Rodney King riots, the salience of sexual identity voting in a new multiracial/multi-identity coalition supporting Councilman Michael Woo became evident. Although gay men and lesbians indicated a strong interest in police protection, more than even the typical Los Angeleno did, they did not tend to vote with the moderately conservative coalition that led to Richard Riordan's election. Instead, they remained an important portion of Los Angeles's liberal coalition.

Los Angeles's Biracial, Prodevelopment Coalition, 1973 to 1989

The institutional arrangement of the city of Los Angeles was heavily influenced by California's progressive tradition. Nonpartisan elections, weak parties, referenda, and executive authority dispersed through commissions (including police and public works) all are common to government in Southern California. The odd geographic definition of the city, a result of the process of annexation, along with the inchoate character of multiple

cities and jurisdictions in the Los Angeles Basin, led some scholars to describe governance in Los Angeles during the 1960s as a matrix of horizontal intergovernmental relationships.[16] One aspect of this fragmental government was that even infrastructure development, which in other locales
would have been the principal source of public leverage over development
patterns, was heavily influenced by private powers, especially the Southern
Pacific Railroad Corporation and the Chandler family of the *Los Angeles
Times*.[17] Indeed, the contemporary debate over the interaction of politics
and economic development policy in the Los Angeles Basin is not over
whether at midcentury, Los Angeles was an entrepreneurial city in Stephen
Elkin's sense—it was—but over the relative influence on development and
thus other issue arenas by private entrepreneurs, local state, and specific private actors.[18]

Post–World War II analysts saw Los Angeles as a modern, entrepreneurial city; indeed, much of the best commentary on the city's politics was
written not by political scientists but by economic geographers, sociologists, and cultural critics. The city's economic transformation in the 1970s
was a major focus of interest for political economists. Many urbanologists
studied Los Angeles through sociological and cultural lenses, as the template whose form other cities would copy. The remaining burden of research on Los Angeles during the 1970s and 1980s was organized around the
political sociology of differing religious, racial, and ethnic identities. Much
of this analysis was intended as ethnographic study, but today it can be seen
as a precursor to contemporary identity politics.

Racial politics and "regime theory" did merge in the political analyses of
Los Angeles's biracial, progrowth regime typified by the years of Mayor
Thomas Bradley. Raphael Sonenshein's study of the city's mayoral politics
identifies two watershed events. The first occurred in early 1960s, when Sam
Yorty built a populist, Democratic biracial electoral coalition that defeated
the conservative, business-centered coalition that had dominated Los Angeles politics since World War II. At first, Yorty's election as mayor was seen
as a victory for the unions and minority power in Los Angeles and also for
the newer and alienated voters in the fast-growing San Fernando Valley.
Basic municipal services in the valley had not kept up with its mounting
population, and taxes seemed to buy little. Yorty's appeal to valley voters defined his political image and became the leading edge of his urban pop-
ulism. But his protection of home owners' property interests frequently
conflicted with minority aspirations, which eventually drove a wedge

through Yorty's coalition. In addition, the isolation of the city's police department from political accountability through the commission form of governance and the professional dominance of its administration, combined with the relatively conservative tone of the city's politics, led to racial tensions in the city dating back at least to the 1950s. These were exacerbated by the ideological and racial tensions of the 1960s. Yorty had promised to fire the city's race-baiting Police Chief William Parker, but after the 1965 Watts riots, Yorty himself began to sound more and more like Parker. The actions of the police department through the 1960s provided the foundation for a generation of suspicion between the Los Angeles Police Department and black youth in South Central. Unlike in Atlanta, Yorty's support for downtown development offered no basis for a coalition with blacks, because minorities received few of the construction contracts or jobs.

The change in Yorty's politics led to a second major event: the loss of most liberals' confidence, especially that of white, liberal, and, mostly, Jewish voters and fund-raisers on the West Side and a large portion of the business community. At the same time, the minority portion of Yorty's initial coalition grew dramatically throughout the 1960s and became the base that defeated him in his third reelection attempt in 1973.

The biracial coalition that directed Bradley's 1973 nonpartisan primary campaign was formed from the intergroup coalitions (and intragroup factions) that fought for position and power in the border areas of South and West Los Angeles. African Americans made up only 15 percent of the city's population in 1973, and most resided on the South Side of the city. Bradley, as the first African American to mount a serious campaign for the mayoralty, could count on their vote. But he never could have succeeded without support from the important Latino vote and from the established white liberals, in many cases Jewish, in West Los Angeles. Although Bradley had the support of the white liberal establishment, the broader acceptance of a black candidate by the white voters was the main focus of his campaign.[19] As in Chicago, the principal interest of upscale white liberals was the reform of urban government and the quality of urban services. Bradley's message to these voters, like that to many multiracial coalitions, was reassurance that change would come but not be dramatic. Assurances regarding downtown redevelopment could be more directly communicated, however. The final component of Bradley's victory was the mobilization of the black vote.

After the nonpartisan primary, Bradley and Yorty faced each other in a runoff. The business community was skeptical about supporting an increasingly strident Yorty for another term, and so they contributed to Bradley's campaign. Blacks in coalition with liberal whites, middle-class Latinos, West Side Jews, and labor were, again, Bradley's greatest supporters.[20]

Bradley was reelected four times—in 1977, 1981, 1985, and 1989. Nevertheless, by the mid-1980s, the coalition supporting him had become unstable. The steady economic growth in Southern California since the 1940s had peaked, and the region's manufacturing sector had begun to decline. Defense cutbacks and the integration of Southern California's economy with East Asia's marked the change. Economic restructuring throughout the Los Angeles region led to a loss of jobs in manufacturing, especially in the industrial areas of the Los Angeles Basin south of the city's border. This was a serious problem for unskilled workers. In the 1980s two types of manufacturing jobs were being created in the Los Angeles area: those requiring a high level of skills, as in aerospace or computers, and those requiring few or no skills, such as low-paying apparel jobs that frequently were taken by undocumented workers. Blacks and second-generation Latinos were the first to lose in Los Angeles's economic change. Most economic and demographic indicators from South Central Los Angeles showed that African Americans had not made any appreciable gains from the economic boom of the Los Angeles Basin or from the fifteen years of Bradley's biracial politics. Then the weakening in aerospace and defense contracting that capped off the 1980s brought the economic decline to Southern California's middle class.

Population changes also took a toll on Bradley's coalition. As in San Francisco, where the African American population had actually declined in both real and percentage terms throughout the 1980s, the changing racial makeup of Los Angeles also influenced the dynamics of mayoral coalitions. The structure of voting in the increasingly important Latino community had begun to mature, losing its coherence as disparities in income and national identity increased. Asians took on new importance in voting, their earliest victory being the election of Michael Woo to the City Council in 1985. But the Asian voting bloc was also divided by the demographic categories of Chinese, Koreans, Japanese, and Pacific islanders, each with their own interests. Although the wealthier whites remained ambivalent to Bradley as crime and the general quality of life in Los Angeles began to deteriorate, liberal whites continued to support him in 1989.

Bradley's attempt to obtain a fourth term in office preceded the Rodney King incident and the rioting that followed the acquittal of the officers who had beaten him. Even though gang activity was common in Los Angeles throughout the 1980s, the full effect of the crack cocaine economy had not been fully realized, and drive-by shootings had yet to win headlines every few days. Nor had the mounting tension between African Americans and Asian Americans, especially Koreans, yet exploded. But the stress was there, even in 1989. The coalition that had sustained Bradley was showing strains. Conflict between blacks in the southern part of the city and many liberals in the Fifth Council District was one part of the stress.

The second source of political strain in Bradley's coalition was common to all cities undergoing economic change: between downtown and suburban interests seeking growth and the amenities of postindustrial, latticelike urban formations, and the environmental, neighborhood, and class interests that emphasized the costs of growth.[21] As Yorty had, Bradley had become immersed in a strategy to redevelop downtown Los Angeles, had campaigned for the 1984 Summer Olympics, and was increasingly seen as more interested in downtown than community development. This strategy led to challenges not only from his own African American base for more equity in hiring by construction firms but also from the environmental component of his liberal coalition.

Finding Gay and Lesbian Voters in Los Angeles

Part of this mix of demographic and economic change was the rising presence of lesbians and gay men in and around Los Angeles. There are several clusters of lesbian and gay residents in Los Angeles County. Not all are in the city of Los Angeles proper, however. Venice, Van Nuys, the southern portion of Santa Monica, and shorefront Long Beach all have large lesbian and gay populations that are not within the Los Angeles city limits. West Hollywood, lying between Beverly Hills on the north and west and the city of Los Angeles on the east and south, is the center of lesbian and gay political activism and culture—as well as nightlife—in the Los Angeles area. But West Hollywood is not part of the city of Los Angeles. It was incorporated as a separate city in the early 1980s, after failing to gain much influence in county government. West Hollywood's substantial lesbian and gay population supported incorporation, eventually electing a lesbian as its first mayor.

The city of Los Angeles itself contains clusters of lesbian and gay residents (in addition to individuals dispersed throughout the city). They can be found on direct mailing lists and also in geocoded exit-poll data from the *Los*

Angeles Times which confirm the mailing list analysis for the city of Los Angeles proper. Areas with large lesbian and gay populations include Silverlake, the lower end of the San Fernando Valley (Studio City, etc.), greater Hollywood, and those portions of Los Angeles bordering West Hollywood.[22]

The most pronounced geographic boundary with voting statistics for gay men and lesbians in Los Angeles is the area defined by the *Los Angeles Times* poll unit as central Los Angeles, essentially greater Hollywood, Silverlake, and downtown. During the April 1993 mayoral primary, 12.1 percent of the voters in sample precincts in the area self-identified as gay or lesbian (n = 66 of 455).[23] This was just about half (51.3 percent) of the total weighted gay and lesbian sample for the city of Los Angeles as a whole. During the June 1993 mayoral runoff, 13.1 percent of the voters in sample precincts in this area were identified as gay or lesbian (n = 88 of 597.)[24] Again, just over 50 percent of the total weighted sample citywide were located in this portion of Los Angeles. Overall, these exit-poll samples reflect many of the patterns seen in chapter 5's analysis of the patterns of self-identified samples: these samples are younger, whiter, slightly better educated, substantially more liberal, more likely to rent than own their home, and more apt to be male—in fact, the gay and lesbian samples in central Los Angeles are two to one male.

The bulk of this *Los Angeles Times*-defined area overlapped with the predominantly white Fourth and Thirteenth Council Districts as drawn in 1989. Both districts also have substantial Latino and Asian populations. In addition to having a more blue-collar lesbian and gay population than that of West Hollywood, this section of Los Angeles overlaps with a small portion of Bradley's home Tenth Council District on its southern side, the portion of the city that Sonenshein identified as an incubator of the biracial coalition that governed Los Angeles from 1973 to 1985.

Michael Woo and a Multiethnic/Multi-Identity Coalition

The key to understanding the gay vote's effect on Bradley's fourth attempt at reelection in 1989—and on the multiracial coalition that supported Councilman Michael Woo's 1993 mayoral campaign—is the continued if hesitant support of Bradley by Central Los Angeles and West Side liberals. The overlap of those white liberal voters that were part of the multiracial coalition supporting Bradley and the city's most identifiable lesbian and gay neighborhoods is a theme often found in urban politics. Not surprisingly, these areas had also elected some of the most liberal politicians from the Los Angeles area, including U.S. Congressmen Henry Waxman (who, along with his assistant, Timothy Westmoreland, was a key figure in most of the early HIV-related legislation passed by Congress) and Howard Berman. Woo himself was elected in 1985 to the Thirteenth Council District seat representing greater Hollywood, including the highest concentrations of gays and lesbians in Los Angeles, and contiguous to West Hollywood. As a council member, Woo was used to dealing with issues of the gay community and had received considerable support from it in the past.

In 1989, Bradley was challenged by several candidates, Nate Holden, an African American who had won Bradley's old council seat in 1985, was the strongest among them. Baxter Ward, a former newscaster and conservative county supervisor, ran in 1989, as he had in 1969, and came in third. But Bradley's greatest opponent in 1989 was Zev Yaroslavsky, the councilman from the Fifth District who strongly identified with slow-growth proponents and represented some portions of the increasingly conservative West Side Jewish community. As Sonenshein stated, a Yaroslavsky candidacy "threatened the existence of coalition politics (especially between Blacks and Jews)."[25] After he (and the Waxman-Berman forces who considered financing a challenge to Bradley) tested the waters for a run, Yaroslavsky withdrew when a internal memo from the campaign surfaced in the *Los Angeles Times*.[26] The memo had racial overtones that made many West Side liberals hesitant to abandon racial coalition politics. His decision not to run in 1989 put off until 1993 the decisive moment in the passing of Bradley's biracial coalition.

There are no direct data on sexual identity voting in the 1989 mayoral race, but in retrospect, it appears not to have been a significant factor. The difference between how the gay and nongay samples voted for Bradley in both the 1989 and the 1993 mayor's race was negligible. Although voters frequently remember incorrectly how they voted in the past,[27] there is no evidence that lesbians and gay men voted in a significantly different patterns than all other voters did.[28] This was true citywide as well in the *Los Angeles Times*–defined central area of the city, which holds the largest portion of lesbian and gay voters. In the end, Bradley won his fourth term with sexual identity playing an almost insignificant part in the outcome.

In 1993, however, as new coalitions were being formed, the lesbian and gay vote became better defined and more important. The residual political effects of the South Central/King riots and the dislocation associated with the continued economic restructuring throughout Southern California, defense cutbacks, and the general recession were the main issues of the campaign. Bradley's approval ratings plummeted in the two years after the Rodney King beating was shown on television. He had failed in an attempt to remove Police Chief Daryl Gates, and after the uprising that followed the acquittal of the Los Angeles police officers who beat King, Bradley announced that he would not seek reelection. With Bradley out of contention for the first time in twenty-five years (he ran and lost in 1968 against Yorty) and with race a key and obvious election factor, Bradley's coalition had finally fallen apart.

The new voting coalitions were defined in the April 1993 nonpartisan primary and coalesced around the two candidates who faced each other in the June runoff: Richard Riordan and Michael Woo. Riordan offered a "businesslike," jobs-generator approach to government. Trying to build on Los Angeles's history of prodevelopment traditions and reform government themes and attempting to diffuse gender and racial issues, Riordan sought a coalition based in the city's worried business community, the San Fernando Valley, and the more conservative voters who identified as Jewish, Asian, and Latino. In short, the coalition cut across the city's ethnic and identity divides and was defined in terms of income, government efficiency, and economic development. Woo put together a community-based, multicultural urban coalition that echoed the coalitions that supported Washington in Chicago, Dinkins in New York, Agnos in San Francisco, and Maynard Jackson in Atlanta. It was a broad but unstable group of liberals and "outsiders" who wanted a greater stake in the city.

Clearly, the biracial coalition that had supported Bradley was changing, with some Anglo voters moving toward a white, moderately conservative coalition and other groups toward a multiracial/multi-identity coalition. The core of this latter coalition was the African American and Mexican American vote, with substantial support among liberal Jews, Asian Americans, and gay men and lesbians. Joel Wachs and Richard Katz, each with varying support among gays, Jews, and liberal whites, dropped out of the race, leaving their supporters to choose between Riordan and Woo. The majority of these voters chose Woo. Riordan's core was among white Catholics, San Fernando Valley voters, conservative and upper-income Latinos (not first- or second-generation Mexicans), half the Asian population (especially Koreans), and a growing portion of the Jewish vote worried about the future of Los Angeles and its mounting crime rates.

In the primary, the lesbian and gay vote was strongly for Woo. With a self-identification rate of slightly less than 5 percent citywide, Woo received almost 40 percent of the total gay vote. Wachs did second best, with 27 percent. Riordan received only 11 percent of the self-identified lesbian and gay sample.

In the runoff against Riordan, more than 72 percent of the gay vote went to Woo. Despite the small size of the sample, the self-identified gay voters who voted for Riordan were disproportionately higher income, white, and male. The voting difference by gender was less than 7 percent. Interestingly, the gender gap between Woo and Riordan was negligible in the June runoff, but the gap based on sexual identity was much greater.

Logit Analysis of Election Results: Who Is the "White Liberal"?

To assess the effect of sexual identity on the voting coalitions for Woo and Riordan, we subjected the June runoff exit-poll data to nonlinear multiple regression analysis. In addition to the dimension of gay and lesbian self-identification, two demographic variables and two political variables showed predictive power: race, religion, political bias (ideology), and party registration. Together, these five dimensions predicted more than 86 percent of the cases in the Los Angeles general mayoral election (82.9 percent of the Riordan votes and 76.58 percent of the Woo votes). Surprisingly, the dimension of sexual identity outweighed the comparative effects of age, gender, income, and educational achievement when their effect was controlled for by the five variables identified through the logit procedure as having explanatory value.

The usual conclusion in the biracial coalition literature is that class, party, or ideology holds disparate racial interests (or identity) together. But in the case of Los Angeles in 1993, class (as defined by income) had negligible power explaining voters' choices after race, party, ideology, religion, and sexual identity all were accounted for (housing tenancy did offer some explanation). Party, however, was much more powerful than income as an explanatory indicator, providing at least some basis for the coalition.

Beyond race and party, ideology offers an interesting result. Ideology is a potent predictor when included in a testable explanatory mode (PBIAS, political bias in the *Los Angeles Times* coding). Since the potency of both sexual identity and religion (especially, in the case of Los Angeles, the category Jewish) is reduced when ideology is not included in the model, we can assume that both sexual identity and religious identity contribute to the definition of ideology. But even though "liberal" may include many Jewish voters, gay men, and lesbians in Los Angeles, both sexual orientation and religion affect election outcomes beyond "political ideology." Because sexual identity and religion become much more powerful dimensions when ideology is removed from the model, this raises the question of which comes first: surely it is sexual identity that leads to liberal political views, not the other way around. The same is true in regard to religious identity, though not as definitively.

Looking at it another way, if we view the variables of race and party through their categories, sexual orientation can compete with "Latino," "Jewish," "Republican," and "Independent" as a cluster of secondary variables, all with some independent explanatory power regarding the election outcomes. But sexual identity is not on the same scale as racial identity, political ideology, or party identification.

The New Poles of the Post-Bradley Electoral Coalitions in Los Angeles

As long as a general biracial, moderate probusiness consensus governed Los Angeles, self-identified lesbian and gay male voters did not stand out significantly in the Bradley coalition. They were included electorally with moderate whites, Jewish voters, moderate forces in the business community, large portions of the Latino and Asian communities, and those African Americans who participated in the process. But when that coalition collapsed, partly around economic issues and partly around crime and the King riots (and thus also around race), the gay vote in Los Angeles became more defined and salient, joining forces with the new, though less stable multiethnic/multi-identity coalition that supported Woo. Despite being aligned with the losing coalition, Riordan did recognize the political importance of the gay community. Even before he took office, Riordan felt it necessary to involve Los Angeles's lesbians and gay men in the city's government, and he obviously also hoped to win their support in any future reelection attempt. One of his first appointments was of a gay man as deputy mayor.

The new mayoral fissures in Los Angeles continued through the April 1997 nonpartisan runoff election. It pitted Riordan in his first reelection bid against State Senator Tom Hayden, a one-time leader of the antiwar and student movements of the 1960s. Although Riordan won by a wide margin grounded in a multiracial, center-right coalition, the poles of urban mayoral coalitions were still evident. Hayden received a plurality of only five demographic groups: African Americans (75 percent for Hayden to 19 percent for Riordan), registered Democrats (49 percent to 47 percent), self-assessed liberals (62 percent to 33 percent), renters (50 percent to 48 percent), and self-identified gay men and lesbians (54 percent to 41 percent).

The 1997 mayoral election also had one of the lowest turnouts (possibly the lowest turnout) in Los Angeles's political history: "as few as one in eight of the city's adult residents, and only one in four of its registered voters, turned up at the polls."[29] The low general turnout combined with voter registration drives associated with what Latinos perceived as anti-immigrant and anti-Latino propositions pushed the Latino vote above the black vote in Los Angeles for the first time. Riordan's margin of victory among Jewish voters was 71 percent to 26 percent, and the liberal West Side, whose southern borders were affected by the King riots, voted for him by a 64 percent to 33 percent margin. And that vote did turn out in 1997.

But Riordan's coalition could not be characterized as containing only one racial identity. He also had wide support among other racial and ethnic groups in the city, including Latinos and Asians, who were added to his (and Yorty's) traditional base of Catholics and voters in the San Fernando Valley. Thus the new poles that emerged in the Woo-versus-Riordan election of 1993 continued into the late 1990s in Los Angeles, but the city's racial polarization in the postriot period had stripped the progressive coalition of many of its important components, especially Latinos. Indeed, only two groups gave Tom Hayden more than 50 percent of their votes in the 1997 mayoral election: African Americans and gay men and lesbians.[30]

New York City: Dinkins Versus Koch and Giuliani Versus Dinkins

In New York City—as in Chicago and Los Angeles—sexual identity voting was an important component in a multiracial coalition that opposed the coalition of moderate, middle-class urban conservatives that were predominantly (though not exclusively) white. The profile of this coalition that supported Koch and Giuliani in New York is similar to the one that elected Riordan in Los Angeles: middle class and upper middle class, Jewish and Catholic, concerned with crime and education, socially conservative, and skeptical of any new government initiatives.

Ed Koch and Post-Fiscal-Crisis New York

Edward Koch was elected as mayor of New York in the aftermath of the city's 1975 financial crisis, which came at the midpoint of a fundamental reorganization of New York's economic base.[31] In the preceding twenty years, New York had become susceptible to the shifting influences of the world economy. Then a combination of local policies and larger economic trends undermined the city's economic position from its high point of the immediate postwar period and brought it to a competitive low point in the mid-1970s. The clearest indicator of this decline was job loss. Between 1967 and 1975, New York lost more than 600,000 jobs, most of these in the manufacturing sector.[32] The relative productivity of New York's skilled workforce, the higher cost of doing business in New York (taxes plus utilities, commercial space, etc.), and the general cost of living which in turn pushed up the price of skilled white-collar labor all made New York a less attractive location for the manufacture of goods for national or worldwide consumption.

The trend toward a service-dominated economy, postindustrial business needs, and the influx of highly skilled white-collar workers was hastened by the internationalization of financial services, the equity markets, law, and the increased importance of the communications industry. New York was the nation's center for each of these industries, and this portion of the city prospered. The outcome of this transition was an economy more focused on services than manufacturing, more on national and international economic domains than local ones, an economy less diverse and more reliant on trends outside the control of both public and private decision makers in the city.

A second problem, initially hidden by the growth in the service sector during the late 1970s and 1980s, was the emergence of a series of economic mismatches. The price of commercial and residential space in New York (as in Boston, San Francisco, and Washington) rose dramatically in the 1970s and 1980s. There was also a growing mismatch between the skills needed for employment in the new economy and the skills of the available labor. The result of the first was the recycling of commercial space for residential use at higher prices (leading to the displacement of poor residents and many small businesses). The second meant that people outside New York would take a substantial number of the new white-collar jobs generated by the city's economy. The city's schools could not produce a qualified workforce as quickly as the economy was generating a need.

In terms of New York's governmental influence, this economic change gave New York's downtown/midtown progrowth alliance greater influence, even predominant, power. Savitch called the emergent regime of the 1970s that prospered after the fiscal crisis a progrowth regime characterized by a corporatist-pluralist hybrid in its internal dynamics.[33] This "corporatist hybrid" regime supported several prodevelopment policies, including public development corporations, tax subsidies, land assemblage, enhanced services through business development agencies, and, in some cases, direct subsidies to sustain the city's economic base. The dominant regime of the 1980s, capped by the Koch administration's budgetary and development policies, clearly wished to position New York to take advantage of the changing world economic dynamics rather than become a victim of it. But while protecting the city as a whole from the negative consequences of change, the governing regime also intensified the social and political effects of the mismatches emerging from those changes in New York.

The transformation of New York's economy was also reflected in the reorganization of the city's politics. There is a clear division between those who were vested in, and gained from, the emerging world city of postindustrial New York and those whose interests were tied to older forms of social organization: unions, public employees, public-sector clients (recipients of services), and those sectors of the middle class tied to traditional forms of interest mobilization (ethnic identities or older communities). This cleavage was frequently reinforced by race.

Koch solidified much of the institutional, managerial politics and social changes that followed the financial crisis into the 1980s. But rather than expand the city's public sector to deal with the changes produced by these economic forces, he encouraged the postindustrial growth and the transformation of Manhattan and downtown Brooklyn and accepted the negative effects of change as the unpleasant but necessary consequences of growth.

Koch's initial 1977 electoral base was a loose coalition of predominantly white middle-class (especially Catholic and Jewish) outer-borough New Yorkers, along with his traditional base of Manhattan liberals and reform Democrats. The Manhattan business community was at first hesitant about Koch but eventually came to support him. He and then political newcomer Mario Cuomo defeated the incumbent, Abraham Beame, in a primary and faced each other in a runoff. During the runoff campaign, Koch sealed a deal with the Brooklyn Democratic organization that ensured his election by denying to Cuomo their support in Brooklyn. This deal, however, came to haunt him eight years later.

Koch's first reelection in 1981 was little more than a coronation. The Republican Party allowed him to run in its primary (which he won, thus heading the two principal parties), but his support among Manhattan liberals and public employee unions was soft. Among blacks, the opposition to Koch was even stronger. Brooklyn State Assemblyman Frank Barbaro, who had long had links to the labor movement, challenged Koch in the Democratic primary. Finding support among Manhattan liberals, officials from the Liberal Party, public-sector labor unions (excluding the uniformed services), and some African American leaders, Barbaro received a surprising 36 percent of the Democratic primary vote, but the turnout was low. Koch did especially poorly in African American districts, where he received as little as 30 percent of the vote.

Koch and Manhattan's Gay Community

The same 1981 election also represented a change in the relationship between Manhattan-based gay activists and Koch. It had been assumed that New York's lesbian and gay voters supported Edward Koch in the 1977 Democratic mayoral runoff against Mario Cuomo. Koch's traditional base in the liberal and reform constituencies of Greenwich Village and Chelsea, which he represented on both the New York City Council and in Congress, overlapped with the city's main gay neighborhoods. An incident that occurred in Cuomo's home base, Queens, and that had homophobic overtones also contributed to the sense that Koch had "gay" support. It was widely reported that a sound truck supporting Cuomo told local residents to "Vote for Cuomo, not the Homo," referring to Koch's being a lifelong bachelor and living in Greenwich Village. The Cuomo campaign denied that the incident had any official sanction, but the damage had been done. In 1977, Koch carried most of what today would be identified as the city's gay neighborhoods.

But in 1981, things were different. In the activist gay community, then almost exclusively in Manhattan, one gay political club supported Barbaro, and the district leader from the Village Independent Democrats—the principal reform Democratic club in Manhattan which also was becoming an arena for the influence of lesbians and gays in Manhattan politics—did not endorse Koch.[34] Barbaro, sensing a new constituency active in mayoral politics, became the first serious citywide candidate to campaign in gay male bars and clubs, a campaign tactic that had begun in San Francisco.[35]

As he did with other segments of Manhattan and Brooklyn's liberal constituents, Koch gradually alienated his initial support, first Manhattan's gay political leadership and finally gay voters in general. His inability to obtain a local ordinance providing civil protections against sexual discrimination chipped away at his support in the gay community. In addition, Koch's joint public appearances (and known private dinners) with John Cardinal O'Connor—an earnest opponent of gay-positive legislation—angered many. The decision to have his campaign organization support an old friend—Council member Carol Greitzer—in a 1985 primary challenge from David Rothenberg, who was mounting an effort to obtain a City Council seat for lesbian or gay representation, further alienated previous supporters in the lesbian and gay community.

But two more significant factors were also taking a toll on Koch's support among lesbians and gay men. The first was a generational shift in the gay leadership. This newer generation was more professional, better educated, no longer exclusively male or white, and both more sophisticated behind the scenes and more aggressive in the streets. It expected more from the gay rights movement than simple tolerance. The second factor was a general perception among nearly everyone in the gay community, the public health community, and, increasingly, minority communities that Koch's administration had responded inadequately to the AIDS crisis. These two factors turned the relationship between Koch and his previous lesbian and gay supporters into a genuinely hostile one.

In 1985, there again was some gay support for Koch's opponents, in this case the Harlem assemblyman and county Democratic leader Denny Farrell and the former City Council president Carol Bellamy. Both Farrell and Bellamy actively sought support among lesbian and gay men in Manhattan and Brooklyn, and Farrell carried many of the gay election districts in Manhattan and also the majority of African American voters. But it was the Latino vote that was becoming the key swing constituency, and Koch nursed it until he obtained a remarkable 65 percent of Latino voters in 1985. In the end, no one could mount an effort serious enough to defeat the coalition that continued to support the mayor.

In three months after being reelected in 1985, however, the reform patina of Koch's administration faded as corruption charges escalated, leading

to the eventual suicide of Queens borough president and county Democratic party chair Donald Manes. Koch was further undermined by the way
that economic growth had affected the city. Rather than improve the quality of life, change was bringing even greater problems. Homelessness,
crime, poor-quality schools (both educationally and literally as infrastructure), and the cost of housing all grew. For the poor, largely black and Latino, economic growth did not mean new opportunities for employment—
the jobs being created could not be filled by poorly educated New
Yorkers—but, instead, a lowering in their standard of living as rents and
other living costs increased in response to the prosperity of more successful
New Yorkers. Even middle-class New Yorkers knew something was wrong
when the cost of housing prevented many of their children from achieving
a middle-class standard of living.

The New Poles of New York City's Mayoral Politics

The coalition of opposition to Koch that tentatively emerged in 1985 was
dubbed a "rainbow coalition" or, as its eventual leader labeled it, a "glorious
mosaic." It consisted of African Americans, public employee unions (excluding police and fire), portions of the Latino communities, newer immigrants (especially Haitian, Dominicans, younger Asians and Irish, Latinos
not from Puerto Rico, and Africans not of American descent), other white
liberals, and the gay community. The mosaic was an appeal to build on Jesse
Jackson's 1984 and 1988 Democratic primary coalition (and 1988 victory in
New York City). Jackson had included gays and lesbians in his coalition,
with some indication that in New York City and California, he carried a
majority of their vote.[36]

The Lesbian and Gay Vote in Dinkins's 1989 Victory

By 1989, the Koch electoral base had shrunk. It was not just the change in
demographics but also the increased dissatisfaction among his own supporters with his divisive personality. Koch's support was now drawn from
what was left of the ethnic Catholic and Jewish middle class, those portions
of the business community that could be termed small businesses, and the
uniformed service unions. In addition to being defined by social conser-
vatism, Koch's coalition was also defined by economic, fiscal, and service issues.[37] The grievances against him accumulated over twelve years in office,

combined with six years of economic boom that had had no significant effect on poverty, homelessness, or employment opportunities for minorities all led to a slim margin of victory by David Dinkins over Koch in his bid for a fourth term in office.

The racial component was also critical, not just in terms of demographics, but also in the way people came to understand policy. Issues of education, welfare, health care, and especially crime all had racial overtones. The 1989 Democratic primary presented the highest rate of black voter participation of any previous election. The combination of Jesse Jackson's two presidential bids—each of which had major voter enrollment drives in African American communities—combined with the possibility of electing the city's first black mayor boosted the African American turnout to a rate even higher than that of Jewish voters—typically the highest voting group.

In 1989, a racial incident in Howard Beach not only mobilized blacks in Brooklyn but also may have increased the gender gap, particularly among many Catholic women seeking some resolution to the racial tension in the city. The continued presence of ethnic voting and the increasing strength of racial identity voting in New York, along with the division between African Americans and Jewish voters, also defined the new voting coalitions partly in ethnic terms.[38]

Lesbians and gay Democrats tended to support Dinkins over Koch in the September 1989 primary. With four candidates in the field, the election was essentially between Dinkins and Koch. The WABC/*New York Daily News* exit poll found a gay and lesbian self-identification rate of 4.2 percent overall, 4.5 percent among Democrats the Republican self-identification rate was negligible).[39] About 50.6 percent of the total sample voted for Dinkins and 41.0 percent for Koch (the remainder went for lawyer Richard Ravitch and City Comptroller Harrison Goldin). Of the gay and lesbian sample, the margin for Dinkins was much greater: 57.6 percent for Dinkins and 34.5 percent for Koch—indicating that Koch still had support among white and middle-class gay men and lesbians. The CBS exit poll for the Democratic primary reported a 4.3 percent gay and lesbian/bisexual self-identification rate among Democrats voting that day. In the smaller CBS gay and lesbian sample, the margin for Dinkins was also 57.6 percent for Dinkins and 36.4 percent for Koch. These were surprisingly similar results for such small samples.[40]

Despite Koch's endorsement of Dinkins on the steps of City Hall the day after the Democratic primary, most of his supporters moved to the Republican candidate, former U.S. Attorney Rudolph Giuliani. Just as Jane Bryne's supporters moved to Republican Bernard Epton in Chicago against Harold Washington, much of Koch's coalition quickly became the core of the Giuliani coalition. But more than 65 percent of self-identified gay men and lesbians voted for Dinkins in the November general election, compared with the total vote of just over 51 percent for Dinkins.[41]

The two coalitions that dominated the 1989 Koch-Dinkins primary and the Dinkins-Giuliani general election also dominated the 1993 Dinkins-Giuliani race. The profile of the 1989 election of Dinkins and the 1993 rejection of him is remarkably similar. The overlap of tax and budget issues with race, personal values, and identity again became major issues in the 1993 rerun of 1989. Without much change in the actual structure of the electorate, Dinkins won by a few points in 1989 and lost by a few points four years later. Changes in turnout rates—higher on Staten Island owing to a referendum on secession and lower among African Americans throughout the city—altered the balance between the electoral coalitions. By taking away a percentage point or two among those groups that had supported Dinkins, Giuliani won by a slight margin in 1993.

Much of Dinkins's "glorious mosaic" of multiracial and gender-based identity politics in City Hall and in the public schools was replaced by the core themes of fiscal responsibility, economic development, crime reduction, "privatization," and budget reduction. In his appointments and statements, Giuliani expressly opposed the kind of identity politics that Dinkins had affirmed. And yet Giuliani played an identity politics of his own. At the January 1, 1990, inauguration of David Dinkins, the New York City Gay Men's Chorus opened the ceremony, whereas at the 1994 inauguration of Rudolph Giuliani, the black POW/MIA flag was displayed with the flags of New York's five boroughs. Giuliani understood identity politics as well as Dinkins did; they just emphasized different identities.

Although the two coalitions' relative size and energy were uneven and unstable at the edges, they continued to dominate politics in New York into the mid-1990s. Philip Thompson attributes the initial Dinkins victory to the mobilization of African Americans in New York and his defeat in 1993 to the lack of such mobilization—largely because Dinkins's own administration did not reinforce its own political base. The lower turnout in the black election districts in 1993, as opposed to 1989, is proof that Thompson is at least partly correct.

Logit Analysis of the 1993 Results

When subjecting the 1993 Giuliani-Dinkins vote to logistic regression, as we did in Los Angeles, the variables that best explain the outcome are race, party identification, political ideology, religion (primarily Catholic but also Jewish as the descriptors), and the variable for self-identified lesbians and gay men (Table 6-1). Together, these variables predicted more than 85 percent of voters' choices (as opposed to 80 percent for Los Angeles). By 1993, the self-identification rate of gay and lesbian voters reached 7.8 percent in New York, second only to San Francisco among major cities as the highest of randomly generated citywide samples of gay and lesbian voters (In San Francisco, the self-identification rates, including bisexual, have been as high as 16 percent.) As in Los Angeles, the tested variables that did not meet the model's usefulness criteria included age, income, education level, and gender. The fact that in both New York and Los Angeles, sexual identity was a more powerful indicator than gender was an interesting and unexpected finding. And again, as in Los Angeles, the inclusion of political ideology lessened the effect of both sexual orientation and—but more significantly—religion on the predictive relationships, reinforcing our conclusion that sexual identity does influence the development of political predispositions.

Although religion and sexual orientation provided only secondary power to the model in addition to the basic variables of party affiliation, race, and political ideology, they did have independent influence in predicting sample voter responses. Again, as in the case of Los Angeles, when the categorization schemes of race, religion, and party identification were broken down and contrasted among themselves, the "lesbigay" (lesbian, bisexual, and gay) variable had roughly the same potency as "Republican," "Latino," and "Jewish."[42] In short, as an important part of the coalition that had twice supported Dinkins, sexual identity voting was independently identifiable as a predictor of voting behavior but certainly was not as decisive as race or party identification as a predictor that structured the 1993 election outcome.

The Gay and Lesbian Vote in Urban Electoral Coalitions

Even though sexual identity showed a measurable and independent influence on electoral outcomes in Los Angeles and New York, it was not strong

TABLE 6.1.

Logit Results for New York City: General/Mayoral Election, November, 1993

Dependent Variable
MAYR_2WY   Vote for Giuliani or Dinkins?
                  [Guiliani vote is referent]

Independent Variable(s) Entered on First Step:

POLPHILY
[Political Philosophy:]   Do You Consider Yourself? [Categorical]
AGE   Age Group You Belong [Categorical]
GENDER   [Gender of Voter] Your Sex:
WHITE   Race: White
BLACK   Race: Black
ASIAN   Race: Asian
LATINO   Race: Latino
INCOME   1992 Total Family Income?: [Categorical]
LESBIGAY   Gay/Lesbian/bisexual
PROTESTN   Religion: Protestant
CATHOLIC   Religion: Roman Catholic
JEWISH   Religion: Jewish
OTH_CHRI   Religion: Other Christian
OTH_REL   Religion: Other Religion
DEMOCRAT   Party ID: Democratic
REPUBLIC   Party ID: Republican
LIBERAL   Party ID: NYS Liberal Party
CONSERV   Party ID: NYS Conservative Party
INDEPEND   Party ID: Independent
EDUCAT   Last Grade of School Completed? [Categorical]

Variable	B	S.E.	Sig	R	Exp(B)
PHILOSOPHY			.0000	.1978	
Liberal	**-1.1764**	**.1581**	**.0000**	**-.1938**	**.3084**
Moderate	**.6039**	**.1496**	**.0001**	**.1003**	**1.8293**
AGE			.4275	.0000	
18–24	.1226	.3285	.7090	.0000	1.1304
23–29	.0531	.2787	.8489	.0000	1.0545
30–39	.1490	.2230	.5041	.0000	1.1607
40–44	−.6127	.2940	.0372	−.0406	.5419
45–49	.0433	.2949	.8832	.0000	1.0443
50–59	.0458	.2771	.8686	.0000	1.0469
60–64	−.2403	.4138	.5614	.0000	.7864
GENDER	−.1399	.2098	.5051	.0000	.8695
WHITE	.4960	.7151	.4879	.0000	1.6421
BLACK	**-4.0345**	**.7868**	**.0000**	**-.1308**	**.0177**

ASIAN	.1736	.9549	.8557	.0000	1.1896
LATINO	−1.1045	.7371	.1340	−.0131	.3314
INCOME			.0884	.0000	
Under $15K	−.5357	.3229	.0971	−.0230	.5852
$15K–$29.9K	−.4599	.2372	.0525	−.0352	.6313
$30K–$49.9K	.0532	.1987	.7891	.0000	1.0546
$50K–$74.9K	.3322	.2278	.1448	.0094	1.3940
$75K–$99.9K	.6664	.3285	.0425	.0386	1.9473
LESBIGAY**	**207**	**.3664**	**.0009**	**.0800**	**3.3895**
PROTESTANT	.7697	.5325	.1483	.0079	2.1592
CATHOLIC	**1.6349**	**.4399**	**.0002**	**.0912**	**5.1290**
JEWISH	1.3623	.4646	.0034	.0681	3.9053
OTH_CHRSTN	.5371	.6282	.3925	.0000	1.7111
OTH_RELGN	.4420	.6257	.4799	.0000	1.5558
DEMOCRATIC	−1.4389	.6374	.0240	−.0467	.2372
REPUBLICAN	2.0134	7321<	.0060	.0626	7.4890
LIBERAL	2.0073	1.0450	.0548	.0345	7.4430
CONSERVTVE	1.3633	.9849	.1663	.0000	3.9090
INDEPENDNT	.0262	.6850	.9695	.0000	1.0265
EDUCATION			.3587	.0000	
Some HS	.0160	.3674	.9653	.0000	1.0161
HS Graduate	.3169	.2253	.1596	.0000	1.3729
Some College	.0790	.2181	.7171	.0000	1.0823
College Grad	−.0182	.2082	.9305	.0000	.9820
Constant	−6.2806	5.4414	.2484		

Significant at <.001. Variables noted in bold.
*Voter News Service, General-Mayoral Exit Poll, November, 1993. Data weighted by VNS formulae with imputed three decimal points. Total number of cases: 1788 (Unweighted); Number of Gay/Lesbian/bisexual cases: 111 before processing. Number of cases: 1788; number rejected due to missing data: 743; number included in the analysis: 1045. Percent cases correctly predicted: Dinkins, 86.04%; Giuliani, 87.76%; Overall, 86.94%
**Positive correlation is the result of coding categories. Scale is "not-Gay."

enough to have a political effect without being merged into broader coalitions. In Chicago, where coalition building both in the lakeshore wards and citywide is required to achieve political influence, the choice facing lesbian and gay voters on the North Side has been between recreating the Washington coalition or accommodating the new Cook County Democratic organization of Richard Daley Jr. But in each case, a political vote organized around sexual identity showed a willingness to become engaged in multiethnic/multi-identity coalition politics in order to pursue identity politics. Thus our final question for this examination of urban voting is, How do voters influenced at least partly by their sexual identity fit into the three current explanatory models of urban voting coalitions? Because direct data are available only for New York, Los Angeles, and San Francisco, we must infer through other techniques whether neighborhoods with large numbers of gay residents offer patterns similar to those in Chicago. One widely applied perspective on citywide electoral combinations contrasts coalitions among citizens as service consumers and as resource providers. A second perspective explores biracial/accommodationist alliances among different racial and economic groups. A third describes the shifting association of groups externally driven by structural economic changes. This we might call the urban transformation/progressive fragmentation thesis.

Service Consumers Versus Resource Providers

The service demander–resource provider model of urban voting views electoral coalitions as a cost-benefit game among rational voters vying for perceived gains and avoiding potential losses in their own taxation/service calculus. Following these principles, big-city voters should coalesce around two poles. The first brings together the poor, the urban professions as service providers, organized municipal workers, and (quietly) segments of the business community seeking dramatic and specific infrastructure investments. The second is made up of taxpaying home owners, residents subject to the various taxes now imposed on middle- and upper-middle-class professionals, small businesses, large businesses, and fiscal reformers in the policy communities.

Martin Shefter's examination of New York City is a good example of this model.[43] Dividing the city's electorate into service demanders and resource providers, Shefter builds on a broader theme in which he sees New York' City's history as a tension between two rationales: one *political*, in which politicians try to maintain sufficient support among political constituencies to be elected, and the other *economic*, in which both government and business elites run the economy for their mutual benefit. In his examination of the Irish political machine, Stephen Erie finds common ground in economic growth between the business sector seeking infrastructure investment and subsidies for economic development, and the machine seeking new tax revenue for patronage and thus votes.[44] In contemporary urban welfare states, in which the bureaucracy has replaced the machine and social services have replaced patronage positions, these tensions will remain if transposed onto new arenas of conflict—over the raising and allocation of public resources.

This rational and singular analysis of urban political behavior focuses on substantive budgetary matters, as opposed to identity (or even ethnic) matters. It appeals to policy analysts and political scientists who use economic models to view urban politics. Whether the model is predictive in the end is less clear, however. Other analysts, building on theoretical critiques, argue that self-interest—in the classic economic sense—is only part of the public opinion and voting behavior story. For example, after studying public opinion in the city and county of Los Angeles, David O. Sears and Carolyn Funk concluded that "self-interest does not have much effect on the mass public's attitudes," even though large tax burdens clearly linked to personal interest do have an effect, if not an overwhelming one.[45]

The data available at the city and national level indicate that lesbian and gay voters are more interested in services than in a reduction in the national deficit (but 30 percent in Los Angeles believed that taxes were too high) and that lesbian and gay self-identifiers are more likely to support health care programs and educational programs than their particular income profiles in cities might predict. (HIV/AIDS is the obvious association with health care, and breast cancer has also become an important issue of cohesion in the gay and lesbian community. Bond and tax referenda for additional educational resources in both Los Angeles and San Francisco have won strong gay and lesbian support in recent years.)

And although it is true that in New York and Los Angeles a substantial number of gay and lesbian self-identifiers voted for Giuliani and Riordan, respectively, in 1993, these voters were typically in the upper-income categories, reported higher education achievement than even the gay and lesbian samples, and tended to be male and white. Also, home ownership by lesbians and gays in Los Angeles tended to induce more conservative voting among the self-identified sample, to a statistically significant degree.[46] Nevertheless, the votes of lesbian and gay self-identifiers cannot be predicted by their income or service requirements.

There is a point at which the resource provider–service consumer model does help explain some aspects of lesbians' and gay men's voting behavior. At the highest income brackets, the coherence of the gay and lesbian vote does appear to break down. This was first evident in the gay and lesbian samples from two 1988 Democratic presidential primaries, in the 1992 presidential exit-poll sample, and in the 1993 general election returns for New York and Los Angeles.[47] Still, it is clear that except in the samples' very highest income categories, voting behavior motivated primarily by gay or lesbian identity goes beyond the values of the simple self-calculating, rational actor model drawn from microeconomic metaphors.

Based on a more sociological definition of interest, William Grimshaw reminds us of Harold Gosnell's finding that Chicago blacks remained loyal to the party of Lincoln well into the 1930s and 1940s, even though their economic interests rested more with the New Deal of the Democrats.[48] (Likewise, some African Americans in the South remained loyal to the Republican Party up to and including the Nixon/Kennedy race of 1960.) Even today, in matters of racial identity and equality in political procedure, the importance of symbolic affirmation clarifies some voting behavior not explained by "rational" support for public service.[49]

Such a conclusion begs for similar reflections on identity voting among lesbians and gay men. The dramatic mobilization around sexual identity since the 1970s has included only a few demands for special budget allocations, with health care and preventive programs associated with the HIV epidemic being the most significant. Symbolic empowerment for lesbians and gay men outweighs any mini-max explanation associated with taxes and spending. Even though self-identified gay men and lesbians voters are better educated and report earning about the mean income for the cities in which they live, they do not vote as their income would predict. This does not mean that some gay voters do not vote according to their personal or household economic interests—clearly, many do—but that the typical self-identified lesbian or gay male is prepared to sacrifice some margin in an economic calculus of voting for symbolic affirmation and self-esteem.

Accommodationist Biracial Coalitions

A second approach to understanding electoral coalitions in urban politics over the past two decades is a model based on biracial coalitions led by moderate or even accommodationist black mayoral candidates. Peter Eisinger's study of Milwaukee in the mid-1970s is an early example of this approach.[50] Browning, Marshall, and Tabb then used this approach to view the accommodation less from the perspective of electoral coalitions than from participation in the governing regimes.[51]

In the early years of African American political incorporation, black mayoral candidates felt required to play down their racial identity and seek accommodationist coalitions of Latinos, liberal whites, other minorities, and the local business community. Portions of the business community aligned themselves with these regimes in the fear that racial division might undermine their city's economic stability. From the late 1960s to the late 1980s, biracial accommodationist coalitions elected black mayors in Cleveland, Newark, Atlanta, Oakland, Los Angeles, Philadelphia, and countless smaller cities.

The electoral success of these individual mayoral candidates and the coalitions that backed them is evident, but the tensions inherent in the political bases of Mayors Stokes, Gibson, Young, Bradley, and Goode eventually caused problems of their own. More community-based and assertive (nationalist?) African Americans frequently criticized black mayors for not paying enough attention to their community's needs. A second criticism of these biracial accommodationist regimes came from both African American and neighborhood organizations. How far were black mayors willing to go to keep the business communities from opposing their reelection?

In Atlanta's case, for example, Clarence Stone describes some of the tensions in the black community as prodevelopment, African American–centered electoral coalitions came to dominate the city's government. Although the black middle class gained from Atlanta's growth, their gains did not come through public services, as in other cities, but through the contracts, construction, and small-business opportunities associated with growth.[52] Nonetheless, many other blacks reaped little or nothing from Atlanta's postwar boom.[53]

Sonenshein saw more stability in Tom Bradley's Los Angeles coalition, but it, too, ultimately developed internal tensions. As the economics and demographics of Los Angeles changed, Bradley depended more and more on his alliance with downtown business interests. And as he did, his support among community activists, environmentalists, and the increasing number of Latinos who could not participate in the emerging economy waned.

A key component of these biracial coalitions is the cluster of "white liberals" that make up a portion of the coalition vote. In Bradley's Los Angeles, this was quite large, and in Dinkins's New York, it was significant. In Washington's Chicago and Richard Arrington's Birmingham, it was small. In all the cities, it was important.

Where biracial coalitions came to power, local journalists and campaign technicians understood the nonminority component of the coalitions as being urban, professional, and typically clustered in at least one geographic portion of the city. Thus their appellations "West Side Jewish voters" in Los Angeles, "Manhattan liberals" in New York, and "lakefront liberals" in Chicago. In each case, these geographic concentrations of white voters saw their interests tied ideologically to progressive politics, but frequently they were also linked to the local governing structure through indirect economic interests. The very presence of these coalitions was associated with the transformation of the central cities' core economic functions. These clusters of younger and professional voters built biracial coalitions with the emerging minority political powers because they tended to express values similar to (or at least compatible with) those of minority voters. The new urban professionals emphasized reformist and environmental values, whereas long-resident blacks and Latinos stressed program, service, and identity issues (especially the racism evident in urban police departments and the criminal justice systems).

The data presented here illustrate the relative importance of the gay vote in bi- or multiracial coalitions in both Los Angeles and New York. In New York, for example, in 1993, 22 percent of Dinkins's total vote was identified as "white," and 69 percent of gay and lesbian self-identified voters cast their ballots for Dinkins. If, however, the gay and lesbian subsample is removed from the overall sample, the "white" percentage of the Dinkins vote falls from 22 percent to 19.4 percent. In Los Angeles, if the gay sample is taken out of the 1993 Riordan-Woo exit-poll data set, the white component of Woo's multiracial coalition drops from 33.3 percent to 31 percent. Clearly, a disportionate segment of the white vote in these biracial coalitions is lesbian or gay.

Looked at in another way, the point can be made more strongly. The 1993 exit-poll data showed that only 27.4 percent of white voters chose Dinkins over Giuliani for mayor. This indeed might seem to be substantial portion of white voters in a biracial coalition, certainly larger than Harold Washington received in Chicago or Richard Arrington received in Birmingham.

But when the white voters—56 percent of the 1993 New York voters— are observed through the prism of sexual identity, new and governmentally worrisome issues appear. Gay and lesbian self-identifiers, 8.2 percent of the white voter sample, cast their ballots about 60 percent to 40 percent for Dinkins.[54] Nongay and lesbian white voters had opposite preferences: about 80 percent for Giuliani and only 20 percent for Dinkins. Similar results were found in the 1993 runoff in Los Angeles. Again, white gay voters cast their ballots in a completely different pattern than did white nongays. Gay and lesbian self-identifiers, 5.1 percent of the Anglo voter sample in the Los Angeles runoff, cast their ballots about 71 percent to 29 percent for Woo.[55] Nongay white voters again had opposite preferences, though not as strong as in New York: about 69 percent for Riordan and 31 percent for Woo—almost a mirror image.

The 1993 demographic profile of the lesbian and gay sample from New York is more representative of the racial makeup of that city than is the Los Angeles sample of Los Angeles (representing the overall low turnout of African Americans that year), but an important portion of what many scholars call the "white liberal vote" in biracial coalition voting still is disproportionately a "white *gay and lesbian* vote."

The biracial coalition model has had both explanatory and tactical problems. Tactically, its cross pressures are apparent. The threads that hold it together are not always as strong as the pressures that pull it apart. These voting coalitions often disagree on foreign policy (or more accurately, ethnic politics expressed as foreign policy disagreements, as in the local impact of pre–Mandela South African and Israeli military cooperation), on how to incorporate other minorities into the coalitions (such as Asians in Los Angeles), or, in the black community, on simple organizational issues (as in the ongoing tension between leaders of the Harlem's Democratic organization and the more activist central Brooklyn leadership). In addition, each group in the coalition either gains or loses when downtown progrowth policies threaten the group's cohesiveness.

The inclusion of a gay and lesbian identity into these coalitions has complicated them further, bringing some resistance from other coalition members. In the mid-1980s, Harold Washington found reaction to a gay rights bill ranging from indifference to outright opposition among black aldermen.

In New York's gay community, some regarded Dinkins's accommodationist strategy with the business community, his reaching out to the Koch-Giuliani coalition, and the effects of internal conflict in the black community on homosexuality as a betrayal of gay support. The delay of domestic partnerships and the arrest on St. Patrick's Day of Irish gay and lesbian protesters and their supporters (including one member of the City Council) were arguments against renewed support for him.

Whether a more assertive multi-identity strategy for elections is wiser than an accommodationist strategy is thus an open question. What is certain is that the bi- or multi-identity coalitions in Los Angeles and New York are less stable than the broad-based, moderately conservative urban coalitions that have propelled into office Mayors Riordan in Los Angeles, Giuliani in New York, Rendell in Philadelphia, and Daley Jr. in Chicago. The inclusion of a gay identity in these multiracial coalitions extends them further but adds another challenge to keeping them together. Whether the coalitions supporting Woo in Los Angeles and Dinkins in New York indicated the rise or the end of an multiracial, multi-identity voting coalition—since both Woo and Dinkins lost—it is clear that identity voting was important to urban mayoral coalitions.

Economic Transformation and Progressive Fragmentation

A third approach to citywide mayoral coalitions links changes in cities' economic structures, and thus ultimately their economic function in the world hierarchy of domains and markets, with the political coalitions that form around expectations for gains and losses in economic change.

The politics of the urban economic transformation model focuses on the generation, distribution, and redistribution of the negative and positive spillovers of economic change. The economic assumption among the critics of modern urban boosterism is that economic transformation has both negative and positive effects on any city: those tied to the industrial/manufacturing base will be losers in the transformation, and those associated with the emerging economic activities of "nodal" or "postindustrial" cities will be winners. Those who survived at the edges of the labor and housing markets during the manufacturing age are threatened with displacement as the transformation process proceeds.

Some writers have tried to identify areas of political liquidity during the process of urban transformation in which neighborhood and community groups can mobilize to influence the economic change. Other scholars seek to define the prerequisites for effective community mobilization. The conclusion of most case studies is that the urban economic transformation generates its own antithesis; that is, the victory of the progrowth coalitions generates forces that limit its own success.

The methodological emphasis on economic development has drawn researchers' attention to divisions in the urban politics of postindustrial cities. The political fault lines exposed by urban economic transformation divided cities into opposing forces. On one side are "the transient elites," those who represent mobile capital and human resources. On the other side are the "resigned residents," those who have a longer-term stake in the city as a community, have fewer resources, and, because of both, are less mobile. This conflict is most obvious in capital expenditures, in which financing for new airports, convention centers, and the other prerequisites of modern urban economies are funded while the older, traditional municipal infrastructure issues such as schools, parks, and sewers deteriorate. The groups on the losing side of the conflict include small homeowners, civil servants whose skills are not marketable outside the local economy, and small businesses.

The second dichotomy is between those who gain immediately from the emerging economy and those who lose. Sassen looks to the likely payoffs in the imposition of the new arrangement of urban economies: "Clearly one class of workers who benefit from this new industrial complex [is] the new professionals, managers, brokers of all types."[56] These "new professionals" are not as secure as industrial owners were in the 1950s or as current senior managers are who have achieved a real stake in their firms. They are hardworking and well paid but are not part of any power elite. They represent a large and new pool of purchasing capacity and generate specialized niches in retail activity, entertainment, and the arts. On the other side of the new divide are those living on the margins of the housing and labor markets, for whom the new urban economies have been a disaster. Competing even with new immigrants, the standard of living of those who were able to survive at the margins of the older economy has been reduced to public assistance or even homelessness.

Building mayoral coalitions from these new urban economies has been difficult. There should be a natural coalition of community activists, small businesses whose base is neighborhood economies, public employees, and workers tied to the declining manufacturing sector. But this is an unwieldy group. DeLeon showed how difficult it was to manage the alliance of the slow-growth movement, gay men and lesbians, blacks, environmentalists, Latinos, new ethnic identities, and the neighborhood movements that propelled George Mosconi and Art Agnos into San Francisco's City Hall. The costs of economic changes are uneven and cut across the usual ethnic, racial, and even class bases of traditional urban politics. Blacks, for example, who might find rapid downtown growth to be a source of jobs sometimes find opposition to such growth from environmentalists in the same liberal coalition. The new young professionals, who in Inglehart's framework are the protagonists of a postindustrial culture shift, conflict with others more concerned with day-to-day economic matters. Those who in-migrated and took jobs in the growing administrative sector forced up housing prices in neighborhoods long identified with particular ethnic groups. The problems with coalition building in the politics of urban transformation are contained in this simple fact: The very economic changes that should align these forces also generate the issues that divide them. Creating and maintaining an alliance among these divergent groups is a stressful task with which mayors supported by progressive coalitions can identify.[57]

Conclusion

The gay vote—women and men who include their sexuality in their assessment of candidates and policies—has had an identifiable and independent effect on mayoral elections in the two largest American cities. Other analysis leads us to believe that similar patterns could be discerned if data were available in cities such as Chicago (and possibly Philadelphia and Washington, D.C.). In New York and Los Angeles, white gay and lesbian voters are willing to cross racial and income divides to join bi-and multiracial coalitions if they support the *deep agenda* of identity politics. There is reason to believe the same was true in Chicago during the latter Washington years.

We have assumed that African American, Latino, and other racial minorities who also identify as gay are predisposed to join such coalitions. Indeed, we have seen no evidence to the contrary, except in rare, outlying cases.[58] There is no reason to think the opposite would be untrue, that gay men and lesbians of color also would be willing to cross racial lines, although data are not yet available to examine such a proposition. In fact, in purely statistical terms, given the data reviewed in this analysis, we have probably underestimated the willingness of the sexual identity group to cross racial lines, especially Latinos and Asians in New York and Chicago and black lesbians and gay men in Los Angeles in 1993. The inferential method we used in Chicago is skewed toward underestimating black lesbians and gay men. In Los Angeles and New York, where we saw that although race, party, and ideology explain much of such coalitions, they do not explain them entirely. And this explanation assumes that ideology and party affiliation are independent of sexual identity, which we have seen they are not.

In the various identity issues here, racial, gender, and sexual constructions interact in ways that are beyond the scope of this book. Suffice it to say that in voting studies, it is not very interesting to show that for example, a unionized African American gay male might vote for Harold Washington. The point is to explain why in so much of urban America, where race determines social and political life, a measurable and consistent portion of white (and

Asian and Latino) voters are ready to cross racial categories on behalf of their sexual identity to create bi-and multiracial coalitions.

We can infer from what we have seen (and from other data) that the cultural and symbolical nature of identity voting operates according to different criteria than do budget-based mini-max voting calculations, except in two regards. The first is when budgetary allocations take on a highly symbolic meaning for identity voting—as in HIV prevention programs and domestic partnership authorization. The second is when gay men and lesbians earning higher incomes find that the tax burden of urban coalition building has reached a point beyond which they refuse further taxation. At this undefined point, household fiscal issues outweigh identity voting (although there is no evidence to suggest that high-income gays would ever vote for a homophobe, regardless of his or her economic and budgetary policies). These would be the lesbian and gay Riordan and Giuliani voters of 1993. In addition are the cross pressures among gay voters based on ethnic or religious identity. These could be seen in New York City during the 1988 Democratic presidential primary and the 1993 Dinkins-Giuliani race. Voters identifying as both gay and Jewish showed voter patterns different from those of the rest of the self-identified lesbian and gay samples.

Tying self-esteem to the ballot box is the essence of identity voting. Where politics is simply the business of government, identity politics is a minor affair. Where past patterns of discrimination and arbitrary behavior are common, the incorporation of identity dimensions into voting models compensates for the decreased value of the simple cost-benefit calculus of linking votes to services.

What seems certain is that analyzing urban elections through the lens of "ethnic voting," or interest groups that focus on budgetary mini-max solutions, detracts us from observing the emerging identities and the cultural aspects of large-city elections. The Dinkins coalition resembles the Woo coalition in Los Angeles, and both resemble the Washington coalition. The emerging culture- and gender-based political identities now discernible in urban politics are not completely explained by older categories of ethnic voting patterns or mini-max budgetary calculations by resource providers and service consumers; they need to be treated as standing on their own.

⣿

PART IV

Sexual Identity and Urban Governance

CHAPTER 7

⣿

The Political Organization of Sexual Identity in
Birmingham, Alabama

The political expression of sexual identity in American cities is organized
around a set of associations sustained by local energy, monies, and commitment. In a few cases, these organizations receive local or state funds,
sometimes affecting their behavior as if they had become part of the local
state. This is especially true in the area of HIV prevention and social services, drug and alcohol rehabilitation, and youth services. But mostly they
are centered in a community, embedded in networks of similar local associations in other cities and organizations across the nation.

The number and diversity of these associations are remarkable. There are
annuals that attempt to catalog them as sets of groups.[1] Some are clearly of
political intent, described as political action committees or legal advocacy
groups, and some are even defined by party affiliation. Others are more direct expressions of identity politics, such as sexual identity, racial identity,
religious identity, gender, or simply avocation.

Underlying these organizations are identifiable patterns indicating
broader influences on their structuring. The most obvious of these is the influence of the American federal system. Organizations in the neighborhood, city, state, region, and nation were established and linked to local
communities by ties both strong and weak. Each locality has similar needs
for organization, and thus similar organizations arise to meet those needs.
Community communications is an example. Until the mid-1990s, few metropolitan dailies covered issues of interest to, and certainly not from the
perspective of, gay men and lesbians. To meet this need, homespun journals
sprang up across the country, largely local and financed through advertising
revenue raised from local lesbian and gay bars, restaurants, professional services, and small businesses. Some grew into important circulation journals,
such as *The Advocate* and *OUT*, or had a sound journalistic reputation,

such as the *Washington Blade*; still others found niches in the diverse lesbian and gay market.

The evolution of these organizational sets can also be seen as a process of cascading replication, in which one city develops a successful new organization that in turn is emulated in other cities. Thus, in most large and medium-size cities in the United States, local communities have developed political action committees, "pride" committees that sponsor parades and other events near the June anniversary of the Stonewall uprising, women's groups, political action committees, HIV prevention and education groups, HIV/AIDS support groups, religious associations, and the like.

In the past, social scientists interested in political organization might have studied these organizations to determine their peak association and the relative influence of each in local policy formulation. Or they might have examined these community-based organizations as instruments of public policy implementation, community filters of policies set at state or national levels. The goal would be to find out how national and local priorities clash during the processes of community implementation.

The intent of this chapter is not to look at the individual organizations in one city or even at a specific type of organization across cities but, rather, to look at the political organization of identity as an organizational field in a single city: not the organization as such, but the field of organizations, centered on and around an unbounded locality. The subject is the organizational field's relation to the community from which it arose and its relationship, if there is one, with the local state. Because identity has political and social meanings, the organizations though which sexual identity mobilizes must be interpreted more broadly than the microeconomic underpinnings of interest-group models often used in urban analysis. This is a perspective informed by social organization theory[2] and differs from the traditional single interest-group perspective in four ways:

1. Individual organizations are not assumed to be separate. The meaning of any one organization in the field is partly derived from the meaning of the field as a whole. One corollary is that although multiple memberships in several groups in the field may lead to some cross pressuring, as they do in an interest-group model, the most important effect is its overall reinforcement of the field as a whole.

2. All these identity organizations are assumed to be open, and although focused locally and named by the geography in which they operate, they also are po-

sitioned in horizontal and vertical networks of political communication. Many of these organizations are true grassroots organizations, but it is not unusual for coordinating committees across different cities to form them if they are needed. Identity is not bound to any one location.

3. In addition to the formal nature of local organizations, with each having its own regulations and rituals, the fact that this organizational field is held together by a common identity introduces normative and semiotic overtones to its descriptions and meanings that go beyond the classic microeconomic understanding of interest.

4. Finally, the relationship of the organizational field as a whole to the local state is different from the relationship of any one organization to the state. Representation and legitimacy—in the informal sense of civil society organizations—rest with the field, not with any one organization.

We use the city of Birmingham as one case of how sexual identity is organized locally for political effect. New York, Boston, Houston, Atlanta, and San Francisco have many more and more varied groupings than Birmingham does, so they—and San Francisco especially—have much more organizational capacity in their local gay and lesbian communities. In a sense, Birmingham serves as one pole in a continuum of what we later describe as the *embeddedness of identity* in the social organization of local governance. We chose Birmingham precisely because it is not known as a major center of lesbian and gay politics, and yet we found clear evidence of sustained community activity and effort.

Birmingham: From Yesterday to Today

Historians hesitate to call Birmingham a southern city. It was, in fact, a Reconstruction-period invention of southern investors, northern engineers, and local speculators. Birmingham's potential as an industrial center had dominated expectations for the city from even before its founding in 1871. Because Birmingham was never bound to the agricultural heritage of cotton, its history stands in marked contrast to the urban centers of Alabama's "black belt" farther south to Selma, Mobile, or even the state capital of Montgomery only one hundred miles away. In Birmingham, there never was any sense of losing the genteel (and slave-based) agrarian way of life left behind in the ashes of the Civil War, no antebellum mansions as in Charleston, no lasting scars of war as in Atlanta. Indeed, nearly all the historical sites in Birmingham relate to the era of pig iron and steel in the 1880s and 1890s or to the events of the civil rights era in the 1960s.[3]

The Political Legacy of Steel, Soil, and Race

Birmingham's industrial legacy, fashioned in the midst of a primarily agricultural economy, made its economic history unique, "Prussian" some have termed it: a path toward industrialization that took advantage of the serflike cheap labor that was leaving the land after the Civil War. But in Birmingham's case, this cheap labor was black freedmen, not a peasant class. In fact, it was one of the few great industrial centers of the United States that did not rely heavily on European emigrants for labor. This is important because for more than seventy-five years, Birmingham relied on cheap labor for its competitive margin over other iron- and steel-producing centers, which also laid the groundwork for racial conflict between black and white industrial laborers: race offered a ready social divide that could be manipulated to the owners' advantage.[4]

Almost from its founding, Birmingham's industrial capacity was largely owned by outside investors.[5] This "Pittsburgh of the South" was dependent on financial powers that did not reside in the city. By the turn of the century and certainly by the time of the Great Depression, almost all the major steel mills of Jefferson County were owned by outside financiers. Birmingham's absentee industrial legacy had lasting effects on the city's social temperament: a suspicion of the power of outsiders; a frightened and vulnerable industrial working class whose economic status rose and fell with coal, iron, and steel; and a history of business's being involved in local affairs only to the point that big steel could be assured that labor would remain cheap and that public expenditures, and thus taxes, would remain low. Industrial owners were not directly vested in the city's future as were the resident business classes in Atlanta or, indeed, in Pittsburgh. No "six families" are identified with the establishment of Birmingham's cultural and educational institutions as they are in Pittsburgh. Except for its private universities, most of the city's formal cultural institutions were built after the 1960s and were paid for by Birmingham taxpayers.

Distant ownership also meant that managers could exacerbate racial tensions between black and white industrial workers without worrying about the possible collateral impact on the civility of their own neighborhoods, as they lived several hundred miles away in Cincinnati, Cleveland, Pittsburgh, or even New York. The social effects of racial division and low wages were far from the neighborhoods of even the local factory managers, who lived in the hills south of the city and beyond Red Mountain. In the heyday of steel, these local corporate leaders were the Big Mules of Alabama politics of which V. O. Key wrote.[6] Through the first half of the century, they formed an alliance with the white owners of the tenant farms who leased their land to the children of former slaves. These whites of the black belt, in the southern half of the state, were primarily interested in restricting the franchise of blacks, and the industrial powers of northern Alabama wanted to keep labor costs down. This conservative bond was sealed in the restrictive 1901 state constitution and continued into the civil rights era. It was strong enough to thwart the labor unions in the 1890s and 1930s, the New Deal Democrats in the 1930s, the populist movements of the 1940s, and the early battles for civil rights in the 1950s.[7]

Birmingham's industrial legacy and race remained the defining characteristics of the city's political and social life long past World War II. Although Birmingham had begun to produce a forward-looking, white professional class similar to Atlanta's, it was not as large or based in an increasingly internationalized business elite as was Atlanta's. Nor did Birmingham's new professional class have much faith in the older industrial elite. Thus, the prudent and development-focused alliance that Clarence Stone describes as forming in Atlanta among the business community, the local government, and the city's African American middle class[8] did not materialize until much later in Birmingham, and when it did, it was much weaker. The first signs of an alliance were not evident until the 1960s, when the civil rights movement had altered the public discourse; steel had declined and, with it, absentee indifference to Birmingham as a place to live; and national policies had helped empower African Americans through voting rights and community organization.

The Emergence of a Tentative, Progressive Coalition

The early 1960s was a critical period of transition from the old Birmingham to the city as it is today. Almost as important as the civil rights movement, at least for Birmingham, was the restructuring of the city's economy. The first signs of the structural decline of steelmaking in Birmingham had already appeared. Although there had been downturns before, such as at the end of the recession in 1958/59, employment in the industrial sector never regained its peak. In 1954, steel accounted for more than 26,000 jobs in the Birmingham MSA, but by 1987, this number was only about 8,000. By the 1990s, health care dominated both the for-profit and the not-for-profit and service sectors of greater Birmingham. The Big Mules of Alabama politics were being replaced by professionals in real estate development, law, services, and the professions (especially health related).

Coinciding with the decline of steel was the slow emergence from the business community of sustained, locally focused, political interests. The forces behind the white, commission form of government were slowly being replaced by more regional business interests whose attention was focused on Birmingham itself.[9] This was not so much a "liberal" wing but one locally vested in the city's long-term commercial interests, a "prudent progressivism" grounded in business interests. As in many other cities, this group of businessmen had a vision of a new Birmingham, a city with a postindustrial economy and a large entertainment/cultural sector. They launched a coordinated, private-sector, master plan for the redevelopment of the city's downtown area. Only a resident business class with locally focused interests would want to redevelop the downtown city.

The civil rights battles of 1963 were the final critical factor in changing the politics of Birmingham. The Birmingham Klavern was one of the more vicious wings of the regional KKK associations in the South. Its members were engaged in a clandestine civil war against the civil rights movement of the 1950s and 1960s. Their actions extended to most of the bombings in Birmingham in the 1950s, including the home of A. G. Gaston, the city's most prominent African American. The local government, which steel interests had confined to keeping the streets clean and maintaining public order, quietly but frequently supported many of the Klan's activities. At best, the local police were indifferent to the Klan's actions.

At the most decisive moment of the civil rights period in Birmingham, local police arrested hundreds of protesters, including children, during a rally in Kelly Ingram Park in April 1963. The park was situated on Sixteenth Street—the border between the white and black business districts of downtown. Martin Luther King Jr. was also arrested at the rally, and it was during his time in jail that he issued his "Letter from a Birmingham Jail." The letter underscored the urgent tone of the civil rights movement but called for a balance between urgency and the discipline needed for nonviolence. In the fall of 1963, the Sixteenth Street Baptist Church was bombed, killing four children. The outcome of all these events was blacks' new sense of political empowerment and the emerging and locally focused business community's abandonment of support for the local government.

These and other events interacted to create a weak and halting yet still progressive coalition in Birmingham that first exercised its influence outside government before it gained governmental powers in the 1970s. The economic base of all these progressive business interests was outside steel, in real estate, law, health services and research, and the professions. Its leaders knew that the image of Birmingham's racist past would have to change, that their success partly depended on easing racial tensions. In fact, it was a segment of the new white business community that first tried to change Birmingham's racist image. Political reform was seen as a prerequisite to the kind of downtown transformation that real estate, finance, and professional interests desired. And for the new, younger leaders of the business community, reform meant eliminating the old commission form of government, now identified with Bull Connor and police abuse, and establishing a modern mayor (manager)/council form of government.

The movement toward a mayor-council from of government was supported by both the African American community and many whites. The civil rights struggle had created a new, assertive, and politically sophisticated class of black Birminghamians. They also saw the need for a change in government, partly as a way to remove Connor and partly as a way to obtain representation on the City Council, especially after the Voting Rights Act of 1965.

The civil rights struggles and the effort to change Birmingham's form of government had another result: the formation of a tentative, biracial, liberal, and reform coalition to deal with the social and governmental issues confronting the city. The working relationships between white liberals and black religious, business, and community leaders that were forged in the civil rights era and in the reform movement of local government lasted well into the 1980s. This coalition set the stage for a new era in the politics of Birmingham: the election of David Vann as mayor in 1975 and of Richard Arrington as the first African American mayor in 1979.

Pre-Stonewall Birmingham: From Underground to Social Visibility

Immediately after World War II, gay life in Birmingham was quieter than in other, larger cities, but the pattern of moving from a fragmented population to an emerging social and political identity was much the same. The social dislocation caused by the war was important to the restructuring of homosexual subcultures throughout the United States and to the reorganization of gay male and lesbian identities. The first domains of same-sex male sensibility in late 1940s Birmingham were spaces similar to those in other cities: the cocktail lounges of the Tutwiler and the Thomas Jefferson, the major downtown hotels, were centers of gay intermingling, but typically the activities were kept covert. Linn Park facing City Hall and the Public Library, and the streets near the Tutwiler were cruise areas for men at night.

Outside the city was a hideaway on the Bessemer Highway, between Birmingham and Bessemer city, where the manager allowed same-sex dancing late at night. A similar club where both gay men and lesbians gathered could be found in Homewood, just south of the city. But as historian John Howard pointed out, access to such gathering spots had class associations, as only those with sufficient income to own cars could get there.

The role of bars for lesbians in Birmingham does not seem as important as they were in Buffalo or in the San Francisco Bay Area. In Birmingham, although lesbians could be found at many of the gay male bars or "bohemian" mixed bars and clubs, they were not as focused on bar culture; there was no women's bar in Birmingham until the 1980s. Instead, regardless of race or professional class, women maintained quiet social networks in Birmingham into the mid-1970s.[10]

But men had options not usually available to women. In the oppressive atmosphere of pre–civil rights Birmingham and despite the availability of bars, private home parties were important to men also. Rather than use family homes, "safe spaces" could be rented as sexual domains for socializing with friends (and also for sexual contacts). They were not always safe, however. During a July Fourth weekend in 1962, after an unrelated murder, one party was raided by the Birmingham city police, and forty-one people from several surrounding states were arrested. Most were released, but the names of all were published in the city's newspaper.[11] Several weeks later, Public Safety Commissioner Bull Connor used the breakup of this "convention of queers" as an example of how his police were working to make Birmingham a decent town.[12] But whether gay men and lesbians met in bars, parks, or homes, there was always the possibility of police harassment, frequently in the enforcement of liquor laws and closing times until bar owners discovered a new mechanism, the private club, to allow for later closing times and exemption from other state liquor authorities' sanctions.[13]

The closeted nature of Birmingham's lesbian and gay social life did have a positive aspect: it allowed for some mixing of the races. The underground "safe spaces" drew the line between private life and public life more sharply than that between black and white. In the parks, clubs, and private spaces, especially in town, the racial lines could be crossed. By bypassing Birmingham's social and political worlds, lesbians and gay men did cross class and racially defined boundaries, but only in the evening and only in marginalized "safe" spaces. In daily public life, Jim Crow prevailed, as did the more subtle enforcement of class and sociosexual codes.

Moving the Gay and Lesbian Identity to South Birmingham

In the late 1960s, the geographic center of gay evening life began to switch from the north side to the south side of Birmingham. Changes in the city's demographics (north Birmingham was becoming increasingly black), the abandonment of some commercial and residential spaces on the south side, and the creation of a "bohemian" culture around the Five Points area of south Birmingham all encouraged the move. The pattern was similar to those in other cities. Lesbians and gay men found a more open atmosphere in bohemian neighborhoods, such as Greenwich Village in New York, North Beach and Polk Valley in San Francisco, and portions of the North Side in Chicago.

Five Point South and the residential areas around the University of Alabama at Birmingham (UAB) served this function in Birmingham. Residential property values fell as a new highway—Interstate 31—cut through Red Mountain, disrupting the quiet residential areas of the south side. In the mid-1960s, gay men and some lesbians began to move into rental apartments near Highland Avenue and in the hills above and east of Five Points. One rental building became almost completely gay in the early 1960s and was known as such.[14] The homes and apartments of the area were being vacated by the departing middle management class associated with the dying steel industry. Suburbanization (as well as the city's racial tension) sent outside the city limits much of the white middle class that survived the decline of the steel industry.

Stage 1: The Early Political Organization of Sexual Identity in Birmingham

The political organization of sexual identity in Birmingham can be traced through at least three stages. The first stage, mostly in the 1970s, transformed sexual identity from a social to a political identity through the founding of incipient organizations. This was followed by the second stage, a period of political consolidation coinciding with the first years of HIV disease. The third stage of institutionalization by means of strong, community-based service organizations characterizes Birmingham's lesbian and gay community today.

The first organizations in Birmingham based on sexual identity were not political but a religious and a social group: the Birmingham chapter of Dignity, an organization of gay and lesbian Roman Catholics, and a "secret" male organization called the Mystic Krewe of Apollo. Both represent enduring themes in the social organization of sexual identity in Alabama and in the Deep South generally.

The Dignity chapter was an early forum not just for the Catholic minority in Birmingham but also for others with strong religious, though non-Catholic, backgrounds. Besides being a center of racial conflict for nearly its entire history, Birmingham was also a center of anti-Catholic bias, especially in the 1920s.[15] Whether Catholics felt as shut out of the city's white political power structure as Jews did is an open question. But the city's Catholic population—gay or not—was certainly aware of the burdens of prejudice. It is not surprising, therefore, that a group of Catholic lesbians and gay men was one of the first identity-centered organizations in Birmingham's gay community. Even though the Dignity affiliate lasted only a few years, the contacts made then later helped establish other organizations, and the religious affiliation hinted at what became a major component of the social organization of sexual identity in Birmingham.[16]

The Mystic Krewe of Apollo, a social grouping of gay men, is Birmingham's version of the Krewes of New Orleans, whose primary ritual is to stage events and parades during Mardi Gras. Similar gay "Krewes" outside New Orleans can be found in Atlanta; Shreveport, Louisiana; Jackson, Mississippi; and other cities of the South. Birmingham's Mystic Krewe of Apollo is all male and maintains strict neutrality in local political matters, but for nearly twenty years its annual ball has been the largest social event identified with Birmingham's gay community. Although its leadership has been hard hit by HIV disease, it continues to be an important social organization for gay men.

An Early Attempt at a "Unified Front"

The first strictly political organizations for gay and lesbian identity in Birmingham were formed in the mid-1970s. A small local chapter of the Society for Individual Rights (SIR), a San Francisco–based group that was predominantly male and drew much of its membership from bar culture, opened in Birmingham. SIR was both political and social, urging individual rights in public settings and resisting harassment of patrons in gay bars and entertainment centers.[17]

More important than Birmingham's SIR chapter was a homegrown political group entitled Lambda, Inc., which was explicitly political and became the hub of a network of social and political organizations in the Birmingham area. When founded, Lambda was "the only publicly recognized gay organization in the State."[18] The vision of its founders was that it would be a political face for lesbians and gay men and also a community coordinating organization of sexual identity.

Lambda, Inc., was incorporated in June 1977 as a nonprofit organization and was reincorporated in 1983 as a tax-exempt educational organization after its tax-exempt status was challenged by the Internal Revenue Service. Although this reincorporation prevented Lambda from supporting political candidates, its social and educational functions were directed toward political ends in a broader sense. As in other cities, but even more so given the history of Birmingham, Lambda's initial leadership was influenced by the civil rights movement and the social consciousness politics of the late 1960s. Its leaders had been children during the years of Bull Connor, and many of its early activists were women "who grew up and 'out' in the women's movement."[19] The Birmingham chapter of NOW, the National Organization for Women, also was supportive of lesbian concerns.

Over the last two decades, Lambda's financial position and primary purpose have changed many times. Its most constructive period was between 1978 and 1988, when it played the role of community center, published the only reliable source of information for the region's lesbian and gay residents, and began representing the gay community to City Hall.

Lambda had problems with class sensibilities and finances, however. Its first organizers were not from the city's professional classes but largely from

Birmingham's blue-collar tradition. In a city with a strong industrial history, this was not surprising and actually was in keeping with some of the initial organizing by working-class and blue-collar activists in Los Angeles, San Francisco, and Chicago. But in Birmingham, where the declining industrial sector was losing its influence in local politics, this blue-collar profile was a problem. Consequently, well into the 1980s, lesbian and gay professionals associated with the emerging postindustrial, largely medical economy kept their distance from local gay and lesbian organizing, as did the older gay men and lesbians of the postwar generation who might have contributed funds to new organizations but rarely would be active in them. These class tensions characteristic of Birmingham's gay politics have remained a source of tension into the 1990s.[20]

Lambda as an Organizational Incubator

Lambda's financial problems prevented it from becoming a single unified front for Birmingham's lesbians and gay men. Its problems partly stemmed from its class roots and partly reflected its founders' managerial skills. The political energy of Lambda's activists did not translate easily into organizational capacity, especially in regard to legal and significant financial issues, and the active role of many lesbians reinforced the class strain and tested the sexism of gay men. The growing importance of Lambda as an institution from the 1970s to the 1980s broadened the organization's identity base but also placed higher demands on its organizational integration, a burden that its leaders could not always carry.

In retrospect, Lambda's most important contribution may have been as an incubator and catalyst for newer organizational forms as more people translated their lesbian and gay identity into political and social action in Birmingham. As Lambda's financial problems threatened to bring down with it several other organizations, some spun off, and others were established independent of Lambda, as follows:

1. The *Alabama Forum* was begun as a newsletter of Lambda but became financially self-sufficient by the mid-1980s. After it became independent from Lambda, it became a statewide journal for Alabama's lesbians and gay men. By the mid-1990s, the *Forum* had a printing run of more than 3,500 and was distributed around the state in local bars, bookstores, and other community venues as well as through subscription.[21]

2. After its reincorporation in 1983, because its new status prevented it from

giving direct financial support to political campaigns, Lambda created a political action committee, PRO-PAC. PRO-PAC raised money from the lesbian and gay community for municipal and state political candidates. But
PRO-PAC stopped operating in the late 1980s when its fund-raising efforts
became stymied.

3. Another spinoff from Lambda was Birmingham's Pride Committee, which
sponsored the annual June pride events—"A Day in the Park" in Rushton Park
and later a parade downtown. A softball league, maybe the community organization with the highest number of participants, and other recreational organizations were also formed through Lambda's sponsorship. More important, perhaps, are two other institutions that evolved were Lambda's
assistance: the Metropolitan Community Church, which initially met in
space provided by Lambda, and the Birmingham AIDS Outreach, the city's
main HIV preventive and service organization. Both were established with the
assistance and support of Lambda.

Organizing Birmingham's Gay Voters

Besides a political organization of identity through Lambda, the Community Center, the *Alabama Forum*, and other community-based organizations,
gay men and lesbians also wanted to be able to influence city politics. Again,
bars and clubs served as a base for political organization and fund-raising.

The 1975 mayoral victory of David Vann was the culmination of a
decade-long struggle led by a biracial liberal coalition rooted in the civil
rights battles of 1960s.[22] For more than ten years, Vann was a business and
governmental notable who pressed for government reform and social integration. In the 1960s, he was a leader of the Young Men's Business Association—a moderate group rooted in the white professional class and a frequent arena for interracial discussion and government reform—and a key
figure in managing the Jefferson County Council for Economic Opportunity, the War on Poverty community board of Birmingham.[23] Even
though Vann's 1975 mayoral election victory was supported by black voters, he still carried most of the white voters. Vann was the first mayor to
make several significant appointments of blacks to policy positions in the
city government.[24]

The situation was different in 1979, however. Between 1975 and 1979,
several factors in Birmingham contributed to a dramatic change in the citywide electoral vote. One factor was the annexation of surrounding lands
and communities by the growing city. Also important were the higher voter

registration rates of blacks and the higher voter participation rates of both blacks and whites, each a continuing effect of the 1965 Voting Rights Act.[25]

But the key event influencing the 1979 mayoral election had nothing to do with demographics: it was the shooting that year of a black woman by a Birmingham police officer. The city eventually admitted that it had made a mistake, but the police officer was exonerated on the grounds that he had followed department procedures in wielding deadly force. Mayor Vann accepted the department's explanation, but the result was a crisis of confidence among his crucial black supporters. In fact, the uproar among the city's black elite led to a challenge to Vann by Richard Arrington, a friend of his, a fellow council member, and a professor of zoology at Miles College.

Arrington represented the new generation of African American leaders in Birmingham who had grown impatient with the slower approaches of A. G. Gaston and A. Shores, legendary figures in African American politics in Birmingham from the 1940s on (and key actors in settling the disruptions of 1963). In seeking white, liberal, and sympathetic voters, Arrington tapped the south side's newly visible and largely white gay community. He campaigned in at least one gay bar in 1979—two years after George Moscone had done so in San Francisco and two years before mayoral candidates did so in New York City—and responded to a questionnaire issued by Lambda asking all the candidates their views on issues of interest to lesbians and gay men. Lambda's board members generally viewed Arrington's responses as positive.[26]

It is difficult to determine whether Arrington's outreach paid off, but it seems to have done so. In those areas of the south side most frequently identified with gay voters, Vann ran strong in the first round of a nonpartisan election. But in the second round, after Vann had been defeated (largely because his black supporters had switched to Arrington), Vann chose to endorse Arrington as the candidate of Birmingham's reformulated biracial liberal coalition. Arrington won over lawyer and businessman Frank Parsons, but by only 2.2 percent. The turnout was a record in Birmingham—68 percent of registered voters. Parsons obtained few black votes, and Arrington received about 10 percent of his total votes from white precincts (called *boxes*). Arrington's strongest white support came from defeated mayor David Vann's old strongholds—the Southside and Forest Park polling places.

Arrington carried none of those white liberal polling sites but did best in the boxes identified with lesbian and gay voters. He was reelected in

1983 by a larger margin. In three of the four 1983 precincts identified with concentrations of gay voters, the percentage of support for Arrington increased over his 1979 vote. Although the City Council president, John Katopodis, was able to form an anti-Arrington coalition from the city's white middle class, it was no longer enough to threaten Arrington's base.[27] The demographics of the city proper had changed with the increasing black percentage of the population, surrounded by a belt of largely— though not exclusively—white suburban towns.[28] The liberal coalition in Birmingham was now centered on African American voters, along with an important component of white voters. A disproportionate share of the white voters were gay and lesbian, a pattern we have already seen with harder data in New York and Los Angeles. Indeed, Arrington's former executive assistant ranked the core of Arrington's support as (1) African Americans, (2) white liberals, and (3) gays and lesbians.[29]

The importance of these white and gay voters was not just in the margin of victory it gave the African American community in a mayoral coalition but also in an expanded claim to legitimate governance that the biracial coalition provided. Even though Arrington never received more than 12 percent of the white vote, the participation of liberal whites and gay men and lesbians of all races in the coalition has had both political and governmental implications. In fact, by 1987, the coalition headed by Arrington persuaded the Jefferson County Citizens Coalition to support his allies— and thus dominate the City Council—by defeating all those council candidates the coalition had not endorsed.[30] This well-organized coalition became known by his detractors as the "Arrington Machine."

Stage 2: The Political Consolidation of Sexual Identity

Birmingham's service economy added a new dimension to the race and class divisions in the lesbian and gay community. Whereas once the class division was between closeted gay men of some means and working-class lesbians and gay men (and defined even further by race), the new class entering the political dynamics of identity politics was neither rich nor poor but middle class, reflecting the skills of Birmingham's new economy. This new economy also included many more professional women whose personal lives were quite different from those of the working-class lesbians of an earlier period.

Although class tension was evident before the mid-1980s, it was the HIV crisis that severely tested and eventually transformed the blue-collar, working-class overtones of many of Birmingham's early gay and lesbian organizations. HIV mobilized the restrained professional gay men (and many lesbians) into political activism as they saw the death toll among their own friends begin to mount. By bringing many professional gay men and lesbians into both older and new political organizations, the HIV crisis broke down some of the social barriers between blue-collar and professional lesbians and gay men. But the disease also made the social disparities in the gay community more apparent because of its organizational and political response.

HIV/AIDS in Alabama

The first identified case of AIDS in Alabama was the result of an apparent early exposure to the HIV-1 virus by a hemophiliac.[31] By 1985, only thirty-four cases of AIDS had been identified in Alabama, about 40 percent of which were men who reported having had sexual contact with other men. The impact of AIDS on Birmingham was not great at first. In fact, into the 1990s, public health researchers still classified it as a "low-incidence city."[32]

The general perception was that Alabama had escaped the initial full force of the HIV epidemic but would be susceptible to a second wave of infection if preventive measures were not taken. Dr. W. James Alexander, the Jefferson County epidemiologist dealing with HIV, concluded in 1985 that "most persons with AIDS in Alabama are members of the same high risk groups which are represented in the national figures" and recommended a strong safe-sex campaign. He also cautioned against taking too much consolation in the relatively stable rates of infection at county screening centers, since those who showed up were self-selecting. Because Birmingham was the state's largest city, most of the suspected vectors of exposure were there.

The earliest attempt in Birmingham's gay community to mobilize political support of preventive services and social service for persons with AIDS (PWAs) was through Lambda. Several Lambda members had attended a 1983 meeting of the Southeastern Conference for Lesbians and Gay Men (SECLGM) in Chapel Hill, North Carolina. They came away convinced that AIDS would be an important item on the gay community's agenda. Seeking to raise the profile of Birmingham's gay and lesbian community, they brought the ninth annual meeting of SECLGM to Birmingham in 1984.[33] This was the first significant regional meeting of lesbian and gay leaders to be held in the city so closely identified with civil rights. Acknowledging that lesbian and gay voters had supported him, Mayor Arrington gave the welcoming remarks at the meeting, but his appearance touched off a storm of protest in the letters column of the local newspapers.

More important, though, this was the place at which southern gay activists began to confront the HIV crisis systematically. After the Birmingham meeting, the Southeastern Conference immediately became active in AIDS policymaking, and the following year, it held a special conference in New Orleans on AIDS policy and prevention. Both meetings were a catalyst for the formation of the first HIV preventive and service organization in Birmingham (and thus Alabama). The need was becoming apparent to Lambda board members, as more and more inquiries regarding AIDS/HIV were being called into their Gay Information Line.

Birmingham AIDS Outreach

In May 1985, Birmingham AIDS Outreach, Inc. (BAO), was formed. The Jefferson County Health Department was supportive of a community-based educational group aimed at controlling the epidemic. During the hepatitis B epidemic among sexually active gay men in the late 1970s, a good working relationship had been established among gay men, gay bars, and county public health officials.[34]

In its first organizational phase, BAO maintained its gay identity and depended on the lesbian and gay community almost exclusively for financial and volunteer support. Its second stage was characterized by conflict both with the state and internally. Because it was less strongly linked to identity and became increasingly professionalized, the tension between the activists and the professionals became apparent. Finally, when BAO was fully institutionalized and receiving federal and local funds as well as grants and donations from many sectors of Birmingham society, some activists started regarding the organization as part of the problem of dealing with HIV.

BAO's first office was attached to a gay club whose owner had donated the space. Its policy prescriptions for dealing with HIV (then referred to as HTLV-III) were similar to those already developed in larger cities hit earlier and harder by the epidemic. Three issues highlighted the gay identity of

BAO in its early years: AIDS preventive materials, HIV-antibody testing, and contact tracing.

The importance of education for risk reduction was emphasized in BAO's earliest newsletters. The materials took a positive attitude toward same-sex sexual contact, combined with a message containing specific warnings to engage in behaviors that would reduce the risk of HIV transmission. In response to moralistic approaches to the spread of HIV, a BAO policy statement concluded that "it is not likely that large numbers of gay or bisexual men, who are not monogamous, are going to consider celibacy a realistically viable solution" to the epidemic.[35] As in other cities, BAO produced explicit information about safer sexual practices, which was distributed in bars and at community events.

Although explicit educational materials could be kept within the bounds of identity spaces, and thus its political consequences controlled, no position taken by BAO in this early period was as controversial as that on HIV-antibody testing. In July 1983, the Alabama State Committee of Public Health designated AIDS as a reportable disease, thereby placing it in the same category as tuberculosis, syphilis, and several other communicable diseases.[36] Although researchers in late 1983 assumed that a nonairborne virus was the likely agent, the specific virus had not yet been identified. Then in March 1984, the U.S. Department of Health and Human Services announced that scientists found what they believed was the cause of AIDS. With the identification of a specific virus whose presence was at least one prerequisite to developing immunodeficiency disease, an antibody assay could be developed, tested, and distributed, probably by late 1984.

The commercial availability of a test for the presence of HTLV-III (LAV) was seen by many gay organizations as a threat—especially since there were (at that time) few legal protections for infected men and women. The fear was greatest in the South. Sodomy laws there were widespread and still occasionally enforced (and, in fact, were upheld by the U.S. Supreme Court in *Bowers v. Hardwick*, a Georgia case, in 1986). Thus a positive test for antibodies meant not only the possibility of sickness but also the potential loss of job and insurance. Besides, many felt there was little to gain in being tested for HIV, since there was no known effective therapy at that time. The actual utility of the test for any reason other than surveillance was thus viewed as dubious.

Birmingham AIDS Outreach formally expressed its concern in July 1985. Its board adopted the joint national statement at a conference of community-based AIDS preventive organizations from around the country and held under the sponsorship of the National Gay and Lesbian Task Force. Nearly all these organizations were gay financed and organized.

Two sometimes confusing messages were being communicated to gay men: The first was cooperation, that gay men should assume that their potential sex partners were HIV positive and thus they should practice safer sex. Second, in the absence of legal protections and the increased unwillingness of life and medical insurers to deal with groups at high risk for HIV exposure, they should be tested only anonymously. The general recommendation to gay men therefore was that they should not be tested, but if they were, to make sure that the testing would be anonymous.

But by the spring of 1986, members of the Alabama state legislature were beginning to get involved in what until then was essentially a policy area that BAO, representing the gay community, and the Jefferson County Department of Health, as the local arm of public health, dominated. Working through the AIDS Task Force, BAO and the Jefferson County Public Health Department lobbied heavily, and with some success, against a bill introduced in Montgomery that would have required mandatory testing for HTLV-III as part of the application process for a marriage license. The successful cooperation between the two shows how they could dominate a policy area that until then was of little interest to state officials. This was a minor victory, though, given what was soon to come.

The situation changed in 1986. By then, the first wave of public reaction to AIDS had passed. The publicity surrounding Rock Hudson's death in 1985 had receded, but there remained a number of incidents that inflamed public alarm.[37] This was also the end of the period when gay-identified social service organizations had sole "proprietorship" of AIDS, HIV, and all the supportive programs and institutions created to deal with the crisis.

The expanding scale of the epidemic and the gradual shift in the caseload toward African-Americans, women, and children—as well as the rapid increase in the cost of treating the disease—created new political problems for gay-identified HIV organizations. Unlike the Jefferson County Department of Health, the Alabama Department of Public Health was more forceful and punitive in its approach to HIV.

BAO became more resistant to state intervention when Alabama state health officials tried to incorporate the BAO into the state's new, activist, agenda. The first statewide coordinating meeting to launch a new HIV education prevention program was held in late July 1986 in Montgomery. It was a planning meeting on how to spend new federal preventive funding being distributed by the Centers of Disease Control (CDC). Despite more than two years of cooperation between the Jefferson County Department of Health and Birmingham AIDS Outreach, there was no indication that state health officials were aware of this. After the meeting, the Alabama Department of Health began to discuss awarding grants to BAO and the AIDS Task Force for printing preventive materials, as the CDC's grant process required including community-based organizations (read gay and minority) in funding plans in order to tap their social and sexual networks for preventive efforts. This required, therefore, the inclusion of Birmingham AIDS Outreach, a gay-identified community group, in administering the state's HIV-prevention funds.

In April 1987, in response to pressure from state legislators, the Alabama Department of Public Health began to circulate a plan for a new program of antibody testing and contact tracing. Contact tracing was seen as a way to forestall the spread of HIV by notifying individuals who had been exposed to persons who had tested positive. Proponents of the plan hoped that by informing the previous sexual partners of newly diagnosed individuals, they would choose to be tested. But contact tracing would inevitably threaten the confidentiality of those already testing positive, and thus the plan might have the opposite effect—driving members of the higher-risk groups away from being tested and finding out their HIV status. Besides, there still were no protections in employment or insurance in Alabama for HIV-positive employees, and an effective therapy had still not been found.

The board of directors of BAO "voted unanimously its opposition to the Proposal for Expansion of AIDS antibody testing and Contact Notification," knowing it risked losing federal and state preventive funds.[38] In July 1987, the state legislature authorized a portion of the mandatory testing and contact-tracing program to be implemented by the Alabama Department of Health. Technically, the law expanded the requirement of local doctors and public health officials to report an HIV-seropositive diagnosis, not just a full diagnosis of AIDS.

Although this legislation increased the legal protections of confidentiality, many public health experts and HIV activists were skeptical, as the legislation contained none of the explicit employment or insurance protections on which the activists had insisted. When the Alabama Department of Public Health promulgated regulations pursuant to the legislature's action, it did so on the basis of the commissioner's emergency powers, so as to bypass the standard regulatory process that in Alabama includes public hearings.

The day after the new rules were promulgated by the state's health department, leaders of Birmingham AIDS Outreach suggested that those who feared they might have been exposed to HIV be tested in another state. For Birminghamians, this generally meant Atlanta.

The recommendation that people take the antibody test outside the state threatened the working relationship between the Jefferson County Department of Health and BAO. Dr. W. James Alexander, normally an ally of BAO, indicated that if indeed BAO referred people out of state, the Jefferson County Health Department might not be able to renew its contract with BAO.[39] Leaders of BAO stated that they were misquoted, but whether or not that was so, the BAO policy was changed to allow telephone volunteers to tell callers about all options available, including in-state and out-of-state anonymous testing. The following year, and in opposition to the recommendations of many public health scientists, the Alabama legislature began to consider whether confidential HIV testing was prudent, given the insistence of some legislators that the state begin contact tracing.

The expansion of the HIV policy arena to include the state health department and especially the state legislature undermined the working relationship of BAO, the Birmingham city government, and the Jefferson County Health Department. This in turn led to a series of conflicts on policy toward HIV—which had been a prerogative of Birmingham's gay community and local public health officials—that would now be challenged by an unsympathetic state legislature.

As AIDS became a more important public policy problem, moving beyond gay men and Jefferson County, there also were changes in BAO's lesbian and gay base that created their own tensions. Birmingham's economic change had created new core industries—health care, research, and medical services and finance and professional services. With them came a new professional middle class that extended into the lesbian and gay community, and their professional skills gave them a measure of independence. Although these professionals were uncomfortable associating directly with open gay rights demonstrations or publicly identifying themselves at the workplace as lesbian or gay, they were available to gay-identified organizations for fund-raising and volunteer work, especially for HIV causes.

But expanding BAO's base into a newer professional class created other problems. One was a conflict among "privacy," identity, and fund-raising.

Birmingham AIDS Outreach's first revenues came from small fund-raising events confined to the gay community. By 1987, however, BAO began receiving a little money from the county, as well as federal funds administered by the state and county. Between 1987 and 1989, BAO's budget increased dramatically. To meet this greater need, BAO held a series of large public fund-raising events in 1989, which often included Mayor Arrington's wife on the sponsoring list. But despite becoming involved both professionally and in fund-raising events for BAO, many middle-class lesbians and gay men still wished to maintain a public distance from a "gay" identity.

The influence of funding from outside the gay community was another issue. Although the support from local fund-raisers and pro-bono services provided by individual gay men and lesbians continued, the great growth in funds came primarily from the state and county governments, corporate donations, service contracts, and large-scale fund-raisers. These new funds consequently brought about the professionalization of BAO as an organization and circumscribed its policymaking, a pattern seen in most of the other cities in which HIV community–based organizations have been studied. The end result of this stage in the history of Birmingham AIDS Outreach was a more professional organization, but one that began to distance itself from exclusively identifying with Birmingham's blue-collar lesbians and gay activists. It expanded its resource base into government and corporate donations, and its service base to African Americans.

Birmingham's "lesbian-gay community" now had two faces. The first group was made up of middle-class professionals who were more attuned to the needs of large bureaucracies and their desire for managerial accountability, financial discipline, and legal prudence. The second group, rooted in the early gay rights movements and more fully politicized by the HIV crisis, pushed for an even more aggressive strategy for lesbian and gay identity. It was this core of older activists and new, younger, post–Stonewall-generation activists who then turned to Birmingham's ACT-UP chapter and the more assertive parade committee that moved June's annual pride events to downtown.

Stage 3: Political Institutionalization via Social Service Organizations

In the early 1990s, the theme that dominated Birmingham's lesbian and gay community was institutionalization. By the mid-1980s, the initial period of almost spontaneous but fragmented organizing had passed. The election of Richard Arrington as mayor and the mounting costs (and psychological burden) of HIV propelled the political organization of sexual identity onto its next stage of development. The attitude of Arrington's administration toward Birmingham's gay community was formed during the benign administration of David Vann. Vann, but especially Arrington, moved the municipal government away from its history of harassing gay bars and bar patrons and the arbitrarily enforcing the city's regulatory policy. But while Vann and Arrington were moving Birmingham's municipal government toward tolerance, the focus of hostile policy debate toward gay men and lesbians switched to the Alabama state legislature, itself spurred on by Christian and other social conservatives to resist reframing the discourse on sexual politics.

After 1987, Birmingham's lesbian and gay community spent much of its energy establishing more formal organizations, setting down financial roots, and creating bureaucratic routines. Indeed, the service organizations have become the forefront of sexual identity politics in Birmingham, being part of a social matrix of identity-focused organizations in a city whose economy is dominated by its services sector.

Gay Identity, Religious Traditions, and the Metropolitan Community Church

One striking characteristic of Birmingham's gay community has been the incorporation of religion into the political organization of sexual identity. From its very first years, when Dignity was meeting in the mid-1970s, to the tremendous growth experienced by the Metropolitan Community Church in Birmingham in the 1990s, there has always been a religious dimension to gay and lesbian identity in Birmingham.

The Ministries of the Metropolitan Community Church (MCC) are a American denomination that ministers primarily to lesbians and gay men. Founded in California in 1968, the church describes itself as being in the mainstream of Christianity. It is heavily influenced by the evangelical traditions of the South, of the American Baptists, and of mainline Protestant churches. The merging of these various religious traditions is most apparent in MCC rituals which include communion, some homilies with Episcopalian, Presbyterian, and Methodist themes, as well as other rituals drawn from Southern Baptist and Evangelical traditions.

The church's first members were lesbians and gay men who had moved to California from the South and Midwest.[40] Although the first MCC congregation—called the Mother Church—is located in the greater Los Angeles area, most members of the Metropolitan Community Churches live outside the major coastal centers of gay life. The Birmingham congregation, for example, is one of thirty congregations in the Gulf-Atlantic region of Metropolitan Community Churches. There also are MCC congregations in other Alabama cities, Mobile, Huntsville, and Montgomery among them.

In its first ten years, Birmingham's Covenant MCC was a small congregation of fewer than fifty. But by 1995, the congregation had an overall membership of six hundred, with a regular church attendance of three hundred each Sunday at two services.[41] The gender and racial makeup of the Covenant congregation better reflects the overall demographics of Birmingham than do many of the political organizations of the gay community. Women and African Americans are prominent. Children are included in the Sunday morning services, and a coffee and community meetings are held afterward. Several weekday evening services also are offered, and Covenant publishes a monthly newsletter mailed to congregation members.

Although some of the long-term members of the Metropolitan Community Church were also present at the early meetings of Dignity in the mid-1970s and many were active in other organizations in the lesbian and gay community, most of the MCC congregation cannot be considered political activists. And yet as an institution with substantial assets and meeting space, MCC's presence has become an important institution in the social network of sexual identity on which lesbian and gay political activity rests.

Whether or not Birmingham is unique in regard to the importance of religion to gay people, religion is clearly important to the general political culture of Alabama and the Deep South. The MCC's success has also affected other denominations. The local Unitarian churches and one Methodist congregation declared themselves "reconciliation" congregations, open to and even seeking out lesbians and gay men to return to their religious traditions. Although we do not know whether the growth and strength of the Metropolitan Community Church in Birmingham is confined to the southern gay identity, the MCC as a service organization supported by lesbians and gay men in Birmingham clearly is important.

Birmingham AIDS Outreach as a Social Service Corporation

In the summer of 1995, thirteen years after a hemophiliac became Birmingham's first confirmed case of what some then still called GRID (Gay Related Immunodeficiency), 983 men, women, and children had developed full-blown AIDS.[42] More than half these patients were gay men. By the 1990s, HIV/AIDS was no longer new to Birmingham. Preventive, social service, and research aspects of the fight against immunodeficiency disease had become institutionalized.

The impact of this institutionalization on Birmingham AIDS Outreach was twofold. First, BAO was no longer alone in the battle against the disease. As the caseload of HIV disease changed and federal and state funds increased, the gay-identified, community-based nature of Birmingham Aids Outreach was eclipsed by the professional needs of preventive services and support care. By 1994, no fewer than five organizations were providing some sort of services to people with HIV. In addition, the city has four clinics associated with hospital and service organizations that provide services to HIV/AIDS patients. BAO now is only one of several organizations dealing with the HIV epidemic: the AIDS Task Force of Alabama, which provides support groups and preventive services for African American men and women with HIV; the United Way, which offers assistance to infants and others; and ASAP, which was created by a board member of AIDS in Minorities and serves women with HIV. In addition, the local United Way created its own internal coordinating committee—Birmingham Response to AIDS. The United Way, Birmingham Response to AIDS, and the National Community AIDS Partnership all are dominated by health care professionals and staff of the traditional not-for-profit and service organizations.

As the number of HIV service organizations and providers has increased, Birmingham AIDS Outreach itself has changed. It has continued to professionalize its service delivery and internal management while diversifying its service base. One result is that BAO is losing the edge of its identity association with the gay community. By the 1990s, the battles in Birmingham over testing and the degree of explicitness in HIV preventive materials had largely been fought. Funding for services was now the critical component of organizational growth. Indeed, BAO's funding no longer comes primarily from small contributions by the lesbian and gay community but now comes from government grants, large annual fund-raising events, and corporate donations. For example, at one time, funds for preventive and social service support supplied by the Ryan White Care Act were appropriated to BAO, and additional funds for preventive services from the Centers for Disease Control were also granted to BAO In addition, BAO applied for and received a competitive grant from the federal AmeriCorps program.

The principal change in BAO's financial condition was the purchase of two buildings. In one case, BAO entered a joint venture with the Children's Aid Society (United Way) to buy a permanent foster care home for babies with HIV. BAO bought the house for the program, and the Children's Aid Society secured state funding for its operations and administered the project. By 1992, financing was secure enough for the home to become an independent organization.[43]

On a larger scale, Birmingham AIDS Outreach purchased a building to house its offices and serve as the center for service delivery. The building had previously been an office and research center on the east side of downtown. Known as the Swann Building, named after a scientist and entrepreneur from Birmingham's industrial past, it had been abandoned and was for sale for $250,000. In 1991, an election year, the city offered to sell the building to BAO. The title was held by the firefighters' union, which wanted a more updated building in another location. The city of Birmingham assisted in the financing of the purchase. BAO did not incur a debt, although the building needed repairs. Supporters for the transfer to BAO included Council Member David Herring, who represented south Birmingham. Herring had one stipulation for BAO to ensure his informal support, that BAO include in its new space an office for Lambda and its Gay/Lesbian Information phone line. Ironically, almost ten years after its founding, BAO was now in a political and resource position to help Lambda, which had been the catalyst for its formation in 1986.

Gay and Lesbian Alliance of Alabama (GALAA)

As the Metropolitan Community Church and Birmingham AIDS Outreach reached the institutionalization stage in the political organization of sexual identity in Birmingham, a new organization, the Gay and Lesbian Alliance of Alabama, took a more aggressive position on lesbian and gay issues statewide. Even though GALAA is formally housed in Montgomery, the core of its organizational and financial support comes from north Alabama, from Birmingham and Tuscaloosa, the home of the main campus of the University of Alabama. Formed in January 1993 at a meeting in Montgomery and formally incorporated in October 1994, GALAA is the first statewide organization representing lesbian and gay issues to the Alabama state legislature.[44] GALAA has two main functions, as a lobby group and political organization focused on state government and as an educational unit attempting to alter the image of gay men and lesbians in Alabama.

GALAA's first two lobbying efforts were to have gender and sexual orientation included in Alabama's hate crimes bill and to modify Alabama's sexual misconduct law, which had been recodified in a sodomy law but not further reformed. GALAA hired a part-time lobbyist to pursue these goals, but the struggle to change either state law was difficult.

GALAA's greatest concern in late 1995 was the continued assertive positions taken by social conservatives in the state legislature. In 1992, after the administration of Auburn University recognized a gay and lesbian student group, the Alabama legislature passed a measure "prohibit[ing] any college or university from spending public funds or using facilities, directly or indirectly, to sanction, recognize or support any group that promotes a lifestyle or actions prohibited by the sodomy and sexual misconduct laws." It further restricted "any group from permitting or encouraging its members or others to engage in or provide materials on how to engage in the lifestyle or actions" prohibited by the state's sodomy or sexual misconduct laws. No criminal penalty was attached to violating the statute, however.

The law was challenged by a student group from the University of South Alabama and was ruled unconstitutional on First Amendment grounds by the federal district court in January of 1996. The state intended to appeal the decision. Despite the law's unresolved legal status, however, members of the state legislature and Governor Fob James used it to question the appropriateness of a conference scheduled to be held at the University of Alabama in February. The Fifth Gay/Lesbian Youth Conference, cosponsored by SECLGM and the university's Gay, Lesbian and Bisexual Alliance, was to be held on the Tuscaloosa campus. All the previous SECLGM youth conferences had been held at Vanderbilt University in Nashville. State Attorney General Jeff Sessions went further than James; he requested a stay of the decision and threatened to obtain a court order to cancel the conference. In the weeks immediately before the conference, both the federal district court and the 11th Circuit Court of Appeals refused the request for stays by the state. And in an April 1997 decision issued by a three-judge federal appeals court the matter was resolved in favor of the students.[45]

One result of the legal challenge was that the state's sodomy and sexual misconduct laws again became the center of attention. The controversy over the youth conference also led the state attorney general to pursue legislation that would force the University of Alabama Law School to allow military recruiters on campus to interview prospective lawyers. The law school had resisted on-campus military recruiters because of the military's continuing ban on openly gay men and lesbians serving in the military.[46]

GALAA also began an extensive education and networking operation, including publishing a "gay Yellow Pages" similar to those in other cities in which gay/lesbian-owned or -friendly businesses, professional groups, and other associations are listed and advertise. Preparation of video materials for educational purposes and a youth service initiative also are long-term goals of GALAA. GALAA's leaders see the organization's educational role as central to a legislative agenda. Whereas GALAA remains a new and largely defensive political organization, its relative stability gives northern Alabama's—indeed, all of Alabama's lesbians and gay men—a face in the halls of the state legislature.

Organizing Identity for Political Intent

Birmingham is only one case of organizing sexual identity for political intent, and our analysis of Birmingham is by no means exhaustive. Although we cannot offer any conclusions from this single case, we can draw insights for other analyses.

Local Political Organizations as an Organizational Field

We earlier defined the unit of analysis for organizational study as the *field of local organizations*, not the individual organizations that make it up.[47] We thus would expect each organization to serve a function in the overall mobilization of identity for political intent. Thus at the same time, the field can both reflect diversity in the identity and emphasize the unifying characteristics of that identity.

When analyzing the individual social and political associations organized around sexual identity in Birmingham, we should not look at them as competitors (though sometimes they certainly are) but as compatible vehicles for organizing political identity. The influences of gender, race, and class are evident in the numbers of organizations, but more important, they are evident also in the development of these organizations. How each has resolved (or not resolved) the inherent tensions associated with diversity in the identity contributes to the organization's characteristics and also its relative effectiveness in the larger political world.

The first question is what the purpose of so many organizations is. The answer might be that the greater the web of local organizations is, the more varied the meanings expressed through the field will be. Thus in an identity grouping, the more varied the identity's diversity is, the more organizations will be formed. But the main demarcation in Birmingham's lesbian- and gay-identified organizations was not by race or gender but by the types of the organizations and their function or, maybe, mission. That is, some are primarily *political*, some are primarily *service*, and some are primarily *social*.

The first category, strictly political organizations, showed a process of evolution and structuration over time, with enhanced definition and functional diversity. From SIR, through Lambda, Inc., and PRO-PAC, to GALAA, we can see the increase in political ambition and the political base. A long-term trend toward greater organizational sophistication becomes apparent. (Any hesitation here derives from the newness of GALAA and its yet undefined organizational complexity.)

But none of these political organizations displays the same degree of formal structuration as the second category does, the primary service organizations of Birmingham's gay community: the Metropolitan Community Church and Birmingham AIDS Outreach. Both derive their models not from organizations initially defined by sexual identity but from other, more professional models: for BAO, from community-based health agencies, and for MCC, from the Protestant tradition of congregation-based religious organizations. But for all their structure, they both more accurately reflect the racial and gender makeup of Birmingham's general population than do the strictly political organizations.

The third dimension, social organizations, exhibits the least amount of structuration and displays a high degree of what Harrison White might call *ambage*, or "a slackness in social ties."[48] These social organizations are, however, better defined in regard to race, gender, and other binding affinities. Birmingham's gay community contains many informal and yet stable gender and racially defined associations. Other binding affinities expand the pool of such associations defined by religion, cultural interest, sport, ethnic group, social event, or sexual practice. These loose social organizations do not express the full degree of structuration that some sociologists might hold to be the minimum to be recognized as formal organizations. Never-

theless, this informal organization of sexual identity challenges the distinction between organization and organizational environment that some theorists posit; instead, they form an ambiguous organizational demarcation.
But each of these groups contributes to the social organization of gay and
lesbian life, though perhaps subsumed under the political organization of
sexual identity in Birmingham.

Last are the links between the different organizations in the field. The
meaning of any one organization in the field is derived from the meaning
of the field as a whole. Organizations in the field are not independent of the
others. Rather, the field contains multiple organizations in networks of
identity ties that feed into and out from the field. Thus the social organization of identity is through patterns of ties, both weak and strong, in a field,
a matrix, of different organizations.

This network raises the question of coordination among the organizational bodies. In Birmingham at least, there was a period in which the formal interorganizational coordination was between the board members and
activists in Lambda, Inc. But when Lambda faltered and the organizations
diversified, especially with the formalization of BAO and MCC, the *formal*
arena of coordination disappeared. Nevertheless, some informal coordination can still be observed in the social, political, and professional ties operating in different networks overlapping in different configurations.

Ultimately, it is the identity itself that provides the interorganizational
coordination. Affirming and emphasizing the commonality in the class of
persons collectively identifying as lesbian and gay (or as any identity, for
that matter) lowers the threshold of experienced interaction necessary to
create stable networks of ties.[49] Despite Lambda's ups and downs over time,
it is clear that most of the major organizations that have come to institu-
tionalize gay identity in Birmingham were established through some cat-
alytic event in Lambda. And although there clearly have been cross pressures within the identity as different diversities are expressed, multiple
memberships are generally a reinforcing aspect of lesbian and gay identity—not a divisive one, as the economic model of intergroup competition
might suggest.

The Unbounded Locality

Just as no local organization can be fully understood outside the context of
the organizational field, no local field can be understood outside the context

of its own larger organizational environment. All the organizations we studied are assumed to be open, and although focused locally and named by the geography in which they operated, they also are positioned in horizontal and vertical networks of organizational and political communication. Lateral lines of communication are local, and vertical and horizontal lines are national. The Covenant Metropolitan Community Church, for example, began as an annex to Atlanta's MCC Church. BAO exists in networks of gay and lesbian identity and professional health care services. PRO-PAC was a copy of similar political action committees in other cities, and GALAA is a copy of other state lobbying organizations. Even the Mystic Krewe of Apollo exists in a social network of southern celebratory tradition.

These influences of both vertical and horizontal communications are a constant concern for leaders of lesbian- and gay-identified organizations. City by city, they are arrayed as a field, and yet they also are weakly tied through networks of similar organizations in other cities. Thus, just as the local organizational field is not simply a local "ecology of games" but operates in a broader framework, the unbounded nature of the locality permits communications with and influence by outside identity–linked organizations. I do not wish to go so far as to say that the field determines the nature of individual organizations, but the field certainly does influence them. Nor do I wish to say that the national organization determines the nature of local ones, but it certainly does influence them. What is so interesting is that from city to city, local communities of sexual identity replicate institutions formed in other cities.

Process, Weak Ties, and Legitimation

In reviewing the primacy of process over decisional outcome, some organizational theorists have seen process as creating bonding rituals for politics.[50] It is well known that the rituals of formal organizations invest meaning in and authority over the outcome of decision processes. Constitutions prescribe procedures through which legitimate law is created. In both a positive and an ethical law framework, extraconstitutional or unconstitutional law is not legitimate. But beyond the normative integrity of their decisions, processes also define members, give identity to institutions, and create links to and through associations.

The organizations we studied were not so formal as governmental institutions, and yet they still require legitimacy in that they present themselves to both community members and state officials as a link between an identity-defined "community" and formal governance. We have observed that the social organization of sexual identity has an explicit, nonlocal dimension in that the signs, symbols, languages, and history through which the identity is defined stretch beyond local boundaries. It is the very diversity of the field that offers a degree of legitimation. As a bloc of organizations, variations in the identity can find expression. Each organization is relieved of major conflicts over definition because of the diversity of the organizational field, since new organizations can be formed easily from latent patterns of social organization. But each organization must find a niche that justifies its existence.

We can apply a insight from March and Olsen, that identity-centered associations not organized primarily for political intent can, even through weak ties, create a latticework of social and political communications that may ultimately be used for political effect. Thus, a softball league, having no other intention than collectively engaging in an avocation, institutes weak ties among members and between each team. If this is true of athletic groups, it certainly is true for larger associations such as the Metropolitan Community Church.[51] Mark Granovetter speculated that extended networks of weak ties are more effective for community mobilization than are several sets of strong ties—close cliques of family and friends—since the former extend the channels of information gathering through a broad array of domains of trust.[52] "Queer" political theorists have held that accepting the name *gay*, *lesbian*, or *bisexual*, or simply *queer* is itself a political act of everyday life. We can say the same here, but from a more organizational perspective: All social ties mediated through identity associations have the potential to be mobilized for political effect. In identity politics, the personal, the social, and the political all are linked.

Relation to the Local State

Traditionally, community organizations have been viewed by social scientists using one of three models: (1) a protest model, (2) a functional model, and (3) a franchise model. All three have a stated or implied relationship to the local state.

At first, we might expect to analyze local lesbian and gay community organizations as essentially protest groups, engaged in symbolic action typically using protest as a political resource. Certainly in the early years of BAO and in the later years of ACT-UP, this is true. But in many other cases, it is not. Much of the social movement literature interprets associations organized around sexual identity as constantly conflicting with the local state. Although this holds for many such groups, especially political organizations, it does not hold for all activities. Both functionalist and what we can call government franchise dimensions can be found in some local lesbian and gay community organizations.

In a functionalist analysis, one that initially grew out of the reassessment of the urban machine by functionalist historians, the recognition of community groups by the local state was caused not just by the need for information but also by a prudent assessment of potential legitimacy problems. The decline of urban political parties opened the door to more Taylorist approaches to public management of the reform movement. The negative aspect of a scientific approach to public administration was that it broke the link between governing regimes and local communities. One response to this decoupling was increased pressure for community control of the delivery of urban services. In most cases, "community control" was a euphemism for linking distanced minorities to the local governing regime, but the impersonal delivery of services affected all urban groups.

The great body of literature on local organizations—especially on the Community Action Program—looks at how community organizing led to the mobilization of new interests in the local policy process. If these programs were successful, however, another problem of legitimation arose. Viewed in reverse, the incorporation of community groups and organizations through community control, especially in the areas of human and community development, presented government with a different issue of problematized legitimacy: By franchising the state to local community organizations, the definition of bureaucratic rule making became imprecise. The governance issue was not the incorporation of alienated groups, however, but the very ability of government to impose its decisions on localities. By incorporating new groups and franchising the state's authority, the legitimacy crisis of local governance was moved from alienated minorities to the groups from whom resources were being extracted and who expected effective governance.

Thus the classic trade-off of the machine era—jobs for votes—was transformed and mediated by the local states across new lines of tension. The

urban middle class and downtown corporate taxpayers were forced to provide services that would diffuse delegitimation processes among minorities
and the poor. In turn, the recipients of these social services would support
the local government, either directly through their votes or indirectly
through their passive support of the resource extraction and allocation
process. Many of the problems currently facing local urban managers relate
to the trade-off of one set of legitimation claims aimed at the middle class
for another directed to the poor.

For lesbian and gay community organizations, these issues are much the
same. In addition to organizing for protests, they also petition the government for intervention and protection against discrimination, for specific
services, and, in some cases, even for a voice in neighborhood development
policies, in which sexual identity and neighborhood locale overlap. These
organizations serve a functional role in linking a portion of a local constituency to government in a way that was not available in the past. But
when many lesbian- and gay-identified community groups received funding from city government, their leadership became embroiled in political
tensions driven by conflicting criteria of identity and profession. Still, for
the government, these groups offer a link between an alienated identity and
the local state.

The ambivalence of the franchised state—with community groups seeking to achieve their purposes through an allocation of government authority and with the government seeking to implement its priorities by taking
advantage of the emerging social networks—is most clearly seen in the formulation and implementation of HIV policy in Birmingham. Since the rise
of HIV, the government has needed information about and access to social
(and sexual) networks that lesbian and gay associations can provide. These
once small and voluntary associations are now instruments of city and state
health and welfare policy. The transformation of BAO in Birmingham is a
pattern reflected in most of the other urban areas where HIV has been a serious problem. As task forces are funded by various government sources,
their accompanying regulations—ranging from accounting procedures to
restrictions on the explicitness of preventive materials—change the organizational patterns of the franchise agency. These once identity-focused and
loose organizations have come to resemble institutionally the government
agencies from which they receive funding. One result is that they have become an arena of conflict and mediation between their initial identity-defined constituency and government policy.

Conclusion

Attempts to organize around a specific identity is different from organizing around a specific economic or fiscal gain. The very affinities that bind an identity group are more cultural (or in the case of sexual identity, social and psychological) and not as distinct, and their goals cannot be measured as easily as can economic, regulatory or fiscal gain. Although identity groups sometimes behave like interest groups in seeking specific goals, the nature and purpose of identity organizations are not exhausted by such discrete and identifiable gains.

Because so many identity organizations are purely social, their political potential might easily be dismissed. How could a lesbian (or gay) softball league or a weakly structured pattern of women's house parties or even a semistructured network of purely sexual contacts have a political effect? We can conclude, nevertheless, that in affirming a problematized identity, the character of such social organizing ultimately has a political effect, since working together in an organizational field, these groupings provide the background for a political identity that eventually can be mobilized for po-litical gain (or defense). We should emphasize here a point made previous-ly: All social ties mediated through identity associations can be mobilized for political effect.

One quite visible aspect of Birmingham's lesbian and gay political setting is that it is disproportionately white, at least when compared with the de-mographic makeup of the city of Birmingham. None of the organizations we examined excluded African Americans as a policy; in fact, most reached out to Birmingham's black lesbians and gay men as an important goal. But at a statewide meeting of GALAA held in Birmingham, not a single African American was present. The visible participation of blacks and other minori-ties in the primary service organizations—the Metropolitan Community Church, Birmingham AIDS Outreach, even the softball league—and their absence in political organizations is telling. On second thought, the fact that Birmingham's African American lesbians and gay men identify politically primarily as black, not gay, is not surprising, especially in a city so closely identified with its racial history. The affirmation of a same-sex sexual identi-ty need not inevitably lead to its primacy in political matters.

CHAPTER 8

◫

Protected and Unprotected Minorities in the Districting of
New York's City Council

In the twenty years separating the Stonewall riots of 1969 and the municipal elections of 1989, political activists in New York's lesbian and gay community made no fewer then five attempts, each of escalating intensity, to
obtain representation on the City Council. The most important efforts
were in the West Village and Chelsea areas of Manhattan. In all, gay candidates raised and spent more than half a million dollars to secure a seat on
the council, but without success. Their failure is usually attributed to two
factors: (1) the advantages of incumbency (Council Member Carol Greitzer
had held office since 1970) and (2) the large size of council districts in New
York City. The absence of gay representation was especially pointed during
the decade-long attempt to have a gay rights bill pass and, more important,
while the death toll from the HIV epidemic among gay men was mounting
throughout the 1980s. The decade ended without a lesbian or gay presence
on the New York City Council.

In 1990, however, the movement for empowerment by other minorities
in New York created an unexpected opportunity for New York's gay community. Federal courts ordered the city to reorganize its central governing
institutions to comply with the "one-person, one-vote" criterion of *Baker v.*
Carr. A successful legal challenge filed on behalf of racial minorities and the
residents of Brooklyn prompted the change. The U.S. Supreme Court
eventually refused to hear the city's appeals.

The prospect of a new council with additional seats was seen as an opportunity for change. Nevertheless, with the possibility of a new council
came a challenge. Since the principal criterion of this reorganization was
enhanced representation as envisioned by the Voting Rights Act of 1965,
those minorities that federal law explicitly protected would influence the
districting process, or challenge the process' outcome if the statutory and

court-established criteria were not met. Numerical minorities without such federal protection would be placed at a disadvantage in the districting process, not simply by their raw numbers, but also by the aspirations of other numerical minorities protected by the law. Lesbians and gay men were an unprotected class under federal law.

New York's gay activists, having no legal standing in voting rights enforcement as a group, responded politically by mobilizing political resources, creating unusual coalitions, and marshaling new data sources to influence the districting process.[1] One result was the deliberate attempt to carve out a legislative district that was termed *gay winnable*, that is, a council district that took into account the residential and voting patterns of gay men and lesbians. New York's districting experience has important implications not only for the study of identity politics but also for representation theory in general as the proliferation of new political identities challenges the continued utility of single-member, plurality-elected legislative districts in the United States.

Representation in the Era of Strong Municipal Executives

During the past fifty years, institutional reform in New York City had been organized around two central themes. The first is to achieve sufficient organizational capacity to direct New York's huge public sector. The second is to integrate new political identities.[2] Both themes have conflicting claims for legitimacy that are linked to two contending political coalitions in the city. The first coalition is made up of the business class and the middle class seeking stability, economic growth, and a refined version of older reform movement principles. The second coalition is composed of all the new groups seeking influence on city policy, equity in the allocation of city services, and a role in urban governance.

In the face of its expanding revenue base and dramatically increased service responsibility, the command and control structures of the New York's public sector showed signs of wear and even an occasional crisis. The greatest of these crises was in 1975, when New York's inability to meet its debt obligations demonstrated the inadequacy of the city's organizational capacity. The political-managerial response to the rapid expansion (and eventual crisis) in New York's public sector was to increase hierarchical controls, install new management technologies, and establish several new oversight bodies at the fiscal, financial, and managerial levels of city government. The increased managerial capacity introduced in response to the 1975 crisis followed other and similar reforms undertaken in the 1960s, all of which were aimed at reinforcing the executive powers of the mayor. These reforms did lead to more predictable fiscal and service patterns and altered the terms of political discourse in the public sector. That was part of their success. Together, and for the first time, they established the mayor of New York as the legal and managerial operating officer overseeing a newly integrated local public sector.

Nevertheless, the attempts at managerial reform in the 1960s and 1970s exacerbated New York's other major problem. Concentrating power in the mayoralty for managerial effectiveness undermined previously useful links between the city's central managerial structures and the emerging political forms that sought influence and accountability in the city's policy process. Politically, as in other cities, the adoption of modern and hierarchical managerial structures undermined the alternative power centers based in party organizations, profession-dominated service delivery bureaucracies, and the municipal employees' unions that had challenged executive authority in the past. And they also closed to communities many channels of political accountability and influence that in the past had successfully diffused legitimation problems.

Seeking Links Between Communities and the Local State

The tension associated with the legitimation challenge to New York City's governance was not managerial but, essentially, political. The aspirations of a growing minority population exposed new questions about the legitimacy of the New York's governance. African Americans increased their demands for a civilian review of the police department. Indeed, the entire community empowerment movement of the 1960s and early 1970s was unmistakable evidence that reform solutions to the city's managerial problems would not necessarily solve the city's increasing legitimacy problems—in fact, managerial reform might make them worse.

Attempts at relegitimation did include changing the distribution of political resources in the city (through the Community Action Program and other initiatives of the 1960s), but the main response to demands for inclusionary politics was to alter or create new community institutions.[3] Mayors

John Lindsay and Abraham Beame established a system of community school boards and community planning boards in New York. But the same bureaucratic forces that had resisted central executive direction also dashed hopes for community influence over service delivery.

Maybe the best case of resistance to community empowerment by bureaucrats was in public education. The once positive aspects of professional dominance and "normalization" of instructional criteria and curricular materials, administered by a central authority, were now incapable of responding to changes in the social and political environment.[4] Frustrated with the continuing failure to influence the central Board of Education, parents began demanding community control of the schools. The end compromise was a halfhearted attempt at reform, in which the state legislature established a decentralized school governance structure that enhanced neither community accountability nor managerial efficiency. Community activists largely saw the compromise as a defeat and, ever since, have vigorously protected what little prerogative community school boards do have.

Despite these and other attempts at community control, a sense of community linkage to City Hall never developed. Academic assessments of the community school boards and service boards began to conclude that even though the activists had achieved some of their goals for decentralization, they had not obtained the full agenda of empowerment.[5] The massive recentralization of managerial and financial control over the city's public sector associated with the 1975 financial crisis also returned the political resources of the service delivery bureaucracies to the central political and managerial authorities of the city's government.[6] The move to link communities with the city's administrative structure through institutional decentralization was limited by the need to centralize budgeting, financial planning, and economic development policy in the post-fiscal-crisis period. Even the City Council had become frustrated by not being able to represent communities.

The New Focus on Institutions: *Andrews v. Koch* and *Morris v. Board of Estimate of the City of New York*

By the late 1970s, the institutional front line in community empowerment switched from community boards and school boards to the apportionment of the city's legislative system. With the community power movement largely contained, legal challenges to the formal manner of representation in the city's central institutions were now one of several new strategies that advocates were using for community empowerment in New York.

A shift in arenas accompanied the shift in strategies. Attempts at decentralization relied on administrative and policy changes at the behest of the mayor, the City Council, and the New York state legislature. In these arenas, blacks, Latinos, and neighborhood movements had little influence, at least when compared with countervailing interests. As 1975 showed, shifting priorities and new political coalitions could alter these administrative policies. The federal courts might offer a more fruitful arena.

One post-1975 legal challenge to the representativeness of New York's government was against a remnant of the City Council's attempt at apportionment that allowed the five constituent counties of New York (its boroughs) to maintain an institutional identity of their own in the council.[7] Under the system remaining after the changes of the late 1940s, the City Council was apportioned partly according to population and partly according to geography. Each borough had an additional two seats on the council that it elected countywide. The result was a mixed system of single-member districts and multiple-member districts at the county level. In *Andrews v. Koch*,[8] the U.S. Court of Appeals for the Second Circuit held that these two additional countywide seats violated the equal protection clause of the Fourteenth Amendment. The city corporation counsel's attempt to appeal the decision was futile, and the court ordered a realignment of these ten seats in the council.

It was through *Morris v. The Board of Estimate*[9] that the challengers to the representativeness of the city's central institutions scored a direct hit. Advocates challenged the Board of Estimate on the grounds that it, too, tended to favor the smaller boroughs over the larger ones. The board as a five-county governing body had been reestablished in the 1898 incorporation of the greater city of New York and was given even broader powers in the 1901 city charter. As had its predecessor—the Board of Estimate and Appropriations established in the 1850s—the Board of Estimate could be seen as a regional government; therefore, it had a central role in franchising, capital construction, contracting, and planning. Still, by 1985, the city had far outgrown the five counties as an economic and social region, and the board had lost much of its higher planning function.[10] Although one purpose of the Board of Estimate was to give Brooklyn a sense of separate political identity, the result was the creation of a board on which each borough, no matter what its population, had equal representation.

At the time that *Morris* was filed, the board consisted of eight members. The five borough presidents had one vote apiece, and the three city-elected officials (the mayor, the City Council president, and the comptroller) had two votes each. The intended calculus was that the city-elected officials together would balance the presumably parochial votes of the boroughs if each group voted together. In reality, however, the overlap of party organization and the ability of the mayor to offer facilities and budgetary preference to individual boroughs allowed the mayor to dominate the board. Whatever the effects in practice, the board's apportionment was legally problematic. Indeed, the point on which the case turned was not on the one person–one vote principle—if the board were a legislature, it surely would need to change—but on whether the board was an executive or a legislative body. Given the board's role in the capital budget process, land-use planning, and franchising, the courts held that it was predominantly a legislative body and so would have to change.

The U.S. Supreme Court refused to overturn the rulings of the lower federal courts in the *Morris* case. New York City would have to alter its institutional makeup to achieve a more balanced system of representation. In the previous twenty years, if community and minority representatives had sought influence over public policy by establishing administrative mechanisms and community channels to influence city agencies, the city was now required by both *Andrews* and *Morris* to find a more fundamental approach to reform in representation.

The Ravitch Commission, the Schwartz Commission, and the Districting Commission

To prepare for a possible restructuring of New York City's central governing institutions, Mayor Edward Koch appointed the Charter Revision Commission under the authority of the older city charter. Richard Ravitch, an attorney who had led the effort to recapitalize the city's subway and commuter rail systems in the early 1980s, chaired the commission. The so-called Ravitch Commission completed its work before appeals of the *Morris* decision had run their course. The commission's members thus were left with recommending only managerial changes aimed at stemming the kind of corruption that had resulted in the Parking Violations Bureau scandal of 1985/86. Although the Ravitch Commission was prepared to take on the more difficult issues of restructuring the city's government, Koch was concerned that Ravitch was interested in running for mayor against him (and indeed, Ravitch announced his candidacy in 1989). As the mayor and potential reelection candidate, Koch needed someone he could trust. So he allowed the Ravitch Commission to expire and appointed a new charter commission (most of the staff members were the same).

F. A. O. (Fritz) Schwarz Jr., a former corporation counsel under Koch and a member of the toy-retailing family, was appointed chair of the new group. The most important challenge facing the Schwarz Commission was dealing with the problem created by the *Morris* case. Was the Board of Estimate to be retained? If so, could it be changed to meet the criteria of *Baker* and *Reynolds*? Could other, acceptable forms of apportionment and voting be established while retaining their executive nature? Would weighted voting solve the problem? Could proportionate representation based on a borough plan remedy the imbalance of the one-vote-per-borough rules of the challenged board? The Schwarz Commission authorized the research on and presentation of many alternative mechanisms of representation, such as both proportional voting and cumulative voting. In the end, the commission decided that the legal vulnerability of a reformulated Board of Estimate would be too great, and so it recommended that the board be eliminated.

If the Board of Estimate was to be eliminated, two subsequent issues were pressing. The first was how the board's executive and legislative responsibilities would be divided between the remaining institutions (the mayoralty and the City Council). The second was how the new council should be apportioned. Without the 134-year-old Board of Estimate[11] to serve as a check on executive power in New York, the new council would now be the primary institutional check on the mayor. It also would be the main arena for voicing and aggregating community and identity interests.

Again, the themes of managerial capacity and representativeness defined the debate. The Board of Estimate had important influence over the capital budget and land use in New York. It was the final authorizer of contracts by the city and was the real base of power for the borough presidents. Until 1960, the board was also the residual holder of title on the city's assets. Since the board was a stabilizing force at the core of the New York's governing institutions, providing an additional arena to manage the sharp political divisions between mayoralty and council that had occurred in many other cities, its elimination was feared by many concerned with issues of governance. Change would also affect the balance between the city government as a whole and the communities and neighborhoods of New York.

The Schwarz Commission saw the new council as the principal check on the powers of the mayor and as the central institution for community and group representation in the city. To achieve these goals, the commission created the new council with three criteria in mind: (1) to enhance its role in budgeting, land use, and capital planning; (2) to professionalize the council staff so that it could compete with the enormous powers of the mayoralty housed in the Office of Management and Budget and the Office of Operations; and (3) to expand the number of seats on the council and thus indirectly to increase the diversity of representation.

After some internal debate and research, the Schwarz Charter Commission voted to increase the size of the council from thirty-five to fifty-one seats. This reduced the mean population of the council districts from about 240,000 people to about 145,000. The commission also decided on and codified the criteria to be used in the districting process. These criteria were a combination of federal statutory and case law, state law, and city tradition.

To accomplish the districting of the new council, the Schwarz Commission created yet another commission—the New York City Districting Commission—whose sole mission was to serve as an independent, nonpartisan (or, better, multipartisan) body to draw the districts' lines. By creating an independent districting commission, the task of creating council lines was again moved outside the council itself and placed it under a body to be appointed jointly by the mayor and the council leadership. With the criteria set for creating district lines, the smaller size of the anticipated council districts, and the evolution in federal case law since the passage of the Voting Rights Act of 1965, minorities had a real chance to redress their underrepresentation in New York City's central institutions.

Protecting the Voting Power of Unprotected Minorities

For the lesbian and gay community, the opportunity presented by the creation of a new City Council was an uneven one. Although no openly gay person had been elected to any city legislative body, neither the federal Voting Rights Act nor the Schwarz Commission explicitly required any special effort by government to redress or even respond to lesbian and gay claims of underrepresentation.

Three fundamental problems were facing the lesbian and gay activists of New York as the districting of the new council began: First, New York's gay community had no real experience with districting, whereas in San Francisco, an entire generation of politically sophisticated operatives understood districting and actively supported single-member, rather than multiple-member, at-large districts (which eventually led to Harvey Milk's election in a district carved out of the Castro/Eureka Valley area of the city).[12] Even in Rochester, New York, less formal discussions between the gay community and the Democratic organization had influenced some districting issues.[13]

Second, even though concentrations of gay men and lesbians living in definable neighborhoods could be identified, none of these neighborhoods was as large as a City Council district, nor were all "gay" neighborhoods contiguous, not even in Manhattan. In fact, there are so many gay and lesbian residential clusters in New York City that they can be further identified by other characteristics, including class (the Upper East Side of Manhattan), race (the large black population in Prospect Heights, Brooklyn), ethnic grouping (the large gay Latino area in Jackson Heights, Queens), gender (the large female population in Boerum Hill, Brooklyn), and other dimensions besides sexual orientation.

Finally, and most important, because of the underrepresentation of minorities on the City Council, New York was covered under the 1965 Voting Rights Act. Any change in legislative lines was subject to a preimplementation review by the U.S. Justice Department. Political operatives in the city thus expected that the districting process would be driven by fear of litigation on behalf of one or all the classes protected by the Voting Rights Act.

The Classes Protected by the 1965 Voting Rights Act

The Voting Rights Act of 1965, along with its 1982 renewal and amendment, is a landmark effort to redress the accumulated effects of segregation, discrimination, and the unequal distribution of political resources among America's politically disadvantaged. Although its direct intent is to protect the voting rights of minority classes, as defined by race and eventually by language, its ultimate purpose is to redress the excesses of majoritarianism.

Before the 1990s, enforcement of the 1965 act as it pertains to redistricting can be divided into two periods. The first began as the courts focused on the use of multiple-member districts and their effect on the dilution of minorities' voting power. The federal courts had become skeptical of "at-large" and "multimember" districts in which black voting blocs could be diluted through districting procedures. What might have been objectively

equal voting procedures were increasingly being tested against election outcomes. In addition, the courts expanded the domain of the Voting Rights
Act as it pertained to districting to include state, county, and municipal districts and school boards.

Although during the 1970s, the Supreme Court generally supported vigorous enforcement of the act, this changed with the 1982 decision of *City
of Mobile v. Bolden*.[14] When the Court turned its attention to evidence of
intent, the justices' differences of opinion began to emerge. The confusion
during the renewal of the law in 1982 had been enough to return the Congress to section 2, amend it, and announce the congressional goal of maximizing the minority voter effect. The Senate staff generated a report that
led to an explicit statement emphasizing *effect* rather than *intent* as the guid-
ing principle in enforcing the act. The general criteria codified in the act
and outlined in the Senate report became known as the *Gingles* criteria (as
a result of the Supreme Court's recognition in *Thornburg v. Gingles* of the
Senate report as being "authoritative").[15] These criteria were a preference
for single-member districts characterized by (1) a geographic compactness
of minority voters, (2) minority voting cohesion, and (3) a polarization in
voting behavior when measured by race.[16] In the immediate post-*Gingles*
environment, the courts were much more open to the admissibility of arith-
metic and regression techniques, particularly in establishing patterns of
"racial bloc voting," a more significant indicator in finding for plaintiffs
claiming discrimination.[17]

The Voting Rights Act also required the preclearance of any change in
election laws or election districts that might dilute the voter effect of protected minorities in "covered jurisdictions." Jurisdictions were determined
to be "covered" under the Voting Rights Act if 5 percent of their residents
were minorities and their voter turnout had been below 50 percent in the
previous presidential election. In addition, any district that required litera-
cy tests or other specific forms of testing or that contained language minorities but did not produce ballots in the language of that minority met
the act's criteria. Three of New York's five counties—the Bronx, Brooklyn,
and Manhattan—met these criteria.

The use of single-member districts, along with the *Gingles* tests, did raise
the possibility of "minority packing" in districts.[18] To prevent minority dilution, the courts had accepted supermajority black or Latino districts of 65
percent or more minorities. The temptation for minority incumbents to
"pack" their districts even above this 65 percent "floor" was especially

strong, even though it might come at the cost of diluting the minority's voting power in an adjacent district or of not creating two winnable but not assured minority districts.

For "secondary" minority groups, competing with primary minorities, the single-member, minority-dominated district created according to the *Gingles* criteria was especially threatening. Although some observers regarded this strategy as only a temporary remedy to redress past voting imbalances, for others, reliance on single-member districts had become the main strategy for dealing with minority voter empowerment.[19] But in cities with very diverse populations, this strategy threatened to dilute the voting power of secondary minorities. Other strategies and voting procedures that might help these numerical minorities (such as cumulative voting or proportional voting) were initially suspect to the courts, especially in those jurisdictions where previous districting and voting policies had left continuing patterns of discrimination. In most of the United States, this was a problem for Latino communities and African American communities living in close proximity. In New York City, San Francisco, Seattle, and Los Angeles, the Asian American community joined, as language groups, this competition among protected minorities. Lani Guinier wrote about the danger of relying solely on the *Gingles*-tested, single-member district for minority empowerment:

> Districting provides no clear theoretical justifications for resolving—and may instead exacerbate—conflict between the interests of competing minority groups. For example, subdistricting may smack of a "political land grab" in which each minority group has a legitimate but potentially unfulfilled claim to representation.
>
> Indeed, in sorting through the competing claims, the districting process may carve up politically viable communities of interest.

Guinier also cited a critical case in districting that originated in New York City, *United Jewish Organizations of Williamsburgh v. Carey*, in which competing ambitions for minority representation—in Brooklyn, between African Americans and Hasidic Jews—had clashed, to the disadvantage of the unprotected class (in this case, Orthodox/Hasidic Jews.[20] There was insufficient proof that the districting process was influenced by religious prejudice). Similarly, because of the close proximity of clusters of gay voters and minority voters in center cities, empowering classes of protected minorities might come at the expense of carving up "gay enclaves" and thus diluting their voting influence.

Mobilizing an Unprotected Minority

Attempts at establishing a legal basis for protecting the interests of geographic clusters of lesbian and gay voters had actually begun under the Schwarz Commission. A self-selected group representing the interests of lesbian and gay New Yorkers had met with the commission's legal and research staff.[21] They were mainly interested that the city's Human Rights Code in the old city charter be incorporated into the new draft charter. The group asked for the codification of the existing ban against discrimination in housing, employment in the private sector, and government that lesbians and gay men—along with all the other categories protected by the city government—had enjoyed. Such a codification would include gay rights in the basic document of city law.

A second issue was the inclusion of "sexual orientation" in the guarantee of equal protection required of contractors seeking business with the city of New York. The requirement, first termed Executive Order 50 and issued by Mayor Edward Koch in 1983, was challenged by some religiously affiliated social service agencies.[22] It was finally implemented by the Board of Estimate as the formal entity of city government that enters into contracts with outside providers, and the gay representatives wanted comparable language codified in the new charter.

A third request was met with caution. It was for an explicit reference to "gay and lesbian" or to sexual orientation in the portion of the charter draft outlining the criteria for creating the new City Council. Schwarz Commission staff members were hesitant, believing that three direct references to the gay community in the new charter might cause some conservative religious groups to oppose the entire charter. Since on balance, the lesbian and gay attorneys saw the new charter as positive for a whole range of issues, an acceptable solution was to give the new Districting Commission the power to define its own notion of community. Thus the word *other,* referring to other characteristics, was added to the section of the new city charter that defined those communities to be given special status. These new, city-protected communities were to have "established ties of common interest and association whether historical, racial, economic, ethnic, religious or other."[23] The staffs of both the Schwarz Commission and the Districting Commission understood the implied meaning of the word *other,* and the Districting Commission accepted this stipulation.[24]

A second attempt to influence the commission's work before its formation came through a demand that at least one of its seven members be lesbian or gay. It was not likely that the speaker, Peter Valone, and his office would voluntarily appoint an openly gay member, so pressure was put on the new mayor, David Dinkins. Even though more than 57 percent of self-identified gay and lesbian voters had supported Dinkins in the primary against Edward Koch and more than 68 percent in the general election against Rudolph Giuliani, the initial response from City Hall was not encouraging.[25] Still caught in the transition between administrations and more concerned with protecting African American voting power, Deputy Mayor Bill Lynch's office listened to the request and interviewed several openly gay candidates. But the inability of the gay leaders to unify behind one candidate, as well as the gay community's general lack of experience in the technical matters of districting, gave Lynch an excuse to duck out of the issue. There was, however, a commitment from Speaker Valone's office to hire openly gay staff. After appointments were made by Dinkins and City Council Speaker Peter Valone, Frank J. Macchiarola, a former school superintendent and professor of business law at Columbia University's Graduate School of Business, was appointed chair.

Identity and Representation in Spatial Terms

Some political scientists interested in economic analysis have examined the influences of extended randomness and party bias in legislative districting.[26] But the burden of commentary in political science looks to groupings as mediators of individual voting behavior. Group identity organized around an industrial class or budgetary alliances or ideology became an intermediate level in representation theory.

Except in the cases of political parties, which are sanctioned by the state in election law, and race, which is sponsored by the state in voting rights statutes and case law, the group basis of representation remains an informal one. But the intergroup dynamic does acquire a formal status through the boundaries around the geographic arenas of representational politics. By drawing legislative district lines, the state either recognizes a dominant political identity or identities in the bounded space or rejects its claims of a formal right to representation. To draw a single-member district around clusters of, say, Asian American residents is thus to recognize the identity's claim to compete as a state-recognized group, to organize its political interest through that identity, and to grant the group a foot up in its attempt to lead an electoral coalition in the bounded territory.

In a system of representation that formally rests on the relationship between geography and demography, the coupling of space and political identity presents a challenge to new groups and identities seeking to break into the state-sanctioned consortium of groups participating in the districting process. To enter the process, they must make their claim on the grounds of coherent identity, political legitimacy, and spatial dimensions—an odd combination, to be sure.

Without having the status of a protected class under federal law and having no further legal basis for entering the districting process than an accepted interpretation of the word *other*, New York's lesbian and gay activists needed to make two persuasive arguments. The first was to show that they indeed were a community in the sense of having a common identity and to demonstrate acceptable manifestations of that identity, including voting behavior. Second, they had to prove that their community had geographic compactness similar to that of other minority groups, so that it could benefit from a single-member district in the system of apportionment.[27] Left unstated was a third criterion: that advancing the interests of the gay community could not come at the cost of the interests of the protected minorities.

For much of 1990, New York City's many group identities, including that of the gay community, mobilized to advance or at least protect their interests in the new council-districting process. To show that the gay community had a common identity and social organization, an information campaign was launched, and presentations were made at as many public hearings in as many different locations around New York as possible. Information on anti-gay violence from the State Division on Human Rights and the Anti-Violence Project was submitted to the Districting Commission.[28]

More persuasive than anecdotes, however, were hard data. Using some techniques generated in San Francisco and some of its own, FAIRPAC (the name was later changed to the Empire State Pride Agenda), the principal political action committee in New York State for lesbian and gay residents, (1) mapped social service, business, and recreational centers serving the city's gay community; (2) analyzed voting patterns in support of openly gay candidates for the City Council and the state legislature in New York City; and (3) focused on fund-raising and direct sales mailing lists for the lesbian and gay community. The effort was coordinated with two of the city's major lesbian and gay political clubs—the Gay and Lesbian Independent Democrats in Manhattan and the Lambda Independent Democrats in Brooklyn. A fourth strategy, similar to studying ethnographic bounding, was pursued by the commission staff itself. All four strategies showed identifiable patterns of lesbian and gay residential clusters—the kind of clustering typically needed in court challenges of districting plans based on a dilution of minority voting power.

GAY AND LESBIAN VOTERS FOR LESBIAN AND GAY CANDIDATES

Voting for an openly lesbian or gay candidate is not an indication of being lesbian or gay. But a consistent pattern of not voting for a lesbian or gay man might be an indication of hostility toward gay men and lesbians. Three elections in Manhattan were important enough to provide some patterns of gay and antigay voting below Fifty-seventh Street: the David Rothenberg–Carol Greitzer Democratic primary for City Council in 1985; the Thomas Duane–Carol Greitzer primary in 1989; and the primary and general election data for Deborah Glick, member of the State Assembly from the Sixty-fourth District (southwest Manhattan) who ran openly as a lesbian.

The analyses of results from the 1985 and 1989 Democratic primaries for City Council showed that the strength of incumbent Carol Greitzer was in the eastern and northern part of the old council district as well as lower Fifth Avenue (just above Washington Square Park near New York University). The strength of Rothenberg and Duane—both gay—was in the western and southern parts of the district, anecdotally known as the heart of New York's gay community. Duane, who had been a tenant activist and district leader in Chelsea, had additional personal strength in the district's northwest portion. In the 1990 Democratic primary for the State Assembly in the Sixty-fourth District, Glick was nominated from a field of five. Again, the area of the Manhattan in which she was strongest was the western and southern parts of Greenwich Village. Her ties to both traditional Jewish liberal groups and women's groups gave her additional strength.

When the Glick results were overlapped with the Democratic primary results from 1985 and 1989 on a GIS system, the geographic concentration of progay voting was apparent. It stretched from the Hudson River on the west to Fifth Avenue on the east, and from Houston Street on the south to Twenty-third Street on the north. This area includes the West Village and Chelsea and parts of Murray Hill.

BREAKDOWN OF GAY AND LESBIAN ORGANIZATIONAL MEMBER LISTS

Advocates from Gay and Lesbian Independent Democrats in Manhattan and the Lambda Independent Democrats in Brooklyn added another technique to those developed by Castells and Murphy (see chapter 4) and by an increasing number of gay and lesbian political geographers. Again, the merged mailing lists of donors and participants in gay and lesbian social, political, health, and other organizations were the database.[29] Borough and city means were calculated, and the individual count from each zip code was compared with the city and county means. With an expected bias toward white men on the main mailing list, FAIRPAC/ESPA applied the same techniques to smaller and even more direct lists of women's organizations, a gay seniors' group, and some disco/club mailing lists that had a higher proportion of young gays and people of color. Again, these less-than-scientific methods tended to agree with the anecdotal information of lesbian and gay neighborhoods and also with the voting data in Manhattan.

The greatest concentrations of gay men and lesbians on the lists were in the Chelsea/West Village areas, the Upper West Side, the East Village, and Murray Hill in Manhattan; Jackson Heights and Forest Hills/Kew Gardens in Queens; St. George on Staten Island; and Park Slope/Boerum Hill/Brooklyn Heights and Prospect Heights in Brooklyn. In the absence of census data, the use of mailing lists offered the best measure of the relative compactness of gay and lesbian New Yorkers: the Bronx appeared to have the greatest dispersion of gay and lesbian population; Brooklyn had the most concentrated; and Manhattan had the most populous gay neighborhoods.

GAY AND LESBIAN ETHNOGRAPHY

As it had with the Asian community in south Manhattan and the Latino community on the Lower East Side (Loisaida), the commission staff interviewed persons familiar with the residential and commercial geography of New York's principal gay community—the West Village/Chelsea—and surveyed it. the Political symbols and signs, history, taverns and entertainment centers, shops, and the like were identified to determine roughly the core and bounds of the gay community. Some shop owners and community leaders were interviewed, and lines of demarcation were identified. This technique was also used in areas with small "downtowns," that is, the commercial strips of New York's neighborhoods. These historical communities also were protected in the criteria of the new city charter, though at a much lower level than those classes protected by the Voting Rights Act.

The cumulative effect of these various techniques was to indicate the clusters of lesbian and gay populations. Chelsea/West Village was clearly the strongest community, followed by the Upper West Side of Manhattan. Greater Park Slope—stretching from Brooklyn Heights and Boerum Hill on the west to Prospect Heights on the east—was the largest community outside Manhattan. Jackson Heights in Queens was the next largest. These became the focus of attention for influencing the districting process.

The Need to Build Alliances

In 1989 there was no reliable estimate of the number of gay men and lesbians in New York City. In addition, given the relative dispersion of lesbian and gay voters, the leaders of FAIRPAC/ESPA quickly recognized the need for building alliances. The most important protected minorities for the alliance were Asian Americans, African Americans, and Latinos(as), especially the Dominicans in upper Manhattan. A pragmatic accommodation with organizational Democrats also was necessary.

ASIAN AMERICANS IN MANHATTAN

In Manhattan, the most important negotiations for the gay community were those with advocates for the Asian community. Representing a protected minority explicitly mentioned in the revised Voting Rights Act, leaders of the Asian community could pursue their group's interest on a firmer legal foundation than was available to advocates for the lesbian and gay community.

New York City's Asian community had greatly expanded. As the number of Italian Americans declined in what is still called Little Italy, traditional "Chinatown" spread both north and west. The Bowery on the east, Canal Street on the north, and Baxter on the south and west still defined the core commercial center of Chinatown. The Asian residential population was pushing across Center Street on the west and Canal Street on the north. Gay residential areas centered in the West Village were expanding also, out of the areas west of Seventh Avenue South toward Houston Street and east toward the East Village. These two neighborhood identities (Asian and gay) were slowly taking over the residential and cultural spaces left behind by older Italians as they died or moved out to the suburbs. Eventually, the communities would clash if they had not decided to cooperate.

The older streets of the Lower East Side became multiethnic Asian as the northern part of Chinatown moved as far north as Fourteenth Street, into what New Yorkers know as Alphabet City, or ABC-land. Bordering the north and eastern part of Chinatown are the traditional Lower East Side neighborhoods where Eastern European Jews once settled and where Latinos (and some African Americans) now live. They are close to (or overlap with) the new multiethnic Asian community. A large cluster of mid-dle-class whites (many Jewish) live in the Grant Street housing complex on the border of the two neighborhoods. In keeping with its historical role in New York, the Lower East Side is a center for new immigrants in Man-hattan. Three out of five residents in the area covered by the local Com-munity Service Board are minorities, many Latinos from Central and South America and non-Chinese Asians. According to the 1990 census, 32 percent of the residents were Latino, and 30.3 percent were Asian or Pacif-ic Islander.

This is also an area of Manhattan that is being "gentrified." In the midst of these neighborhoods is Tompkins Square Park, a focus of conflict be-tween the remnants of the older and bohemian Lower East Side of the 1960s and 1970s, and the newer forces of gentrification. The New York City police and homeless residents living in the park clashed for control of this small piece of urban space in 1988 and 1991.[30]

The (initially) cheap rents on the Lower East Side also attracted a new wave of younger gay and lesbian residents who were priced out of the hous-ing markets in the Village and Chelsea. In fact, zip code information about residents on gay and lesbian community mailing lists reveals that in the late 1980s, the East Village was the fastest-growing area of gay residents in Man-hattan. In New York's gay networks, the Lower East Side was known as a neighborhood with a "new wave" gay identity—younger, multicultural, and more prone to street action than established channels of political ac-cess. By the late 1980s, if ACT-UP and Queer Nation had become the or-ganizations at the cutting edges of the "queer" identity movement, then the first ACT-UP's meeting at Cooper Union on the edge of the East Village of-fers proof of the change in generations and maybe as well in the geograph-ic center of queer culture in New York.[31]

Although there were significant clusters of Asian voters in other areas of the city—Chinese, Korean, and Vietnamese Americans in Flushing; Chi-nese in Sunset Park and Flatbush, Brooklyn; Koreans in midtown Manhat-tan; South Asians in central Queens—only one place in the New York con-tained a residential cluster large enough to serve as a population core around which an Asian-identified council district could be drawn. That was lower Manhattan. Yet simple demographics indicated that there were not enough Asian American residents in greater Chinatown—already a misap-plied title even before the new waves of immigration of the 1980s—to cre-ate an Asian-dominant, single-member district.

Advocates in the Asian community devised two strategies. The first was for Chinatown to become the core of a council district that would also include the new housing centers created as part of the 1980s boom in lower Manhattan's real estate market.[32] These "new" neighborhoods included Soho, TriBeCa, Washington Market, Independence Plaza, Battery Park City, the South Street developments, and the array of residential lofts that had once been centers of light manufacturing. The other option was to join Chinatown in a council district with the Latino residents of the Lower East Side, creating what some called a "multicultural district."

The debate over geography really was over one identity. How did Asian Americans in lower Manhattan wish to be identified, and with whom? The 1990 census indicated that the Asian community itself was becoming less Chinese and more ethnically diverse. The growth rates of all Asian identities in lower Manhattan meant that the Asian community would eventually be large enough to dominate a district—but not in 1991. The census also indicated that most Asian residents were moving west (not north, as they had in the 1980s and as the advocates of a multiracial district assumed). Further complicating the issue were fissures in the dominant Chinese community, caused by class, the history of twentieth-century Chinese politics, the decade of immigration, and the experience of discrimination in the United States. Older Chinese, established in local commerce, were bound together by business organizations and a continued identification with the Kuomintang; these Chinese were haunted by memories of both the 1949 Chinese revolution and the cultural revolution of the 1960s. Set against this older view of politics were the younger Chinese and newer Asian immigrants who were less hostile to the Beijing government and open to an ideal of multiculturalism, gender equality, and the protection of marginal workers.[33] Not surprisingly, many of these activists had had their faith shaken by the 1989 events in Tiananmen Square.

The division in the Chinese community was largely reflected in the different positions on districting. The new professionals represented by Ken Chin, the one Asian on the Districting Commission, and the AAFE (Asian Americans for Equality) saw a Chinese-centered district aligned with the newer middle-class professionals in the financial district. Younger Chinese, along with advocates for workers in the "new sweatshops" and some community activists, supported the multicultural position—a district dominated by Latinos and Asians, with smaller representations of Jews, what was left of the Ukrainian community on the Lower East Side, and the younger gays and lesbians moving into the area. On behalf of the Asian American Legal Defense Fund, Margaret Fung argued in support of such a district on the grounds that the economic, language, and immigration problems faced by Asians were similar to those faced by Latinos. Thus a merged district would meet the needs of both communities.[34] Because one advocate of the Chinatown–Wall Street proposal lived south of Chinatown and had been expected to run for the City Council when the district lines were drawn, this proposal was dubbed a "candidate-focused" plan—drawn up for either an incumbent or a specific candidate from the Asian community.[35] As for those aligned with the older business association, in keeping with tradition, they did not involve themselves at all.

The greatest problem in a merged Latino and Asian district was that it did not meet one test of the *Gingles* criteria: the voting patterns of Latinos and Asian Americans did not match. Self-described Asians tended to vote more conservatively than Latinos. So if there was an objective appearance of common interest, the voting patterns did not bear it out.[36]

For the gay community, the decision of the Latinos and Asian Americans to merge was central. If a multicultural district was established—even though it would include some younger gay men and lesbians on the Lower East Side—the gay community would not be able to dominate its politics. Moreover, this multicultural district would force the creation of a Lower West Side district that would either dilute the gay vote throughout the financial district or result in a division at Fourteenth Street between the lesbian and gay voter clusters in Greenwich Village and Chelsea. The latter possibility was most feared by the ESPA and locally active gay leaders.

Advocates for the lesbian and gay position in Manhattan determined that the line to be drawn between an "Asian district" (eventually the First District) and a "gay district" (the Third District) was key. The Districting Commission staff indicated informally that it would review whatever the two communities agreed on. Such a discussion would have substance, however, only if the Asian community chose to ask for an Asian–Financial Center District and not a multicultural Lower East Side district. Gay activists from the Village were working with Margaret Chin, a young and liberal activist who identified with Chinatown but did not live in it. Even though Chin (no relation to Commission Member Ken Chin) was ideologically sympathetic to a multicultural district, she sided with the Asian-dominated lower Manhattan district. This partly was the result of her own sympathy for the gay community and partly because she lived near Wall Street and would be outside the Asian district if it were merged northward into the Lower East Side.[37] She had been working with supporters of Tom Duane, a district leader from Chelsea, who also intended to run for the City Council. It was in both their interests to cooperate in creating a negotiable line between a "gay" district and an "Asian" district.

After intense lobbying from both sides, Ken Chin took the side of an Asian–middle-class district that would include all of lower Manhattan but be centered in Chinatown. By allowing Chinatown to merge into one district with the increasingly residential Wall Street and Battery Park City areas, Chin identified Manhattan's Asian community with their aspirations rather than their problems. Advocates of the gay community and some members of the Asian community agreed on a proposal making Houston Street the north-south dividing line and Thompson Street[38] the east-west dividing line of two new council districts (see figure 8-1).[39] The commission accepted the proposal.

"GAY WINNABLE" DISTRICTS, "GAY VETO" DISTRICTS, AND A "GAY INFLUENCED" DISTRICT IN QUEENS

A second target of lesbian and gay activists was the area known as Jackson Heights, in Queens. A planned community built in the 1920s, its residents in the 1970s were largely middle-class apartment dwellers and small-home owners. As early as the 1920s, it also had a quiet gay presence.[40] Adjacent to it is Woodside, one of the last Irish-identified neighborhoods in New York City.[41] To the east is Corona, once Italian and now largely black and Latino, and to the north is Elmhurst, whose eastern portion is heavily black.

Apartment dwellers dominate most of central Jackson Heights. Since the 1970s, the area has acquired an outwardly Latino (especially Colombian) appearance, together with a large Asian population (many non-Chinese). There also is a strong presence of both Latino and Anglo lesbian and gay renters who support several bars and social organizations along the main commercial strip. Jackson Heights has the greatest concentration of gay and lesbian residents in Queens and the most important one outside Brooklyn and Manhattan. It also has the largest concentration of gay Latino(a) residents in New York City.[42] The second strongest lesbian and gay neighborhood in Queens is in Forest Hills/Kew Gardens, a slightly more upscale but still middle-class neighborhood of apartment dwellers along Queens Boulevard.

Despite the strong lesbian and gay presence in Jackson Heights and the adjacent Sunnyside, the gay vote was not large enough to dominate the

MANHATTAN

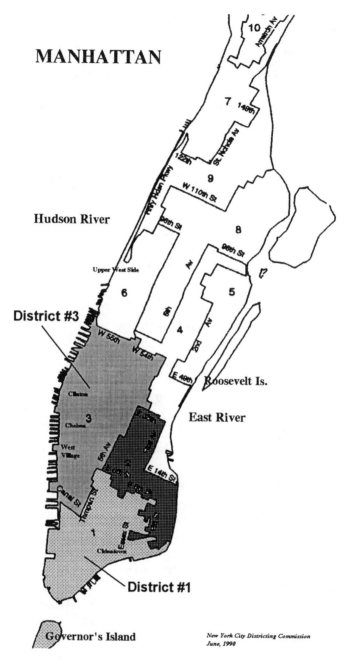

Hudson River

Upper West Side

District #3

Roosevelt Is.

East River

District #1

Governor's Island

New York City Districting Commission
June, 1990

FIGURE 8-1.
Manhattan.

area's politics. Yet the polyglot ethnic makeup of the area made it one of the few sections of Queens whose voting record became increasingly liberal as its demographics changed. In the past, this section of Queens had been carved up in a classic case of diluting minority votes (of all kinds), to the advantage of organizational Democrat and conservative interests. For several terms, the area was represented on the City Council by Joseph Lisa, a middle-of-the-road Democrat associated with the Queens Democratic machine of Donald Manes and Congressman Thomas Manton. Lisa had been appointed chair of the City Council Health Committee and became a particular target of AIDS activists. Not only did they disagree with Lisa on some key policy issues, but they were convinced that he knew too little about the public policy issues of HIV to be chair of the Council Health Committee during the epidemic.[43]

The strategy pursued by lesbian and gay groups in Queens was to create a "gay-influenced" district, where gay interests would have to be taken into account by candidates for the council seat but would not necessarily prevail. This could be compared with a "gay veto" district, in which the gay vote was so significant that if mobilized, it could ensure that no candidate opposing the gay community's interests could be elected. These two could be further distinguished from a "gay winnable" district, in which the gay and lesbian presence was so dominant that if mobilized, it would have a strong possibility of electing one of its own. (There can be no "safe" gay seat in New York—even in the West Village and Chelsea—if that means the presence of a fully cohesive, majority vote of lesbians and gay men.)

The Manhattan district was thought to be gay winnable. A second gay-winnable seat might be possible in Brooklyn. A multiracial, gay-influenced district in Jackson Heights was possible if the area's differing but relatively progressive constituents cooperated. An informal alliance among Latinos, Asian Americans, white liberals (largely Jewish), and gay leaders pursued this goal, which would also meet the Districting Commission's goal of dramatically increasing the number of minority-competitive districts in the city.

The only parties to oppose the creation of this new multiracial, progressive district was the Queens organization and—at least initially—the City Council leadership. John Sabatini, a liberal Democratic leader whose roots were among the remnants of the white ethnic population in larger Jackson Heights, used the occasion to challenge the party organization. Once cooperation was secured among the leaders of the Asian community, African

American and Latino advocacy groups, liberal whites, and the lesbian and gay community in Jackson Heights, the alliance could not be resisted. Seeing his future on the City Council coming to an end, Council Member Lisa resigned his seat to accept a judgeship that had been arranged by the Queens County Democratic party organization.

The outcome was a multi-identity district drawn around Jackson Heights that cut into some of the apartment complexes of central Queens. The Twenty-fifth District had a population that was 33 percent white, 29 percent Asian, and 33 percent Latino, which made it a "majority-minority" district under the *Gingles* criteria. Census tracts with a large African American population were placed in an adjacent district to create a another mixed black/Latino "majority-minority" district. Sabatini was elected to the seat with support from the gay community, Asians, and Latinos, as well as women and labor groups.

PROTECTED AND UNPROTECTED CLASSES IN BROOKLYN

The gay community in Jackson Heights succeeded largely because its interests were aligned with those of the two major "protected" classes—Asian Americans and Latinos—and its goals were appropriately modest. In Brooklyn, however, those same interests were in opposition.

The concentration of gay and, particularly, lesbian residents in Brooklyn tended to be identified with the brownstone belt, the portions of Brooklyn built when it was a separate city. Brooklyn Heights, Cobble Hill and Carroll Gardens, Boerum Hill, Park Slope, Fort Green, and Prospect Heights were areas whose residents ranged from Brooklyn's nineteenth-century elite to its largely Irish and Italian working class. All these neighborhoods had fallen on hard times since World War II, and most were being gentrified by the 1970s. Some, such as Cobble Hill and Carroll Gardens, were renamed portions of south Brooklyn. Fort Green and Prospect Heights were the integrated border neighborhoods between the gentrification movement and the core (and poorer) African American neighborhoods of central Brooklyn.

Overall, Brooklyn does not have as strong an African American middle class as does Queens. Brooklyn was one of New York City's counties whose minority voter participation rates triggered the applicability of the Voting Rights Act and the Justice Department's oversight of New York City. White voters in south and eastern Brooklyn tended to vote conservative. Even though the area has a heavy Democratic registration rate, the ten assembly districts in Brooklyn with the highest percentages of white residents together supported Ronald Reagan over Michael Dukakis by 53 percent in 1984.[44] They voted for Ed Koch in all his reelection bids and for Rudolph Giuliani in his 1989 and 1993 mayoral bids.

The central issue in drawing district lines in western Brooklyn concerned Park Slope, an older Italian and Irish neighborhood that has become a center of women's activism in New York City. It also is the commercial and entertainment center of the "new Brooklyn." Would it be retained in its present form and become the core of a new brownstone belt (and gay-friendly) district? Or would its predominantly white and, in many cases, liberal voting clusters be broken up and dispersed among the surrounding minority-centered districts? The neighborhoods immediately to the east, northeast, and southwest of "the Slope" are all minority.

The effort of lesbian and gay residents in Brooklyn's districting process was led by the Lambda Independent Democrats (LID), the strongest gay political organization in Brooklyn. In the early 1990s, LID had 600 active members and a mailing list of 3,500 prime "A" registered Democrats that it could mobilize. The strategy was to form "friendly alliances"[45] with community and neighborhood activists who wanted to maintain the coherence of greater Park Slope in one unified council district. Alliances were forged with the Park Slope Civic Council, the Boerum Hill Neighborhood Association, and the Cobble Hill Neighborhood. To these essentially neighborhood organizations, the quality of education and various quality-of-life issues were critical. On the agenda of lesbians and gay men were identity issues such as abortion rights, domestic partnerships, HIV education, and affirmative education policies. The two agendas were compatible.

Using data from several Brooklyn mailing lists focused on lesbians and gay men, Lambda Independent Democrats compiled a map of western Brooklyn neighborhoods identifying concentrations of lesbians and gay men. The LID data are similar to the Strubco data but are considerably more detailed in greater Park Slope, Boerum Hill, and Brooklyn Heights. Block by block, Lambda Independent Democrats laid out the residential clusters by sexual identity. As in the case with citywide data, mailing lists could be used only as an indicator of concentrations, not for the actual numbers of residents. Still, the data reinforced years of anecdotal information that Brooklyn had become a major center of lesbian and gay life in the United States.[46]

In its first presentation to the commission, LID argued that Brooklyn's gay community was a community of interest as described by the new city charter, had grievances and specific needs that had not been met, and also had a geographic definition. In a subsequent hearing, LID proposed a district that stretched like a triangle including all of Park Slope to the Brooklyn Heights Promenade on the west, to Fort Greene on the north. This was Brooklyn's "brownstone belt."

Despite the relative coherence of the proposed district and its essential overlap of the gay and lesbian community with the neighboring communities, the criteria of the Voting Rights Act held the day. Park Slope as a commercial center was left intact, and portions of the surrounding residential neighborhoods were divided among five adjacent council districts. What ended as the Thirty-sixth District was intended as a Latino district but also included Park Slope and Boerum Hill. In the end, it voted for an Irish woman, largely because the Latino community did not unite behind one candidate. The Thirty-third District took in the core of Park Slope but also included the Hasidic communities in Williamsburg and Greenpoint, which made it a more conservative district than it would otherwise have been. In the Thirty-fifth District, one of the overwhelmingly black districts that acquired a portion of the liberal white Park Slope residents, Council Member Mary Pinket, an African American, was elected. She had become more sensitive to the gay community's needs, in part spurred by the knowledge that Fort Green and Prospect Heights, both in her district, had identifiable clusters of gay black male and, especially, lesbian residents. Finally, in the Thirty-ninth District, Sal Albanese, a young, liberal, Italian American who was an incumbent, was reelected.

Although the outcome did not include the election of a lesbian or gay man to the City Council from Brooklyn, some influence is now evident in each of the districts covering a portion of the "brownstone belt." In addition, the election of a lesbian to the community school board that covers the Park Slope area (despite citywide resistance from the two Roman Catholic dioceses and the Christian Coalition) gave notice to all council members in western Brooklyn of the voting power of gay men and lesbians. The widespread if diverse influence was an unexpected result of the final districting outcome, but the actual district lines were what was feared when some of New York's lesbian and gay activists first confronted the districting process. The centers of lesbian and gay voters in Brooklyn are now largely dispersed among four new council districts: one identified as African American; one as Latino; one as white, with a 10 percent Asian population that voted 55 percent to 35 percent for Rudolph Giuliani as mayor in 1989; and a second heavily white district in northern Brooklyn that included the Orthodox Jews of Williamsburg.[47]

Identity, Space, and the Search for Representative Proportionality

The final result of New York's districting process was a plan creating fifty-one new districts, largely based on race with other factors taken into account. Twelve districts had a majority of African American voters; twenty-four had a majority of white voters (with one expected to elect a lesbian or gay candidate); nine had a majority of Latino voters (with one heavily populated by Dominican Americans); and six had multiracial characteristics (though one had a plurality of Asian American residents). Up to seven districts contained enough registered Republicans to be competitive in regard to party.

The plan submitted to the Justice Department was challenged by representatives of the Latino community, with some success. Because of the residential dispersion of many middle-class Latino voters, some of the new Latino-identified council districts fell below the 65 percent floor that analysts had concluded was the minimum necessary to elect a minority. Litigation regarding the plan continued for more than a year, but the new fifty-one-seat council plan was put in place. The council leadership promised Latino advocates that the lines could be modified in two years. The actual electoral outcome in 1991 was twelve African Americans, nine Latinos (one Domincan, the first non–Puerto Rican Latino elected to the City Council), two gays (one from the Third District, emphasizing his gay identity, and a second from the Second District, Latino, and not emphasizing his gay identity), and five Republicans. No Asian American was elected.[48] Nevertheless, at least one goal of the new New York City Council had been met: the new council was more diverse than any since the 1930s.

Space, Identity, and the Limits of Single-Member Districting

American representation theory has rarely investigated its presumptive association between geography and community. This relationship is not just between numbers and space but also its implied definition of political identity. Guinier makes the point that the spatial definition of representation is, in effect, a group definition of representation, since space is linked to group identity both a priori and a posteriori. An ethnic group that settles into a section of a city or state will eventually be represented in accordance with the district lines drawn around it. Racial identification with separate legislative districts reinforces this link. More subtly, the district itself builds a set of interests and identities that have their own political viability. "Political boundaries traditionally define communities of interest," Guinier noted.[49] Contiguousness, voter coherence (in a bounded space), geographic boundaries, compactness, and the like all are geographic ideas in both modern and postmodern frameworks that contribute to the construction of political identities.

The racial and language minority categories on which the past twenty years of statutory and case law on districting rests divides the electorate among discrete categories of racial identity: black, white, Latino, and Asian. Under the system of single-member, plurality-elected districts, a dispersed minority with a strong sense of individual and collective identity can in fact seek paths of representation in the older framework of single-member districts—but it is at a disadvantage. In a sense, this is what also can be learned from the experience of New York's gay community in 1991. Just as modern technology problematized urban geography, postmodern social life has problematized identity: the category "African American," for example, never as solid a category of identity as the law assumed, is even more problematic today: consider black women or, further, black lesbians. An ever more refined sense of political identity inevitably clashes with a geographic basis of interest organization and representation. The link between community and geography that once could be assumed has slowly—maybe irreparably—been broken.

The struggle to expand the "representativeness" of New York's City Council shows the problems that many other jurisdictions have had in using districting for empowerment. The single-member district system on which the courts and Congress relied as the remedy of choice for past discrimination began to have problems in the mid-1980s. Social science and legal commentary began to document its limits in obtaining a greater variety of political voices in state and local legislatures. Empirical research identified other problems. Two of the *Gingles* criteria that were especially useful in empowering African Americans through districting were not as useful with other protected minorities. One is racially polarized voting. Although race is a good—if not the best—predictor of voting cleavages in many cities, when other variables are added to regression models to control for income, education, and religion, the potency of race in explaining voter differences is typically undermined.[50] This is especially true for Latino and Asian voters. Another *Gingles* criterion—geographic compactness—actually worked against Latino and especially Asian voters in New York. As these groups moved into the middle class, they became more dispersed than did urban African Americans.

A second problem with using districting to redress past discriminatory policy was the collateral effect of maximizing the effect of white voters as "white." Constructing single-member districts around clusters of racial minorities necessarily creates adjacent majority-majority districts. In such districts, numerical minorities with a strong sense of racial, religious, or other identity would have little effect on election outcomes if each group voted strictly according to identity. The possibilities of alliance building and thus policy influence would be minimized as the majority position in each single-member district made way for other minority-dominated districts. The minority-dominated, single-member, plurality district was most effective in redressing past discrimination in which multiple-member or at-large districting was used intentionally to dilute protected voting strength.[51] Most of the social science literature concluded, however, that at-large districts would be an institutional impediment to minority representation in proportion to its percentage of the population (unless it was a near majority of the city), and this, in turn, became one of the criteria imposed by the courts.

Recent legal commentaries also question whether the single-member, plurality district can lead to equity of minority representation.[52] Indeed, it was in raising the standard of scrutiny of multimember districts that the Supreme Court issued its guidance to the lower courts in *Thornburg v. Gingles*, clarifying the mixed messages sent in *Bolden*. By the late 1980s, the courts had given mixed signals on its continued support for enforcing the Voting Rights Act through districting. In the early 1990s' most important ruling on districting, *Shaw v. Reno* (and two subsequent rulings, *Johnson v. Miller* and *Shaw v. Hunt*), the Supreme Court held that race-conscious districting is admissible, especially to redress past discrimination, but that race consciousness remains suspect.[53] Furthermore, compactness, contiguousness, geographic boundaries, and established governmental demarcations (such as counties or cities) do not in themselves permit any dilution of the minority voting effect, but they still are pertinent to drawing representational districts. Whereas minority voter dilution had been the major justification for race-conscious districting, the courts have begun to allow districting plans that fall short of fully maximizing minority voting power in favor of plans that show effort and intent to redress past inequities.

The most recent case law on districting can be viewed as a slow withdrawal from the vigorous enforcement of the Voting Rights Act through districting. In a New York State case[54] concerning runoffs for office nominations, the Supreme Court allowed two overriding bases to challenge districting plans: those that "deter members of a class from voting" and those that "diminish a class's opportunity to elect representatives in proportion to its members," thus explicitly stating the test of proportionality.[55] In *Johnson v. DeGrandy*, the Supreme Court confronted "proportionality" directly.[56] Finding against a Latino group of litigants that had challenged a district plan for not maximizing the potential voter effect of a protected class, the Court held that under the plan, Latinos' voting strength was "roughly proportional" to their share of the general population.[57] In a 1987 case, the Court permitted the introduction of a negotiated cumulative voting system (a type of voting system that achieves proportional representation) in Alamogordo, New Mexico, as a remedy for the dilution of Latino and African American voting strength.[58] And in what may be the most important case exploring alternatives to single-member districts the Court took a different tack toward protecting minority voting strength in *Cane v. Worcester Co.*[59] Viteritti notes that the key differences between *DeGrandy* and *Worcester Co.* were that in *DeGrandy* cumulative voting was permitted, whereas in *Worcester* it was imposed—after discussion with the plaintiffs.[60] If the *Gingles* criteria had seen indirect proportionality as a floor, *Worcester* allowed for a broader set of options to enforce the Voting Rights Act, including more direct channels to proportional representation.

Regardless of the disposition of tenuous claims for representation made on the basis of sexual orientation, the more general issues are identity and representation among numerical minorities. The gay community was not the only identity without recognition under the Voting Rights Act to seek representation that was frustrated in New York's case. Single-member districts seeking proportional representation for protected minorities, regardless of intent, place two groups at a disadvantage: concentrated minorities without protected status and dispersed minorities with or without protected status. This latter problem confronted the Asian American voting bloc, large sections of which had moved into middle-class neighborhoods in

Queens and Brooklyn. Middle-class Latinos had much the same problem. Although the single-member districts did result in greater diversity and increased minority representation in the new City Council, the core problem of identity representation for unprotected minorities had not been resolved. With both party and race embedded in election and voting rights law, other mediating groups—whether economic, ethnic, or other identities (such as sexual)—are left to compete for the indirect state sponsorship of legislative representation through the boundaries of legislative districts.

Proportional Representation in Urban Politics

Bruce Cain argued that the attempt to use the Voting Rights Act to redress generations of discrimination against African Americans and language group–defined minorities was an indirect attempt to achieve proportional representation.[61] By encouraging an overall representation system of single-member districts, each written around minority voting clusters, the direct intent was to maximize the number of minority-dominated districts. The proportionality rests in the *districting system as a whole*, not in the individual districts or the voting method.

The system rests on an understanding of space that is increasingly problematized and of identity that is increasingly diverse. An interactive dynamic of bounded spaces, each identified by differing racially defined groups, should raise the representational index of the largest of the protected minorities (and it has). But relying on single-member districts has never resolved the issue of dispersed or smaller minorities who seek formal identity representation through the maze of single-member districts. The operational scheme of proportional representation that Cain notes has come about as a result of the Voting Rights Act's picking apart multimember and at-large apportionment systems, thereby enhancing African American or Latino voting strength.

In some ways, the whole enterprise of enforcing proportionality through a matrix of single-member districts misses the point. Beyond the protection of a dominant minority, the system of single-member, plurality-elected districts is not a solution to other proportional issues in representation theory. In fact, it presents a challenge to other numerical identities. The attempt to create a gay legislative district in New York was in fact a defensive effort. The initial fear was that since its voting clusters are frequently adjacent to Latino, black, and—in the cases of New York and San Francisco—Asian communities, the vote tally of lesbians and gay men might be subverted to advance the legitimate goals of the Voting Rights Act. If the case of New York shows how sexual identity can be mobilized to achieve a political goal, it also raises questions of how other numerical minorities not as well organized as New York's gay community were left out in the final districting outcome. The underrepresentativeness of Asians, Orthodox Jews, and other groups in New York's system of single-member districts is the end result of a representative scheme that still tends toward a centrist majoritarianism in a postmodern social environment that spins off new identities with increased ease.

We can put aside for a moment the normative issue of whether representation should be based on ascriptive characteristics such as race, gender, religion, or sexual orientation or on other factors generally and review the instrumentalist issues in New York City. Through accommodation, a political solution could be advanced in the West Village/Chelsea area of Manhattan. In Brooklyn, events turned out as political advocates for lesbians and gay men feared. In Queens, a common solution was found in which all the major minority actors joined together to establish an enclave amidst a majority culture. Their "victory" was thus mixed.

The search for some more formal criteria of legal proportionality in which diverse and multiple minority interests can be expressed more effectively is of increasing interest to the courts. Proportional voting has two great advantages. First, it lowers the threshold at which a numerical minority, if they vote coherently, can be elected to office. Second, unlike the *Gingles* criteria, which organize political identity around court-interpreted definitions of racial identity, proportional voting allows the individual voters to define themselves politically. In Guinier's words,

> Ultimately, what the one-vote, one-value principle does is to transform the unit or representation from a territorial or racial constituency to a political or psychological one. This affirms [the] view of social group as one based on self- and historical identification, and it rejects representational groups based simply on the joint possession of externally observable attributes or the choice of residence.[62]

In the vocabulary we have used here, proportional voting minimizes the essentialist aspects of voter protection and maximizes the range of self-constructed (and -interpreted) political identities.

This "self- and historical identification" aspect of proportional voting is also seen as an advantage by Bernard Grofman. His commentary on the problems of subminorities in single-member districts (such as the Dominicans in New York City) is illustrative:

> Persons of the Spanish Heritage—the category mentioned in the Voting Rights Act—should be interpreted as synonymous with persons of Spanish origin as self-identified on the census, rather than in terms of country of birth, country of parental origin, or any other designation. Similarly, I would use census self-identification to define the other groupings identified in the census including Native Americans.[63]

Guinier's sense that proportional voting allows for self- or historical construction of identity and Grofman's belief that self-identification even through the census is the preferred route of racial categorization both resist the "essentialization" of racial categories. Imputed characteristics derived by general observation tend not to define the individual as being in the majority but as determining his or her minority status. In proportional voting, the individual can chose to identify with or against the range of political and personal identities—what we earlier called the *matrix of identities*—in their voting.[64] The search for an appropriate balance between voting strength and the actual numbers of voters in different groups is a search not just for proportionality but also for the appropriate definition of political identity.

Conclusion

For the student of public policy, the districting issues described here are less ones of voting rights than of continuing influence over public policy through the legislative body. The right to vote is both an individual and a group right—an identity right in the terminology and framework here. If the apportioning system—even after the Voting Rights Act and the evolution of case law attached to it—is heavily weighted toward a majoritarianism, the many, many voices and perspectives now left out of the electoral process are also left out of group influence on legislation.

Ironically, between 1937 and 1945, New York City had a proportional representative system of legislative apportionment. The change in the structure of New York's legislative process led to a system of proportionality based on party preference. It was a time when the party organized interests (or interests were organized around the party). In the years during

World War II and immediately before it, proportional voting resulted in a diversity of party identification: fourteen Democrats, three Republicans, two Liberals, two American Labor, and two Communists.[65] It was, in fact, the victory of the Communist candidates that led the city back to single-member districts.

What has changed in the intervening fifty years is not just the alteration in the perceived threat of leftist parties in the United States but the primary mode of representational organization. Whereas proportional representation offered a diversity of economic and class-based party organizations, proportional representation today would offer a range of racial, ethnic, religious, and sexual identities. That urban legislatures could be apportioned on such identities is a telling change in America urban politics.

⠿

CHAPTER 9

Sexual Identity and Police Practices in Philadelphia

For nearly four decades, politics in Philadelphia has had a special connection to police practices. Frank Rizzo was not the only officer to rise through police ranks to the mayoralty of a large city—Tom Bradley in Los Angeles and Frank Jordan in San Francisco are conspicuous West Coast examples— but Rizzo's influence was a unique link between the police and Philadelphia politics that the careers of Bradley and Jordan could only suggest. The effects of Rizzo's years of police district leadership in West and South Philadelphia and finally in Center City, as police commissioner and finally as mayor, left the Philadelphia Police Department with an independence that was and still is rare in American cities, at least in those with a strong-mayor form of government.[1] Rizzo's very success as an aggressive police commissioner and later mayor created its own barriers to changing the strong organizational culture of the Philadelphia Police Department.

Even when the police became an increasing embarrassment to the city in the 1970s, 1980s, and even the 1990s, professional isolation remained the enduring pattern. From abuses of African Americans in the 1950s and 1960s through Rizzo's confrontational leadership during the unrest of the mid-1960s, his political alliance with Richard Nixon on crime (even though he was a big-city Democratic mayor), the corruption scandals of the 1970s,[2] and the preparations for the eventual assault on MOVE's headquarters that left an entire city block in flames in the 1980s,[3] the resistance to reform in Philadelphia Police Department has been legend. In fact, it was not until the aftermath of the fiasco on Osage Avenue that genuine attempts at police reform were possible—only after the credibility of the department that Rizzo had largely created had, quite literally, gone up in smoke.

A minor chapter in the history of police reform from the 1950s to the 1990s was police practices pertaining to the Delaware Valley's lesbian and gay residents. The change in policing and in the attitudes of police toward gay men and lesbians is less an issue in itself than a reflection of organizational change in the police department. This change in attitude is only a small part of the long struggle to make Philadelphia's police more responsive to community interests, but it is a significant chapter in the history of gay people in the "City of Brotherly Love." The indifference to and even abuse of lesbians and gay men at the hands of the Philadelphia police were major motivations for the area's lesbian and gay community to organize. The police ignored crimes, frequently violent, against lesbians and gay men; rather, the average gay or lesbian business person experienced police practices as harassment and demands for illegal payments. Change—albeit incomplete—came only with the increased visibility of the lesbian and gay community and its growing prominence in the economic revitalization of Center City in the 1970s and 1980s.

Marginal Spaces, Marginal Lives: Center City, 1950 TO 1976

Since gay bars and clubs were the most visible manifestations of what in the 1950s and 1960s was largely an underground culture, for outsiders gay identity was associated with evening entertainment strips, and all the vice and morals problems attached to them. This association conditioned the police's attitudes toward lesbians and gay men: homosexual lifestyles were not only "socially deviant" but also corrupt. Even though senior police frequently expressed their disapproval, sometimes contempt, in moral terms, the average patrolman more likely felt disdain for the homosexual's social marginality. Some police might have not have been homophobic; others may have been; but regardless of their personal moral or sexual attitudes, it was the close association in the 1950s and 1960s of gay men and lesbians with the seedier areas of the city and the underground nature of homosexual sexual lives that compounded their treatment as objects of local state regulation through policing.

In the minds of police officials, lesbians and gay men, who both lived and congregated in Center City, were often linked to other activities of the area—prostitution, organized crime, and violations of liquor laws—all adding to a perception of their being marginal, even threatening, to the life of the city. The attitude of ordinary policemen in 1974 (there were no policewomen in Philadelphia at that time) was clearly articulated during a hearing held by the city's Commission on Human Relations as part of the general attempt to pass a municipal "gay rights" ordinance.[4] A spokesman from the Fraternal Order of Police (FOP), the Philadelphia police union, warned that if the bill passed, "there might be more crime in the streets."[5] The FOP had always resisted formal protections for gay men and lesbians through local ordinances, since they usually included nondiscrimination clauses covering the police, but the view that homosexuals were a *source* of crime, rather than its *potential victims*, reveals the underlying attitude of the police patrolling Center City.

In terms of practical policing, this perception of marginality had three implications: First, the commercial venues of simple gay and lesbian socialization—the bars, discos, and coffeehouses—were viewed by the police through the defining characteristic of their clients, that is, through their sexuality. These sites were subjected to specific and enhanced enforcement as part of more comprehensive activities aimed at regulating sexual commerce and its presumed socially (and economically) debilitating effects. Second, the use of public space for the expression of same-sex affection or culture or for sexual contact was a major issue for regulation and policing, whereas almost the same activity by opposite-gendered couples would be perceived, at worst, as a minor neighborhood annoyance. Finally, and most important, the police held an attitude of near indifference toward crimes aimed at lesbians and gay men—violent crimes included. These three themes did change between the 1960s and the 1980s in Philadelphia, but not without a struggle.

Postwar Honky-Tonk Versus Postindustrial Center

In the mid-1950s, Center City Philadelphia was the "honky-tonk" zone of a deteriorating urban region. Its clubs, after-hours bars, strip joints, and illegal gambling establishments were a late night attraction for many adult Philadelphians, out-of-towners, visiting servicemen (especially those docking at the Navy Yard), and others wanting to sample the adult offerings. Both the post–World War II decline of Philadelphia's industrial sector and the movement of a substantial portion of the city's white population to the suburbs were linked to the drop in Center City's property values and its role as a legitimate retail and evening entertainment center. In turn, the new availability of downtown space permitted the growth of the seedier forms of adult entertainment. The most notorious section of Center City, the Locust Street strip, was a product of this regional decline. Most of its establishments served nongay clients, but gay clubs—frequently owned by organized crime—coexisted peacefully in one adult commercial space of Center City.

The openness of the late night adult activities, along with the visible presence of transients, alcoholics, and other "marginals," was seen by leaders of the religious community as a sign of moral degeneration. For the leaders of the business community, however, the problematic social and moral overtones of Center City were not as important as the issue of space utilization itself. That is, the appropriation of these declining urban spaces for late night activities impeded the redevelopment of downtown Philadelphia.

It was not the city's industrial powers that were concerned with the effects of adult commerce but the emerging downtown financial community, insurance, entertainment, and retail enterprises. Like their counterparts in Chicago, San Francisco, Boston, and New York, new elements of Philadelphia's business community wanted to revitalize the downtown area. The Greater Philadelphia Movement was created in 1951 as a reform and downtown progrowth organization. The movement reflected similar progrowth coalitions in other cities. Its first goal was political reform—especially a new city charter granting broader home rule powers and a stronger executive mayoralty. Throughout the 1950s, the organization pressed for a series of changes and programs typically identified with other reform- and pro-growth-minded business elite coalitions: land clearance and urban renewal, redevelopment of older downtown areas, preservation/gentrification of inner-city housing (in Philadelphia's case, this was especially important), waterfront development, arterial transportation planning, and so forth. Gambling, after-hours bars, drugs, strip clubs, and the like were not conducive to these plans for development.

In addition to the business community's concern about the economic vitality of Center City, more traditional proponents of reform named police corruption as one of their targets. Throughout the century, the Philadelphia Police Department had resisted organizational reform and police professionalization, with petty corruption being one result. Much of this resistance was blamed on the long reign of the city's Republican political machine, which had used police positions as patronage. In 1952, several decades of Republican control of City Hall were ended by Joseph Clark, the first reform mayor that Philadelphia had had in many years. A coalition of businesses, the reform movement, African Americans, and the press had finally succeeded in overturning decades of Republican rule. In the same election, Richard Dilworth, another reformer, was elected district attorney for the county.

As part of the reform of police practices and the cleanup of Center City, the new reform police commissioner, Thomas Gibbons, chose Frank Rizzo, a young, fast-rising, and public relations–savvy district captain with experience in West and South Philadelphia, to run Police District 6, the district covering Center City east of Broad Street. In his brief command in West Philadelphia, Rizzo had already earned a reputation for cracking down on gambling and enforcing tax laws on private, mostly African American, clubs. Although he had incurred the wrath of some local African American leaders in West Philly for his rough and troubled attitudes toward policing (including the skepticism of Cecil B. Moore, an important black leader of postwar Philadelphia), he did win the respect of the reform-minded City Hall and its reform police commissioner. It was Rizzo's no-nonsense and corruption-free reputation that brought him to Center City to regulate its seedy evening activities as preparation for changing the face of Center City.

As part of his general crackdown on adult activity in Center City, Rizzo also hit most of the gay social and entertainment spaces. Sodomy laws were still enforced in the city—albeit selectively—and some gay bars operated after hours. Rizzo shut down one club offering a "Gay Boy Review"; a judge later dismissed the case and released the manager.

But Rizzo went beyond sex clubs and unlicensed and after-hours bars to monitor and control the coffeehouses around Rittenhouse Square and near South Twelfth Street. The coffeehouses were not licensed taverns or spots known for prostitution or gambling in the usual sense of vice control. Typically, their clients included young college students associated with the beat culture, musicians, and, yes, lesbians and gay men. As in other cities, Philadelphia's bohemian and beat culture provided a setting for the emerging lesbian and gay identity. Even though the coffeehouses were not primarily identified as gay, their availability as venues for same-sex identification added to their perception by reformers and—to the degree that they cared—the business community as attracting an "undesirable" element.[6]

Rizzo also was bothered by men in women's dress (regardless of the men's actual sexual orientation; Rizzo assumed they all were homosexual) who congregated around the bars and clubs near Thirteenth Street and Locust year-round, but especially during the Halloween season. This was both a moral and a practical problem for Rizzo, since on-leave navy personnel frequently came in contact with cross-dressing men. For a variety of reasons—including prostitution—such dress often led to fights between cross-dressers and sailors. Rizzo refused to allow shore patrols or the base commander to handle infractions by naval personnel. Although his refusal did not endear him to the U.S. Navy, his crackdowns on prostitution and rowdiness did win him the support of the business community, religious leaders, and the editorial pages. "Rizzo's Raiders," as the press dubbed his officers, told state liquor license holders that if they allowed cross-dressers in their bars, especially during the Halloween season, the city would challenge their licenses.[7] Through its police department, the city was using its regulatory powers over commerce to enforce cultural norms, and most people in the gay community understood this.

Rizzo's enthusiasm for these exercises would have no historical significance except for his presence in the 1950s and 1960s, his elevation to police commissioner, his later election as mayor, and his actions as a symbol of racial division in Philadelphia. Regardless of who headed the Center City Police Districts in the 1950s and 1960s, the same policies would have been pursued, though perhaps not with the same vigor. The stakeholders in Center City—the business community, real estate, and financial interests—allied with the traditional moral reformers and church groups, the editorial page of the *Philadelphia Inquirer*, and the local residents who objected to the noise associated with the bars and coffeehouses. The effort to curb the adult entertainment in Center City predated Rizzo and would have been made even without his presence in Center City. The gay clubs and bars would still have been harassed. After all, the police made similar raids in San Francisco into the mid-1960s and in New York until the late 1960s.

The perception of women's and gay spaces as marginal and thus subject to arbitrary enforcement activity without any repercussions for the police continued into the 1970s. But unlike raids in the 1950s, during which most patrons ran or tried to prevent being revealed as homosexual, in the 1970s patrons only became radicalized, thereby advancing the lesbian and gay identity as a basis for a political movement.[8] Rizzo's actions against the coffeehouses and gay bars thus left a permanent imprint in Philadelphia's lesbian and gay community, leading lesbians and gay men to support a three-decade-long effort to bring the city's police department under greater civilian control.

Loitering and Sodomy Laws

The second major area of legal interaction between police and lesbians and especially gay men was the enforcement of loitering and sodomy laws. Again, Philadelphia was not unlike other cities that enforced laws regulating open, if subtle, sexual propositions and, indirectly, also sodomy laws.[9] From the perspective of males "cruising" for sex in public places, police enforcement was seen as entrapment, centered in places where homosexual men often gathered for sexual contact. In Philadelphia, this included Center City parks, Suburban Station, underground pedestrian malls, the larger departments stores, and the streets around Locust and Thirteenth. The pattern of enforcement was usually arrest, imposition of a fine, release, and publication of names. In the 1950s and 1960s, it was the publication of names that was the true punishment.

Pennsylvania's sexual offense laws were changed in 1952, following a broader national trend toward stricter laws for and enforcement of sex crimes—a trend that accelerated after several child molestations and rape-murder cases. As in many other states, Pennsylvania began to include psychiatric norms and assessments in its adjudicatory procedures. In some respects, this was intended as a reform—that is, requiring therapy for chronic sex offenders—but in many cases, the states also used psychiatric assessments as a basis for preventive incarceration.[10] Unfortunately, in Pennsylvania's new statute, as in many other states, "sodomy and solicitation for sodomy" were deemed sex offenses, along with the more serious crimes of "indecent assault, incest, assault with intent to commit sodomy...[and] assault with intent to ravish or rape."[11]

These new laws were the basis of much of the police's action against gay men cruising in the evening in parks and streets for sexual contact. In the 1950s, many bar managers did not allow direct sexual expression on their premises (including kissing), for fear that the police might use it as grounds to close them down. Thus the streets and parks had became common venues.

Enforcing sodomy and solicitation laws was difficult for the police. The often subtle and covert manner of gay people's communication tested the department's perceptiveness. It also raised issues of selective enforcement, since solicitation arrests were few, unless the department made a concerted effort or a sweep of the parks. The most common practice of police enforcement was through undercover police decoys assigned to spaces for gay male congregation. The use of police decoys was a contentious and legally problematic practice, however. Although it may have resulted in many arrests, it did not result in as many criminal convictions. The very process of making oneself available for sexual contact can also be understood as enticing the "felon" into acts which he (or she) may not normally engage. Thus, the usual defense if a case actually went to trial was entrapment. And if entrapment was not a viable defense, prosecutors were still required to show "clear communication of willingness," that the communication first came from the defendant, that is, that intent was present. If the officer had offered any indication of consent—intentionally or not—the case would collapse.[12]

But the anticipation of conviction assumed that the charges would be brought to trial and that the defendant would not plead to a lesser charge— if it went that far. The difficulties in achieving a successful prosecution still left those arrested with formal charges and the availability of their names to the press. Disapproval and the imposition of real personal sanctions by family and employers almost always followed. Avoiding publicity—well into the 1980s, for some—was the first priority of those arrested. Thus there was little actual restraint on the police. Even the successes of the movement for sexual identity and the proliferation of gay (male) sex clubs in many urban areas through the 1970s into the early years of the HIV epidemic did not stop the "cat and mouse" game between police and gay men.

Murder Comes Out of the Closet

The third theme of police-gay interaction before the mid-1970s was the indifference of both the police and the media in Philadelphia to crimes committed against lesbians and gay men. The underground nature of premovement gay social contact meant that death also was underground—to say nothing of less serious crimes. In the 1950s or 1960s, because of the personal cost to the victim of exposure as homosexual, minor hate crimes—targeted robberies, beatings, extortion, and simple harassment, even by the police—were unevenly reported. The social sanctions of having one's name appear in the press or on the police blotter was far greater than the immediate cost of medical attention, the loss from theft, or even physical pain. Only when the effects of a hate crime escalated to the point of severe harm or death did it receive police attention, often instigated by unwitting third parties who brought the victim to the hospital or reported the presence of a corpse. As late as the 1970s, murders of gay men and lesbians were given little attention by police or were kept quiet at the family's request. The desire to find the perpetrator was less important than keeping a family secret. The first major crime to break the silence of violence against gay people in Philadelphia was the 1975 murder of John S. Knight, the thirty-year-old grandson of John Knight, owner and chairman of the Knight-Ridder newspaper group. (The younger Knight worked on special editorial projects for a Knight-Ridder newspaper, the *Philadelphia Daily News*.) In 1970, the Knight-Ridder service bought the *Philadelphia Inquirer* from Walter Annenburg. The older Knight wanted to upgrade the quality of the *Inquirer* and so began a head-to-head competition with the *Evening Bulletin* to become Philadelphia's premier newspaper. Knight-Ridder also brought to Philadelphia a skepticism of Rizzo and the police that made the senior Knight a presence in Philadelphia politics.

One morning in 1975, John S. Knight was found dead in his Center City apartment near Rittenhouse Square. There were no signs of a break-in. The body had been mutilated, and robbery was only ancillary to the main crime. It was a textbook case of a gay-related hate murder. Except for the prominence of the victim's family, the Knight murder was not very different from other such cases. But because this family was involved in Philadelphia's competitive newspaper business, the matter could not be kept quiet, and leaks to the *Inquirer*'s competing newspapers—especially the *Bulletin*, which was protective of the Rizzo administration—from the police department and from Rizzo's City Hall ensured intense scrutiny.[13] Although the Knight murder case had no lasting effect on the internal workings of the police department, there now was a new openness (and sensationalism) regarding violent crimes against gay men and lesbians.

Only after the murder of John Knight did the press begin routinely to cover the murders of gay men and lesbians. But murder is only one hate crime against lesbians and gay men. Nearly none of the other crimes motivated by the victim's sexual orientation were reported by the press, or the role of sexual identity in the crime was never mentioned.[14] This was especially true of crimes committed against the most vulnerable in the gay community: lesbians, transvestites, effeminate or older gay men, and S/M practitioners. In each case, either a false image of "weakness"—as in women, effeminate men, and transsexuals—or "hidden-ness"—as in older gay men and S/M practitioners—invites serious crime. The combination of racist and homophobic hate crimes often make Latinos, Asian Americans, and African Americans particular targets for undisciplined anger. But no sub-group in the lesbian and gay community was immune. Furthermore, except for vice charges, loitering, and sodomy, neither the police nor other equally important institutions kept specific information about sexual identity. That is, even those who collected crime data associated sexual identity with the perpetrator of the crime rather than with its victim. Finally, lesbians and gay men still suspected that crimes committed against them were routinely ignored.

Support for and Isolation of the Police

During the years that Rizzo was the district commander for Center City, the police commissioner, and, finally, the mayor, the Philadelphia Police Department became even more autonomous. The department had been formally under the control of the mayor since the creation of the commissioner's office in 1952, so when Rizzo became mayor, he had an active hand in managing the department and maintaining its independence. Although he did succeed in keeping petty party politics and machine patronage out of the police force, his strong support of individual members of the department also increased its isolation from the community and from the oversight of other criminal justice institutions. This isolation had three results: (1) an organizational culture that sustained petty corruption in the force; (2) the continuation of excessive force in police practices, especially in regard to minorities; and (3) a general resistance to outside influence on the professional training of the officer corps.

Partly because of the vice laws and partly because of poor pay, the Philadelphia Police Department had a long history of petty corruption that was encouraged by both the organizational culture and the department's actual practices. A 1975 report by the Pennsylvania Crime Commission found that "police corruption in Philadelphia is ongoing, widespread, systematic, and occurring at all levels of the Police Department."[15] This included routine corruption in the enforcement of liquor laws, prostitution, gambling, and narcotics:

> This condition results from the interaction of many factors, including the Police Department's attitude toward the corruption problem, the vice enforcement policy of the Department, various societal pressures on the individual police officers, and the reaction to police corruption of other parts of the criminal justice system and the public.[16]

The report documented how officers solicited cash payments when stopping suspected stolen cars or fugitives. "Car stops are one of the first ways a rookie will be tested by his peers to see if he is 'trustworthy' in terms of accepting 'notes.' "[17] The commission also concluded that enforcement of the state liquor laws in late night clubs, and prostitution were particular problems in Center City. Interestingly, the commission recommended ceasing the enforcement of "vice crimes such as enforcement against homosexuals" to reduce the potential for corruption.

In personnel matters, too, the Pennsylvania Crime Commission was critical of the Philadelphia police. Specifically in regard to women and minorities, the commission discovered patterns of discrimination in hiring, promotion, and assignments, which in turn had exacerbated other departmental effectiveness issues, especially in dealing with Philadelphia's large minority communities. (Background checks of the "moral character" of potential recruits prevented most lesbians and gay men from entering the Philadelphia police force.)

The very fact that neither Rizzo as mayor nor Joseph F. O'Neill as commissioner cooperated with the 1975 state commission was cited as creating an atmosphere that accepted petty corruption. The commission also found that individual police officers and even supervisory personnel would not hesitate to perjure themselves in court testimony. In commenting on the court system's reaction to such widespread corruption, the commission concluded:

> One would expect the Police Department and entire criminal justice system to react harshly against any member who has betrayed the Department or the system of law enforcement. Philadelphia has witnessed just the opposite reaction. For reasons not entirely clear, the Police Department, the FOP [Fraternal Order of Police], and the criminal justice system have sought in many complex and sophisticated ways to protect any member accused of betrayal.[18]

The isolation of Philadelphia's police department made it nearly impossible for outside authorities or political reformers to chip away at its petty corruption.

A second consequence of the department's isolation was that it was insulated from charges of brutality. Complaints of excess force by the Philadelphia police had been made for decades, especially by African Americans. In Rizzo's early years as mayor, the U.S. Civil Rights Commission urged the U.S. attorney general to file suit against Philadelphia, a decision

based on confidential hearings held in the city on actions taken during
Rizzo's years as police commissioner. Almost as soon as Rizzo became
mayor, the U.S. Justice Department requested authorization to investigate
allegations of harsh police practices against blacks in Philadelphia. The
White House, however, refused the request. Rizzo's relationship with President Nixon protected the mayor—but it also meant that for almost another whole decade the Philadelphia police were secured from the legitimate oversight of external authorities.[19]

Excessive police force against minorities came up in the 1977 reelection
effort of District Attorney F. Emmett Fitzpatrick. Although they were not
close allies, Rizzo supported him. Fitzpatrick already had serious problems—he had been accused of personal corruption— when he began his reelection campaign, and after a series of Pulitzer Prize–winning articles in
the *Philadelphia Inquirer*, exposing violations of procedure (and law) in the
police's Homicide Division, Fitzpatrick's prospects dimmed further. Officers had engaged in torture and threats that generally shocked the average
Philadelphian. After the *Inquirer*'s reports, Fitzpatrick's 1977 opponent (and
later mayor), Edward Rendell, made police brutality a central issue of his
campaign, thus legitimizing the issue for future political inquiry. Rendell
promised to establish a police brutality division in the Philadelphia's district
attorney's office. The *Inquirer* articles had already reinforced the general
perception of African Americans and liberal whites that Rizzo's police department was unregulated and out of control, and so even Rendell's efforts
as district attorney were not enough to forestall the police's continued abuse
of authority, especially toward minorities.[20]

The department's isolation was evident as well in personnel matters and
in the police academy's curriculum and training. In the mid-1970s,
Philadelphia police recruits received about five hundred hours of training,
nearly all at the police academy. Most of the training was in departmental
operations; firearms training; criminal procedures in regard to arrest and
evidence collection; arrest procedures; and the responsibilities of city, state,
and federal agencies. Very little of the training pertained to corruption prevention or community relations. In 1974, of the police forces in the ten
largest American cities, New York had the longest period of recruit training—910 hours. Philadelphia had the second shortest. This was even more
of a problem when one considers that Philadelphia did not have an educational achievement standard for new recruits—an unusual oversight for
an urban police department. In regard to the temptations of corruption,

New York had thirty hours of integrity training; Philadelphia only one.[21] In narcotics training, too, Philadelphia lagged. Drugs, a major venue for police corruption, were part of the academy's general department curriculum, with fourteen additional hours of training if a candidate were to be assigned to the Narcotics Division. In the mid-1970s, the International Police Chiefs Association recommended a minimum of eighty hours of training in narcotics for all police officers.[22]

In addition to the relative weakness in recruit training, the force had two other problems. One was that officers had very little in-service training after leaving the academy. The second problem was that in the mid-1970s, nearly the whole curriculum was formulated by departmental officers. Only one component was subject to outside input, a social science module taught by the criminal justice program at Temple University. Only fifty-one hours, or about 10 percent of the total curriculum, was dedicated to the social sciences. Furthermore, the subject matter was not geared toward sensitizing apprentice officers to different racial, ethnic, and other identity groupings but instead concentrated on the more traditional topics of police training: the psychodynamics of youthful crime, social issues in family disputes, teenage and juvenile behavior, the history of urban policing, and general human behavior.

On January 1, 1980, Philadelphia was scheduled to begin a new decade without Frank Rizzo holding public office. Under Philadelphia's home rule charter, mayors were limited to two terms. But in a divisive attempt to change the term limit, Rizzo began a campaign to amend the charter. Because of Philadelphia's changing demographics and the expectation that an African American mayor would soon be elected, the charter campaign had deep racial overtones. Some even quoted Rizzo's supporters as suggesting that voters in the northeast section of the city should "vote white" in the 1979 referendum. The movement to amend the charter failed, and the result of the 1979 election cycle was the election of Mayor Bill Green, a reform mayor. Both Green and his city administrator, Wilson Goode, later to be mayor, stated that police reform was one of the new administration's highest priorities.[23]

Respectability and Reform in the Immediate Post-Rizzo Era

One irony in the attempt to regulate adult commerce in Center City was that the gay community was about to become a strong supporter of its cleanup, not as individuals seeking quiet evening outings but increasingly as property holders, business owners, and residents. This change in position coincided with a brief opportunity for police reform in the immediate post-Rizzo era. Both led to changes in police practices toward lesbians and gay men in Center City Philadelphia.

Green's appointment of a reform commissioner, Morton Solomon, began a new effort by a wide coalition of interested parties, including members of the Delaware Valley's gay community, to influence police practices. A working group from the lesbian and gay communities began meeting in the summer of 1980 to discuss issues between the police and the gay community. The group was organized by Mark Segal, publisher of the *Philadelphia Gay News*, and was named the Police-Gay Community Relations Committee. Its members were activists and education and psychology professionals interested in changing the relationship between an isolated police culture and a still marginalized sexual identity group. The specific issues of concern were hate crimes, harassment by police,[24] rules for gay men in parks, and internal police procedures. In addition, the committee wanted gay and lesbian activists to be aware of the problems the police confronted in enforcing the law in Center City.[25]

The first priority for the committee was to revise the "perceptions gays and police had of each other."[26] The group wanted police officers to receive instruction on gay culture and crime issues that particularly affected lesbians and gay men. An education committee was established, and it drafted a detailed proposal for training at the police academy that would include

- The problems that gay men and lesbians have in "coming out."
- The ways in which lesbians and gay men are responsible citizens.
- The ways in which gay men and lesbians are harassed in Center City.
- The need to use nonjudgmental language.
- The special problems of the Sixth and Ninth Police Districts, those covering Center City.
- An attempt to disprove some of the stereotypes of homosexuals, especially their relationships with children.[27]

There was some anticipation that the effort might be successful. The local district captain called and indicated that Commissioner Solomon thought the effort was important and had ordered the local captain to start communicating with representatives of the gay community. The precinct commander and a community relations officer from one of the Center City police districts attended a meeting in September 1980 at which the representatives of the gay and lesbian communities tried to convince them that a ninety-minute seminar on lesbian and gay issues would benefit both the police and the community. This first meeting, however, accomplished little except to establish communication with the local police districts.

The change in senior police officials' attitudes raised hopes that there also might be a change in recruitment policy. In a tantalizing offhand comment, Commissioner Solomon indicated that the department might drop its opposition to homosexuals on the force when the police department again began hiring new officers in 1981.[28] But the departmental culture was so strongly hostile to lesbian or gay officers that it was not until the mid-1990s that the first lesbian officer made public her sexuality.[29] As of 1996, no gay male police officer had done so, and there was no Philadelphia group associated with LEGAL—the international Law Enforcement Gays and Lesbians association.[30]

Respectability and Real Estate

Another set of issues on the Police-Gay Community Relations Committee's agenda concerned the general living conditions of the Center City neighborhoods, especially an effort to remove the increasing number of prostitutes from the area around Locust and Thirteenth Streets.

Similar to that of other cities, the growth in Center City's commercial space was reflected in the local housing market. Changes included the creation of condominiums and the conversion of warehouse, industrial, and other space into residential housing. Although Philadelphia's Center City housing market was better balanced than, say, New York's or San Francisco's, the tensions associated with gentrification were not unlike those in other cities.

Washington Park West—the section of Center City stretching from Washington Park (Eighth Street) to Juniper Street, and Walnut to South Street—then inhabited by a diverse mix of eight thousand to nine thousand people, had become a center of gay and lesbian residence and gentrification. The area offered a mix of residential, commercial, and institutional uses. The public commitment to urban renewal in this area had resulted in the development of market-rate housing units: abandonment had decreased by 40 percent in the previous decade because of residential rehabilitation and the demolition of unsafe structures. As one measure of the area's growth between 1975 and 1982, the price of single-family houses rose 108 percent.[31]

The growing presence of young, middle-class, gay and nongay residents put pressure on the older uses of land in this section of Center City. Most of the prostitution was concentrated in what residents called the "Merry-Go-Round," a city block between Locust and Spruce, Twelfth and Thirteenth. It was here that the city's seedier sections conflicted with the newer residents and businesses, many owned by lesbians and gay men.

Neither gay nor nongay establishments wanted the tawdry reputation of the area to continue. In 1983 the Thirteenth Street Business Association was formed, cochaired by Mark Segal and Michael Guzzardi, a local realtor. The *Philadelphia Business Journal* described the group as "an unusual coalition of traditional business people, gay activists and bar owners...trying to clean up Center City."[32] The association pressured both Mayor Green and then District Attorney Edward Rendell to enforce the loitering laws. It was an odd turn of events: The association was looking for law enforcement officials to enforce just the laws that had been used to harass lesbians and gay men in the same area of the city fifteen years earlier.

Whether the Thirteenth Street Business Association accomplished anything permanent is difficult to ascertain. Although trafficking in prostitution declined in Washington Park West, it probably just moved to other sections of town. Today, the new identification of Washington Park West as an increasingly middle-class neighborhood open to gay and lesbian residents came about in part because of the new respectability of a sexual minority once marginalized and policed in Center City. It also, however, revealed divisions in that sexual minority along class and race lines and in the sexual identity itself.

Gay Bars and "Steady Notes" in Center City

The incidence of petty corruption among Philadelphia police is a well-documented theme of the department's history. Ignored by both Rizzo and his police commissioners, the 1974 State Crime Commission Report resulted in virtually no reforms. This investigation was followed ten years later by a series of federal investigations between 1982 and 1985. The U.S. attorney for Philadelphia, a federal grand jury, and the FBI cooperated to produce one of the largest systematic attacks on police corruption in American urban history.

The federal grand jury came to much the same conclusion as had the State Crime Commission: that corruption in the Philadelphia Police Department was sustained, systematic, and nearly universal. The U.S. attorney began his prosecutions in West and Southwest Philadelphia and then moved to the Center City police districts. In Center City, the corruption mainly involved street patrol officers and their enforcement activities against taverns, bars, clubs, and prostitutes. The police had even tried to extort protection money from a part-time private detective who also owned two brothels and an after-hours club in Center City.[33] He decided to cooperate with the FBI's investigation of the force. The overall investigation, which began in November 1982, revealed that more than $350,000 in "business notes" or bribes were accepted from Center City activities between January 1983 and April 1984. It is telling that it was the FBI, not the police department's Internal Affairs Division, that documented the general pattern of extortion from bar, tavern, and club owners.

Many of the clubs covered in the Center City investigation were predominantly or all gay. The DCA, a club on Chancellor Street just off 13th and Locust, was one prime target of extortion. A bar, disco, and sex club all in one, district police sought payments in exchange for protection. Also involved was the Back Street Baths, the major gay male bathhouse in the 1970s and early 1980s and only a few dozen feet from the DCA. The DCA Club and the Back Street Baths were the venues most associated with the sexual freedom and experimentation among male homosexuals in the 1970s. Although there was no equivalent in Philadelphia to some of the sex establishments that existed in San Francisco or New York, the DCA and Back Street came closest. This made them especially vulnerable to police shake-downs. The DCA was to pay $60 a week for each of the rotating midnight–to–8 A.M. shifts of officers. By mid-1980, the DCA Club's payments had grown to $200 a week, according to federal prosecutors. The club's bookkeeper recorded the protection payoffs as expenses for "ice." The Back Street bathhouse paid $50 a week per shift.[34] But these gay venues were not the only ones targeted for payoffs. Even some of the more tame taverns in Center City were also required to offer "notes" to police.

In February 1985, the U.S. attorney began to issue indictments for corruption against members of the Philadelphia police. "Three current and three former Philadelphia police officers" were charged with extorting about $40,000 "from businesses and individuals including Center City taverns, gay clubs and bars, a pimp and two numbers writers" between 1975 and 1982. The prosecutors used the RICO statutes and federal extortion laws, claiming that a consistent pattern of payoffs that went up the police precinct hierarchy essentially formed a racketeering enterprise. At one trial, two witnesses from gay bars testified that the payments went to patrolmen, sergeants, and even lieutenants.

These incidents were similar to the type of corruption reported in the state's investigation of the Philadelphia police in 1974.[35] The testimony of all the witnesses who worked at the gay bars indicated that they paid off the police for three reasons: (1) to protect their clientele from police harassment, (2) to ensure that the police would respond quickly when needed, and (3) to reduce the chance that patrons' cars parked on the street would be ticketed.

The major difference between these investigations and enforcement activities of the 1950s was that the reformers and prosecutors directed some of their attention to gay establishments, not as sources of crimes, but as victims of racketeering. The police were not seen as a force to clean up businesses serving a marginal sexuality but as perpetrators of harassment and extortion against them. The fact of corruption in the city's police was certainly not new, nor was its extortion from gay bars; what was new to the federal investigation was that an external authority concentrated on corruption by the police and took a stand on behalf of gay establishments. In this investigation, no owners were indicted; many even cooperated with the investigators. No clients were arrested, and no unwanted names appeared in the press. The change in bar ownership from organized crime to gay entrepreneurs, a process that also took place in many other cities, had stimulated a change in the bar managers' attitude toward corruption. More important was a change in the attitude toward gay and lesbian bars by the established powers interested in Center City's development. In the twenty years between 1965 and 1985, a robust lesbian and gay night life was no longer seen as a part of a declining Center City but was now associated with its revitalization. It was part of a new respectability for a lesbian and gay identity.

Out of the Ashes: New Possibilities for Police Reform: 1985–1990

Despite attempts at reform by both Mayors Green and Wilson Goode, the Philadelphia police's isolation and strong organizational culture limited its extent. This situation changed markedly in May 1985, however, when the police attacked the headquarters and residence on Osage Avenue in West Philadelphia of a antiurban and black nationalist group called MOVE.[36] To dislocate what the police department said was a nest atop the building, the police dropped a C-4 bomb from a helicopter, whose explosion ignited fuel on the roof.[37] For fear of weapons fire, the fire commissioner reported that he ordered his forces not to extinguish the ensuing conflagration. By nightfall, an entire city block of wooden frame homes had burned to the ground. Even more troublesome were charges that some police officers had used unauthorized weapons to fire on the MOVE contingent (which included children) as they tried to flee the fire.[38] In all, six adults and five children died at 6221 Osage Avenue. In 1996, the city of Philadelphia was found liable for the incident and ordered to pay more than $1.5 million to the survivors of the MOVE organization. It cost an additional $37 million to rebuild the houses on Osage Avenue.

The deaths and fire were a disaster not only to the residents of West Philadelphia but also (and obviously) to the police department's reputation. It reinforced every criticism that had been leveled against it in the previous twenty years: racism, resistance to control by outside forces—including the mayor—a lack of quality social and tactical police training, senior officers' refusal to accept responsibility for the actions of lower-level police officers, and a general suspicion of press scrutiny. The Osage Avenue fire broke the back of support for the police by the city elite if not by all its citizens and ironically made way for the first new wave of serious police reform since Frank Rizzo left office.

In issuing its recommendations, the commission that investigated the attack focused on the police's history of racism, poor training, and poor accountability. Mayor Goode used the opportunity to force from office his city administrator, who, Goode was convinced, had lied to him. Goode wanted the new police commissioner to be an outsider with a professional and reform agenda, so he appointed Kevin Tucker.[39] Tucker had headed up the regional office of the Secret Service and agreed with Goode's reform agenda for the police, especially the need for more careful recruitment, better in-service training, and stepped-up corruption prevention programs. Tucker became the most reform-minded commissioner that Philadelphia had had since Thomas Gibbons in the early 1950s. Tucker's agenda included community policing, management overhaul, adoption of new technologies, enhanced training, managerial decentralization, an upgrade of the department's financial management capacity, and greater sensitivity to Philadelphia's diverse communities.

The New Organizational Capacity of the Lesbian and Gay Community

The Osage Avenue incident did not lead to renewed organizing by lesbians and gay men for political influence. But it did create opportunities to build alliances with others who were seeking changes in police practices, who now were spurred on by a new sense of expectation for reform. Nevertheless, the fire did coincide with a new attempt in the gay community to influence police practices. Their effort moved from the ad-hoc, informal group that had represented the interests of lesbians and gay men to the police since 1980 to a group with new organizational capacity. Founded in 1979, the Philadelphia Lesbian and Gay Task Force (PLGTF) became the focus of political activism toward the police department from 1985 onward.

The first task for the PLGTF was to document both hate crimes and abuses inflicted on lesbians and gay men by the police. The police department did not keep separate data on the victims of crimes, even if a defining characteristic of the crime was the victim's sexual identity. Philadelphia was not alone; most other large city police departments did not consider sexuality a category significant enough to warrant collecting data on it. Violent crimes were "treated like all other crimes"—though they were routinely devalued in practice—and harassment of gays and lesbians was not generally thought to be a crime. But the department did frequently record the sexual orientation of arrestees, partly because up to the 1980s, it was common practice to refer homosexuals arrested by the police to mental health clinicians associated with the department.

Both to document patterns of hate crimes against lesbians and gay men and as a basis for lobbying the police department and state legislature to take these crimes more seriously, the PLGTF began to collect data on crimes based on the sexual identity of their victims. Their first report was released in 1986 and used data gathered in 1985. The data collection sheets were distributed in places where gay men and lesbians congregated—mostly in Center City, at specific meetings, or at sites outside Center City identified with lesbians or gay men. Although this method could not produce scientifically accurate results (the total n was only 167, and the sample was not randomly compiled), the aggregate data did reveal the following:

- Thirty-nine percent of the women and 63 percent of the men surveyed indicated that they had experienced some form of criminal violence (usually assault) during their lifetimes, which they saw as being directed at them because they were lesbians or gay men.
- In the year before the survey was taken (1985), 10 percent of the women and 24 percent of the men reported that they had been victims of violent crime solely because of their sexual orientation.[40]

The results of the report were communicated to the incoming commissioner, and the task force requested a meeting with Tucker, who agreed.

At the November 1986 meeting of Commissioner Tucker, Deputy Commissioner Robert Armstrong, and members of the PLGTF, the task force's recommendations were formally conveyed to the department. These included enhanced training, especially in diversity issues; outside civilian review of police actions; an antibias curriculum in the schools; and the passage of bias-crime legislation at the commonwealth level. Although Tucker was generally supportive of the police professionalization and anticorruption programs, he was not sympathetic to curricular materials centering on the sociology of group victims. He accepted only a few of the recommendations made by the PLGTF, and then only after they had been watered down.[41] He rejected an independent directive to all police personnel to investigate incidents of harassment or violence against lesbians or gay people (but he did issue a short memo the following year on the same subject). Tucker also rejected the recommendations for a civilian review board, increased police protection in the Sixth and Ninth Districts covering Center City, and the immediate introduction of a pilot training program covering topics of crime and sexual identity in the same precincts. He did, however, hold out the possibility that some lesbian/gay concerns would be incorporated into future training programs. Tucker also added the role of liaison to the gay community to the responsibilities of his deputy commissioners.[42]

A second PLGTF report issued in 1988, covering the city and Philadelphia suburbs with a much larger sample, contained much the same information as did the 1986 report. Likewise, a study in 1992, with a total sample of more than four thousand, had similar results. Twenty-four percent of the gay male Philadelphia residents sampled and 16 percent of the self-identified lesbian or bisexual women reported that they had been the victim of some form of criminal violence in the previous twelve months, based, in their view, on their sexual orientation. Sixty-five percent of Philadelphia's gay men and 40 percent of lesbian or bisexual women reported some form of verbal abuse in the previous twelve months. Of more concern for the professionalization of the police, 11 percent of men and 5 percent of women in the Philadelphia sample reported some form of harassment or abuse by the police themselves in the previous twelve months.[43]

Some First Successes

Commissioner Tucker's initial resistance to some of the PLGTF recommendations was misleading, however. Upon taking office, Tucker appointed a thirteen-member panel of civilians to review the department and its operations. This Police Study Task Force concluded that the Philadelphia police was "unfocused, unmanaged, undertrained, underequipped and unaccountable."[44] Among other things, it recommended a dramatic increase in recruit and in-service training. It also recommended that the department consider using training initiatives tried in other cities and in the business community. Tucker was convinced that the training of new recruits was currently inadequate. Following the task force's report and sympathetic himself, Tucker announced the hiring of a training consultant from outside the department. Professor Jack Greene of Temple University was the lead outside expert brought in to assess and redesign much of the police academy's training program.[45] He reviewed the academy's entire curriculum, particularly its anticorruption curriculum, community sensitivity discussions, and the overall recruit and in-service training. He was especially interested in creating a transitional curriculum to introduce an early form of community policing to Philadelphia.

As part of the process, Greene reached out to many groups in the city, including the Philadelphia Lesbian and Gay Task Force. In developing the curriculum, both Tucker and Greene wanted to balance input from many groups in the city without franchising the curriculum to various advocacy groups. The PLGTF recommended a nine-day social science package, one day of which would be an overview, with each of the remaining days dedicated to a different urban identity group, gay men and lesbians among them. Even though Greene and the commissioner rejected this proposal, in 1987 Tucker did introduce to the academy curriculum its first diversity training component, which included an hour of lesbian and gay issues. Tucker's initiative was only a first step; by 1992, under Commissioner Willie Williams, a one day in-service training program on diversity issues was established for patrolmen and -women, as well as officers already on duty.

Tucker was also the first commissioner to deal seriously with bias crimes, including those against lesbians and gay men. In December 1986, he instituted the Conflict Prevention and Resolution Unit in the department to investigate bias crimes motivated by race, religion, ethnic affiliation, or (explicitly mentioned) sexual orientation. Then, the following June, Tucker issued a memo to be read at the morning roll call: "All acts of violence or threats related to racial, ethnic, religious or sexual orientation will be viewed as serious and the investigations will be given priority attention. Such acts generate fear and concern among victims and result in loss of public confidence."[46]

Tucker's announcement followed by only three weeks one of most contentious incidents between the gay community and the police. Whether they were related is an open matter. In May 1987, an off-duty police officer, Thomas Duffy, was arrested with five others in Center City and charged with beating and kicking two gay men after shouting antigay comments at them.[47] Tucker suspended Duffy, but a few months later a Philadelphia judge cleared the police officer and another defendant of the charges. A third man was convicted of simple assault.[48]

After the charges were dropped, Duffy began a five-year campaign to regain his job. He had the support of the Fraternal Order of Police and, it seemed, much of the local judicial system. His attempts to erase the record of his arrest so he could apply for reinstatement were opposed by both the commissioner's office and the district attorney's office on the grounds that Duffy "is not the kind of man the city wants on its police force." Duffy's attorney argued that he had been "a fine and decorated officer for more than six years."[49] In 1989, Duffy had his arrest and trial expunged from his record. In 1993, after a series of hearings, an arbitrator ruled that Duffy should be reinstated and receive almost five years of back pay lost during his suspension. Under Mayor Edward Rendell, the city appealed the ruling. What was new in the Duffy case was that the elite of the criminal justice system—the commissioner, the mayor, the district attorney, the city solicitor—were ahead of the culture of the department (and of the municipal court system). The experience added to the pressure for change in the police rank and file.

The Duffy case illustrated the wide range of frustration felt not only by the gay community but also by African Americans, Latinos, and other minorities who were subjected to arbitrary behavior by the police. The protective channels in the department, the general sympathy of local municipal courts toward the police, and the resources of the FOP were frequently sufficient to block even the commissioner's attempts to increase accountability in the force. As in Duffy's case, an officer fired by the police commissioner was able to submit the case to arbitration, in which the Fraternal Order of Police had a strong record of overturning cases or reducing punishment.[50]

The Siege at the Bellevue and Civilian Review

The gay community learned two lessons in the 1980s regarding police practices. First, consistent pressure for police reform might result in change, but only if it were placed in the context of broader attempts at police professionalization. The coincidence of the PLGTF's recommendations on training with Tucker's desire to enhance the training of new officers and senior brass expanded the political base for the commissioner's agenda into the gay community and other identity communities in the city whose representatives had taken similar positions. Second, success was much more likely if pursued in conjunction with representatives of other groups. The PLGTF had cooperated with the local chapters of the ACLU, the NAACP, Latino groups, and academics experienced in police professionalization strategies. The appointment of a commissioner at least willing to talk and seriously consider recommendations that in the past would simply have been dismissed out of hand was also a factor in some of the changes.

ACT-UP, the Police, and Outside Review

These lessons were reinforced by the politics of the Civilian Review Board toward the police department which—in the case of the lesbian and gay community—followed a particularly ugly incident between the police and demonstrators at an early evening fund-raising dinner for President George Bush at the Bellevue Hotel in April 1991. Among others, ACT-UP planned to be part of a large demonstration protesting the Republican administration's position on a wide variety of social and health issues. ACT-UP was specifically opposed to what they saw as inadequate support of HIV research and service programs. More than one thousand demonstrators were outside the Bellevue.

After the president was safely inside the hotel, a scuffle broke out between ACT-UP and the Philadelphia police that eventually escalated into a more severe confrontation. The demonstrators began a "die-in," a standard demonstration technique of ACT-UP. They had a coffin representing those who had died from HIV, and some members lay on the ground as if dead. As they pushed close to the police lines, the "coffin" fell and accidentally hit a police sergeant. Officers then either overreacted or reacted in an undisciplined manner. The crowd was pushed back forcefully, with some injuries from being pushed and more serious injuries from swinging batons. Charges against the police included homophobia, assault, irrational fear of HIV/AIDS, excessive use of force, and "name-calling."[51] Videotapes of the event showed that officers were not being given clear directions by their superiors. Since many of the young officers had been brought in from outside Center City police districts to deal with the demonstrations, they did not have adequate training in crowd control. The Civil Affairs Unit of the Philadelphia Police Department, which usually handled demonstrations and maintained a liaison with the protesting groups, made up only 10 percent of the total force around the Bellevue. Police sources also indicated that the U.S. Secret Service had not clarified its plans to protect the president in the midst of the expected demonstration.

The incident itself may not have been startling, given the history of the Philadelphia police force, but what was a sign of change was the commissioner's willingness to form a civilian advisory group to investigate the incident and recommend policy changes to avoid similar future events. Although he initially defended the police's actions, after viewing tapes of the events around the hotel, Rendell's commissioner—Willie Williams—announced he would set up an investigation of the police response to the demonstrators. Among others, he appointed a cochair of the Philadelphia Lesbian and Gay Task Force, a deputy police commissioner, a council member, several attorneys, a member of the commissioner's staff, and the president of the Fraternal Order of Police. The FOP appointee, however, refused to take part in the investigation, claiming that the police had acted professionally. Williams also termed the advisory group a "civilian review board," which FOP opposed.

The advisory group completed its work in March 1992, finding that "some but by no means all members of the Philadelphia Police Department over-reacted to peaceful, non-violent acts of civil disobedience by the AIDS activist group ACT-UP and other demonstrators." The report also stated that "for some officers, an irrational fear of AIDS, hostility to gay people, and heightened tensions due to the presence of the President contributed to the over-reaction." The advisory group offered a wide range of recommendations on training, tactics, specific education on AIDS/HIV for all supervisors and all officers and the upgrading of access to the Civil Affairs Unit. But their most important recommendation was the establishment for the department of a permanent Civilian Review Board, similar to the temporary advisory group.[52]

After the advisory group's report was released, the commissioner directed the police department's Internal Affairs Division to conduct its own investigation into possible police misconduct based on the report's evidence. In its March 1993 report, the Internal Affairs Division challenged several of the civilian group's conclusions, determining that "despite the chaos and confusion of the initial confrontation . . . the officers were able to respond to the situation effectively and with the minimum amount of force necessary."[53] It further indicated that all the recommendations of the advisory group had already been implemented. The recommendations regarding training were met with the assertion that the subjects had been part of academy and in-service training "for several years" and that the division supported the "continued utilization of civilian police advisory councils" to work with the commissioner.[54] In short, the two reports contradicted each other.

In June 1993, four members of the advisory group, including the principal representative of the gay community, Professor Larry Gross of the University of Pennsylvania, issued a final report in response to the Internal Affairs Division report, charging that it was a "study in systematic bias." The issues surrounding President Bush's April 1991 visit to Philadelphia were thus left unresolved.

The Struggle to Re-create a Civilian Review Board

The most important effect of the entire process was to renew the interest of leaders of the lesbian and gay community in creating a Civilian Police Review Board. A police review board in Philadelphia had been established in 1957 by another reform mayor and former district attorney, Richard Dilworth. In the six years before the founding of the earlier review board, the local branch of the ACLU could find no documented case in which an officer had been disciplined for any inappropriate conduct directed toward a civilian. Much (though not all) of the African American leadership and many from the Italian American community supported a board. Dilworth then established it by executive order when the City Council refused to do so. Interestingly, this board was established before the dramatic change in Philadelphia's demographics.

From 1980 to the Bellevue incident, representatives of the lesbian and gay community focused most of their attention on establishing communications with the police leadership and instituting some form of diversity training at the academy. For accountability of arbitrary actions by police officers, individuals and groups attempted to use the civil courts to obtain some redress. Several cases were filed, using strategies similar to those employed in the past by African American and Latino groups. Either large settlements or changes in police policies as stipulated in the settlements were used to leverage change in the department. The strategy was not as successful for lesbians and gay men, however, although several cases were settled in the 1980s. In 1992, the city agreed to payments ranging from $750 to $12,500 to fourteen individuals and six organizations in litigation that followed the Bellevue Hotel demonstrations, but these were not based on sexual orientation as a class.

Nevertheless, in a consent decree associated with the Bellevue case, the police agreed not to "restrict, disrupt, punish, prevent or otherwise interfere with the free exercise of speech, association, assembly or petition for redress of grievance" in the future.[55] A 1996 settlement with the ACLU, NAACP, and the Police-Barrio Relations Project was a major success for the black and Latino communities. But despite efforts by the ACLU and independent attorneys, sexual orientation was not established as the basis for a "class" settlement. In many cases, individuals harassed or even assaulted by police did not want to pursue their legal rights or to be used as the basis of defining a legal class because they feared exposure in the press.[56]

Changes in the political environment, as well as a general failure by the courts to hold the police accountable for their actions against gay men and lesbians, made a civilian review of the department a more attractive option to gay leadership. In July 1992, the PLGTF reunited with the revitalized Coalition for Police Accountability, a group initially formed in response to the MOVE events of 1986 and composed of twenty of the city's leading civil rights, civil liberties, community, and advocacy groups demanded the creation of a permanent advisory board.[57] Commissioner Williams, who was about to become Los Angeles's police chief, would not endorse a permanent police advisory board, and the Fraternity of Police opposed it in the strongest terms.

The issue did not die, however. When the advisory group on the Bush visit was preparing to respond to the Internal Affairs Division report, three civilians were killed by police in ten days in May 1993. At least two of the three were questionable shootings, especially one that resulted in the death of a mentally ill homeless man who had thrown an empty bottle at a police officer. That shooting occurred the day before the City Council was about to hold hearings on the issue of a review board.

In its final draft, the bill would create a thirteen-member panel and have a budget of $525,000. Most of the council members, especially the minority council members, supported it, and the bill had the strong support of Council President John Street, arguably the most powerful African American politician in Philadelphia. Also an early sponsor of a similar bill was Angel Ortiz, the most important Latino member of the council. Most of the opponents were white. Furthermore, for more than a year, Mayor Rendell had opposed the review board as constructed by the council, saying that he feared for the morale of the police force.[58]

Ironically, the gay community became involved in the issue once again, but not as victims of arbitrary police authority. As a tactic to pressure Rendell to support the Civilian Review Board, several members of the City Council began to withdraw their support from Rendell's domestic partnership bill, which was geared toward and strongly supported by the city's lesbian and gay constituency. Liberal council members offered a quid pro quo: If the mayor wanted the domestic partnership bill, he would also have to accept the Civilian Review Board. Many assumed that John Street, president of the City Council, was the author of this strategy, though his staff denied it. Civilian review of the police was clearly seen as a minority issue, although some did not regard it also as a lesbian and gay issue. From Street's perspective,

> it would be very difficult to explain to people in my district why we have a gay bill, a domestic partnership bill, and we can't have a police oversight bill. We feel very strongly. We feel in North Philadelphia that we've been the victim of a lot of abuses of power demonstrated by a minority of members of the police department.

As a result of the linkage, the vote on the Civilian Review Board was put off for two weeks, and the vote on the domestic partnership bill was put off for months.

On May 21, the Civilian Review Board bill passed, eleven to six.[59] Even though the margin of victory in the council was a strong one, it was not sufficient to overturn a veto—and Rendell had threatened to veto the bill. Two weeks after the council passed the legislation, Rendell issued an extensive veto message that included the creation of a review board by executive order. Rendell's board was not as independent as that designed by the City Council, but the concession did establish a consensus that outside review of police actions was needed. Nevertheless, Rendell's plan was thwarted when one member of the council who had voted against the initial bill switched his vote and supported those forces trying to overturn Rendell's veto.

Conclusion

The struggle of Philadelphia's communities and even its mayors to obtain greater influence over police practices has been a long one. Although only a minor part of the long battle to make Philadelphia's police more responsive to community interests, their contention with the Philadelphia Police Department is a significant chapter in the history of gay people in the City of Brotherly Love. The organizational culture that built up around Philadelphia's isolated police department seemed to have gone beyond what other cities experienced. It made even more tense an already tense relationship between two cultures: the culture that grew up and around police rituals and regulations and the culture built around sexual identity. The uneasiness between these two cultures was not unique to Philadelphia, but the role of the police department in the postwar politics of Philadelphia was.

Without exaggerating the actual amount of change in Philadelphia's police department, a review of the past twenty years of attitudes toward sexual identity groups in Philadelphia reveals two overriding factors.

The first was the change in the status of Philadelphia's gay community. The marginal nature of lesbian and gay life in the 1940s and 1950s had largely disappeared—at least for white, middle-class gay men and lesbians—by the early 1990s. The commerce now associated with sexual identity was investment in residential and commercial space, and a legitimate nightlife. Whereas once the attempt to regulate adult commerce in Center City targeted both the social and the sexual practices of lesbians and especially gay men, a portion of the gay community had now become a strong supporter of the "cleanup" of Center City. Change—though certainly not complete change—came only with the greater visibility of the lesbian and gay community in Philadelphia and its growing prominence in the economic revitalization of Center City in the 1970s and 1980s.

The second factor is the series of crises in police professionalism that opened specific and time-bound windows of opportunity for external influence over police practices. The end of the Rizzo era opened one window of opportunity. The gay community's earliest efforts at police reform largely failed; it was not until the departure of Frank Rizzo and the election of a new, reform mayor that change became possible. There were several points at which intervention was attempted. The most prominent—though not specifically related to sexual identity—was the Osage Avenue incident. Other points at which new initiatives were taken at reform came after the federal investigation of police extortion of Center City's gay bar owners, the visit of President Bush and the police overreaction to the demonstration, and the Duffey case. It was at these points that the political resources of the lesbian and gay community could be used for efforts at reform.

The history of attempting to alter police practices—not only in Philadelphia, but also in most of urban America—tests the persuasiveness of several models of organizational behavior. Specifically, it calls into question the tradition of organizational theory that sees bureaucracies as open arenas of political conflict through which larger social forces operate. According to this view, the policy outputs of service delivery bureaucrats are predominantly driven by environmental forces—the social and political variables in which the bureaucracy operates.

The behavior of large city police departments has never quite fit this "open systems" model of organizations. The resistance to community control, often even mayoral control, combined with the paramilitary élan and internal bonding of service personnel challenges both hierarchical and open systems models of bureaucratic behavior. In many ways, the policy outputs of urban police bureaucracies are independent of environments and formal hierarchical control. Instead, they are determined by the very rationale of the organization itself. The entire community-policing movement is yet another attempt to control these pressures to isolate police departments by establishing congruent beliefs about the police among the patrolling forces and communities. But even here, the open systems model does not really explain this common response to the challenge of police legitimacy in (minority) communities. It was not imposed externally by police review boards or outside political forces. Rather, community policing was a response by the urban criminal justice professions to the delegitimation of the police.

The themes of the community-policing movement have never challenged the central rationale of urban police departments. The effect that leaders of Philadelphia's lesbian and gay community have had on police practices has not been through political force or external review. Instead, it has been the result of exploiting inconsistencies in bureaucratic universalism that are behaviorally expressed in police practices. Why, when the police are responsible for protecting person and property, do they harass gay men and lesbians? Why are data on sexual identity collected only when gay men or lesbians commit crimes, but not when they are victims of crimes? Why is it rational for homosexuals to be prevented from becoming police officers? These and many other questions challenge the legitimacy of the police and require a defense with which the department's actions are not necessarily consistent. To use sociologist John Meyer's phrase, the legitimacy of police organizations rests on a "cultural accounting," an accounting that now includes criteria established by an identity organized around sexuality.[60] "A completely legitimate organization would be one about which no question could be raised." Needless to say, most urban police departments do not meet this criterion.

From the perspective of activists, their actions against the department were not just a call for bureaucratic universalism, but an effort to problematize social processes, attitudes, and imputed attributes associated with homosexuality that were embedded in the department's procedures (both formal and informal).[61] In offering such a challenge, the intent of activists goes beyond just questioning past practices, but toward embedding aspects of their sexual identity into the procedures and discourses of the criminal justice system. There has been some success here. The end of a formal barrier to lesbians and gay men being admitted as officers; the collection of data on hate crimes with specific reference to actual or perceived sexual orientation; the incorporation of antigay hate crimes as in issue in a Federal-Commonwealth-City criminal justice interagency council on hate crimes;[62] and the incorporation of lesbian and gay concerns into the social science curriculum at the Police Academy. These are important if subtle organizational changes that will have their own direct and ancillary effects on the police culture.

###

CHAPTER 10

*Regime Theory and Identity Theory: Development Politics, School
Politics, and Domestic Partnerships in San Francisco*

As the quintessential postindustrial American city and a center of lesbian
and gay political influence, San Francisco is a good setting in which to investigate the interaction of urban regime theory and identity politics. What
happens when a group not defined by ethnicity or common economic interest but by sexual identity becomes part of a jurisdiction's governing
regime? Does participation in the governing coalition amplify tensions in
the group, since participation in a governing regime necessarily leads to involvement in issues not directly relevant to the identity themes that initially defined the group? Or does the burden of participating in urban governance make the identity even more complex?

   In the contemporary literature of urban affairs, regime theory has been
primarily identified with issues of economic development and the interaction of markets and the local state.[1] Progrowth regimes have been studied
in Los Angeles, Pittsburgh, Chicago, Houston, and Atlanta, among other
places. In these cases, through the sustained, informal overlap of economic
resources and public instrumentalities, the regime coalition forms its strategic economic perspective. The very informality of this "purposive coordination of efforts" highlights both informal networks of communication and
a common "vision." Typically there is no central and coordinating arena—
formal or informal—in which policies and broad strategies are determined,
but there is a matrix of relationships through which leaders of differing
groups are able to become comfortable with one another and generate the
regime's perspective.

   Although development policies have been the principal focus of regime
theory during the past decade, some applications to urban politics of
regime theory refer to broader frameworks. Greenstone and Peterson, for
example, took a more social and macro approach to regime theory, seeing

the ultimate impact of the Community Action Program of the 1960s as altering the relationship between race and the sometimes conflicting legitimation principles of American civic culture.[2] Although they used cities as the settings in a conflict between latent regime interests and the underlying legitimating themes of American governance, their approach centered on the social organization of institution building. They saw the incorporation of African American interests in city regimes as uncertain in the short term, with institutionalization coming only after the initial leaders' agenda was passed on to the next set of leaders—if it ever was.

Others, looking to individual urban regimes and de-emphasizing contextual issues, described coalitions built around noneconomic agendas. Adolph Reed used this approach to describe "bi-racial regimes."[3] Regimes not primarily defined as "progrowth" may arise from other informal matrices defined by racial or ethnic background, gender, ideology, or less tangible binding ties.[4] Although particularistic economic gains by a regime's members define much of its politics, the bonding ideology can be broader than a simple economic perspective. It can be ethnic or cultural or, more likely, a political discourse that mixes economic interest with cultural characteristics.

The "tacit understanding" or "regime perspective" that keeps a regime together can be seen as either ideology or—again through a social organization lens, in which the "rhetoric" of the regime is a "native statement"— "a robust abstraction from linguistic practices generated by the intersection of style together with institutions."[5] It is important not just that leaders of the regime's component networks negotiate with one another to define common ends but that they also have a common language—what postmodernists would call a *discourse*—that is not problematic to them and, furthermore, renders other positions literally "meaning-*less*" in the terms of the rhetoric.

In San Francisco, the politics of the 1990s seems best characterized by a view that merges an identity model with a model describing the tension between a progrowth regime and its community-based opponents. Can we find evidence of political influence outside the areas of immediate interest to identity-defined groups? Coalitions based on election mobilization and influence cut across the traditional progrowth/growth-control division that San Francisco development politics exemplifies. In some cases, interests organized around identity groups may divide the component groups of the coalitions organized around economic conflict.

To explore these themes, we chose several cases in three policy areas to examine the problematization of policymaking criteria by an emerging identity, the political tensions surrounding the policy effects of such policymaking, and the information such politics offers to a better understanding of regime theory in general. The three policy areas are (1) the ambivalent role of lesbians and gay men in San Francisco's economic development practice, (2) the establishment of a special counseling program for lesbian and gay students in San Francisco's public schools, and (3) the drive to legitimize domestic partnerships for lesbians and gay men (and cohabiting nongay couples also). These broad issues include both specific and general interests of lesbians and gay men in San Francisco. The goal is to broaden the framework of our discussion of regimes to include identity and ultimately its embedding in urban governing structures. We will return to this latter theme in the concluding section of the book.

Sexual Identity and Growth-Control Politics in San Francisco

Most lesbians and gay men remember November 27, 1978, as the day Harvey Milk was assassinated, but for the history of San Francisco, it was George Moscone's murder that more truly altered the city's political future. Moscone had put together a coalition of neighborhood and community groups, minorities, and new immigrants—gay men and lesbians among them—to confront the local effects of San Francisco's rapid economic change. The neighborhood effects of urban change included a rapid rise in the cost of residential and commercial space, the destruction of much of the lower-income (albeit inadequate) housing near downtown, the displacement of its population, and the loss of many manufacturing jobs. Blocks of near downtown were leveled, and thirty years later, some, still vacant, were being used as parking lots.

The economic transformation of San Francisco was pursued and, in part, directed by what Mollenkopf called San Francisco's progrowth coalition. As early as the war years of the 1940s, the business community and public officials worked together to sustain the economic boom in the Bay Area that the wartime spending had stimulated. The Bay Area Council, growing out of war coordination efforts, looked toward a fully integrated plan for greater Bay Area development. Despite conflicting individual business perspectives, the unifying vision for the central city was as a postindustrial service center city. In many ways, the "new" San Francisco would be a model "nodal" city with its downtown business space, convention center and stadia, arterial highways connecting satellites of economic activity, high-speed commuter rail to the region's business core, enhanced retail and arts facilities, and a modern airport with commuter, international, and air-freight capacities.

Although not every part of the plan was implemented (the convention center was constructed, but a downtown stadium never was), the San Francisco that resulted changed the scale and dimensions of the city, bringing more people into the urban core, threatening older neighborhoods near the central business district. In addition to being a model postindustrial city (and region), San Francisco became a textbook case of a city experiencing the social tensions of an economy in transition from one based on manufacturing and commerce to one with finance, real estate, and advanced business services.

Well into the 1970s, the local government generally supported the emergence of the new San Francisco. What came to be called the "Manhattanization" of the city proceeded with the full support of Mayors George Christopher, John Shelly, and Joseph Alioto.[6] Fainstein, Fainstein, and Armistead describe the role of the city government (including its authorities, the city's role as a county, and its other public instrumentalities) in San Francisco's development in three time-bound stages.[7] The first, roughly from 1950 to 1964, was a period of unopposed clearance. Using federal urban renewal and housing funds, state and federal highway monies, special taxes to fund bonds for BART (Bay Area Rapid Transit), and the broad Western Addition project, Christopher—as both a reform and a progrowth mayor—firmly pressed on with the plans for a Manhattanized San Francisco, working with corporate and business groups. One result was that whole swaths of central-business-district (CBD) land were leveled, justified as necessary for urban renewal.

The second stage of San Francisco's development was instigated by activists seeking federal assistance for community service. Community activists had begun to use funds made available through the Equal Opportunity Act and the Community Action Program and other antipoverty programs to confront the social effects of redevelopment. Even though the antipoverty programs of the mid- and late 1960s did help the community movement, especially in the Mission district, private investors continued the destruction of lower-income housing and commercial space. During the Christopher years, only minor concessions were made to neighborhoods. When Joseph Alioto was first elected in 1969, he brought the major unions—especially the building unions—into the progrowth coalition. In exchange, Alioto was able to obtain a more generous package for those unionized employees displaced by the destruction of low-income housing and commercial space downtown. More important to the future, neighborhood activists began to win some victories in the courts.

Fainstein, Fainstein, and Armistead considered the years between 1975 and 1980 to be a period of consolidation for the progrowth forces.[8] Despite the work of neighborhood activists and the mounting signs of displacement, Alioto's slum clearance and redevelopment policies were generally supported by San Francisco's voters. The city's middle class and blue-collar ethnic voters had not yet been on the losing side of the progrowth policies. Although Alioto's election could be described as a victory for ethnically defined groups (largely Italian and Irish Catholics) and for the continuing influence of organized labor, the San Francisco of the postwar era was passing.

Accordingly, near the end of Alioto's second term, Frederick Wirt described San Francisco's politics as a *hyperpluralist system*, a term frequently used for New York City's politics.[9] San Francisco had become a meeting place for many different communities and identities, a resource that George Moscone was able to exploit. Asians and Latinos were asserting their political presence, and African Americans were at their demographic peak. The West Coast city most closely identified with the beat generation and the cultural politics of the 1960s attracted a new wave of domestic in-migration of younger, better-educated non-Californians, many of whom were lesbian or gay (see figure 10-1). By the time of Moscone's 1975 election, the basic plan for the new San Francisco had been laid out. Investment was now principally private, with the public sector already committed to investing in the infrastructure. For the next twenty years, city government was less an instrument of progrowth forces than an arena in which the slow-growth and progrowth forces fought, seeking an accommodation to be administered by city government.

The Conflicting Roots of Lesbian and Gay Involvement in Growth Politics

The rise of lesbian and gay political and cultural influence in San Francisco is usually linked to this fundamental reorganization of the city's political economy during the 1960s and 1970s. The need for educated personnel to

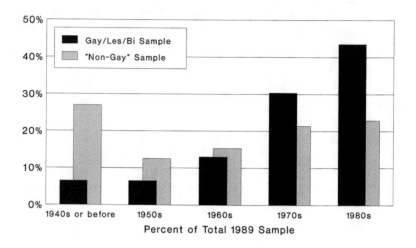

FIGURE 10.1

Lesbians/gays arrive in San Francisco
(year respondents arrived/were born in SF).
(Source: State of the City Poll, San Francisco State University, R. DeLeon.
Valid totals n = 373; gay/les/bi = 46.)

fill the new service-sector jobs was met by the city's new residents, which included lesbians and gay men. From this point on, the gay community acquired enough economic power, political resources, and local influence to
pursue its interests in city affairs.

The interest of urban specialists in the emergence of gay and lesbian
identity enclaves coincided with the economic and spatial restructuring of
postindustrial cities. Until the mid-1990s, most of the references to gay men
and lesbians in the literature on urban affairs concerned their relation to the
gentrification process. Some of these references are to the initial work done
by Castells and Murphy in the early 1980s, who observed that homosexuals
were among the gentrifiers of the older ethnic neighborhoods of San Francisco, especially the old Irish working-class communities in Eureka Valley
(whose central commercial strip is Castro Street) and in the northwestern
portion of the Mission district.[10] But as we saw in chapter 4, an influx of
lesbian and gay residents does not necessarily lead to an outflow of minorities and the poor.

The lesbian and gay presence in San Francisco long predated both the

1969 Stonewall uprising in New York and the dramatic demographic and economic changes in San Francisco during the late 1960s to 1980s. San Francisco's gay- and lesbian-friendly bars proliferated during World War II, although this relative freedom was accompanied by periods of arrests and shutdowns by the city police, state liquor authorities, and, in some cases, military police. In fact, the political weakness of lesbians and gay men in San Francisco can be measured by these various crackdowns on gay-friendly bars and establishments, which lasted well into the 1960s with arrests of patrons and charges filed against owners.

Nonetheless, the original homophile movement did find an early home in San Francisco. Both the Mattachine Society and the Daughters of Bilitis were located in San Francisco by the late 1950s, as well as a new local group called SIR, which led to informational forums and candidates' nights attended by many of San Francisco's then emerging liberal stars, such as Philip Burton, James Morrison, Willie Brown, and John Burton. The organizers' goal was to bring attention to the city's gay voting power.[11] As the 1960s proceeded, politicians seeking office began to believe that the "gay vote" was substantial and that liberals in particular needed to court it. The "Burton machine" especially nurtured the gay vote and was rewarded for it well into the 1990s. Still, as late as 1970, the main concern of gay politics was ending police harassment and applying due process to lesbian and gay men. Their ultimate goal was the repeal of California's sodomy law.

The initial gay involvement in San Francisco's community politics did not come about as a result of the city's urban transformation but in opposition to it. Throughout the 1960s, the geographic center of San Francisco's gay community was still in the Tenderloin, North Beach, and Polk Valley (or Polk Gulch) areas of the city. It had begun to expand into the Western Addition, a largely black neighborhood bordering the civic center on the northwest, which was slated for urban renewal by the San Francisco Redevelopment Agency (SFRA) and thus destruction. For some gay residents, this was an opportunity for an upgrade in housing, but for others it threatened displacement.[12] The Yerba Buena site south of Market Street also threatened the newer gay residential clusters there.

In the 1970s, a rougher gay community became established south of Market and below the Mission. This area eventually became the center of the city's leather community. The destruction of inexpensive rentals and resident hotels south of Market thus would threaten what was becoming a gay-friendly neighborhood. If the demolition of inexpensive housing were extensive, the expected relocation of poor, transients, and some gay men and lesbians into the Tenderloin would put pressure on housing prices there. Therefore, maintaining these neighborhoods was, at best, a marginal goal in the central strategy of downtown development envisioned by the SFRA and the Shelly and Alioto administrations. That the gay identity centered here also shows the marginalized nature of homosexualities as communities in the late 1960s. The proposed destruction of low-income commercial and residential space near downtown threatened not only the remnants of the city's white ethnic communities, the elderly, lower-income blacks, Latinos, poorer Asians, and small businesses but also those areas of the city where gay-friendly establishments were socially assigned and where gay political activity found its first, insecure, base.

It was in the Tenderloin that gay participation in San Francisco's policy-making first received governmental (as opposed to political) recognition. It was in regard not to human rights or health care but to issues of relocation, community development, and social services to the young, including gay youth. The Tenderloin area was declared an antipoverty district under the federal Equal Opportunity Act, and funds were made available for community development. (The Mission area was declared a Model Cities district in the 1970s.) As part of the Community Action Program, two openly gay men, among the first organizers of SIR, were hired to provide program support for adolescent homosexuals hustling in the city's "red-light" district. Education and social services were seen as a way out of prostitution and street life.

These initial gay political and governmental actions in the Tenderloin conflict with the more popular image that gay political influence and even identity first emerged in San Francisco as a result of an influx of well-educated, middle-income gay men and lesbians in the 1970s. Rather, the first gay and lesbian political identification was community based and service oriented, centered not in the Castro but in some of the poorest and most troubled sections of San Francisco. Nor were the initial organizations fueled by self-confidence and a confrontational style. Instead, their agenda was a simple one—survival—and their strategies were often self-conscious and hesitant.

This does not mean that the large influx of gay men and lesbians in the 1970s had no effect. To the experience of San Francisco's first gay activists were added the resources and expectations of the lesbian and gay <ea>migr<ea>s of the 1970s. San Francisco's economy was generating jobs at a rapid pace. Like many others moving into the Bay Area, these

<ea>migr<ea> gay men and lesbians were taking advantage of the city's eco-
nomic transformation as well as public and private investments in amenities. In this sense, urban transformation did indeed create an environment
that helped San Francisco become a center of gay and lesbian politics. (Even
so, Boston, Minneapolis, and Seattle went through much the same transition without becoming the major site of gay identity in the United States.)

The new lesbian and gay émigrés both overlapped with the older generation of activists in San Francisco and frequently clashed with them. The
older group found its home in the subculture of lesbian and gay identity in
the beat, bohemian, and counterculture movements of the 1950s and 1960s.
Many were native Bay Area residents or people who had moved to San
Francisco after World War II and organized through Mattachine, Daughters of Bilitis, and SIR. They did lay the foundation for the political activism of the next generation, but their agenda was narrow and specific.

These pioneer activists and organizers, however, were familiar with the
actors and powers of San Francisco politics, which in most cases was an
asset, but in some ways, their experience with San Francisco city politics
limited their expectations for political success. They had already challenged
or reached some accommodation with the unions, the Democratic machine, the Roman Catholic archdiocese, and government social service bureaucracies. Ironically, nearly all these groups lost power and influence as
the city moved toward a postindustrial economy. The newer <ea>migr<ea>s
found their home in the corporate world, social and human services, or the
spillover economies and markets that "gay money" was generating through
the bars, clubs, real estate, retail outlets, and personal services. This new
group took advantage of the emerging economy that older San Franciscans—gay or not—sometimes saw as a threat.

Writers seeking to recapture San Francisco's lesbian and gay political history have made much of the tension between the older gay leadership in
San Francisco and the younger, more militant leadership that had taken
shape in the 1970s.[13] Much of this conflict concerned the tactics of advancing gay rights, not the place of gay men and lesbians in growth politics.
But in retrospect, it is clear that several conflicting themes were joined in
San Francisco's gay community regarding growth politics as a result of the
struggle between two generations of leaders.

The first theme was an early recognition of the costs of unbridled growth
to lower-income groups, which included a large portion of the initial Bay
Area sexual identity cohort. For the earlier activists, the marginalization of

gay and especially lesbian life was real, not just symbolic. It meant menial positions and low wages and real ceilings on professional careers, if entry-level positions could even be found. City government and the education sector were not the safe havens they would be in the 1980s but instead were hostile to hiring openly gay people. To this group, identifying with work-ing-class problems and poorer San Franciscans was taken for granted.

The second theme was the economic and social pressure that the "newer" lesbian and gay male <ea>migr<ea>s were adding to the forces of urban transformation and gentrification. The effect of these trends, which in part were instigated by new gay residents, can be seen in the housing markets. Gentrification in Eureka Valley (the Castro) and Duboce Trian-gle—in which the city's older Victorian homes were remodeled and up-graded—was especially identified with "gay money." The results were a doubling, tripling, and sometimes even quadrupling of housing prices in a relatively short period of time.

As these new <ea>migr<ea>s became established residents, a third theme emerged. Portions of the new lesbian and gay population began behaving like many other new San Franciscans: they resisted the effects of continued economic dislocation on their own neighborhoods, seeking to preserve their quality of life by supporting controls on further and potentially dis-ruptive growth.

These three themes present conflicting ways in which lesbians and gay men approached the growth-control battles of the 1980s in San Francisco. If the lesbian and gay community was to become a formidable political force in the city, it had to reach a consensus on a wide range of concerns, growth-control issues among them. If not, the uneven effects of class and race could tear apart the gay community as development patterns and growth-control issues inevitably and unevenly affected different compo-nents of the sexual identity grouping. Outwardly, too, the gay and lesbian community needed to take a position that did not immediately align new gay residents in San Francisco with the gentrification movement. Some res-idents—especially Latinos, since they frequently lived adjacent to lesbian- and gay-identified housing clusters—suspected that the "gay community" had become part of the forces displacing the city's poor. In matters of growth control, sexual identity voters became a pivotal force in the balance of power between progrowth and slow-growth forces in San Francisco, but they were not always allies of the most "progressive" slow-growth advocates.

Identity Politics and Neighborhood Activism

By the mid-1970s, the residential and political focus of San Francisco's gay community had shifted from the Tenderloin and Polk Gulch to the Castro (the center of Eureka Valley). This change had political implications that went beyond simple urban geography. The Castro was an old, blue-collar, largely Irish neighborhood of well-maintained if not luxurious housing. The political dialogue that took place here was quite different from that in areas closer to downtown. Many fewer poor and many fewer "marginalized identities" lived in Eureka Valley. When gay life was centered in the Tenderloin and Polk Gulch, it was not surprising that the interaction with government was about dislocation and social services to young male prostitutes and gay and lesbian drug users, but these were not the main issues for the Castro's gay community.

On the broader stage of San Francisco's politics, Harvey Milk was one of several supervisors elected in 1977 in the new system of single-member districts, itself a product of the neighborhood movement and demands by minority groups for better representation. The new Board of Supervisors replaced the older board which, with its at-large apportionment, tended to be white and conservative—in both politics and temperament. The new board was elected two years after George Moscone was elected as mayor, giving growth-control forces their first real foothold in City Hall.

Within the bounds of lesbian and gay politics, Milk brought together several themes that could lead to internal conflict. Most important to our purposes, Milk merged identity politics with neighborhood politics. Many older veterans of the homophile and original Gay Liberation organizations objected to Milk's ambition to be San Francisco's first openly gay elected official. Others saw him as yet another "non–San Franciscan" seeking public office in San Francisco. By 1977, however, a coalition of movement and neighborhood forces began to form. Because they were organized through an identity-based movement, lesbians and gay men instinctively supported other identity movements of Asians, Latinos, and African Americans—understanding from experience that alliances among identity movements were the only way for any one of them to achieve its goals. Milk had also calmed the suspicions of some labor figures by organizing a boycott against the Coors brewery on issues of gay rights. The policy themes that Milk put together in his district—largely reflecting the themes of the Moscone years—represented the new groups taking shape in San Francisco: identity-and neighborhood-based organizations with a strong emphasis on community and neighborhood service and combined with resentment of the progrowth coalition's nearly twenty-five years of dominating San Francisco's politics. Similar coalitions were evident in other new districts of the city.

Propositions O, P, Q, V, and M: The Role of the Gay Vote in Early Slow-Growth Failures and Victories

Whereas Milk persuaded a large portion of the gay community to join the emerging political alliances in San Francisco, it was Moscone who validated the gay community's new status in San Francisco politics (a role he also played in the ascendancy of Asians, Latinos, and the neighborhood development movement). The themes and strategies that elected George Moscone in 1975 as the first mayor of what Richard DeLeon calls the "anti-regime regime" were also the ones that galvanized the various other identity and neighborhood coalitions around the city, including Milk's.[14] In the period between Moscone's election and his and Milk's assassinations, an "anti-regime" regime in San Francisco began to take shape, a regime that grew up in opposition to, and was fueled by, the negative effects of the three-decade-long dominance of San Francisco's politics by the progrowth coalition.

The first major policy effects of the neighborhood-based, growth-control movement came after Moscone's death. Proposition O in 1979, the high-rise-control referendum, would have limited the height of downtown office towers. Although the measure did not pass, the surprising amount of support for it indicated that the mood of San Franciscans toward unrestricted growth was changing.

In addition were the several corporate and property tax measures, all of which sought to impose additional revenue responsibilities on downtown development, using different revenue instruments. Generally, these tax initiatives would transfer a greater portion of the tax burden in San Francisco from residential property to downtown commercial property. The effort followed the passage of California State Proposition 13, which capped local property taxes. Increasing corporate taxes could forestall the service cutbacks that would likely follow the passage of Proposition 13, by forcing downtown businesses to contribute a larger share of the city's own-raised tax revenues. Some of these corporate tax measures were severe and rejected by voters. But Proposition M was a broadly directed tax measure and was seen as moderate. It passed.

Even though many lesbians and gay men worked in downtown businesses, the geographic outline of the residential areas identified with a gay presence indicates that these precincts voted for—though not as strongly as other sections of the city did—the measures perceived as a part of the anti-corporate, neighborhood coalition agenda. For example, the vote for Proposition O (high-rise-growth controls) was strong in gay neighborhoods. Much of the lesbian and gay leadership also endorsed the new corporate tax initiatives, especially the moderate Proposition M, which passed. But even here, there was ambivalence in areas with a heavy gay and lesbian population. The margin of victory from Harry Britt's (Milk's successor) Fifth District, especially the Eureka Valley/Noe Valley neighborhood, was not as dramatic as it was in the predominantly African American neighborhoods of Bayview and Hunters Point. The margin of support for Proposition M in the Fifth District's precincts ranged from 50 percent to 69 percent, with a 61 percent margin in the Eureka Valley/Noe Valley neighborhoods. This made the general Castro area only the twelfth strongest of San Francisco's thirty-eight neighborhoods supporting Proposition M.[15] And Eureka Valley/Noe Valley did not support Proposition V, one of the more radical and unsuccessful of the four corporate tax initiatives in 1979/80. Thus, although there was some predisposition in the gay community to align with neighborhood activists—especially among lesbians and gay leaders—as a group, they did not have a definitive, cohesive, and consistent position toward the stronger corporate tax measures.

The gathering strength of the antidowntown and neighborhood coalition movement, especially the strong support for Proposition O in 1979 and the successful vote on Proposition M in 1980, spurred the Board of Supervisors and Mayor Dianne Feinstein to offer a less extreme approach, one that linked a growth-control position with a "tax" on downtown economic power. A housing trust-linkage program (OHHP) was less a growth-control program than a policy device to skim off excess demand for office space in downtown San Francisco to mitigate the impacts of growth on the housing market.[16] In implementation, project by project, the program never achieved the kind of funding that its proponents anticipated. It did, however, begin a series of other linkage or exactive programs—including transit impact, open spaces, public art, and even child care—that remain a central theme of San Francisco's growth-control policy.

But as DeLeon properly describes Feinstein's years as mayor, they were an interregnum when the emerging slow-growth coalition lost much of its influence. The halfhearted administration of the OHHP program certainly did not satisfy slow-growth proponents, nor did it really affect downtown development. The greatest expansion of office and hotel space in postwar San Francisco occurred during the early years of the Feinstein administration, when any modifications in the developers' plans were made largely to gain votes or defuse mounting community opposition. The Feinstein administration did begin to incorporate the agendas of slow-growth and environmental advocates, but it could have done so more energetically. Even with the rapid expansion of office space and at the depths of the 1983 recession, the vacancy rate in office space was no higher than 19 percent in San Francisco.

The next and most important success of the growth-control movement in San Francisco was the final passage in 1986 of its planning initiative— Proposition M—another, but stronger, high-rise-growth-control initiative. The approval followed a previous and similar initiative in 1983 that had failed. The social base of those supporting the 1986 initiative included "renters," Latinos, blacks, environmentalists, and those with a middle-level socioeconomic status.[17] The role of the gay community in this important initiative of the slow-growth coalition is a bit clearer than in previous growth-control referenda. The evidence that those election districts usually identified as having a strong gay and lesbian presence supported Proposition M in 1986 is persuasive. In his analysis, DeLeon used a dummy variable of "gay precincts" in determining the effect of sexual identity on the vote on Proposition M in 1986.[18] He found that gay men and lesbians generally did support Proposition M. But since there was no exit poll in which the vote itself might be analyzed against other variables, we do not know whether race or income level in the sexual identity voting cohort affected voters' preferences.

The gay community probably did support Proposition O (high-rise control) in 1979 and Proposition M (a moderate corporate tax measure) in 1980. Moreover, Richard DeLeon is probably right that a majority of gay men and lesbians living in gay neighborhoods supported Proposition M (the San Francisco planning initiative) in 1986, but the strength of this support is unknown. In fact, there is some reason to believe that by the 1990s, the support for antigrowth or slow-growth measures was waning in the gay community. As evidence, two additional and important initiatives for which there is available exit-poll information show important divisions in the gay community on development policies: (1) the 1989 proposal for a downtown replacement for Candlestick Park and (2) the Mission Bay development project and its 1990 proposition. Accordingly, we can change the focus of our analysis of the gay community's attitude toward economic development and growth-control issues, to attitudes within it.

Proposition P: The Downtown Ballpark

Over the years, there had been several proposals for a new stadium to replace Candlestick Park. Like those in many other cities, the owners of the professional baseball franchise had threatened to move the San Francisco Giants from the city or even to sell the franchise if city officials did not accede to their demands. By the time Agnos had become mayor, voters in San Francisco and the north Bay Area had already rejected one referendum proposal each for a new stadium. In 1989, the pressure by owners for a new stadium was strong, and another referendum authorizing the construction of a new ballpark downtown and assisting in its financing was to be on the ballot. But two unexpected events changed the coalitions and votes regarding Proposition P: (1) the fact that the San Francisco Giants were in the World Series for the first time in decades and (2) the Loma Prieta earthquake, which struck on October 17, 1989.

The slow-growth movement had won a victory in the 1988 election of Art Agnos, who ran on much the same neighborhood-based, identity-supportive, and growth-control platform that Moscone had. Thus it was a surprise to many not only that the newly elected Art Agnos supported a new downtown stadium but also that he strongly supported it. Agnos argued that a new stadium would generate new revenues for social services, drug rehabilitation, AIDS prevention programs, and housing for PWAs (persons with AIDS). The promise of a new revenue stream in a city hard hit by unemployment and HIV was attractive to many, and advocates for African American, Latino, and gay social service agencies supported the proposal on these grounds. Roberta Achtenberg, then a lawyer and expert on lesbian rights issues, announced her support. In addition, other odd alliances were formed around the ballpark.

In a phone poll taken late in the summer before the balloting—and, more important, before both the World Series and the earthquake—support for a new, downtown ballpark was wide and cut across some of the usual divisions created by development issues.[19] Gender had a much more important effect on attitudes toward the ballpark than did variables more typically predictive of voter preferences on development issues. When testing for the likelihood that different demographic groups would have different attitudes toward the stadium than would the population as a whole, gender was found to be the most powerful factor.[20] Men supported the stadium vote 46 percent to 41 percent, whereas women opposed it 53 percent to 41 percent (the remainder were undecided). Preferences among racial and identity groupings showed broad support:[21] African Americans supported the ballpark 51 percent to 39 percent; whites opposed it 48 to 38; Latinos supported it 53 to 48; and Asians opposed it 47 to 45. At least before the earthquake, blacks and Latinos tended to agree that the stadium presented an opportunity for jobs and the new revenues that Agnos had promised for their communities.

Self-identified gay and lesbian voters contacted in the same August phone poll were almost evenly split, with 51.2 percent supporting the proposition and 48.8 opposing it. Although the sample size was small, an analysis of cleavages among gay and lesbian/bisexual respondents showed higher-income households, and younger voters, tended to support the stadium. In fact, income defined the division in gay and lesbian opinion on the stadium better than it did in the nongay population. These data support the more general observations expressed in interviews with local political operatives in San Francisco linked to the gay community. As one knowledgeable activist put it: "Those gays living up there [the east side of Twin Peaks and in the Buena Vista section] were for it, while those in the valley [Castro/Eureka] were opposed."[22]

As the campaign proceeded, Agnos called on leaders of the gay community to support the ballpark proposal and secured the vote of the Harvey Milk Democratic Club. But many others were not won over. Some supporters of the stadium and allies of Agnos attempted to link the ballpark proposition with a domestic partnership vote that also was to be on the ballot that November. Agnos, however, did not see this as a specific strategy, although he and his staff did call in some chips for his past support of lesbian and gay issues.

The October 17 earthquake struck during the first game of the 1989 World Series at Candlestick Park. The collapsed interstate on the East Bay as well as Highway 101 in San Francisco immediately became long-term planning problems. The Bay Bridge also suffered severe damage. The fires in the Marina section of the city were extensive, and many public buildings were damaged.

After the earthquake, Agnos put even more energy and prestige into the campaign, leaving the impression among some in the gay and lesbian community that he cared more about the stadium than for the domestic partnership vote that was also on the ballot in 1989. (Proposition S was a voter initiative to overturn the San Francisco Board of Supervisors' passage of a domestic partners bill.) Despite the resources dedicated to the campaign, opposition to the new stadium grew rapidly after the quake. Indeed, a *San Francisco Chronicle* poll indicated a huge drop in support between July and October (see table 10-1). With portions of the city now in ruins, voters were much more concerned about costs. There was some recovery (a preelection poll indicated that support for the ballpark was behind by only 5 percent, with 11 percent undecided), but the vote would be close.[23] Supporters of the ballpark measure believed that conservative absentee voters would vote against the plan, and they did. An attempt to compensate with a get-out-the-vote drive among people likely to vote yes could not match the heavy opposition to the ballpark by absentee voters, largely senior citizens and business people in California.

On election day, those who actually voted gave the stadium proposition a slight positive margin. But the absentee ballots were not as supportive,

TABLE 10-1
Effect of October 17 Quake on Ballpark Vote (%)

Would You Vote Yes or No on the Ballot Measure This November to Build a New Giants Baseball Stadium in Downtown San Francisco?

	Yes	No	Don't Know
July	48	34	18
August	46	40	14
October 21–25	34	55	11

Since the Recent Earthquake, Are You More Inclined or Less Inclined to Vote Yes on the New Giants Stadium?

	During World Series	After Earthquake
More inclined	10	7
Less inclined	6	26
Same	82	65
Don't know	2	2

Source: *San Francisco Chronicle*, October 27, 1989

nor was the turnout in African American districts as strong in 1989 as it had been in the 1987 stadium vote (Proposition W). Support in black neighborhoods had been strong for the ballpark in the summer, but by election day more blacks opposed the stadium than supported it—at least among those who went to the polls. Turnout was only 33 percent of registered voters, and the proposition lost in the Bayview/Hunters Point districts (the center of the black vote in San Francisco) by more than five hundred votes.

In neighborhoods identified as gay and lesbian strongholds, the stadium vote was mixed. In Upper Market/Eureka, which covers most of the Castro area, the vote was 6,347 for the ballpark and 6,028 against it. In Noe Valley/Diamond Heights, the result was similar: 3,825 for and 3,295 against a new home for the Giants. Indeed, the outcome was mixed.

Proposition I: Mission Bay and Gays in Governance

The Mission Bay project was another long-running growth battle in San Francisco, engaging the interest of many groups in the city, including the gay community. As in many other cities, abandoned track, car float, and storage facilities held by the railroads were being recycled, with new uses. In San Francisco's case, the areas around China Basin and the old Southern Pacific and Santa Fe rail yards encompassed more than three hundred acres, the largest site open to development in San Francisco. On its west, the site bordered the city's Mission section and the South of Market area—both neighborhoods sensitive to development and displacement issues. The site was within walking distance of Potrero Hills, a site of middle- and lower-middle-class housing for many African Americans and Latinos.

Both commercial and residential development was being planned, with the city's encouragement, and with profit-making commercial rentals cross-subsidizing the housing portion. One working plan for the area had a broad framework for community input, which was an important victory for San Francisco's slow-growth forces. Although many people still opposed large-scale development of the Mission Bay area, the more participatory process allowed for additional service and tax extractions as well as height and scale limitations. But it was the passage of Proposition M in 1986 that gave neighborhood groups their most powerful tool to influence the development of a Mission Bay plan: either the plan would meet Proposition M's requirements, or it would require a waiver voted on in a referendum.

Mayor Agnos, who had supported Proposition M, announced his support also for the development of Mission Bay. He and his staff expected the project to be positive on balance, since it would provide revenue for services and an increase in the acreage of land for recreational purposes, especially for children from the Mission district and Potrero. Four of the nine supervisors sponsored the required referendum to approve a waiver—including Harry Britt—and the rest supported it. Even the community groups that were working against the specific proposition were not completely opposed to some of the projects.

The opposition to Mission Bay brought together an odd but understandable combination of what normally would be opposing forces in any city: the big downtown developers and real estate managers, on the one hand, and local neighborhood groups from around the city but especially in the Mission and South of Market areas, on the other hand. Although there was a general predisposition in the city against passing waivers on high-rise control, support for the Mission Bay project and for the required exemption under Proposition M was strong in the early part of the referendum campaign. In the third week of September, the Mission Bay project was winning handily, but only four weeks later, in a poll conducted on October 25–27, 1989, support for it had dropped, especially among women, senior citizens, and households with incomes under $20,000 a year. The focus of the anti–Proposition I campaign was on lower-income voters, residents, and small businesses in neighborhoods around the proposed project, as well as environmental groups and the gay community—not as a sexual identity group but as a core group in the liberal alliance that had so much influence in San Francisco.

Again, lesbian and gay leaders were on both sides of a critical economic development issue. Dick Pabich, for example, a former aide to Harvey Milk, was the campaign manager and consultant for the pro–Proposition I campaign. T. J. Anthony, an openly gay aide to Supervisor Richard Hongisto, was active in the opposition. Supervisor Hongisto's staff had threatened to work against the proposal if changes were not made, such as the addition of a community health clinic with HIV facilities. This was a demand by representatives of both the gay community and the Latino community. Anthony used the rules of the Board of Supervisors to hold hearings, in Hongisto's name, on the project throughout the city. The hearings then became venues for community opposition to the project to gain press attention.[24] When the final vote was cast, it was clear that the campaign against the project had won the information battle: 49.8 percent voted yes, and 50.1 percent voted no.

But the 1990 defeat of Proposition I did not end the controversy. The project was scaled down and developers made several concessions on amenities and exactions. Many of those who continued to opposed the Mission Bay project were not opposed to development of the site per se but felt that city officials could get a better deal from developers. The city school district, for example, sought a new school for children of the complex; advocates for the poor sought more housing; environmentalists sought a smaller overall plan and greater assurances of protection of the wetlands; and neighborhood residents and the arts community sought a public arts program. Using the basic theme of exactive approval processes that San Francisco had been a leader in, representatives from the gay and Latino communities sought a health center with specializations that included HIV/AIDS. The needs of the Mission District's Latino community, along with the projected needs of the incoming residents, justified a health center in the view of advocates for people with HIV. Developers agreed to provide capital funds to build the center and operational funds to staff it.[25] They also agreed to add 250 units of low-cost housing and promised to dedicate a revenue stream to support all 3,250 low-cost units from new sources.[26] With these changes, the opposition to the Mission Bay project that remained within the gay community subsided. Other communities also agreed to the new changes and the Board of Supervisors agreed to the plan with only one negative vote.[27] On April 2, 1991 authorizing and contract documents were signed by Agnos and the developers.

Although we certainly cannot draw any definitive conclusions from this very brief and incomplete review of development policy in San Francisco, two things do seem fairly clear.

First, throughout the 1970s into the 1980s, lesbian and gay voters tended to align with the growth-control movement in San Francisco. Richard DeLeon describes the components of what he terms "the three lefts" in San Francisco politics, with gay voters demonstrating an affinity with at least two of his three dimensions of the "progressive left" (traditional liberalism and environmentalism). (Those electoral precincts identified with lesbians and gay voters scored comparatively low on his "populist" dimension.)[28] The initial predisposition to align with the slow-growth forces was prompted by two traditions in lesbian and gay politics in San Francisco. One was the political activism of those lesbians and gay advocates of the 1960s whose first exposure to politics in San Francisco (except for gay rights issues) was in community services and efforts to resist neighborhood dislocation and the threat it posed to new lesbian and gay residential clusters. The other was the tactical alliance that Milk, Britt, and others had built with neighborhood activists in the 1970s. The middle-class values of many gay San Franciscans were what DeLeon calls "postmaterialist" values, but not because of their sexual identity. Gay and lesbian newcomers to the city did not differ greatly from many other new Bay Area residents in their desire to preserve the environment and their neighborhood.

The second realization regarding lesbians and gay men is that they could not always be counted on to join the growth-control coalition. Even though both Harvey Milk and Harry Britt supported many of the neighborhood activists' policy initiatives and the gay community in general seems to have supported the early corporate taxation initiatives to replace revenues lost by Proposition 13 and voted for the critical Proposition M in 1986, their support of growth control was never unanimous and in fact appeared to be waning. The division on the downtown ballpark and the willingness to accept the Mission Bay complex in return for fulfilling particular projects of interest to gay men indicate the division within the identity grouping over growth-control politics.

It may also be true, especially as lesbians and gay men become even more influential in San Francisco politics, that the gay community as a voting bloc on development matters may become even more divided. The evidence is already accumulating if the actual November ballot vote on the 1991 rent vacancy control initiative is an example. The single most important wedge in the vote was, not surprisingly, housing tenancy. Nearly one-third of self-identified gay men and lesbians voted against Proposition M in 1991, which was clearly a neighborhood and growth-control issue. Age (young) and income (lower categories) also defined support for the initiative. Sexual orientation was significant on a chi-square test, but in a nonlinear regression, after housing tenancy and age were accounted for, sexual orientation was unimportant.

Similarly, the 1994 proposition concerning BART access to San Francisco International Airport also divided the gay community. Some gay and lesbian leaders supported access to the terminal itself—the position associated with the progrowth coalition—and others supported access to the perimeter of the airport, with bus links to the terminal—the position of environmentalists and slow-growth proponents. As of the middle of 1994, the gay community had

not taken a unified position on BART access to the airport. Clearly, these are
not identity-defining or -mobilizing issues for lesbians and gay men.

Identity and Professional Isolation: Project 10% in the Schools

Lesbians and gay men were not as divided over the schools as they were on
economic development issues in San Francisco. In the city's public schools,
the proposal of an affirmative gay and lesbian counseling program generated significant conflict throughout much of the late 1980s. When it was confined to the educational arena, the discussion was largely about professional concerns and the allocation of resources. But like other identity and
participatory issues in school politics, the conflict could not be confined
and so became a mobilizing issue for lesbians and gay men in San Francisco, an issue directly impinging on the identity concerns of students, lesbian
and gay parents, and taxpayers.

The Multi-Identity Setting of San Francisco's Public Schools

The San Francisco school system is relatively small compared with other
big-city school districts in the United States. Its total enrollment in 1992
was 63,800. In many ways the system is either the same as or slightly better
than other urban school districts. It has a substantial dropout rate; 28 percent of the enrolled students are entitled to receive free or subsidized
meals—an indication of the number of children from poor families—and
reading scores are below the national average, though only slightly so. Nine
percent of the children are in special education—about the national average—and 10 percent are in gifted and talented programs.[29]

What is unique to San Francisco is the diversity of the student body. Although African Americans or Latinos represent a greater portion of students in some urban school systems (such as Detroit's or San Antonio's),
none is as diverse in terms of racial, ethnic, and sexual identities as San
Francisco's. The proportion of African American students enrolled in San
Francisco's schools peaked in 1972 at about 30 percent citywide; by 1992,
this number had fallen to 18.7 percent. Almost 20 percent of the students
are from Spanish-speaking households; 14.3 percent are Anglo/white; 24.3
percent are Chinese; 8 percent are Filipino; 1 percent each are Japanese and
Korean; and 6 percent are other nonwhite, mostly Southeast Asian, other

Pacific Islander (especially Samoan), or Native American. In a sense, the word *minority* has no meaning at all in San Francisco's schools.

In fact, the central theme in terms of racial and ethnic identities in San Francisco schools is the relative decline of both Anglo/white and African American students. The fastest-growing student population between 1967 and 1991 was Asian and Pacific Islanders of all national backgrounds.[30] Thus, the usual politics between African Americans and whites over racial balance in enrollment, teacher appointments, school governance, and principal appointments was not as urgent in the mid-1990s as it was in the mid-1970s.

These changes in the San Francisco Unified School District's demographic profile were reflected in its politics. Identity politics entered school politics in San Francisco not first through the influence of the women's movement or gay politics but through the multitude of ethnic and language identities that had acquired enough influence to press for their own traditions and cultures. San Francisco has long been an important legal arena for issues of language and cultural rights in education. A critical case affirming the rights of minorities filed on behalf of Asian American children—*Lau v. Nichols*[31]—was initiated in San Francisco and expanded the court's interpretation of language minority rights.[32] As David Kirp described it, *Lau* was "an invitation to press demands for bilingual-bicultural education."[33] Kirp quotes a 1975 report of the Parents Task Force on Bi-lingualism arguing that the burden of reponsibility for effective languge instruction "should be on the school to adapt its educational approach so that the culture, language and learning style of all children ... (not just those of an Anglo middle class background) are accepted and valued."[34] The multiethnic diversity of San Francisco schools was already a fertile ground for identity politics.

Sexual Identity and Urban Pedagogy

Into this mix of identity politics, the declining influence of both white and black political leaders over the schools, and constraints on resources, the issue of lesbian and gay identity came to the fore. The defeat of the Briggs amendment in 1979 was a major victory for lesbians and gay men in California, for it would have excluded openly gay and lesbian teachers from schools in California. But in primary and secondary schools, the political sensitivity of sexual identity was still significant to many straight San Franciscans.

A formal proposal for a lesbian- and gay-affirming counseling program in the San Francisco schools was submitted to school board members in the spring of 1989. The projected program was drawn up with contributions from Bay Area gay and lesbian teachers and support staff and was modeled on the Los Angeles Unified School District's "Project 10%." The program was designed partly as a counseling and support service for students and partly as sensitivity training for teachers and staff, especially counselors. Customized high school holding programs were a major strategy of the 1980s to reverse the growing dropout rates in America's urban schools.[35] Some of the programs were directed to Latino(a) youth, African American males, women (and pregnant women), and other ethnic identities. "Project 10%" was a gay/lesbian reflection of these efforts.

The developmental issue underlying Project 10% was linked to the identity formation of lesbian and gay adolescents and how this might conflict with a school culture that was predominantly nongay.[36] Students who were having sexual identity problems at home or at school or who were being harassed by other pupils, staff, or even parents may disengage emotionally or, at its worst, completely withdraw from typical arenas of adolescent development, especially school.[37] The final educational result could be leaving high school before graduation.

Anthropologist Gilbert Herdt, using an ethnographic identity model to explore the formation of sexual identity in a sample of self-identifying gay and lesbian adolescents in Chicago, outlined the problem. Students identifying as lesbian or gay typically confront (1) the presumption of heterosexuality in school and society in general, (2) the imposition of the stigma of being gay, (3) the assumption by others of gay people's homogeneity, and (4) the presumption of inversion (by which Herdt means the adolescents' assuming some aspects of the socially constructed characteristics of gay men and lesbians while working though the issues of "coming out"). This last item means that the adolescents with no support tend to assume the socially imputed characteristics of being gay or lesbian, as opposed to simply being himself or herself.[38] The processes that adolescent homosexuals go through are similar for men and women and yet also different. The difference is less attributed to physiology than to the social construction of women as women and women as lesbians and men as men and men as gay men. Adolescents take these into account in their identity formation and incorporate some parts of these images in the process.

Richard Friend defines the problem precisely: In a school atmosphere of (at best) silence regarding sexual orientation, self-esteem becomes problematic among youth whose sexual identity is different from others.' Fearing discovery of their sexuality, "lesbian and gay youth become increasingly uncomfortable engaging in school activities and cut themselves off from others emotionally as well as psychologically." This "withdrawal" can lead to poor grades, truancy, or eventually just dropping out because they have failed to develop trusting relations with fellow pupils or at least one member of the school staff.[39] Public schools usually offer no counseling support for such students.[40]

In the late 1980s, research on the identity development of gay and lesbian adolescents indicated that parents' support for the maintenance of self-esteem was both important and problematic. To deal with the outward isolation of students in high school and the possible loss of self-esteem at home owing to parental rejection or indifference, "Project 10%" programs sought to provide both affirmative counseling for the students and sensitivity training for the high school staff. But outside the schools, the programs were viewed much differently, as a symbolic focus of identity politics for both opponents and supporters.

Under a plan formally submitted to the school board by member Libby Denebeim, a Project 10% program would be established in the San Francisco public schools, in which workers would be hired to coordinate dropout prevention, HIV/AIDS prevention, and support services for gay students. The same staff members would also be responsible for overseeing gay-sensitive curricula and school staff training. After several weeks of controversy, San Francisco Unified School District (SFUSD) Superintendent Ramon Cortines sent a memo to the board members in April 1990 opposing the proposal on the grounds that the SFUSD had insufficient funds for any new programs aimed at a special group. Since the Project 10% program was being justified in part as an HIV prevention program, Cortines also told school board members that the special health needs of gay students were being met by several AIDS/HIV and family life programs already in place.

In one regard at least, Cortines was correct. The SFUSD's counseling facilities were already stretched to their limits. Like nearly all school districts in the United States, San Francisco's schools were subject to court intervention and mandated services, fiscal restrictions generally, and the impact of Proposition 13 specifically in California. For a counselor in a San Francisco school, the typical caseload was between six hundred and one thousand. There also was conflict between professionals who saw a program modeled on Los Angeles's as a genuine high school holding program and those who saw a specialized program for lesbians and gay men as "compartmentalizing them." Still others saw such an affirmative program as extending the notion of high school holding programs to an area too controversial for the public schools. Furthermore, many in San Francisco's liberal circles who usually supported sexual orientation issues were not as enthusiastic about affirmative counseling for gay and lesbians youth.

The debate could not be kept within a professional cloister, however. Taking on affirmative counseling for lesbian and gay students was specifically justified on the grounds that it was almost never available at home—which of course was also the concern of much of the political conflict over the program from religious and social conservative groups. For gay men and lesbians the debate over a "Project 10%" type of program was more than a simple question of allocating funds for a high school holding program; it was an invitation to reexperience unpleasant and homophobic events in their own school experience.

Superintendent Cortines's initial position was to side with those who saw a Project 10% as a "special" service. This escalated the symbolic content of the debate and moved it firmly outside professional circles. In explaining his position, however, an unfortunate quote was to be attributed to Cortines. According to a local San Francisco paper, Cortines also said, "We have to be very, very careful about enticing young people as it relates to their sexual orientation."[41]

Whether the quote was an accurate one or not, the word *entice* had done its damage. Cortines was now suspect among the city's lesbian and gay activists. The resistance to change in the schools was especially annoying to the new and younger gay leadership, which was more militant and confrontational than Milk's generation. Spurned by HIV and higher levels of expectation for success, this new generation, associated with Queer Nation and ACT-UP, was more adept at media-focused tactics than traditional political organization.[42] But in doing so they alienated some old friends.

The debate over Project 10% brought together both the older gay and lesbian political leaders and the younger representatives of symbolic and cultural politics. The coalition that came together in the spring of 1990 to protect the affirmative counseling program included lesbian and gay activists and parents. In the past, other groups tried to break the hold of bureaucracies and professionals on education policy by obtaining access to policymaking at the highest levels of school governance, and there was no reason to think that the gay community would be any different. Accordingly, sensing that their interests and values were being excluded from educational policymaking, lesbian and gay activists began a campaign to obtain a seat on the school board.

School Board Election Politics

There were three school board seats opening in 1991. The San Francisco school board was elected at large with a form of limited voting: with three seats open, each voter had three votes. Then on election night, the candidates were ranked by the total number of votes received.

Tom Ammiano, a leader in BANGLE (Bay Area Network of Gay and Lesbian Educators) and one of the spokespeople for the coalition that pressed for the Project 10% program, announced that he would run for a seat. Ammiano's candidacy attracted considerable support in the gay community and beyond to include some labor figures, neighborhood groups, and parents active in school politics. He had run once before and thus was known; he and his lover had a daughter in the public schools. Ammiano announced that the reason he was running was to ensure that an affirmative counseling program would be established and that the gay community would have a voice in education policy.[43] His own training was in special education,[44] and he developed a reputation as a progressive, especially in his advocacy for minority children in the controversies surrounding special education classification. He had been a friend and political supporter of Harvey Milk and knew the history of practical politics on behalf of lesbians and gay men in San Francisco. Ammiano also had the advantage of an enormous "pull" operation put together that year by the city's lesbian and gay political organizations on behalf of all lesbian and gay candidates.

Carlota del Portillo, who worked for the Community College District, and Dan Kelly, a pediatrician who was active in the movements of the 1960s, were viewed along with Ammiano as the most liberal of the candidates who could win. And all three did win, displacing the two most senior board members.

Although Ammiano's election virtually ensured the continuation of the Project 10% program, the district's continuing fiscal problems did put its extent into question. The outgoing school board president, Fred Rodriguez, expected that state budget cuts might mean that some schools would have to be merged or even closed. Sacramento could no longer be relied on to make up its portion of funds lost after the passage of Proposition 13 in 1979.

Thus, even though the policy issues regarding an affirmative counseling program were settled through political means, as a fiscal matter some issues were left unresolved.

Summary

A central insight from political scientists' nearly twenty years of studying school governance is the relative isolation of educational policymaking from community, market, and parental influence.[45] The victory of educational professionals over local party organizations was important to the professionalization of urban education. But the victory did not depoliticize the schools as the reformers intended; it just isolated local educational decision making from trivial partisan politics. The ascendancy of bureaucratic and professional dominance also kept the schools from genuine accountability to community interests.[46] The main goal of those who try to resolve such problems is usually to alter the institutional structure of school governance and the accompanying vestiges of power that dominate local education.[47] Decentralization, recentralization, at-large elections, district elections, advisory boards, or even radical decentralization to the school level (such as Chicago's restructuring has tried to achieve)[48] all have been enlisted in attempts to increase community and parent access to school decision making.

In a formal sense, elected school boards should provide a channel of accountability to different communities and political identities. Nearly all rural and suburban school districts and even many large-city districts—such as San Francisco and Boston—have elected boards of education. For numerical minorities, though, elected school boards are not always the best route to community accountability. Indeed, it could be argued that African Americans, parents of handicapped children, and parents of language minority children have had a much better response from the federal courts to their demands for change. School board members often are elected from candidate pools put forward by groups with direct and substantial interests in school policies and resource allocations, such as unionized employees, professional associations, the business community, middle-class parents, religious groups seeking access to school facilities, and taxpayers generally. Imbalances in community resources are thus reflected in the makeup of the school board.

As a project that initially came from professionals, particularly those working in the area of high school holding programs and counselors who linked self-esteem with student achievement, the Project 10% program was not an astonishing suggestion. But it was also clear that other programs similarly focused on an ethnic or language minority would have attracted little or no political discussion. Rather, it was the sexual overtones, the problematization of customary values that sexual orientation presents in public spaces—particularly as it concerns adolescents—that invited the politicization. Moreover, the identity aspects politicized the issue outside the professional domain. Precluded from pursuing a legal strategy, the gay community therefore relied on what in San Francisco has been its most effective strategy: political mobilization to the polls.

Local Government and the Restructured Family

The most intensive and extended clash over a sexual identity–related issue in San Francisco was how the city government would deal with the increased demand to recognize alternative family structures through domestic partnership and registry legislation. The battle lasted throughout the 1980s, culminating in the referendum on Proposition K in 1991. Like the affirmative counseling program, domestic partnership mobilized San Francisco's lesbian and gay community toward an eventual electoral victory. But it also mobilized social and religious conservatives to resist governmental affirmation—financial or symbolic—of changes in the meaning of "the family."

The term *domestic partnership* covers many different concepts. Generally, it refers to the conferring of legal status to cohabiting partners in same-sex or unmarried opposite-sex partners. Obviously, no city can grant any legal status beyond its own authorization by state law. So typically the options available to localities are "marriage-like" entitlements: a neutral partnership registry, a set of fringe benefits for the domestic partners of public employees, and specific family or spouse entitlements that can be granted by the local government. Among these are bereavement leave and family/paternity/maternity leave offered by contract to the partner of civil servants and public employees.

In the past few years, the understanding of "family" by either the state courts or the state legislature has broadened. New York State's highest court has recognized in regard to rent-controlled or rent-stabilized apartments in New York City the succession rights of the long-term cohabiting partners of lessees in the event of death. In Massachusetts, through executive orders and collective bargaining agreements, all the fringe benefits for state public employees are available to same-sex cohabitants if they meet certain criteria. In other jurisdictions, legislative or regulatory decisions have allowed long-term partners to be included as "immediate family members" in emergency medical procedures and hospital visits. This was largely a concession made in response to the HIV/AIDS epidemic, in which many persons with AIDS were estranged from their biological families and wished to have their lovers or partners serve as their primary health care advisers. In most of these circumstances, the government simply, and in some cases informally, recognized the changes in household relationships that had taken place over time.

The most controversial aspect of domestic partnership ordinances is the change in values they imply. The establishment of a procedure to register partners in a way similar to, but not carrying the full legal weight of, a marriage license is seen as an affront to many with traditional values. Typically, the kind of city registry that local governments can administer carries no legal weight (unlike a marriage license, which implies the entire body of domestic law in the referent state). But a domestic registry can be used by third parties such as private businesses as an acceptable and objective mode of certification of partnership if they wish to grant "family" benefits to same-sex couples. Similarly, the granting of family benefits to public employees, regardless of sexual identity, is seen by many as a public affirmation of an alternative way of life that many taxpayers regard as objectionable.

Round 1: Feinstein's Veto, 1982

The formal battle started early in 1982. Supervisor Harry Britt submitted a broadly worded domestic partnership bill that included a domestic registry, full health care visitation rights for partners of hospitalized lesbians and gays, bereavement leave and health benefits to the partners of public employees of the city and county. Although Britt submitted the plan on behalf of the gay community, it covered unmarried heterosexual couples as well. The Board of Supervisors passed the legislation, thereby deferring the controversy to Mayor Dianne Feinstein.

The political pressures on Feinstein to sign or veto the local bill were strong. The gay community demanded approval, since the hardest part of the effort, getting the measure through the Board of Superintendents, had already been accomplished. Roman Catholic Archbishop John Quinn personally and publicly called on Feinstein to veto the legislation. Leaders of the city's Episcopal diocese and some Jewish leaders also opposed the bill.

In the case of all these religious leaders, the concern was the legislation's implication for the definition of "family." Yet even among those who might have supported the registry provisions, some found the possible cost of the fringe benefit package for public employees as too uncertain for approval. Citing the costs of the health package, not the cultural issues surrounding the changing family, Feinstein vetoed the bill.

Even though the mayor said she had expected the storm her veto would cause, it is doubtful she had foreseen its immensity. A previous recall petition begun by the White Panthers because of Feinstein's position on gun control became the surprising vehicle to record the disappointment in her on the domestic partnership legislation. After Feinstein's veto of the domestic partnership legislation, the White Panthers began to concentrate their petition drive in neighborhoods with a high number of lesbian and gay residents. The result was thirty thousand signatures and a recall referendum scheduled for April 1984. Feinstein's opponents tried to piece together a recall coalition, arguing that she had abandoned Moscone's coalition and policies. Feinstein's supporters, however, focused the debate on the fairness of the recall and the controversial history of the White Panthers, thus trying avoid having the ballot become a referendum on Feinstein herself. In the end, the strategy may have backfired, as the recall strategy became an unquestioned victory for Feinstein, who won with 80 percent of the vote. This ended the issue of the city's certification of domestic partnerships as long as Feinstein was mayor of San Francisco.

The Election of Agnos and the Reemergence of the Moscone Coalition

The expectations of gay and lesbian activists for a second chance at a domestic partnership policy rose as the 1987 mayoral election approached. Art Agnos, a member of the State Assembly from central San Francisco and a longtime associate of the old "Burton machine," was one of the candidates who supported the growth-control forces, as well as many other positions of the San Francisco left. Agnos had been the initial author of Assembly Bill 101 in Sacramento, the statewide "gay rights" bill. And he received wide support in the lesbian and gay community in his run for mayor.

Agnos was a bridge between the traditional liberals of San Francisco politics and much of the city's new "identity-centered" politics. In the first round of the 1987 mayoral election, Agnos received almost 50 percent of the total vote, defeating two other liberals—John Molinari and Frank Boas. In an analysis of precinct results from the November 1987 election, Richard DeLeon concluded that

1. Renters and Latinos voted overwhelming for Agnos.
2. Gay and African American voters split their support between Agnos and Molinari.
3. Asian voters gave the least support to Agnos and the most to Molinari.[49]

DeLeon's analysis further indicated that "middle class voters gave major support to Agnos while low SES and high SES votes divided about equally among the three candidates."[50] Put another way, the Agnos supporters were a blue-collar/middle-class, multi-identity coalition that included all the city's minorities except Asians. It could be defined as middle class not because Agnos reflected the middle-class values of what was left of San Francisco's Catholic, ethnic, blue-collar vote, but because the wealthy and poor went other ways. Despite Agnos's strength, he did not obtain a majority of the vote, so a runoff was scheduled for early December, in which he easily defeated Molinari. DeLeon's analysis of the December runoff vote showed that Agnos received a majority of his votes from San Francisco's black, Latino, and gay and lesbian citizens.

Round 2: Proposition S and the 1989 Earthquake

With Agnos's landslide victory in the mayoral runoff, domestic partnership legislation was again a possibility. The position Agnos took during the campaign was that he not only would sign a domestic partnership bill if passed (which was the "safe" position) but also would support it in the Board of Supervisors. Accordingly, in 1989, Harry Britt submitted a new version of his domestic partnership legislation.

As it had in 1982, the 1989 domestic partnership bill included both domestic registry provisions and a fringe benefit section for partners of public employees. The law would allow unmarried, cohabiting couples—regardless of gender—to register their relationship with the city clerk for a fee of $35. It granted to city and county public-sector employees bereavement and hospital visitation rights as if they were married couples under California law. It offered fewer fringe benefits than the 1982 version had, however, and the health coverage was not clearly spelled out. Again, the measure passed the Board of Supervisors, and this time the mayor, Agnos, signed the bill.

Before the law took effect, however, opponents from several conservative groups gathered enough signatures for a referendum challenging the measure. Thus the first of three San Francisco referenda on domestic partnerships took shape. But the political atmosphere in San Francisco was different in 1989. Between 1982 and 1989, the impact of AIDS and HIV-spectrum diseases had hit San Francisco hard, harder per capita than any other city in the United States. In addition, in no other major city with such a high HIV/AIDS caseload did gay men represent such an overwhelming percentage. Even in New York City well into the 1990s, where the majority of cases were men exposed through sex with other men, there always were a substantial number of reported cases among other categories defined by the Centers for Disease Control as "high risk for HIV." In San Francisco, the number of HIV-seropositive men who reported having sex with other men dominated the statistics.

The effect of HIV on politics in San Francisco cannot be underestimated, and not just among gay men. It put a tremendous strain on the city's health budget and all health and hospital facilities. It also led to a change in the leadership and style of lesbian and gay organizing. ACT-UP used some of its most innovative tactics in San Francisco. Queer Nation, teasing seemingly middle-class solidity with postmodern tactics, fashioned new approaches to pursuing gay and lesbian issues that were focused more on cultural conflict than the service and distributional aspects of local government.

The effect of HIV on the politics of domestic partnership was twofold. First, using both old and new tactics, it hastened the mobilization of the gay community. Issues such as bereavement leave, hospital visitation rights, power of attorney for living wills, and staggering health expenses were now part of the gay community's daily experience. In such an atmosphere, it was both politically prudent and humane for public officials and private medical officers to support changes in health programs.

The second effect of HIV was the uncertainty of cost. Health insurance benefits, the most expensive part of any fringe benefits package, were not included in the 1989 proposal. Nevertheless, some opponents claimed that passage of a domestic partnership benefits package—even if it did not include health insurance—would inevitably lead to it and its costs. Even though more public officials and many in the center and on the liberal wing of San Francisco's political spectrum were sympathetic to gay men and lesbians in 1989 than in the 1983 campaign, some of the older opponents remained steadfast. San Francisco's Roman Catholic archdiocese still argued that recognition of "domestic partners" would undermine "the sanctity of the family," but other religious leaders were not as firmly opposed as they had been in 1982. The Episcopal diocese, for example, now supported the measure.

Another change had taken place as a result of the HIV/AIDS epidemic. Even lesbians and gay men who might have been indifferent to institutional politics in 1982 were now mobilized in a way that San Francisco had not seen since the days of union power. In a fascinating footnote to his book *Left Coast City*, DeLeon notes that of "all the groups in the City [only gays and lesbians] felt they could influence public policy," a startling testimony of faith given the government's past indifference or outright opposition to lesbian and gay affirmation, even in San Francisco.[51]

The support for domestic partnerships had also shifted since 1982. Analysis of the same August 1989 phone poll used in assessing support for a downtown ballpark showed that most San Franciscans supported—albeit with some reservations—the idea of some form of domestic partnership legislation.[52] A regression analysis indicated that the core coalition supporting the proposal was defined by sexual orientation and marital status, particularly among younger voters. Lesbians, gay men, and young, single heterosexuals—the groups most likely to gain from the proposal—all supported the measure in significant numbers (see table 10-2).

Opposition to the measure was not organized around any specific religion but around religiosity in general and conservative political ideology. Analysis of the results of the poll taken several months before the referendum vote indicated that Catholics, for example, despite the lobbying by the archdiocese, were divided by age and sexual orientation in their support of or opposition to the issue. When a dummy variable for "Catholic" was tested for predictive power, it also indicated that despite the archdiocese's call for repeal, self-identified Catholics were much more divided than might have been expected. Even though the majority did not support the measure, a strong minority, especially young Catholics, did. Self-identified Jews showed no statistical differences from the overall citywide profile. In fact, the most influential category of religious identity was "No Religion," a category that included a disproportionate number of self-identified gay men and lesbians. In addition to the effect of religiosity, younger and unmarried voters tended to support the proposition, and older voters opposed it.

The number of voters who were undecided about domestic registry in the summer before the 1989 earthquake was high—22 percent. Younger and older voters held firmly to their position, as did self-identified gay men and lesbians. Most racial categories did not show any specific pattern of decided or

TABLE 10.2

Descriptors of Vote Supporting Repeal of Domestic Partnerships
(multiple regression analysis) (ordinary least squares)

Variable	B	SE B	Beta	T	Sig T
Asian	-.166236	.171668	-.092195	-.968	.3335
Latino	-.199037	.173587	-.101828	-1.147	.2523
Black	-.177929	.171931	-.109385	-1.035	.3014
White	-.172219	.157270	-.154754	-1.095	.2742
Age	.002461	.001404	.087267	1.754	.0804
Gender	.012418	.044854	.012483	.277	.7821
Married	.107478	.067009	.106698	1.604	.1096
Single Heterosexual	**-.262785**	**.073268**	**-.242112**	**-3.587**	**.0004**[a]
Lesbigay	**-.295836**	**.045614**	**-.399781**	**-6.486**	**.0000**[a]
Catholic	.015491	.052229	.015417	.297	.7670
Jewish	.036103	.090217	.018795	.400	.6893
No religion	.132956	.066901	.098810	1.987	.0477[b]
Religiosity	**-.041160**	**.013372**	**-.145253**	**-3.078**	**.0022**[a]
Education	-.016905	.019653	-.040305	-.860	.3903
Own/rent housing	-.083836	.043802	-.083623	-1.914	.0564
Income	.009649	.011620	.038221	.830	.4069
Ideology	**.067056**	**.014361**	**.218877**	**4.669**	**.0000**[a]
(Constant)	2.517066	.842097		2.989	.0030

Source: David Binder Associates, telephone poll, August 1989

[a] Significant at <.01

[b] Significant at <.05

Multiple r = .61014; r square = .37228; adjusted r square = .34230; standard error = 0.40371
   (f = 12.41934; signif. f = .0000)

*Scale is conservative.

not decided. Instead, when the summer ended, the defining dimensions for the undecided cohort were (1) those who displayed little knowledge of the proposal's content and (2) those who were concerned about its possible costs.

The mayor, the *San Francisco Chronicle*, and most elected officials in San Francisco supported the initiative. The business community in San Francisco and in the Bay Area generally had already begun incorporating domestic partnership into their own personnel policies. But the voters who were undecided in August slowly moved toward the negative column. The great majority of voters polled supported visitation rights, bereavement benefits, and some formal recognition of same-sex aspirations "because it's only fair, since gays cannot marry."[53] But if the earthquake had a positive effect on Agnos's popularity, it had a negative effect on voter turnout (the locations of some polling places were changed as a result of damage to public buildings), thus increasing the proportion of absentee ballots in the general count. And absentee ballots were disproportionately used by the "older" age categories, those voters who opposed domestic partnership. More than 16 percent of all the ballots were absentee. And as it had in regard to the ballpark veto, the quake raised concerns about the cost of domestic partner legislation. Although those people who actually went to the polls on election day supported the domestic partnership measure (as they did with the downtown ballpark), the absentee ballots provided sufficient opposition to defeat domestic registry and some aspects of domestic partnership benefits for the second time in San Francisco.

Round 3: Partner Registry and Proposition K, 1990

In the spring after the defeat of Proposition S, the drive for domestic partnership policy changed its tactics. New and more specific venues were sought for individual aspects of previous domestic partnership legislation. Mayor Agnos, for example, established the Family Policy Task Force to review how changes in the structure of families and households should be reflected in public policy. As chair, he appointed Roberta Achtenberg, a civil liberties attorney and executive director of the Center of Lesbian Rights. The recommendations of the Family Policy Task Force, released in its March 1990 report, included extending health and child care benefits to unmarried partners of city workers, granting longer leaves for family illnesses, and creating a mechanism to register relationships between unwed cohabitants, essentially the same domestic registry that had just been defeated. Agnos immediately announced his own support for the task force's suggestions.

In 1989, the earthquake and uncertainty about health benefits killed the domestic partnership measure. This year, lesbian and gay voters had many reasons to go to the polls. Not only would Proposition K be on the ballot, but 1990 offered the possibility of electing the first openly gay man to the Board of Education and two lesbians to the Board of Supervisors. One was Achtenberg. The other was Carol Migden, who had been active in the domestic partnership referenda campaigns. In addition, another lesbian was running for a judgeship on the Superior Court. No citywide election since 1977, when Harvey Milk was elected, was as important to the San Francisco's lesbian and gay community.

On election day, the turnout in lesbian and gay neighborhoods reached as high as 66 percent (Eureka Valley/Noe Valley),and these neighborhoods overwhelmingly supported Proposition K. Also important was the change in black voters' attitudes. In 1989, the largely black Bayview/Hunters Point area voted against Proposition S (38.7 percent supported the measure and 61.7 percent opposed it). In 1990, however, political operatives from the gay community had supported the election of blacks to the Board of Supervisors and the school board. In 1990, therefore, black voters decided to vote for Proposition K, though by only a thin margin.

The gay community was about to assume a new role in San Francisco's governance. On the same day that Proposition K passed, Carole Migden and Roberta Achtenberg were elected to the Board of Supervisors. Doris Ward, an African American and an incumbent who was supported by most leaders of the gay community, received the highest number of votes. In addition, Tom Ammiano was elected to the Board of Education. The day was, as the press termed it, a "Lavender Sweep."[54]

Round 4: Proposition K, the Consolidation of the Domestic Partnership Consensus

The 1990 Proposition K did not include health benefits. On the recommendation of the mayor's Family Policy Task Force, the city's Health Services Board approved a measure to extend health care coverage to the partners of city employees. Since much of the actual cost of health benefits was paid by payroll premiums, the domestic partnership option was now pursued in the context of restructuring the city-funded insurance programs for its employees. The recommended financial arrangement was extended to domestic partners by making newer and more diverse family packages available to the entire municipal workforce and requiring a minimum payment from those who previously had paid nothing. The new Board of Supervisors passed the plan unanimously, and Agnos signed it.

The 1990 success of the domestic registry vote and the election victory of two openly lesbian candidates to the Board of Supervisor put the social conservatives on notice. Petitions were circulated for yet another referendum, to repeal the domestic registry. This time the major opposition force was the Catholic archdiocese.

In 1991, however, the vote did not appear close at all. An early *Chronicle* poll had the repeal measure failing: no, 62 percent; yes, 33 percent; with 5 percent undecided.[55] When the data from a phone poll on the repeal of domestic registry taken in late October 1991 were run through logistic regression, patterns seen in the past were found.[56] "Age" and "sexual identity" were again the most important predictors of the referendum's outcome. Along with a constant, they explained more than 70 percent of the responses, including 80 percent of the negative responses, to repeal. New residents, who were an important focus for gay voter registration efforts, were more than four to one opposed to repeal.

In the final exit polls, Asians were the only racial group to support repeal.[57] And even though African Americans were less enthusiastic than whites or Latinos about sustaining the registry, a majority still supported it. The gains of the gay community in the 1990 elections may have become a source of concern among blacks who already sensed that they were losing their influence in San Francisco politics. Indeed, throughout the battle over domestic partnerships, African Americans in the city were the most undecided racial or ethnic identity. Those reporting that they had voted on the measure were evenly split. Age, too, had become less important; only a majority of voters above age sixty-five supported repeal. But the final outcome was a strong vote of confidence for domestic partner registry: yes, 72,798 (40.5 percent), and no, 105,866 (59.5 percent) to repeal. Opposition was restricted to Republicans, older voters (especially men), and Asians. But after ten years of fighting and three referenda, the measure was now secure.

Conclusion

The attention given to lesbian and gay voters in the slow-growth movement's decade-long attempt to use referenda as its principal strategy in San Francisco is a testament to their growing importance in the city's politics—and not just in identity matters. Yet an ambivalence toward development issues in the sexual identity grouping is evident and likely to grow if the diversity in the grouping's incomes continues to grow. Calculating the differential gains and losses of further economic changes in the racial and class cross-currents among lesbians and gay men is not easy, but we can assume that about one-third of the gay vote in San Francisco never was part of the slow-growth coalition or has abandoned it. But the issues of economic development that nearly a generation of academic writers on the politics of San Francisco have seen as the defining ones are not strong enough to undermine the essential coherence of sexual identity in other policy arenas.

Even though Agnos lost the mayoralty in 1991 to the more conservative former police commissioner, Frank Jordan, the gay community has preserved many of its gains. In 1994, one openly gay male candidate, school board member Tom Ammiano, was elected to the Board of Supervisors, and two lesbian incumbents were reelected: Carol Migden and Susan Lead. Two gay candidates (one of whom was Asian American) also were elected to the San Francisco Community College Board—all this in the face of the nationwide Republican sweep.

In the fall of 1995, the first serious attempt by a gay man or lesbian to become San Francisco's mayor was made by the former superintendent and assistant secretary of housing and urban development Roberta Achtenberg. Achtenberg lost to former State Assembly Speaker Willie Brown in the first round of San Francisco's nonpartisan mayoral election. But this could not be regarded as a complete defeat for San Francisco's gay community. Brown, who was widely regarded as the most powerful Democrat and certainly the most powerful African American Democrat in California politics, had attended those very first candidate nights sponsored by SIR in the Tenderloin back in the mid-1960s when he was a young man. When leading the California State Assembly, he had consistently supported a gay rights bill and the necessary funding for HIV research and social services. In many cases, therefore, leaders of lesbian and gay organizations backed Brown over Achtenberg, given his strong progay positions in the past. Mayor Jordan, who had defeated Agnos only four years earlier, ran a poor second to Brown, who won the December 12 runoff in a landslide. In March 1996, former San Francisco Supervisor Carole Migden, a lesbian, was sworn in to serve the remaining nine months of Mayor Willie Brown's term in the State Assembly.

Despite the ups and downs of election cycles, referenda, and actions by the Board of Supervisors, the trend in San Francisco politics is the gradual incorporation of lesbian and gay identity into its governance. San Francisco has been an important object of study for regime theory. But the application of regime theory as used in political economy today cannot explain some important events in its recent politics as analyzed here. It cannot explain the outcome or the intensity of the battle over domestic partnership or the mobilizing effect of affirmative counseling in schools, enabling the gay community to be better represented than the African American community on the school board.

In the past decade and a half, political economists have made the most important contributions to regime theory in urban politics. As used in the analysis of political economy and development policy, a regime is a coalition that can sustain an electoral base sufficient to be elected and yet flexible enough to accommodate potential powerful opponents so that the regime's goals are not jeopardized, especially when nonregime interests are mobilized. The regime coalition acts through the informal overlap of private economic resources and public instrumentalities to carry out its economic strategy. Through the governing skills of its members, the mobilization of public and private resources implements the regime's vision.

The emergence of a sexual identity grouping, with a deep agenda not always describable in microeconomic terms, has had a potent, complex, and not necessarily anticipated impact on San Francisco's politics that cannot be explained by urban economism and can be understood only partially using current urban regime theory. Through a social organization perspective on identity, we can expand the concept of regime and assume that an ongoing regime—a structure that might be either strong or weak—exists and that differing regimes limit portions of a city's history, as do the regimes described by political economists. The difference is that the historical boundaries of regimes are not exclusively economic, nor is its policy breadth simply in the area of development policy. In such a broad framework, the embeddedness of political identities becomes the central subject for students of urban governance. The embedding of sexual identity (and other identity movements) in everyday political discourse, in the instruments of policy implementation (essentially the bureaucracies of policymaking and service delivery in city government), in the legitimating institutions of governance, and eventually in the regime itself is what identity theory can contribute to regime theory. These themes have much more to do with political development than with economic development. To these issues of the embedding of identities in urban governance and the limits of the urban economism model we turn next.

▦

PART V

Conclusion: Cities as Places in Which People Live

CHAPTER II

⣿

*Conclusions on the Micro Level: Identity, Embeddedness,
and Urban Governance*

The four cities and policy subjects investigated in part IV were chosen to display the breadth of lesbian and gay activity and the variety of its influences in urban politics and policymaking. Even though no systematic comparative analysis is possible, we can make some general observations about the effects of sexual identity on policymaking at the level of these individual cities—at their micro level.

In Birmingham, we do not see a rising political community poised to influence public decisions outside its own areas of concern, but a community organized largely for defense, internal social support and social services, and some political activity whose effects do not extend much farther than the south side or as a small but legitimating component in Mayor Arrington's electoral coalition. The reform of police practices in Philadelphia, a city in which politics and police are intimately linked, shows how the police department finally has come to consider sexual identity in its day-to-day operations. Incorporating a gay and lesbian perspective into recruits' training, permitting homosexuals to become Philadelphia police officers, and changing the attitude of senior police toward gay men and lesbians all are evidence of the struggle between two disparate cultures. Similarly, in the case of districting New York's City Council, the indirect legitimation of sexual identity as a competitive and state-sponsored grouping through the recognition of the gay community's dominance of a bounded space—Greenwich Village and Chelsea—is a sign of political incorporation. In both Philadelphia and New York, the target of change was the deeper structures of urban governance. Last, in San Francisco, the areas of political activity in which sexual identity became a useful category for policy process analysis are seen to be broad and to include education policy, economic development policy, and civil service regulations in regard to domestic partnerships.

Despite the limitations on a strictly comparative analysis, a general theme in these case cities is the degree to which sexual identity has become an ongoing part of their governance. In a sense, Birmingham serves as one pole in a continuum of what we can call the *embeddedness of identity* in the social organization of local governance. San Francisco serves as the other pole. The effects of identity politics are best understood as appearing along a scale of identity embeddedness in urban governance—how marginal changes in discourse, rules, regulations, and broad policymaking criteria have gradually and unevenly incorporated sexual identity into the structure of local governance. Once established and with resources at its command, the process of embedding identity interests and discourse can proceed, though not unchallenged.

Such an analysis is not contrary to regime theory. As a synthesis of political economy and group theory, regime theory offers important insights into fiscal and development policies. Early treatments of urban regime theory seemed to incorporate identity-based movements in its metaphors. Greenstone and Peterson, for example, took a more functionalist and macro approach to regime theory, seeing the ultimate impact of the Community Action Program of the 1960s as altering the relationship between race and the sometimes conflicting legitimation principles of American civic culture. Writing in the early 1970s and following Dahrendorf, they turned away from macrosociological (Marxist and Parsonian) perspectives of regime theory and instead identified latent regime interests with a group's stake in "the preservation of...existing authority structures."[1]

Since Greenstone and Peterson were studying the Community Action Program, they did not limit the conflict to economics but extended it to cultural identity. Furthermore, they understood that emerging interests not only needed to be included in the bargaining order but also had to be infused into the structures of authority so as to be sustained over time. Most important, they distinguished between the *vesting* of interests and the more important *institutionalization* of political interests.[2]

Economism Versus the Embeddedness of Action in Social Ties

Keeping in mind the theoretical developments since the 1970s, the theme of institutionalization still remains central, but the subject becomes the embedding of identities in the various layers of political structuration. Identities and social action are embedded in networks of social ties that exist both in and across organizations (civil and state). These real-time networks of social ties crosscut both the individual anomic precepts of the market model and the imputed hierarchical power systems of pure and formal organizational models. The difference between Greenstone and Peterson's notion of "institutionalization of interests" and the "embeddedness of identities" is that the latter presents a much more fluid, dynamic, and comprehensive perspective on what is essentially the same social process. "Attempts at purposive action are embedded in concrete, ongoing systems of social relations," not as atomized actors or clumps of economically defined actors clustered in a group.[3] An ascending identity has its own values, languages, and frame of reference and attempts to embed them into the structure of local governance. This is the implicit goal of all the identity's political actions, its *deep agenda.*

The embeddedness argument draws much of its theoretical strength from sociologists interested in reexamining the role of social structure in the economic theory of action. To what degree are economic actions actually embedded in social networks, as opposed to being discrete actions occurring in impersonal markets? Or, more simply, how do personal relations and networks of social relations affect economic actions?[4] As applied to business organizations, the concept of embeddedness is usually contrasted with the pure, neoclassical market model, in which resource allocation and firm-to-firm interaction are conducted as "arm's-length" relationships in markets. Or the concept is contrasted with pure hierarchial organizational structures, in which seemingly stable organizational structures are in fact embedded in the social processes of the organization itself.[5]

This embeddedness perspective has important theoretical implications for the efficiency of business organizations and casts doubt on the applicability to all firms of the neoclassical economic model of decision making.[6] When subjected to empirical investigation, the embeddedness of economic action in social networks is found to be important to the informal accumulation of information on labor markets and the informal coordination of interfirm planning or is defined by specific types of networks, such as immigrants.[7] For economic sociologist Mark Granovetter, economic actions embedded in networks of personal relations offer important sources of information but may also impede needed adjustments to change in an organizational environment.[8] Organizational theorist Brian Uzzi argues that social ties sometimes allow firms to adapt to a new environment by informally

326

cooperating with key decision makers in other firms.[9] All these scholars agree that the embeddedness of economic activity in social ties offers a counterpoint to the pure neoclassical and market explanation for economic behavior.

When looking at the relationships between organizations and social context, some scholars have identified different levels of embeddedness of social ties. For example, Zukin and DiMaggio describe four such levels for the corporate sector of the economy: (1) an embeddedness in cognitive structures that influences and sometimes limits thought about economic action, (2) a cultural embeddedness that refers to "shared collective understanding in shaping economic strategies and goals," (3) a structural level similar to Granovetter's notion of embeddedness as it "concerns the material quality and structure of ties among [economic] actors," and (4) a political level referring to nonmarket institutions, particularly the state and social classes as they limit and condition economic power and incentives.[10]

The embeddedness argument has also been made by political scientists using development theory. John Echeverri-Gent named the social ties that link state administrative organizations with their social environment as the embeddedness of state organizations in a societal context.[11] Echeverri-Gent went beyond the traditional recommendation for cultural neutrality in implementing development policies to argue that agencies need to be sensitive to cultural differences and also to become embedded in their target social bases. He regards successful implementing agencies as being both embedded in local social networks and also having independent resources, so that they can be autonomous and thus able to effect public policy goals in the agency's social context.

For Echeverri-Gent, the interaction of the state and the political organization of identities are at a (1) regime level, (2) a policy mandates level, and (3) an implementing procedures level. At each of these levels, "the capacity of public policy to shape the interests and organization of social groups has important consequences for understanding the relationship between implementing agencies and their social environment."[12] Echeverri-Gent sees the link between the state's implementing agencies and identities as where the state can influence and manage the formulation of political identities. But in this case, he is dealing with social, ethnic, and professional identities, not gender or sexual identities.

The argument for understanding the effects of identity politics on urban governance as the embedding of identities in the social organization of gov-

ernance was made by those scholars who look to nonmarket, horizontal social relations and their effects on information gathering, cultural context,
values, and decision making. Here, when dealing with the interaction of
identity and urban governance, however, we understand the flow of influence as opposite to that described by Echeverri-Gent. It is not from an autonomous state and its agencies to the societal context but an opposite flow,
from the social emergence of identities to their (problematic) embedding in
the structures of urban governance.

The Embedding of Identity in Urban Governance

In the world of urban governance, identities whose values and attempts at
control have been successfully mobilized in the past, or around which organizations have grown over time, are already embedded in the structures
of urban governance. We can see, for example, how the interests and assumptions of the business community have been incorporated into the assumptions of urban policymaking—whether imposed from without, as
Paul Peterson would have it—or from within—as regime theorists would
have it. These embedded aspects of identity become matters for contention
or, in postmodern language, are problematized by new contending identities. Viewed, then, as an aspect of governance and not political theory, identity politics becomes a struggle by a rising identity grouping against the pre-
emptory signs, languages, and symbols that represent the embedded
structures of contrary power and authority.

All this moves from theory to urban governance when the entire complex of public instrumentalities comes into play. Indeed, the understanding
of identity politics moves beyond the New Social Movements literature in
this very notion of embeddedness: that social movements and identity politics are not always urging change from outside the state but can actually influence the discourse within the local state or even become part of the local
state. There is no reason to think that the embedding of a sexual identity
would be all that different from, say, language minorities or religious identities. The terms of the discourse and the objects of policy contention
would be marked by conflicting identities—those already embedded in a
city's governing structures and those challenging the embeddings.

This contention between identities could be a zero-sum game, a culture
war, as some might label it, in which there is only one victor between con-

tending views of the world. Or it could be seen as a means of expanding the framework of political discourse to encompass both (and many other) identities, to allow for what Charles Taylor calls the politics of recognition, permitting formal representation to be based on both an individual identity and a group identity.[13]

Having established this argument for embeddedness, we can explore its various levels in urban governance. The embedding of newer identities is gradual and occurs unevenly on several levels. In reference to local governance, we can distinguish at least four levels of potential embedding: (1) enveloping discourses and emerging rhetorics; (2) policy-implementing bureaucracies and their consequent rules and regulations; (3) formal executive, judicial, and regulatory bodies of policy formulation that serve as legitimating institutions; and (4) regime.

The Enveloping Political Discourse

One theme of postmodern theory in urban regime theorists' analysis is the importance of a unifying and peremptory perspective, sometimes expressed directly in policy statements but more likely embedded in an implicit but pervasive political and policy discourse. In development policy, the most common of these is the convergent "vision" for the modern postindustrial city, the vision that contextualizes a new education initiative (which, in this context, would immediately be reformulated into a human resource policy) or a new infrastructure proposal that would be enhanced not because of its amenity qualities but because of its potential contribution to the regional economy's value-added capacity. Such infrastructure initiatives in the "vision" for American cities are now standard: a new airport with substantial air freight capacity, a downtown hotel/convention center/civic center complex, suburban high-speed rail service, a downtown arts/theater/historical "preservation" (read tourist) complex, professional sports arena and stadia, office retail commercial centers, and so forth. This is the "vision" automatically offered by regional development analysts and usually supported by progrowth coalitions in both business and government arenas. It serves as the base of consensus for the regime coalition and the governing skills and resources implementing it.

In our framework, this general perspective is the "rhetoric" of the regime, "generated by style together with institution."[14] It is important that the leaders of the coalition's components not just negotiate with one another to define common ends but that they also have a common language, an uncontested political discourse. In a sense, it is the implicitness of the regime's rhetoric, the field of symbols and languages across groups and state and private organizations that invests meaning in everyday political discourse, that is striking. Indeed, some important actions may never be collectively conscious, since the regime vision is embedded in the political discourse, making opposition to it seem futile or, perhaps, *in*comprehensible.

The discourses of urban developmental regimes differ from those of a rising identity grouping. The languages of each are bewildering to the other. Those engaged in a discourse of development find the language of multiidentity politics and the sensitivity to recognition that comes with it to be, at best, an inconvenience that can easily be devalued by dubbing it "political correctness" or, at worst, an intolerable obfuscation of what is seen as an impediment to effective governance. Similarly, those who organize their political identities primarily around a sense of self might see urban competitiveness, embedded in the language of growth politics, either as irrelevant to their lives or as a baseless claim against public finances for the benefit of private gain.

In many larger cities, the discourse of a multicultural identity perspective has influenced the more general political discourse. Language minorities and gender- and sexual identity–based movements together have had the effect of dramatically expanding the popular discourse of urban policymaking beyond the discourses of economic action and ethnic identity. Although the language of identity can be found in many American cities, especially when dealing with education and social issues, in San Francisco it seems that the pattern has taken a grand turn.

In alliance with other language, racial, and ethnic identity movements, the lesbian and gay identities have created a rhetoric of identity affirmation and heterogeneous cultural influences that conflict with the rhetorics of more traditional politics in urban America. As noted in chapter 10, even before the assertion of feminist, lesbian, and gay affirmative agendas, identity politics in school politics was largely played out in the conflicts surrounding multilingualism and cultural affirmation. The reorganization of political discourse and the effects of identity movements on political rhetoric in San Francisco can be seen in how labor leaders have changed their political language—from images of class and labor struggles to multi-identity discourse. Whereas once union officials talked about strikes and compensation, job security, and government expenditures, today even they speak the language of identity politics, in San Francisco especially. *Diverse, empowered*, and the like are words that have crept into the vocabulary. This is an effect not just of the sexual identity movement but of all identity movements in the city.

Policy-Implementing Bureaucracies

Similarly, the embedding of sexual identity (and other identities) into the social instruments of policy implementation—essentially the various administrative levels, bureaucracies, and instrumentalities of service delivery and regulation—is another aspect of change that identity movements have sought. What is most striking about investigating urban gay politics and public administration is not the prominence of so many lesbian and gay leaders but how many less visible gay men and lesbians occupy second- and third-tier administrative and service delivery positions in city and county governments and school boards. Although this may not be true in all American cities, it is not unique to San Francisco or New York. Similar patterns can be detected in Philadelphia; Rochester, New York; Washington, D.C.; Seattle; Boston; and Brooklyn, as well as in some federal administrative centers. With the protections of civil service and the promulgation of nondiscrimination ordinances and executives orders in many city governments protecting gay men and lesbians, local public management and service delivery have been areas of professional gain for those concerned with the possibility of discrimination in private institutions.

The more open presence of lesbians and gay men in administrative structures—and the openness is what is important—has continued unobstructed (except in the uniformed services) in some cities since the mid-1970s. In San Francisco, even in the days of the Feinstein administration when many of the most prominent gay leaders opposed her because of her position on domestic partnership and economic development policy, gay men and lesbians still occupied positions in city government. In New York, both the Koch and Dinkins administrations found the presence of openly gay staff and mid-level executives to be an asset. Many gay men and lesbians are now prominent in the mid- and upper management levels of urban public health agencies, a result of HIV's first affecting gay men. The response of the lesbian and gay community was to develop many of the social and nursing support service models for HIV patients that are now used for others needing chronic care. The accumulated influence of so many working in the administrative apparatus of city government is a resource available to the gay community that cannot be underestimated.

Policy formation and interpretation are other areas in which the perspectives, values, and languages of emerging identity groupings are important. Urban regime theorists recognized that regulatory and interpretive settings are areas of policy formulation, but they limited their commentary to how these areas restrict the acceptable discourse of development policy. Going beyond development to the full range of identity politics, a challenging identity needs access to such areas both to influence the interpretation of law already codified and to alter the basic language of the policy debate. Appointments to executive-level policymaking boards, commissions, and regulatory boards all provide access to formal policymaking and allow the identity to influence the policy dialogue. To have an effective political organization capable of pressuring government is one thing; to be part of the policy debate and influence the policy formulation process is another. Thus, the meaning of the word *family* had to be changed through the Civil Service and Health Commissions in San Francisco so as to begin the serious policy debate on domestic partnerships. Likewise, including representatives of gay and lesbian protective organizations on police advisory boards—as in New York and Philadelphia—ensures that some issues will be raised that otherwise might have been ignored.

Legitimating Executive, Judicial, and Legislative Institutions

Although they used the city as the setting in a conflict between latent regime interests and the ideologies of the American regime, Greenstone and Peterson's approach was an institutionalizing one. They saw the incorporation of African American interests in cities as uncertain in the short term, with institutionalization coming only after the initial leaders' agenda has passed to the next set of leaders—if in fact it ever does. The victories of black politicians as city council members or even mayors have always threatened to be transitory successes if not matched by deeper changes in urban bureaucracies, civil service rules, and, eventually, the black community's organizational capacity to influence local discretionary decisions as a whole: in a sense, to be vested in or even to "own" the urban bureaucracy.

Many American cities have now elected openly lesbian or gay members to their city councils, school boards, or judicial posts. Among these are many of the ten largest cities. But whether the election of "identity" candidates to city councils is matched by influence in policymaking remains an open question. Ironically, it sometimes seems that access to formal institutions is easiest for problematized identities. Nearly every major American city has elected a black or Latino mayor over the past twenty years; nearly all have had African American school superintendents and police commissioners (arguably a city government's two most important positions after the mayor); but the social problem of urban minorities remain largely unresolved.

By adding coalitions and alliances to their organizational base, nearly all institutions, including institutions of urban governance, grow if they are not confronted with some fundamental challenge. Culturally, identities and professions build up around the new institution, and the institution begins to legitimate the identities and professions. The incorporation of sexual identity into urban governing institutions through election as well though the active solicitation by party organizations expands the base of governance and is another step toward the embedding of identity.

Regime

An identity's presence in legitimating institutions is not the same as access to the regime.[15] To be a regime, the coalition of which it is composed must remain in place over an extended period of time—usually more than a single mayoral term of office. The coalition must be able to re-create itself in response to changing circumstances, or it will decline and a new regime will emerge. A regime is thus seen organizationally, in a Weberian sense, as the effective overlap of political resources, government apparatus, and a coherent vision. To be embedded at the regime level means sufficient political organization, sufficient presence in the administrative bureaucracy, and the addition of its issues to the political agenda and its language to the regime's discourse. Finally, it requires admission to the points of overlap between private power and public instrumentalities.

Cultural identity and organizational capacity are two themes emphasized in different definitions of regime. Regimes not primarily defined as "progrowth" regimes may grow out of other informal matrices defined by racial or ethnic backgrounds, ideology, or less tangible binding ties. Although particular economic gains by regime members define much of a regime's politics, the bonding ideology can be broader than a simple economic perspective. It can in fact be ethnic or cultural or, more likely, a political discourse that mixes economic interest with cultural characteristics.

In his analysis of Atlanta, Clarence Stone included racial identity as one aspect of regime governance. Stone's formulation of regime theory is attractive because of his reformulation of urban power in the framework of regime theory. He moved away from urban power theorists' previous emphasis on a social control model of power to a formulation as both preemptive power and the social production of power—the view that when rooted in a broad-based constituency, power is (or could be) a social resource. He sees governability as a public asset; regimes operate less often in a passive and restrictive mode by controlling the public agenda than as the "power to do," to carry out a broad strategy or visualization of how their city should be.[16]

According to Stone, in situations of relatively low coherence and weak political authority, urban governance requires the overlap of formal, local state institutions and the informal collaboration of a city's network of institutional powers. If effective and stable, this combination is a governing regime. The absence of a regime, or a too narrowly based regime, offers the opposite of a social resource—a lack of governance and general social powerlessness.[17]

At the level of regime, at which governance can be seen as a public resource, the embedding of a sexual identity can be assessed according to several important criteria that together might give it sufficient standing to obtain a role in the governing regime:

- A perspective expressed by activity in multiple areas of public policy, with implications beyond the initial mobilizing interest.
- Participation in the creation of the overall regime agenda.
- Networks of political communication that intersect, interact, and overlap with other regime coalition members both in formal areas and through informal contacts.
- A sufficiently large cadre of technically proficient professionals in a wide range of policy matters.
- The ability to mobilize political support for itself and on behalf of its electoral and policy allies.
- Appointment or election to office (with an electoral machine) at the highest levels of city government and in key positions in specific policy areas.

These criteria are strict and would be difficult for any identity movement to satisfy. It would only be in San Francisco, of all major American cities, that sexual identity might not be automatically excluded from the social forces participating in a governing regime. But even in San Francisco, where identity and political power have somewhat merged, the absence of economic power as an aspect of "identity" creates a glass ceiling for participants in the regime. Although many see San Francisco's gay community as having substantial economic power, this is a perspective largely of poorer and middle-class citizens.

The link between regime and identity is not new to urban regime theory. Elkin articulated his own regime theory as a prologue to reasserting the formative aspects of institutions. Institutions rested on and were dominated by regimes, which in turn operated through legitimating institutions. Thus for Elkin, regimes—the extended political solution to the tension between exogenous market forces and citizen aspiration—ultimately affected the general character of the citizens.[18]

Although Elkin implicitly recognized the link between identity and regimes, his understanding was only one way: that regimes would structure the balance between the public and the market and this would lead to political socialization and education through procedural politics. Like Echeverri-Gent, Elkin understood the flow of influence as being from the state or regime to the identity, consciously constructing new identities or managing older ones according to its interests. But again, the flow opposite to what Elkin described is also true: that the self, seeking recognition in the public arena as an identity, acting individually and with others, seeks to influence the structure of institutions and the politics of regimes. And in so doing, the self reformulates or reconstitutes his or her own identity while also helping construct the legitimating principles of the evolving regime.

Conclusion

What is different among these four case cities is the extent to which each local lesbian and gay community has been able to embed its identity themes in the social organization of governance. In San Francisco, a lesbian could mount a serious effort to run for mayor. In Birmingham, the goal of the gay and lesbian community has been to sustain itself almost independently of city government, to protect and establish some influence in the most important public policy issue area—HIV policy—and to build local social (read civil) institutions for support in the sexually identified community. Other cities could be similarly assessed according to this continuum of embeddedness of identity.

In a broader social understanding of regime, identity theory and regime theory can find common ground. Sexual (gender, racial, religious, or cultural) identities can become part of a regime when an intermediary organization takes a formal position in the regime's network. The identity's values not only are embedded in its own political and social networks but also overlap with a portion of the regime's informal network.

This is the main difference between identity politics and interest-group politics. In interest-group politics, groups are organized into coherent blocs with definable boundaries, whose ultimate strategy is to maximize gains or minimize loses in min-max situations created by the state. In identity politics, the social (political) movements are instead aimed at the embedded characteristics attributed to the group in the past or, hoping to alter those embedded attributes, problematize those seemingly neutral aspects of context that in fact resist the expression of the identity. It is a politics regarding the acceptance and challenge of embedded attributes associated with the name of the identity and the attempts of the individual alone and in a group to alter the meanings of those attributes and identity. Identity politics is thus partly the excavation of past associations with the identity and partly about the embedding of the emerging identity.

What frequently makes the politics of gender, race, and sexuality into identity politics is that each of these categories was codified in law with attributes that defined as second-class citizens those to whom the categories applied. Group representation never started with the emerging identity groups but were created in law by stigmatizing the groups—whether racial, gender, or sexual identities. In this sense, identity politics does not begin in the identity grouping but in the dissonance created between the claim of neutrality by the state and its codification in law of negative qualities attributed to the identity grouping—in our case, gay men and lesbians.

⬚

CHAPTER 12

*Conclusions on the Macro Level: Identity and Economics
in the Urban Setting*

Throughout this book, I have been making the empirical argument that cities as habitats, as arenas of identity development and expression, show the results of this expression, at least in their politics. This argument does not exclude economic influences but instead is set as a bounding axiom to the economic explanations for politics and policymaking that have become so influential in urban analysis. This economic perspective has three dimensions.

First, it asserts that the description of the person in the city is the same as that of the person who operates in the marketplace. *Homo economicus*—the self-calculating, anomic, rational actor engaged in mini-max calculations and having a single, stable, and static identity throughout his or her lifetime—is seen as the prime actor in politics. This assertion is rarely stated but instead rests below the surface of the analysis in the metaphors that have been transferred from microeconomic and public-choice theory to urban political theory. The assumptions about the actor as a person are even more remote in regime theory, since it is built on the foundations of group theory and historical analysis. But here, too, the initial formal theorizing about group theory was influenced by microeconomic metaphors. Like perfect competition and perfect information, both also stipulated in much microeconomic modeling, the assertion of the static unitary self is required if the advances in formal microeconomic theory is to be applied to the study of urban policymaking. Identity theory highlights the social construction of identities, the active role of the individual in her or his own identity formation, and assumes a multiplexing of identities in the person. The person is neither static nor even unified but instead is conceived through a richer and more interactive understanding of identify formation.[1]

Second, economism has asserted, with increasing detail, a model of urban policymaking whose rational goal is taking maximum advantage of location, human skills, and regional resources for economic growth.[2] As a coordinating goal, the policymaking system deviates from this organizing criterion only enough to maintain an electoral base.[3] The system of intercity economic competition is seen to be the principal mover in urban politics and imposes on localities an almost predetermined basket of development focused public policies.

In assuming that the intercity competitive system drives the politics of each component city, economism had some troublesome policy implications for cities that bore a disproportionate share of the nation's social welfare and public health programs. It may have been the goal of Peterson's theory, as in portions of Musgrave and Musgrave's work before him, to urge Congress to reorganize the finances of redistributive programs so that they would be supported by as broad a tax base as possible, that is, away from cities and counties to full federal financing of transfers.[4] But when their theories were appropriated by business and conservative forces, the outcome was that the cities' social largess would undermine the economic competitiveness of socially concerned urban polities. Then a near consensus was reached in public discourse: that cities are in no position to fund transfer payments and that public policy must recognize that cities are constantly competing with one another for human skills and capital in a highly mobile marketplace. In everyday political discourse, this means that reducing taxes encourages local economic growth and that expanding social services encourages the in-migration of dependent citizens.

Third, both urban economism and regime theory, as well as the academic debates surrounding them, have led to a dramatic refocusing of political study toward urban finance, economic development, and community resistance to the effects of growth politics. The result has been the incorporation of location and trade theory into urban politics, historical analysis through regime theory, and a generally more sophisticated approach to the study of urban politics and policymaking. Or maybe a better way of explaining this is that so much research effort has been invested in development policy that the theoretical development in this one area of study has outpaced developments in other areas of urban social and political life.

The research outcome of this work was a series of highly informative case studies describing the political dynamics of growth regimes and the accompanying community resistance to unbalanced and antisocial growth. These urban studies described a new class line between residents who want low taxes and neighborhood and traditional municipal services (such as schools, police, and parks) and skilled individuals tied more to career than to place who want public investment in the kind of infrastructure required of the "postindustrial city."

Although studies of development have been useful in describing fiscal and debt policy in urban politics, they have been much less useful in examining, for example, education policy, public health, or mental health policy. For example, in education—usually the largest or second largest consumer of locally raised resources—the economism model has little explanatory usefulness.

But the evidence examined here through an identity lens adds little to the persuasiveness of the economist's propositions. In fact, it raises other questions that economism cannot answer. What, then, have we seen?

First, even though the urban transformation literature and the associated growth politics literature can explain the recycling of some downtown space in those cities—such as New York and San Francisco—with a high demand for it, they cannot explain why among all possible neighborhood forms, at least one identified with a same-sex ethos stands out. Indeed, it cannot show why even in cities—such as Buffalo or Indianapolis—that have not gone through a full recycling of downtown space and that have a low demand for commercial and residential space, a residential cluster of gay men and lesbians still emerges. Such neighborhoods do exist and are defined not by economic variables (including income, housing valuation, cash rent, or vacancy rates) but by defining variables such as household structure and age.

Second, we have sufficient evidence that a cohesive voter grouping structured around sexual identity is active in New York City, San Francisco, and Los Angeles (and probably Birmingham and Chicago) and is willing to participate in multi-identity, cross-racial coalitions. Exit polls offer only snapshots of attitudes in time, and admittedly a time-series analysis of several sources would provide better information, but the reality is that the voting group organized around sexual identity breaks up on some economic issues but is cohesive on most other issues. That is, for the so-called gay vote, household income and attitude toward development issues are the exceptions to the general pattern of voting, not indications of those themes. Moreover, it is clear that gay and lesbian voters are more willing to be taxed for education, and health, expenditures than their nongay neighbors.

Third, acting on the basis of sexual identity, not economic interest, gay communities across the nation have created their own community-based organizations. In this book, we looked at Birmingham partly as an illustration of how well gay men and lesbians have become integrated in American cities, but it is only one example. If our assessment of Birmingham is correct, then it is surely true for Boston, Chicago, the Los Angeles area, Seattle, and Atlanta. Occasionally, these community-based organizations and less formal groups act in consort with other neighborhood and community organizations, seeking to protect neighborhoods, provide youth services, and the like. But neither regime theory nor an economism drawn from pure microeconomics would explain the political aspects of this social organization of identity.

Fourth, conflict over the embeddedness of different identities in the social organization of urban governance has become a focus of conflict in many cities. In some cases, the embedding of sexual identity may be only a minor change, but in other cases, we can detect the change in administration procedures, civil service protections, policymaking and legitimating institutions, and even, in San Francisco, the governing structure. In still other cases, past embeddings of contrary identities have formalized negative stereotypes of gay men and lesbians, and so these still exist in the social structures of urban governance. They have (or will) become objects of political conflict.

Finally, and maybe most important, we have seen how the gay or lesbian identity itself has changed over time. Since the beginning of the homophile movement of the 1950s, when a more assertive and self-confident sense of building a gay and lesbian personhood took hold, this identity (or, rather, identities) has changed. Today there is no one single "gay identity" such as the butch-femme dichotomy or the foppish "fairy" of the early twentieth century. The contemporary gay male and lesbian (and bisexual) identity now is broader, not just racially and by gender ascription, but also by generation, style, and other defining affinities. The partly successful struggle to destigmatize the categories "gay" and "lesbian" has allowed the proliferation of many differing and nuanced sexual identities. Economic models cannot comprehend these changes because their understanding of the person is indifferent to the development of identity. Indeed, throughout this book, we have not assumed that either individual identity or the categories of identity are stable. Indeed, we see change in the simplest issue in self-identification in purely empirical data, that there is a continuing variance in the rates of self-identification and thus in the underlying structures that reflect the ongoing construction of identity as a grouping.

Recent work on racial, sexual, and gender identity in urban politics and policymaking would seem to be outside the framework developed under this influence of economics, not in dialogue with it. But even though economic metaphors do not explain the effects of identity movements on urban politics, we cannot say that these economic models offer no important insights into the patterns of political conflict in urban politics over the past twenty years. It may well be that the time for metanarratives in urban politics has passed, just as it has in literary criticism and sociology. Still, we need to construct an architecture to support multiple models, if only for the purposes of mutual recognition and common vocabulary. Cities are both vibrant economies and the domains of a wide variety of identities.

Economics and Identity: Complementary Metaphors in the Urban Setting

If we are to construct an architecture of multiple metaphors to take into account both economic and identity influences on urban politics, we must understand that economic incentives and social ties are in conflict. Marxist theory posits that all social activity can be ultimately understood as an expression of an underlying economic superstructure. Economism reduces all social interaction to what Granovetter calls the undersocialized self-calculating person. A better metaphor, however, is the ongoing tension between market and identity principles, the complementarity between social ties and economic incentives. Having examined some of the effects of sexual identity in urban politics, we can now return to the distinction between identity and economic metaphors introduced in our opening chapters with greater confidence. There, we listed five points of distinction. (See Table 3.1 for a summary.)

Politics "Imposed" by a System of Competing Cities Versus Cities Suspended in Networks of Aligned Political Identities

The political-economy model sees cities as firms competing in a consumer market for available investment, human skills, and potential tax revenue in an ever changing intercity market. At its best, such competition creates incentives to eliminate waste in service delivery and enhance public-sector productivity. But it also creates disincentives to helping those in need. In such circumstances, the rational policymaker pursues progrowth policies.

The central revelation of this intercity competition is that the system as a whole imposes on local urban policymakers an agenda, a set of forces that push toward policy outcomes favoring development policies that exploit local advantages of location, skills, resources, and access to markets. This theme of the political-economy model is both an explanation of how policy is made and a goal recommended by many economists. Regime theory offers a modification of this theory by acknowledging the external structuring of local politics, but it also recognizes some local political fluidity and actor agency in how those structuring forces actually affect local policymaking.

But identity politics is not about identities imposed from above. Rather, it is a struggle against embedded identities and their assumptions in policy, law, and language resulting from past struggles over identity. Identities are not products of urban politics or formulated around economic criteria so much as they are phenomena that form and are expressed in an urban setting. Nor do they necessarily need local reaffirmation and support as a precondition for political action in a time of mass media and rapid personal communications. From the perspective of the more powerful, identities present themselves through individual and group activity supported by an identity network. They emerge and are defined in contention with other identities, necessarily moving across borders as networks of symbols, communications, and transportation bringing people together or driving them apart. Identity politics concerns social ties, and political action draws strength from those ties—both strong and weak—not from competition.

Cities as Nodes in an Economic Hierarchy Versus Cities as Settings for Political Action

A second constant theme in urban political economy is the hierarchy of specialized nodes of economic activity—cities divided into "world cities," "national centers," "regional capitals," and the like, with sector specialization increasing as the domain shrinks. Beyond the simple premise that development must precede redistributive programs, the incorporation of trade and location theory brings export and production into the model. Location theory draws the attention of policymakers to those factors of production—labor, transportation facilities, capital, access to markets—to seek strategies that maximize their economic advantage. The end result is that those cities seeking to take the greatest advantage of location and production factors also end up specializing in an economic function.

In addition to becoming specialized economically, cities also form primary or secondary (or even tertiary) relationships to other cities in their regions, relating to one another in functional patterns. World cities at the highest level, encompassing capital directive and communication functions, coordinate other cities in their production and regional administrative functions down to local centers of consumption and marginal production. When combined, the joint model contains an array of cities arranged vertically in terms of domains of administration and market saturation and horizontally in competition for capital and human skills.

Identity politics has no such hierarchy based on market dominance, no formal specialization, although gay culture does rank those cities most closely identified with gay- and lesbian-friendly spaces (Manhattan; Northampton, Massachusetts; San Francisco; West and Central Los Angeles; and the gay and lesbian vacation archipelago stretching from Ogunquit, Maine, to Guerneville, California). The movement and deep agenda are the same in each place, but the politics in each city concerns the locally specific agenda. This does not mean that the politics is separate—as in the opposition to a particular arterial highway or office tower—only that it has adapted to the local political powers, opportunities, and levers of political influence. Thus, "gay politics" in one area may focus on AIDS prevention and social support or school curricula or women's shelters or attempts to create lesbian/gay electoral districts. Identity politics does, however, have a deep agenda that is presented in local policy agendas. The deep agenda is the recognition of the identity as legitimate and the struggle for some control of space for its expression.

Seen in this light, cities are "nodes" not in hierarchical economic forms but as settings for the expression of gay and lesbian identity through issues and groups embedded in lateral identity networks. We could compare this notion to a topological map in which the contours of identity rise and fall across the political plane. Hills and mountains represent various intensities of expression with different "geologies" of issues. Or we could contrast this topology with the bounded and separated group game that is a common metaphor in urban political analysis.

Urban Space as an Ecology of Economic Functions Versus Urban Space as an Arena for Identity Development

In the economic model, spaces in cities have specific functions. Urban space becomes an ecology of functionally specific areas defined by economics.

The relationship of residential space (initially defined by class, race, and ethnicity), production space, consumption space, and transportation space is key and changes over time. The first theoreticians of urban space as an ecology of economic function saw "rings" around the central business district. The effects of transformation (or economic restructuring) in the current era "leapfrog" from the first ring to the third, leaving the second to decline, its support manufacturing, transportation, warehousing, and shipping functions having lost their utility.

The economism model of cities judges urban space mainly for its economic value—space arranged for production or consumption—as defined in its relation to the city's economic function and specialization. For many in the urban transformation school, the change in space utilization is a result of economic activity decentralizing along with changes in transformation infrastructure and production modes. Urban studies informed by social movement studies, as well as critical economic studies, have come to view urban space less in terms of its economic function and more as an ecology of identity havens. Seeing urban geography itself as a social construct, some analysts have attempted to reconceptualize urban space as a historically specific idea that changes over time. Still others see the same regions of urban space as different for each group, since each ascribes a different meaning to the space and its contents over time.

Some of the first works on gay and lesbian history and politics discussed cities as "safe havens" for sexual minorities. Whether or not this is accurate, urban space does have a bearing on gay politics, particularly in our framework of analysis. Chapter 4 examined the patterns of urban lesbian and gay residential clusters. Here the difference between the economism model and the model of embedded social ties may be most apparent: the economic rationale pushes space toward commodification, whereas identity pushes space toward a site infused with meaning by the attributes of the identity. These may not be exclusive of each other, but they are literally in tension.

The Primacy of Economics Versus the Primacy of Identity over Politics

The acceptance of microeconomic assumptions and the analogy of cities as firms in a competitive marketplace leads to various political themes. Like the public-choice model that informs it, the economic model emphasizes growth, in this case, economic growth. More economic growth leads to a stronger tax base, which produces more revenues to finance new services, or so the argument goes. Although the economic model has helped explain many tendencies in urban policymaking, it has overstated the consensus of urban politics and understated the contentiousness of the policies the model would prescribe. The economic model implies that economic growth depoliticizes the urban system by expanding the public pie. But even though development does change the patterns of politics, it does not depoliticize the system.

The relationship between politics and economics in identity politics and identity networks is different. The expressions of some social movements clearly have economic bases in postindustrial politics or focus on economic patterns that have a social effect, but none names economics as the primary motivator in politics. Identity politics, in particular, sees deeper motivations for politics.

My argument is not that economic factors are unimportant but that the hegemony that economics has claimed for urban politics has gone too far. Even though it can explain much of development policy, the model is not powerful enough to relegate all other political phenomena—whether tied directly to economic change or completely separate from it—to the catchall category "postindustrial politics." Identity is not at the periphery but at the core of urban life.

The Isolation of Cities Versus the Open Polity

Tied to the competitive market of cities as firms and the primacy of economics over politics is the ultimate issue for students of urban political movements: Are cities isolated political systems, or are they arenas in which larger social forces express their political agendas? In short, the economic model draws its fundamental themes from the open nature of the urban economy, but it does not make a similar assumption about an open political system. There are links among cities—or, better stated, among identities among cities—that are manifested in cities pursuing different strategies. The economic model has always underestimated the political interaction of urban life, and indeed, it must, since it assumes the preeminence of microeconomics and the separateness of cities as competing "firms." But the Afro-nationalist movements in Chicago and Atlanta, Detroit and Oakland, New York and Montgomery were never separate. Nor are the urban manifestations of the women's movement fundamentally different in Boston or Seattle or even Provincetown. Today, the lesbian and gay rights movement, the Asian and Latino agendas, and even the Christian fundamentalist agenda and other identity movements are not different from city to city.

The great irony here is that the entire political-economy model proceeds from Norton Long's revision of Weber's description of urban politics as occurring in an "Unwalled City." The end point seems to be a model of a city open economically but closed politically. Even the critics of the economism model, still largely working in the model, have become victims of this aspect of economism. The "urban transformationists" properly pursued the politics of the price shift that naturally followed urban transformation. The uneven distribution of the negative consequences of growth in accordance with class, race, and group became the focus of their work. Neighborhood politics and community mobilization were thus incorporated into the economic model—as if community-based politics could not have other motivations. Identity was sometimes incorporated into the economic model through this channel, but here, identity largely referred to Latino or African identity as a pole of political mobilization played out in neighborhood politics as "losers" in the economic change associated with urban transformation. In the end, much of the criticism of the economism model was in fact conducted within the political-economy model, using its language and categories to modify its excesses.

The identity politics metaphor I have outlined assumes both an open economy and an open political system. It does not leave out neighborhood- and community-based politics challenging the effects of larger economic trends on localities but sees urban politics as going beyond such phenomena. Symbols and people move as fast or faster than capital and skills do. The economic and political walls were brought down together.

Warning: Discard Identities After Use

Asserting the status of the social in urban politics need not come at the exclusion of the economic. While pressing for an understanding of social connectedness in economic matters and organization theory, Mark Granovetter also recognized the value of rational actor models as a source of good working hypotheses: "What looks to the analysts like nonrational behavior may be quite sensible when situational constraints, especially those of embeddedness, are fully appreciated."[5] Similarly, the idea of attaching a policy agenda to the local urban policy process through the system of competing cities acting as firms need not, and should not, be abandoned.

These economic axioms, however, explain only a portion of the real conflict and patterns of political mobilization and cohesion in American cities, at least as they refer to one identity. The same globalizing forces that opened the regional economies of American cities are also creating an environment with new social ties and the cultural identities associated with them. Indeed, the very process of economic change, with its accompanying destruction of long-standing patterns of community, strains other social ties not linked to the newer economic patterns. The globalization of the economy has made American cities into spawning grounds for new identities seeking new social connections.

The breakdown of previously effective social connections—along with increased diversity of populations, multiple languages, and modes of living—has engendered two decades of negative imagery of the American city. The evolving postmodern urban form, with a leveling of narratives, the juxtaposition of differing signs from different cultures, and the decentering of social and political meanings, is a frightening, nihilistic prospect for many—the city as "satanic creche," in Akbar Ahmed's arresting phrase. It is against this image of the "city as hell" that much religious orthodoxy has risen.[6] The multiplicity of discourses that now characterize our major cities makes their governability seem even more tenuous than in the mid-1970s, when Douglas Yates was worried about the capacity to govern more simply as a matter of process and organizational capacity.[7]

Again, note that I am making an empirical argument here. The very proliferation of identities in our cities makes meaningless any argument about supporting or resisting identity politics.[8] As there was a debate within political science two generations ago over how to deal with groups organized around economic interests, challenging as they did an imputed and transcendent "public interest" itself usually defined by conservative forces,[9] today the assertion of identities is seen to some as a challenge to a functional, bonding culture. It might well be true that the tempering of interest groups would make for a more universal notion of the public interest, but all attempts in the past have been hampered by the association of the "public interest" with the interests of dominant economic powers. Similarly, those engaged in identity politics see the attempt to reassert a bonding culture over American politics as a conservative reaction to change centered in a dominant identity.

The issue for politics as a discipline is to find metaphors to deal with these new political identities as it did 40 years ago to incorporate economic interest groups in the analysis. The initial attempts to deal with identity politics was to mimic the models of interest groups politics, so "gay politics" was seen as an interest group, or even as "single interest group." Although lesbian and gay politics is not about interests in the usual sense, it certainly is not a "single interest" group. Better sources for theoretical insight into the politics of identity are not in economics, but in social organization theory, cultural anthropology, and postmodern theory.

Finally, we need to look back at our own method and speak to the problems of the category "identity." As an analytical category, identity does not have the geometric consistency of pure economic and rational models. The elegance of economic modeling comes at the price of its primary stipulations: assumptions regarding the person and an initial disregard for the costs of information, the social or economic impediments to mobility and the accounting of transaction costs. The geometric rules of economic modeling allow for a firmer definition of the bounds of interest groups. Because the groups are defined by their potential for public policy gains, likely winners can be identified, even if they do not yet understand the potential for gain. Some portion of the cost of organizing can then be imposed back onto these "free riders"; or enforcement activity could deny to "free riders" any gains achieved by the group.

The borders of identity groups cannot be as clearly defined. They trail off into other identities. Policing the borders of identity groups does not give rise directly to issues of free riders, but to the essentialist definition of identities and the differences among them. The borders between black and gay, if understood as a distinct line drawn between an essentialist understanding of these two identity groups, can never be reconciled. Only in "soft" edges can a solution to such conflicts be found.

The great risk of identity theory is that a single, historically specific, identity may be "reified," and thus its very application may threaten new ways of thinking. Single identit-*ies* always threaten to impute universal characteristics to members of an identity group to whom such characteristics do not necessarily apply. Thus "gay" can be used—and has been in the past—as meaning white, male, well educated, and middle class. Likewise, "gay media" often refer to magazines adorned with young, white, handsome gay men. And "gay ghetto" may be a code for an enclave of white male residences. We should therefore emphasize that the category "identity" should be included in urban politics as a genus category, in this case as a broadly defined identity associated with same-sex affinity, but not with a specific identity at a specific time. As we have seen in this book, even a measure of identity as seemingly "objective" as exit polls' self-identification rates has associated constructions that will change over time.

Political scientists must learn to use "identity" as a general category but recognize that "identit-*ies*" are not stable. Identity is always applicable as a category, whereas identities are finer tools with more subtle edges, research tools whose subjects participate in their definition. After their application, identit-*ies* should be allowed to dissolve, as they should be used only as a temporary analytic category in a tactical essentialist method and, as with Wittgenstein's ladder, discarded after use.

Closing

The struggle to introduce a lesbian and gay identity into the governance of urban America has been an important story in American urban politics during the past thirty years. Once police felt free to raid gay bars and clubs under the pretext of state liquor laws and criminal statutes on vagrancy and sodomy, but today lesbians and gay men—free and firm in expressing their identities—sit on city councils and serve on the staffs of mayors. They have become officials to whom police departments report. Solid and stable neighborhoods have been built by citizens who were once termed intrinsically unstable and unreliable because of their sexual affinities.

In most cities, the support of lesbian and gay voters is now sought by liberal and center politicians, even if they sometimes do it quietly so as not to upset other voting members of their electoral coalitions. In Chicago, the Cook County Democratic organization has found it worthwhile to incorporate sexual identity into its own grassroots base on the North Side. It has supported domestic partnerships legislation for Chicago City employees and declared the North Halstead Street area as an official urbanscape of the city. In San Francisco, even the business community recognizes the need to deal with the policy interests of lesbians and gay men if it wishes to pursue its growth agenda. The medicalization of homosexuality by psychiatry and psychology, and the interventions they offered into the 1960s to deal with the "problem of homosexuality" are now seen as an embarrassment to these professions. In retrospect, changing the social context oppressive to the emerging sexual identity was easier than changing the identity itself.

As political and cultural identities have become a mainstay in comparative and international politics, so too have they become increasingly important in urban phenomena. As larger economic forces impose their limitations, and state and federal mandates and financial regulations have restricted the fiscal discretion of urban policy-making systems, the realm of identity politics has expanded. Lesbians and gay men are not unique in this regard. The language and sign politics of identity make symbolic and cultural demands on urban political systems far beyond the ethnic politics of older urban machines. Ironically, much of the new identity politics requires little real resources at least when compared with the older ethnic machines and their investment-hungry business community partners. With few slack resources what else do mayors have to define their constituencies, mobilize them to the polls, and unify a coalition sufficient to govern? Identity politics in the American urban setting is here to stay.

⁞⁞⁞

Notes

CHAPTER I

1. In a probit analysis of the effects of socioeconomic variables on the passage of "gay rights" ordinances on the local level, Steven Haeberle found that the three most significant correlates of a city implementing a local "gay rights" ordinance were (1) a turnover in population, (2) a strong "nonfamily" cohort in the residential mix, and (3) dramatic changes in the employment patterns. Steven Haeberle, "Gay Men and Lesbians at City Hall," *Social Science Quarterly*, Spring 1996, 190–97.

2. See J. Buttons, B. Rienzo, and K. Wald, "The Politics of Gay Rights in American Communities" (paper presented at the annual meeting of the American Political Science Association, New York, 1993), 5. For a broader survey and set of case studies on the passage of such ordinances, see, by the same authors, *Private Lives, Public Conflicts: Battles over Gay Rights in American Communities* (Washington, D.C.: Congressional Quarterly Press, 1997).

3. See Todd Swanstrom, "Beyond Economism: Urban Political Economy and the Post-Modern Challenge," *Journal of Urban Affairs* 15, no. 1 (1993): 55–78.

4. See Dennis Altman, *Coming Out in the Seventies* (Boston: Alyson Publications, 1976), and *The Homosexualization of America* (Boston: Beacon Press, 1982); Barbara Ponse, *Identities in the Lesbian World: The Social Construction of Self* (Westport, Conn.: Greenwood Press, 1978); Stephen O. Murray, *Social Theory, Homosexual Realities* (New York: Gay Academic Union/Gai Saber Monographs, 1984); and Jeffrey Weeks, *Coming: Homosexual Politics in Britain from the Nineteenth Century to the Present* (London: Quartet Books, 1977).

5. See Derrick Sherwin Bailey, *Homosexuality and the Western Christian Tradition* (London: Longmans, Green, 1955); John Boswell, *Christianity, Social Tolerance and Homosexuality* (New Haven, Conn.: Yale University Press, 1980); John D'Emelio, *Sexual Politics; Sexual Communities: The Making of a Homosexual Minority in the United States, 1940–1970* (Chicago: University of Chicago Press, 1983), and his "Gay History," in John D'Emelio, ed., *Making Trouble: Essays on Gay History, Politics and the Univer-*

sity (New York: Routledge, 1992); Richard Plant, *The Pink Triangle, The Nazi War Against Homosexuals* (New York: Henry Holt, 1983); Elizabeth Lapovsky Kennedy and Madeline D. Davis, *Boots of Leather, Slippers of Gold: The History of a Lesbian Community* (New York: Routledge, 1993); and George Chauncey, *Gay New York: Gender, Urban Culture and the Making of the Gay Male World: 1890–1940* (New York: Basic Books, 1994).

6. See, for example, Randy Shilts, *The Mayor of Castro Street: The Life and Times of Harvey Milk* (New York: St. Martin's Press, 19982); and David J. Thomas, "San Francisco's White Night Riot: Injustice, Vengeance and Beyond," in William Paul et al., eds., *Homosexuality: Social, Psychological and Biological Issues* (Beverly Hills, Calif.: Sage, 1982).

7. Dennis Altman, "Legitimation Through Disaster: AIDS and the Gay Movement," paper presented to the annual meeting of the American Political Science Association, Chicago, 1987.

8. Bob Bailey and Ken Sherrill, "Poll Shows Jackson Attracted a Majority of the 'Gay Vote'," *Washington Blade*, June 24, 1988, 1.

9. Rudder Schmitt-Beck, "A Myth Institutionalized: Theory and Research on New Social Movements in Germany," *European Journal of Political Research* 21 (1992): 359, 366.

10. Michel Foucault, *The History of Sexuality*, trans. Robert Hurely (New York: Vintage Books, 1990).

11. Ronald Inglehart, *Culture Shift in Advanced Industrial Societies* (Princeton, N.J.: Princeton University Press, 1990). The references to lesbian and gay activism are very sparse when compared with those to feminism, the "Greens," and other social movements.

12. Ronald Inglehart and Paul Abramson, "Economic Security and Value Change," *American Political Science Review* 88, no. 2 (1994): 336–53.

13. On feminism and psychoanalysis, see Carol Gilligan, *In a Different Voice: Psychological Theory and Women's Development* (Cambridge, Mass.: Harvard University Press, 1982); and Judith Butler, *Gender Trouble: Feminism and the Subversion of Identity* (New York: Routledge, 1990). On feminism and epistemology, see Lynn Hankinson Miller, *Who Knows: From Quine to a Feminist Empiricism* (Philadelphia: Temple University Press, 1990). On the dangers of identity as an essentialized category, see Shane Phelan, *Getting Specific: Postmodern Lesbian Politics* (Minneapolis: University of Minnesota Press, 1995). On comparative politics, see Anthony Smith, *National Identity* (Reno: University of Nevada Press, 1991); and Benedict Anderson, *Imagined Communities* (London: Verso, 1983). On Islamic identity, as an example, see G. W. Choudhury, *Islam and the Contemporary World* (London: Indus Thames, 1990). On international politics, see Crawford Young, ed., *The Rising Tide of Cultural Pluralism; The Nation-State at Bay?* (Madison: University of Wisconsin Press, 1994); Alexander Wendt, "Collective Identity Formation and the International State," *American Political Science Review* 88, no. 2 (1994): 384; and John Ruggie, "Territoriality and Beyond:

Problematizing Modernity in International Relations," *International Organization* 47 (1993): 139.

14. I mean the word *metaphor* to be taken seriously, as the opposite of model. If a model is a "picture," a metaphor is part myth (an expression of common experience in symbolic form) and part mirror. Some might use the word *narrative* or *script*. A metaphor is not a model that is separate from experience and above it. Nor does it exclude other metaphors. Following Richard Rorty, the "political economy 'model' " and the "identity field 'model' " are seen here as competing and possibly compatible metaphors. In short, I conceive of these myths as being in competition but also complementary. See Richard Rorty, "Philosophy as Science, as Metaphor and as Politics," in Richard Rorty, *Essays on Heidegger and Others* (Cambridge: Cambridge University Press, 1991).

15. See Norton E. Long, "The Local Community as an Ecology of Games," in Norton E. Long, ed., *The Polity* (Chicago: Rand McNally, 1962).

CHAPTER 2

1. For example, see Todd Gitlin, "The Left Lost in the Politics of Identity," *Harpers*, September 1993, 16–20.

2. See Don Teal, *The Gay Militants* (Briarcliff Manor, N.Y.: Stein & Day, 1971), 75.

3. Although there was tension between men and women from the start of both the Gay Liberation Front and the Gay Activist Alliance, a landmark essay, "The Women-Identified Woman," *Come Out!* June/July 1970, asserted a lesbian identity independent of both the women's movement and the gay rights movement. To this day, the role of lesbians as an organizational and theoretical bridge between the women's movement and the (male) gay rights movement has been a fundamental contribution of lesbian political theory. See Mark Blasius and Shane Phelan, eds., *We Are Everywhere: An Historical Sourcebook of Gay and Lesbian Politics* (New York: Routledge, 1997), 396–399.

4. Angus Campbell, Philip E. Converse, Warren E. Miller, and Donald Stokes, *The American Voter: Unabridged Edition* (Chicago: University of Chicago Press, Midway reprint, 1976), 147, 151.

5. Gabriel Almond and Sidney Verba, *The Civic Culture: Political Attitudes and Democracy in Five Nations* (Boston: Little, Brown, 1965). (Italics in original.)

6. Ibid., 43–44.

7. Ibid., 13.

8. At the time of the survey, they found that "large majorities of American, Britons and Germans see their national governments as having some impact on their lives. Mexicans are at the opposite extreme, with 66 per cent attributing no effect to their national government. The Italians are in between" (ibid., 47). Almond and Verba also use identification with "types" of governments. Identification with more traditionalist forms of political culture—by which they mean tribal, feudal, or autocratic—are transitional states of identity that will eventually move toward participant-subject forms of govern-

ment, typically the British parliamentary and constitutional system. From the perspective of these dominant cultures, the atavistic structures of some civic cultures is an issue of political regulation rather than self-actualization (ibid., 26–28).

9. David Busby Edwards, "Frontiers, Boundaries and Frames: The Marginal Identity of Afghan Refugees," in Akbar S. Ahmed, ed., *Pakistan: The Social Sciences' Perspective* (Karachi: Oxford University Press, 1990).

10. See, for example, G. W. Choudhury, *Islam and the Contemporary World* (London: Indus Thames, 1990); Akbar S. Ahmed, *Postmodernism and Islam: Predicament and Promise* (London: Routledge, 1992).

11. See Bobby Sayyid, "Sign 'O Times: Kaffirs and Infidels Fighting the Ninth Crusade," in Ernesto Lachau, ed., *The Making of Political Identities* (London: Verso, 1994).

12. See Benedict Anderson, *Imagined Communities: Reflections on the Origin and Spread of Nationalism* (London: Verso, 1983); and Partha Chatterjee, *The Nation and Its Fragments: Colonial and Postcolonial Histories* (Princeton, N.J.: Princeton University Press, 1993).

13. Especially from Harrison C. White, *Identity and Control: A Structural Theory of Social Action* (Princeton, N.J.: Princeton University Press, 1992).

14. Erving Goffman, *The Presentation of the Self in Everyday Life* (New York: Doubleday/Anchor, 1959).

15. See White, *Identity and Control*, 2–6.

16. Erving Goffman, *Stigma: Notes on the Management of Spoiled Identity* (New York: Simon & Schuster, 1963), 73–74, 83.

17. For example, see Mark Blasius, *Gay and Lesbian Politics: The Emergence of a New Ethos* (Philadelphia: Temple University Press, 1995); and Shane Phelan, *Identity Politics: Lesbian Feminism and the Limits of Community* (Philadelphia: Temple University Press, 1989).

18. Robert J. Stoller (with Gilbert H. Herdt), "Theories of Male Homosexuality: A Cross-Cultural Look," in Robert J. Stoller, *Observing the Erotic Imagination* (New Haven, Conn.: Yale University Press, 1985), 102 (italics in original).

19. Shane Phelan, "(Be)Coming Out: Lesbian Identity and Politics," *Signs: Journal of Women in Culture and Society* 18, no. 4 (1993): 774.

20. Goffman was explicit in how the problem for the homosexual was "passing," not social change. In his *Stigma* (73), he specifically deals with this.

21. Mancur Olson, *The Logic of Collective Action: Public Goods and the Theory of Groupings* (Cambridge, Mass.: Harvard University Press, 1965).

22. Ibid., 60–61 (italics in original).

23. White, *Identity and Control*, 14.

24. Michel Maffesoli, "Identification or the Pluralism of the Person," in Rommel Mendes-Leite and Pierre-Oliver de Brusscher, eds., *Gay Studies from the French Cultures: Voices from France, Belgium, Brazil, Canada and the Netherlands* (Binghamton, N.Y.: Harrington Park Press, 1993).

25. Iris Marion Young, "The Ideal of Community and the Politics of Difference," in Linda J. Nicholson, ed., *Feminism/Postmodernism* (New York: Routledge, 1990), 300.

CHAPTER 3

1. Edward Blakely, *Planning Local Economic Development: Theory and Practice* (Newbury Park, Calif.: Sage, 1989).

2. Paul Peterson, *City Limits* (Chicago: University of Chicago Press, 1981).

3. Albert Breton, "The Theory of Local Government Finance and the Debt Regulation of Local Government," *Public Finance/Finances publiques* (The Hague) 32, no. 1 (1977): 16–28.

4. Stephen Elkin, *City and Regime in the American Republic* (Chicago: University of Chicago Press, 1987).

5. See Paul Kantor with Steven David, *The Dependent City: The Changing Political Economy of Urban America* (Glenview, Ill.: Scott-Foresman, 1988); and Douglas Muzzio and Robert W. Bailey, "Economic Development, Housing and Zoning: A Tale of Two Cities," *Journal of Urban Affairs* 6, no. 1 (1986).

6. John Mollenkopf, *The Contested City* (Princeton, N.J.: Princeton University Press, 1983); Chester Hartman, *The Transformation of San Francisco* (Towtowa, N.J.: Rowan and Allanshield, 1984); Manual Castells, *The City and the Grassroots* (Berkeley and Los Angeles: University of California Press, 1983); and Susan I. Fainstein et al., eds., *Restructuring of the City: Political Economy of Urban Development* (New York: Longman, 1984).

7. Richard DeLeon, *Left Coast City* (Lawrence, Kans.: University Press of Kansas, 1992).

8. John Mollenkopf, *A Phoenix in the Ashes* (Princeton, N.J.: Princeton University Press, 1992).

9. Clarence Stone, *Regime Politics: Governing Atlanta, 1946–1988* (Lawrence: University of Kansas Press, 1989).

10. See Harrison White, *Identity and Control: A Structural Theory of Action* (Princeton, N.J.: Princeton University Press, 1993), chap. 1 and 759.

11. See Saskia Sassen, *Global Cities: New York, London, Tokyo* (Princeton, N.J.: Princeton University Press, 1991), chap. 7.

12. See J. Vernon Henderson, *Urban Development: Theory, Fact and Illusion* (New York: Oxford University Press, 1988).

13. See H. V. Savitch, *Post Industrial Cities: London, Paris and New York* (Princeton, N.J.: Princeton University Press, 1988).

14. See Benno Werlen, *Society, Action and Space: An Alternative Human Geography* (London: Routledge, 1993).

15. For example, see Stephen O. Murray, *Social Theory/Homosexual Realities*, a Gai Saber Monograph (New York: Gay Academic Union); and Deborah Wolf, *The Lesbian Community* (Berkeley and Los Angeles: University of California Press, 1980).

CHAPTER 4

1. Sociologists, especially Stephen O. Murray and Martin Levine, made the first and most important contributions to the theory of these domains of sexual identity. See Stephen O. Murray, "The Institutional Elaboration of a Quasi-Ethnic Community," *International Review of Modern Sociology* 9 (1979): 165–78, and *Social Theory, Homosexual Realities* (New York: Gay Academic Union/Gai Saber Monographs, 1984); and Martin Levine, "Gay Ghetto," *Journal of Homosexuality* 4 (1979): 363–77.

2. Timothy J. Gilfoyle, *City of Eros: New York City, Prostitution and the Commercialization of Sex 1790–1920* (New York: Norton, 1992), 135.

3. See Stephen Elkin, *City and Regime in the American Republic* (Chicago: University of Chicago Press, 1987); and Theodore Lowi, *At the Pleasure of the Mayor* (Glencoe, Ill.: Free Press, 1964).

4. The flowering of Harlem in the 1920s offered an especially rich atmosphere for gay men and lesbians, though there is some controversy here. For some first hand accounts see the oral histories of Bruce Nugent (pp.228–229) and Stretch Johnson (pp.322–323) in Jeff Kisseloff, *You Must Remember This: An Oral History of Manhattan From the 1880s to World War II* (New York: Schocken Books, 1989).

5. The Bowery, associated with New York's skid row from the Depression era through to the coop-conversion era of the 1980s, was the center of New York night life especially for working people at the turn of the century. The social dynamics of Harlem in the 1920s and 1930s was more complicated. Whites looked at Harlem night life as an area they could engage in things that they normally would not — jazz, Southern food, and a general bohemian culture of "the Other." Drag balls and lesbianism was especially acceptable in these entertainment domains. George Chauncey, *Gay New York: Gender Urban Culture and the Making of the Gay Male World, 1890–1940* (New York: Basic Books, 1994; especially chapters 1, 8 and 9]. Up until the early 1980s there remained two gay bars on (or just off) 125th Street at mid-island and another on West 72nd street off Broadway. By the 1990s, however, African American gay males had come to socialize more openly in the Christopher Street establishments with particular bars geared toward black and mixed clientele between Hudson Street and the Hudson River.

6. Chauncey, *Gay New York.*, p. 136.

7. Faderman, *Odd Girls and Twilight Lovers*, p. 107.

8. The role of bars for women coming to identify as lesbians may be overemphasized in some of the literature. Monika Kehoe's 1984 study of senior lesbians indicated that "only 7% of those who grew up in urban areas . . . met other lesbians in bars."Monika Kehoe, *Lesbians Over 60 Speak for Themselves* (New York: Harrington Park Press, 1989), pp. 19–20; and p.108–109.

9. Elizabeth Lapovsky Kennedy and Madeline D. Davis, *Boots of Leather, Slippers of Gold: The History of a Lesbian Community* (New York: Routledge, 1993), pp. 34–42.

10. See Alan Berube, *Coming out under Fire: The History of Gay Men and Women in World War Two* (New York: Free Press, 1990), 99–100, 115.

11. I. M. Young has critiqued the limits of community as an ideal and goal when applying it to a political clustering in which diversity remains evident. See I. M. Young, "The Ideal of Community and the Politics of Difference," in Linda Nicholson, ed., *Feminism/Postmodernism* (New York: Routledge, 1990); also Steven Seidman, "Identity and Politics in Postmodern Gay Culture: Some Historical and Conceptual Notes," in Michael Warner, ed., *Fear of a Queer Planet: Queer Politics and Social Theory* (Minneapolis: University of Minnesota Press, 1993), 105.

12. Edward O. Laumann, John H. Gagnon, Robert T. Michael, and Stuart Michaels, *The Social Organization of Sexuality*, National Opinion Research Center (Chicago: University of Chicago Press, 1994). Stuart Michaels was the principal author of the chapter on homosexual sexual relations.

13. Ibid., 306.

14. See S. N. Roger and C. F. Turner, "Male-Male Sexual Contact in the U.S.: Findings of Five Sample Surveys, 1970–1990," *Journal of Sex Research*, November 1991, 491.

15. This is largely because of the small number of cities with a population of more than 1 million. It would exclude, for example, all of the San Francisco Bay Area but would include Chicago, New York, Los Angeles, Philadelphia, and Houston.

16. The measures were (1) the presence of gay/lesbian-owned businesses, (2) the presence of gay bars and entertainment centers, (3) areas including census tracts with dual male households, (4) census tracts containing those election precincts that gave Harvey Milk a majority or higher vote in the city's 1975 Board of Supervisors race, and (5) reports of "knowledgeable residents" on the boundaries of the neighborhood. See Manuel Castells and Karen Murphy, "Cultural Identity and Urban Structure: The Spatial Organization of San Francisco's Gay Community," in Norman I. Fainstein and Susan S. Fainstein, eds., *Urban Policy under Capitalism* (Beverly Hills, Calif.: Sage, 1982).

17. Gay bars, for example, which had a long history in the Tenderloin district of the city, and newer ones established in the South of Market area during the late 1970s would not have been good indicators of the actual residential patterns.

18. More technically, Castells performed a T-test analysis on gay versus nongay territories, seeking to disprove a null hypothesis of nonassociation. The data used were from the 1970 decennial census. Why he chose percentages below eighteen years old rather than other possible variables available from the U.S. Census is not explained. For the property variable, Castells used the "percentage of housing units that were owner occupied." He further applied Spearman rank order analysis to refine his conclusions. Castells, *The City and the Grassroots*, 152–53.

19. Ibid., 151.

20. The technique was the Spearman correlation of ranked variables. Ibid., 153.

21. The 1990 decennial census did, however, provide one new indicator that could be used to screen a portion of the nation's gay men and lesbians. On the long census form, under household descriptor, "unmarried partner" is one of the twelve categories of reference relationships. The inclusion of this new category was primarily a reaction to the proliferation of opposite-sex unmarried couples, but it was also true that the increased presence of lesbian and gay couples made the category useful. With additional screening for the related partner's gender, one can find the number of such households that are defined as made up of same-sex, as well as opposite-sex, partners.

22. The data were provided by Strubco, Inc./Quotient Research, a data collection and direct mailing firm based in New York City. The list, a national community master file, is built from local community groups, health groups, gay press subscriptions, donor lists from some lesbian- and gay-identified political candidates, HIV/AIDS service organizations, and several national organizations (National Gay and Lesbian Task Force, the Campaign for Human Rights Funds, and the Victory Fund).

23. Biases in the list are more difficult to deal with. Whereas white, gay, middle-class males are overrepresented, women, lower-income groups, and minorities are not unrepresented. And because it is possible to merge census data with concentrations on the mailing list at the zip code level, this was the method chosen.

24. See Daphne Spain, "Gender Dualities and Urban Decline" (paper presented at the Urban Affairs Association, Cleveland, May 1992). Also see Judith Garber and Robyne S. Turner, eds., *Gender in Urban Research* (Thousand Oaks, Calif.: Sage, 1995).

25. Gregory D. Squires et al., *Chicago: Race, Class and the Response to Urban Decline* (Philadelphia: Temple University Press, 1987), chap. 4.

26. Two results that just miss that threshold point should be noted: the percentage of gay and lesbian residents correlates positively with the percentage of white residents ($r = .3831$, $p = .053$) and negatively with the percentage of Asian residents ($r = <ms>.3844$, $p = .053$).

27. Although most correlations in this analysis were assessed at two-tailed significance with .01 or .001 being considered significant, for the analysis of gender, one-tailed significance and a 0.05 level were used.

28. This is important because if men and women are not separated in the analysis, the relationship with Latino residents would wash out and show no correlation between the sexual identity group and Latinos in San Francisco.

29. In his dissent in *Evans v. Romer*, Justice Antonio Scalia assumed this to be true. There is considerable disagreement on this question, however. See the work of M. V. Lee Badgett in "The Wage Effects of Sexual Orientation Discrimination," *Industrial and Labor Relations Review*, July 1995, F26–F39.

30. See Garber and Turner, eds., *Gender in Urban Research*.

31. According to Soja, "Cities are distinguished by their size, density, heterogeneity,

anomie, functional solidarities, geographic concentricities and axialities [*sic*]." Edward W. Soja, *Post Modern Geographies: The Reassertion of Space in Critical Social Theory* (London, Verso, 1989), 153.

32. See David Harvey, *The Condition of Postmodernity* (Cambridge, Mass.: Blackwell, 1990), chaps. 9 and 22.

33. The cities that did not go through the process and remained stuck as others moved into postindustrial forms could not sustain their past functions and largely declined in output and quality of life. The rust belt cities of the Midwest, upstate New York, and the secondary cities around major urban centers such as Gary, Indiana, Camden, New Jersey, East St. Louis, and Newark, New Jersey, are testaments to disinvestment without new functions.

34. Dennis Altman, *The Homosexualization of America* (Boston: Beacon Press, 1983), chap. 3.

35. Ira Katznelson, *City Trenches: Urban Politics and the Patterning of Class in the United States* (Chicago: University of Chicago Press, 1981).

36. David Harvey, *The Limits to Capital* (Chicago: University of Chicago Press, 1989), 374–75.

37. Benno Werlin, *Society, Action and Space: An Alternative Human Geography* (London: Routledge, 1993).

CHAPTER 5

1. This analysis rests specifically on the 1988 Democratic presidential primaries from New York and California (CBS), the 1988 Democratic presidential primaries (ABC), and the 1990 national elections exit-poll data sets (Voter Research and Surveys/CBS News). (These last data are in fact two data sets, the national data set drawn using national sampling techniques [VRS], the state-by-state data set drawn using state-based sampling techniques.) The New York State and the California State 1992 VRS exit-poll data sheets also had a gay/lesbian self-identifier available, but the other state-specific data sheets did not. A smaller sample from the VNS 1994 national election exit poll and the 1996 presidential exit poll also was used to check specific demographic dimensions.

In addition, the local exit polls used in this analysis include the 1989 WABC/*New York Daily News* local primary and November general exit polls, the 1989 *New York Times*/WCBS-TV NYC mayoral primary and general election exit polls, the Voter News Service (VNS) 1993 New Jersey gubernatorial general election, the 1993 Voter News Service (VNS) New York City general municipal/mayoral election exit poll, and the 1993 *Los Angeles Times* Los Angeles city mayoral primary and runoff election exit poll. Several local elections and referenda in San Francisco and surrounding community surveys with gay/lesbian indicators were made available by David Binder, a San Francisco–based consultant, and by Richard DeLeon of San Francisco State University. I also used data from the 1990 New York State Sixty-fourth Assembly District primary exit poll conducted by Eddie Baca, an independent consultant in New York; Kenneth Sherrill, Hunter College/CUNY; Candida Scott Piel, FAIRPAC (now ESPA); Murray Edelman, CBS/VRS (now VNS); John Leitner, an independent consultant; and myself. In addition, during the 1992 presidential election, I managed an exit poll in heavily gay/lesbian neighborhoods of New York City, which was sponsored by the Gay and Lesbian Alliance against Defamation.

2. When subjected to a chi-square test, the gay/lesbian self-identified and nongay self-identified samples diverged from age at a statistically significant level.

3. For the specific age cohort important to a discussion of the "sixties" generation (in this case, post-Stonewall), see Michael Della Carpini, *Stability and Change in American Politics: The Coming of Age of the Generation of the 1960s* (New York: New York University Press, 1986). More generally, see Warren E. Miller, "Generational Changes and Party Identification," *Political Behavior* 14, no. 3 (1992): 333; and Robert G. Niemi and M. Kent Jennings, "Issues and Inheritance in the Formation of Party Identification," *American Journal of Political Science* 35, no. 4 (1991).

4. The total sample from the ABC New York State 1988 Democratic primary exit poll was 2,883, of which 54 percent were female and 46 percent were male.

5. VNS New York City general election exit poll, November 1993.

6. Changes in the women's self-identification rates may be the result of three technical changes: (1) the larger overall gay/lesbian sample in 1992 compared with 1990, which decreased error through sampling; (2) the fact that the 1992 sample was drawn nationally, whereas about half the 1990 sample was drawn from the states; and (3) the inclusion of the word *bisexual* in the self-identification indicator.

7. VNS 1994 national exit poll, "Questionnaire W," gay/lesbian n = 92, total n = 5,504.

8. For an exploration of sexual identity formation among women as lesbians or bisexuals, see Paula Rust, " 'Coming Out' in the Age of Social Constructionism: Sexual Identity Formation Among Lesbian and Bisexual Women," *Gender and Society* 7, no. 1 (1993): 55–77.

9. Sarah Hoagland, *Lesbian Ethics: Toward New Value* (Palo Alto, Calif.: Institute of Lesbian Studies, 1988).

10. Naomi Schor, "The Essentialism Which Is Not One: Coming to Grips with Irigaray," in Carolyn Burke, Naomi Schor, and Margaret Whittford, eds., *Engaging with Irigaray: Feminist Philosophy and Modern European Thought* (New York: Columbia University Press, 1994).

11. Elizabeth D. Daumer, "Queer Ethics, or the Challenge of Bisexuality to Lesbian Ethics," in *Hypatia* (special issue), Fall 1992.

12. David Binder, an independent consultant and pollster in San Francisco, discovered that a separate category for bisexual would result in an additional 2 percent self-

identification in San Francisco and that women were better represented in this category than in a gay indicator (interview, May 10, 1994, San Francisco).

13. Paula Rust, "The Politics of Sexual Identity: Sexual Attraction and Behavior Among Lesbian and Bisexual Women," *Social Problems* 29, no. 4 (1992).

14. For a fuller exploration of this data set, see Mark W. Hertzog, *The Lavender Vote: Lesbians, Gay Men and Bisexuals in American Electoral Politics* (New York: New York University Press, 1996).

15. We should emphasize that these numbers are small and indicate only representativeness within the samples, not within the population of these cities.

16. *Los Angeles Times*, national exit poll: total $n = 12,741$, and gay/lesbian $n = 333$ (weighted by *Los Angeles Times* formulas). The variance in the gay versus nongay response to the question was statistically significant.

17. VNS 1994 national congressional exit poll, "W Version" Questionnaire, November 1994.

18. Ibid.: total $n = 5,732$, and gay/lesbian/bisexual $n = 92$.

19. VRS 1992 national presidential exit poll, weighted.

20. VNS 1993 New York City general election exit poll, November 1993, weighted by VNS formulas.

21. *Los Angeles Times*, mayoral runoff election, June 1993.

22. When the party identification of the entire 1992 VRS national sample was subjected to a chi-square test, there was a statistically significant difference in party identification between the gay and the nongay samples at the suburban and medium-size city dimensions. For the very largest cities (more than 500,000) and small towns and rural areas, there was no significant difference, as all voters tended to identify as Democratic.

23. The 1989 (ABC/*New York Daily News* and WCBS-TV) primary and general New York City exit polls; the 1993 (Voter News Service) primary and general New York City exit polls; the 1993 (*Los Angeles Times*) Los Angeles primary and mayoral runoff mayoral samples; the national VRS 1990 and 1992 samples; the 1990 New York State Sixty-fourth Assembly District exit poll (sometimes called the Glick poll); the 1988 CBS presidential primary exit polls; and the 1992 CBS and ABC presidential primaries.

24. See Timothy E. Cook, "The Psychological Theory of Political Socialization and the Political Theory of Child Development: The Dangers of Normal Science," *Human Development* 32 (1989): 24–34.

25. Angus Campbell, Philip E. Converse, Warren E. Miller, and Donald E. Stokes, *The American Voter: Unabridged Edition* (Chicago: University of Chicago Press, 1980). More recently, political psychologists concluded that even though party identification could not be traced to early childhood personality development, some did seek explanations for political values, such as diffuse support for government or democratic values, in childhood experiences and common civic education.

26. Norman H. Nie, Sidney Verba, and John R. Petrocik, *The Changing American Voter* (enlarged ed.) (Cambridge, Mass.: Harvard University Press, 1976), 106.

27. Jeffery Henig, "Race and Voting: Continuity and Change in the District of Columbia," *Urban Affairs Quarterly* 28, no. 4 (1993); Ethel Klein, *Gender Politics: From Consciousness to Mass Politics* (Cambridge, Mass.: Harvard University Press, 1984); and Roberta S. Sigel and Marilyn B. Hoskin, *The Political Involvement of Adolescents* (New Brunswick, N.J.: Rutgers University Press, 1981).

28. Gary Marks, "Intra- and Extra-familial Political Socialization: The Australian Case and Changes over Time: 1967–1990," *Electoral Studies* 2, no. 2 (1993).

29. M. Kent Jennings and Richard G. Niemi, *Generation and Politics: A Panel Study of Young Adults and Their Parents* (Princeton, N.J.: Princeton University Press, 1981).

30. Morris Fiorina, *Retrospective Voting in American National Elections* (New Haven, Conn.: Yale University Press, 1981).

31. Richard G. Niemi and M. Kent Jennings, "Issues and Inheritance in the Formation of Party Identification," in Jennings and Niemi, *Generation and Politics.*

32. Arthur H. Miller, Christopher Wlezien, and Anne Hildreth, "A Reference Group Theory of Partisan Coalitions," *Journal of Politics* 54, no. 4 (1991).

33. Klein, *Gender Politics,* 89.

34. Sue Tolleson Rinehart, *Gender Consciousness and Politics* (New York: Routledge, 1992), 149.

35. H. Eric Schockman and Nadine Koch, "The Continuing Political Incorporation of Gays and Lesbians in California: Attitudes, Motivations and Political Development" (paper presented at the annual meeting of the Western Political Science Association, Portland, Oregon, March 16–18, 1995. Their sample was heavily weighted toward men: 71 percent male and 29 percent female.

36. Of all of New York State and California State voters going to the polls in the 1984 Reagan–Mondale election only 1.2 percent self-identified as lesbian or gay. The number of Democratic exit voters willing to self-identify in the 1988 New York State and California Democratic presidential primaries was low: less than 3 percent of all New York State Democratic voters interviewed by ABC News as they left the primary poll self-identified as gay or lesbian and 4 percent in California. In the 1988 Democratic presidential primary in New York City, 73 white Democratic voters exiting primary polls— 6 percent of the total white sample—self-identified to exit pollsters as gay or lesbian, according to ABC News. But when the white sample was recombined with the Latino and black samples, the rate dropped precipitously—indicating an underrepresentation of black and Latino lesbians and gays. In the 1989 New York City Democratic Mayoral primary the rate combing all races was 4 percent on the CBS method. But in the 1993 general mayoral race, VNS (using CBS/VRS methods) captured a self-identified sample of approximately 7.8 percent. In Los Angeles, by 1993 the rate of self-identification was about 5 percent in Los Angeles city—*excluding* the city of West Hollywood, the core of the Los Angeles area's lesbian and gay community. Finally, the self-identification rate in the 1990 national Voter Research and Surveys sample was less about 1.3 percent. The 1992 VRS national sample was about 2.2 percent.

37. Robert W. Bailey, "Out and Voting: The Lesbian and Gay Vote in Congressional House Elections: 1990–1996" (Washington, D.C.; National Gay and Lesbian Task Force, mimeographed, September, 1998).

38. The notions of "turnout" and "self-identification" are different concepts in theory but strongly linked when one actually examines data on gay and lesbian voting behavior. It should be remembered that the rate of self-identification among gays, lesbians, and bisexuals in exit polls is a measure against the total exit-poll sample. Changes in the GLB self-identification rates are a measure of the share of the total vote that can be attributed to those who identify as lesbian, gay, or bisexual in a specific election. In contrast to the long-term increase in self-identification rates there also is a pattern of short-term variations in self-identification that mirror a more extreme version of the standard off-year/presidential year turnout cycles. These swings in gay "turnout" may be due in part to the relative youth of the voter group that identifies as lesbian or gay. Young voters tend to have lower and less stable turnout patterns than older voters. Or it may be that off-year congressional elections simply do not have the kind mobilizing issues related to sexual identity that presidential or mayoral elections may have.

39. The increase in self-identification rates in cities is not necessarily due to an objective increase in the number of gay men and lesbians living in New York City, San Francisco, or Los Angeles. In fact, to the degree that there is anecdotal information, the influx of gay men and lesbians to these cities came in the 1970s and early 1980s, before the late 1980s and early 1990s, when most of the current samples were drawn.

40. Harrison C. White, *Identity and Control: A Structural Theory of Social Action* (Princeton, N.J.: Princeton University Press, 1992), 67.

41. Hertzog, *The Lavender Vote.*

42. This analysis indicates only whether the vote is observable and meets the standard of statistical significance, not whether it had a determining effect on election outcomes. In some cases it probably did, and in many others it probably did not.

CHAPTER 6

1. See, for example, Bernard Grofman's methodological response to criticism of "ecological inference" when used in the enforcement of the Voting Rights Act on the local level: "The Use of Ecological Regression to Estimate Racial Bloc Voting," *University of San Francisco Law Review*, Spring 1993. Although Grofman's central issue is the "bloc voting" criterion associated with the VRA, his review of inferential methods in assessing the effects of group voting is at the cutting edge of the issue.

2. Tim Davis, "The Diversity of Queer Politics and the Redefinition of Sexual Identity and Community in Urban Space," in David G. Bell and Gill Valentine, eds., *Mapping Desire: Geographies of Sexualities* (London: Routledge, 1995). For a longer version, see Robert W. Bailey, "Protecting an Unprotected Minority in Urban Districting: The

Case of Gay Voters in the Districting of New York City's Council" (paper presented at the annual meeting of the New York State Political Science Association, Albany, 1994).

3. Richard DeLeon, *Left Coast City: Progressive Politics in San Francisco, 1975–1991* (Lawrence: University of Kansas Press, 1992), 177–78.

4. Alan H. Spear, *Black Chicago: The Making of a Negro Ghetto, 1980–1920* (Chicago: University of Chicago Press, 1967), chaps. 1 and 7; and Nicholas Lehmann, *The Promised Land: The Great Black Migration and How It Changed America* (New York: Knopf, 1991), 73–77.

5. R. Allen Hays, *The Federal Government and Urban Housing* (Albany: State University of New York Press, 1985), 131–32.

6. Abdul Alkalimat, "Chicago: Black Power Politics and the Crisis of the Black Middle Class," *The Black Scholar*, March/April 1988, 45.

7. Gregory Squire, Larry Bennett, Kathleen McCourt, and Philip Nyden, *Chicago: Race, Class and the Response to Urban Decline* (Philadelphia: Temple University Press, 1987), 74–80.

8. Robert Y. Shapiro and Ester Fuchs, "Government Performance as a Basis for Machine Support," *Urban Affairs Quarterly* 18, no. 4 (1983).

9. Alkalimat, "Chicago: Black Power Politics," 47.

10. In the February 1983 primary, Congressman Washington received 79 percent of the black vote, 25 percent of the Latino vote, and 2 percent of the white vote against two candidates (Jane Byrne among them). But in the April general election, Washington received 98 percent of the black vote, 74 percent of the Latino vote, and 12 percent of the white vote against Republican Bernard Epton.

11. Manning Marable, "Harold Washington and the Politics of Race in Chicago," *The Black Scholar*, November/December 1986, 20.

12. David K. Fremon, *Chicago Politics Ward by Ward* (Bloomington: Indiana University Press, 1988), 291–97, 303–10.

13. These data are from the 1989 Strub-Dawson Company list (now Strubco, Inc.), containing 1,989 names. Just under 63 percent of these households were located in zip codes 60657, 60613, 60614, 60610, and 60640. The list does not represent a random sample and can be used only for analysis within the boundaries of the list itself. Nevertheless, we can infer from these indicators of residential concentration that the area contains a disproportionate share of Chicago's gay vote. A 1994 updated list showed much the same but with more detail, since more households were on the list.

14. There is no direct, random data set of gay voting in Chicago in the early or mid-1980s and certainly not for the 1983 election. Key-ward analysis such as this is the only disciplined way of looking at the question.

15. Paul Kleppner, *Chicago Divided: The Making of a Black Mayor* (DeKalb: Northern Illinois University Press, 1991), 161.

16. Winston W. Crounch and Beatrice Dinerman, *Southern California Metropolis: A*

Study in Development of Government for a Metropolitan Area (Berkeley and Los Angeles: University of California Press, 1964).

17. Stephen Erie, "How the Urban West Was Won: The Local State and Economic Growth in Los Angeles, 1880–1932," *Urban Affairs Quarterly* 27, no. 4 (1992): 519.

18. Stephen Elkin, *City and Regime in the American Republic* (Chicago: University of Chicago Press, 1987), chap. 4.

19. Raphael Sonenshein, *Politics in Black and White: Race and Politics in Los Angeles* (Princeton, N.J.: Princeton University Press, 1993), 103–12.

20. James A. Regualado, "Organized Labor and Los Angeles City Politics: An Assessment of the Bradley Years, 1973–1989," *Urban Affairs Quarterly* 27, no. 1 (1991).

21. Raphael Sonenshein, "The Dynamics of Biracial Coalitions: Crossover Politics in Los Angeles," *Western Political Quarterly* 42, no. 2 (1989).

22. Strubco data, 1989, 1994.

23. In the 1993 primary sample, the *Los Angeles Times* total sample from the central Los Angeles area was $n = 455$. Those who self-identified as gay or lesbian in the central area were $n = 66$.

24. Again, this was about half of the total unweighted gay/lesbian sample for the city as a whole. In the 1993 general election sample, the *Times* total sample from the central Los Angeles area was $n = 597$. Those who self-identified as gay or lesbian in the central area were $n = 88$.

25. Sonenshein, *Politics in Black and White*, 200.

26. Mike Davis, *City of Quartz* (New York: Vintage Books, 1990), 140–43.

27. The source here is a question on the 1993 *Los Angeles Times* exit poll in which voters were asked who they voted for in 1989. The gay/lesbian self-identifier was not on the 1989 questionnaire, so this 1993 question is the only source of direct information on 1989 gay/lesbian voting. I am grateful to Kathy Frankovic of CBS News for reminding me how faulty voters' memories sometimes are.

28. Because of age and mobility, a higher percentage of gay men and lesbians did not vote in that 1989 race. See the *Los Angeles Times* mayoral runoff exit poll, June 1993.

29. Ted Rohrlich, "Record Percentage of Latinos Turn out to Vote, Exit Poll Finds," *Los Angles Times*, April 9, 1997.

30. *Los Angles Times* mayoral exit poll, complete results, April 9. 1997.

31. See Martin Shefter, *Political Crisis/Fiscal Crisis: The Collapse and Revival of New York City* (New York: Columbia University Press, 1993); Ester Fuchs, *Mayors and Money* (Chicago: University of Chicago Press, 1992); and Robert W. Bailey, *The Crisis Regime: The M.A.C., the E.F.C.B. and the Political Impact of the New York City Financial Crisis* (Albany: State University of New York Press, 1984).

32. Raymond Horton, *The City in Transition: Prospects and Policies for New York*, Final Report of the New York State Temporary Commission on City Finances (New York: Arno Press/New York Times Co., 1978).

33. H. V. Savitch, *Post Industrial Cities: London, Paris and New York* (Princeton, N.J.: Princeton University Press, 1988).

34. Edward I. Koch, *Mayor: An Autobiography* (New York: Simon & Schuster, 1984), 303–18.

35. Interview with Allen Roskoff, former chair of Americans for Democratic Action, New York City, and an activist in Manhattan gay politics for almost twenty years.

36. Bob Bailey and Kenneth S. Sherrill, "Polls Indicate Gays, Lesbians Went for Jackson," *Washington Blade*, June 24, 1988, 1.

37. John Mollenkopf, *A Phoenix in the Ashes: The Rise and Fall of the Koch Coalition in New York City Politics* (Princeton, N.J.: Princeton University Press, 1993).

38. See Jerome S. Legge Jr., "The Persistence of Ethnic Voting: African-Americans and Jews in the 1989 New York Mayoral Campaign" (paper presented at the annual meeting of the American Political Science Association, Chicago, September 3–6, 1992).

39. Total Democratic n = 2,727, gay and lesbian n = 125 (unweighted). The weighted gay/lesbian self-identification rate for Democrats was 4.6 percent. Only three registered Republicans caught by the exit poll–sampling technique self-identified as gay or lesbian.

40. The total CBS/*New York Times* September 1989 primary sample of Democrats was n = 1,540, gay/lesbian n = 66 (4.3 valid percentage); and of Republicans, n = 397 (gay/lesbian Republicans a negligible n of 7). The ABC/*New York Daily News* concurrently conducted its own exit poll, which had an overall n = 2,977 for all primary voters; n = 128 for gays and lesbians (for a 4.2 valid percentage weighted by network formulas).

41. WABC/*New York Daily News* exit poll, municipal general election, November 1989. The gay/Lesbian self-identification rate was 3.1 percent.

42. Forced entry logistical regression was used with categorical variables identified as race, party self-identification, political ideology, and religion. Dummy variables for the most significant categories were created for subsequent logit runs. Additional variables tested for the model but found negligible or marginal in predicting other cases included age, gender, income (in this case, education level in the Los Angeles case), and a variable constructed through the interaction of education and income.

43. Shefter's *Political Crisis/Fiscal Crisis*, especially 119–24, describes the role of this divide in the years leading up to the 1975 fiscal crisis.

44. Stephen Erie, *Rainbow's End: Irish-Americans and the Dilemmas of Urban Machine Politics, 1840–1985* (Berkeley and Los Angeles: University of California Press, 1988), 50, 196–220, esp. 210–14.

45. David O. Sears and Carolyn L. Funk, "Self-Interest in Americans' Political Opinion," in Jane J. Mansbridge, ed., *Beyond Self-Interest* (Chicago: University of Chicago Press, 1990), 170.

46. When the own/rent variable was crossed with the mayoral vote variable in the self-identified gay and lesbian sample and subjected to chi-square testing, the samples differed to a significance of <lt> .001.

47. Robert W. Bailey, "The Gay and Lesbian Vote in the 1988 Election: Issues of Method and Identity" (paper presented at the annual meeting of the American Political Science Association, Atlanta, August 1989.

48. See William J. Grimshaw, *Bitter Fruit: Black Politics and the Chicago Machine, 1931–1991* (Chicago: University of Chicago Press, 1992).

49. Gregory Bovasso analyzed the symbolic nature of identity voting in New York's black community and concluded that "nonwhites strive for symbolic group empowerment, regardless of whether it results in improved resource redistribution, because it enhances self-esteem. However, neither blacks nor whites are likely to trade symbolic empowerment for decreased public services." Gregory Bovasso, "Self, Group and Public Interests Motivating Racial Politics," *Political Psychology* 14, no. 1 (1993): 3.

50. Peter Eisinger, *Patterns of Interracial Politics: Conflict or Cooperation in the City* (New York: Academic Press, 1976).

51. Rufus D. Browning, Dale Marshall, and William Tabb, *Protest Is Not Enough: The Struggle of Blacks and Hispanics for Equality in City Politics* (Berkeley and Los Angeles: University of California Press, 1984).

52. Clarence Stone, *Regime Politics: Governing Atlanta, 1946–1988* (Lawrence: University of Kansas Press, 1989).

53. Gary Orfield and Carole Askkinaze, *The Closing Door: Conservative Policy and Black Opportunities* (Chicago: University of Chicago Press, 1991).

54. Weighted by VNS formulas. Total raw "white" sample: $n = 698$, "white" gay/lesbian sample: $n = 67$ unweighted.

55. *Los Angeles Times* mayoral runoff exit poll, June 1993. Data weighted by *Los Angeles Times* polling unit formulas. Total unweighted white sample: $n = 1,932$, "white" gay/lesbian sample: $n = 121$.

56. Saskia Sassen, *Global Cities: New York, London, Tokyo* (Princeton, N.J.: Princeton University Press, 1991), 334–36.

57. Interview with Art Agnos, former mayor of San Francisco, May 10, 1994, San Francisco.

58. When the *Los Angeles Times* data for the June 1993 runoff were analyzed, the only racial subcategory that indicated some ambivalence toward Woo was a small group identifying as non-Mexican Latinos.

CHAPTER 7

1. Francis Green, ed., *Ga Yellow Pages: The National Edition* (New York: Renaissance House, 1993).

2. As distinguished from social organization theorists who see "field" as not being locale centered and those who see it as having a functional base such the art market, community colleges, or multinational corporations. The bounds of the field are of interest and frequently contentious. See Harrison White and Cynthia White, *Canvases and Careers: In-*

stitutional Change in the French Painting World (Chicago: University of Chicago Press, 1993); and Steven Brint and Jerome Karabel, *The Diverted Dream: Community Colleges and the Promise of Educational Opportunity in America, 1900–1985* (New York: Oxford University Press, 1989). I have changed the focus to organizations defined by an identity in one unbounded locale.

3. See Paul Hempill, *Leaving Birmingham: Notes of a Native Son* (New York: Viking Press, 1993).

4. See Bobby M. Wilson, "Structural Incentives Behind Racial Change in Birmingham," *Antipode* 24, no. 3 (1992): 171–202, esp. 178–80; and Henry McIven Jr., *Iron and Steel: Class, Race and Community in Birmingham, Alabama, 1875–1920* (Chapel Hill: University of North Carolina Press, 1985). For a black perspective on the role of U.S. Steel in Birmingham's racial history before the civil rights era, see Howard Mann Bond, *Negro Education in Alabama: A Study in Cotton and Steel* (1939; reprint, Tuscaloosa: University of Alabama Press, 1995).

5. At the turn of the century, the three largest producers of steel and iron—Tennessee Coal, Iron and Railroad; Republic Iron and Steel Company; and Sloss-Sheffield Coal and Iron Company—were owned by northern holding companies. See Edward S. LaMonte, *Politics and Welfare in Birmingham, 1900–1975* (Tuscaloosa: University of Alabama Press, 1995), 4.

6. V. O. Key Jr., *Southern Politics in State and Nation* (New York: Vintage Books, 1949), chap. 3, esp. 48–50.

7. See William Warren Rogers, Robert David Ward, Leah Rawls Atkins, and Wayne Flynt, *Alabama: The History of a Deep South State* (Tuscaloosa: University of Alabama Press, 1994), chap. 21; and Robert David Ward, *Labor Revolt in Alabama: The Great Strike of 1894* (Tuscaloosa: University of Alabama Press, 1965).

8. Clarence Stone, *Regime Politics: Governing Atlanta, 1946–1988* (Lawrence: University of Kansas Press, 1989).

9. James D. Thomas and William H. Stewart, *Alabama Government and Politics* (Lincoln: University of Nebraska Press, 1988).

10. Kathy Kemp, "Most Lesbians Focus on Relationships, Not the Gay Bar Scene," *Birmingham Post-Herald*, December 2, 1986, A.

11. *Birmingham News*, June 31, 1962.

12. John Howard, "Not the Only One in the World: Chronicle of a Post-WWII Gay Man in Birmingham," *Crossroads: A Journal of Southern Culture* 3, no. 1 (1995): 27.

13. Interview with Patrick Cather, August 18, 1995, Birmingham.

14. Howard, "Not the Only One," 28–29.

15. Interview with Rick Adams, August 23, 1995, Birmingham.

16. The newly appointed Roman Catholic archbishop of Birmingham distanced the church from the local Dignity group by refusing to allow church property to be used for its meetings.

17. Phone interview with Howard Cruse, September 14, 1995, New York. Also see

John D'Emilio, *Sexual Politics, Sexual Communities: The Making of a Sexual Minority in the United States, 1940–1970* (Chicago: University of Chicago Press, 1983), for a description of SIR in San Francisco in the mid-1960s.

18. J. Levine, "Editor's Corner," *The Podium* 1, no. 2 (1978): 3.

19. Interview with Cather.

20. In many of the interviews I conducted for this book, I found this conflict to be a constant if subtle theme, evident in phrases such as "white trash," "closeted gay yuppies," and "secretive professional lesbians" often used. In addition, one member of the professional classes noted the resentment attached to professional gay men's becoming active in local institutions even before HIV and fund-raising became an issue.

21. Jay Reeves, "Virtually Unknown Paper Serves as Vital Link for Alabama's Gays," Associated Press Service, Birmingham, November 7, 1995.

22. Huey L. Perry, "The Evolution and Impact of Bi-Racial Coalitions and Black Mayors in Birmingham and New Orleans," in Rufus P. Browning, Dale Rogers Marshall, and David H. Tabb, *Protest Is Not Enough: The Struggle of Blacks and Hispanics for Equality in Urban Politics* (Berkeley and Los Angeles: University of California Press, 1984), p. 145.

23. See LaMonte, *Politics and Welfare in Birmingham*, 166–69; and William Nunnelley, *Bull Connor* (Tuscaloosa: University of Alabama Press, 1991), 125–26.

24. Perry, "Evolution and Impact."

25. Using multiple regression analysis to examine the increased voter participation rates in the South after passage of the Voter Rights Act, Harold Stanley argues that in fact it was not simply the decline of barriers to African American voting and the reaction to it by whites that increased both black and white participation rates, but also the higher levels of educational attainment of both races, the increased competitiveness in elections, the media, and a switch toward postindustrial economic structures. See Harold W. Stanley, *Voter Mobilization and the Politics of Race: The South and Universal Suffrage, 1952–1984* (New York: Praeger, 1987). Also see Peyton McCrary, Jerome A. Gray, Edward Still, and Huey L. Perry, "Alabama," in Chandler Davidson and Bernard Grofman, eds., *Quiet Revolution in the South: The Impact of the Voting Rights Act, 1965–1990* (Princeton, N.J.: Princeton University Press, 1994), 38–66.

26. Interview with Allen Francis, August 21, 1995, Birmingham. The questionnaire was frequently cited as a basis for the disappointment of some in the lesbian and gay community, because they felt that Arrington did not fulfill many of his promises.

27. "Results by Box," *Birmingham News*, October 12, 1983, 12C; and Kitty Frieden, "Arrington Takes Victory Ride on Solidly Black Bandwagon," *Birmingham News*, October 12, 1983, A1.

28. Geographer Bobby Wilson analyzed the housing patterns of black and white in Birmingham's suburbs and found that race rather than income accounted for housing patterns even outside the city proper. See Bobby Wilson, "Structural Imperatives Behind Racial Change," as well as "Birmingham Segregation: Is It a Product of Black-White Socio-economic Differences?" *Southeast Geographer* 29, no. 2 (1989).

29. Interview with Edward LaMonte, Birmingham-Southern University, Birmingham, August 18, 1995. LaMonte is a political scientist.

30. Susan Cullen and Betsy Butgeiter, "Graffeo, Hinton Won Seats with Three Incumbents," *Birmingham News*, October 14, 1987, A1.

31. The case, confirmed in mid-1982, was one of the first three in the nation in recipients of the "clotting factor." The Birmingham case was the longest survivor of these three. The Centers for Disease Control monitored the case closely, sending its own representative to record the patient's progress. The result was that much of the early work on HIV disease in hemophiliacs was done by the CDC and the University of Alabama at Birmingham Medical Center staffs. See W. James Alexander, "AIDS in Alabama: The First 1000 Days" (paper presented at the UAB Briefing on the AIDS Epidemic, UAB School of Public Health, November 28, 1985). Alexander was the Jefferson County epidemiologist and the director of communicable diseases, Jefferson County Department of Health.

32. J. S. St. Lawrence, H. V. Hood, T. L. Brasfield, and J. A. Kelly, "Difference in Gay Men's AIDS Risk Knowledge and Behavior Patterns Across High- and Low-AIDS Prevalence Cities," *Public Health Reports* 104 (1989): 391–95.

33. Interview with Rick Adams, August 23, Birmingham.

34. "A Brief History of Birmingham AIDS Outreach," *Newsletter* (Birmingham AIDS Outreach, Inc.) 1, no. 1: 1.

35. Ibid., 3.

36. Alexander, "AIDS in Alabama," 3.

37. For example, how the concern about AIDS in regard to children affected educational decision making. See David Kirp et al., *Learning by Heart: AIDS and Schoolchildren in American Communities* (New Brunswick, N.J.: Rutgers University Press, 1989).

38. Letter from Rick Adams, administrative assistant, Birmingham AIDS Outreach, to Dr. Claude Earl Fox, state health officer, Alabama State Department of Public Health, Montgomery, May 12, 1987.

39. Letter from Dr. W. James Alexander, Bureau of Communicable Diseases, Jefferson County Department of Health, to Ms. Denise Auger, Birmingham AIDS Outreach, October 1, 1987.

40. Rev. Troy D. Perry (with Thomas l. P. Swicegood), *Don't Be Afraid Anymore: The Story of Reverend Troy Perry and the Metropolitan Community Churches* (New York: St, Martin's Press, 1990). During its first decade, MCC was viewed with suspicion by many lesbian feminists. Although it was founded in 1968, it was not until 1972 that the first women clergy were licensed to the MCC Universal Fellowship (chap. 7, esp. 117).

41. Interview with Dennis Luft, August 25, 1995, Birmingham.

42. HIV/AIDS Division of the Alabama Department of Health, *Update* 6, no. 2 (1995).

43. Patricia Todd, "The Impact of Ryan White Care Act Funding on Alabama" (master's thesis, University of Alabama at Birmingham, 1994), 51.

44. Interview with Mason Meyer, August 18, 1995, Birmingham.

45. *Gay/Lesbian and Bisexual Alliance* v. *State of Alabama* (Eleventh Circuit Appellate Court No. 96-614).

46. Associated Press wire report, January 26, 1996.

47. Scholars interested in the study of organizational fields are usually drawn to three areas: (1) the structural characteristics and behaviors of individual organizational units, (2) the variety of organizational forms, and (3) the nature and extent of linkages between these organizations and the kinds of interorganizational activities they facilitate or constrain.

48. Harrison White, *Identity and Control: A Structural Theory of Action* (Princeton, N.J.: Princeton University Press, 1993), 17, 106–7.

49. Walter Powell, *Getting into Print: The Decision-Making Process in Scholarly Publishing* (Chicago: University of Chicago Press, 1985), 326.

50. As March and Olsen, for example, note: "We are led to a perspective that challenges the first premise of many theories of politics, the premise that life is organized around choice. Rather, we might observe that life is not only, or primarily, choice but also interpretation. Outcomes can be less significant—both behaviorally and ethically—than process." James G. March and John P. Olsen, *Rediscovering Institutions: The Organizational Basis of Politics* (New York: Basic Books, 1989), 51.

51. Just as Mark Granovetter noted that weak ties—sets of social acquaintances—can provide valuable information that militates against the uncertainties of business markets, so too can weak ties of identity, not intended for political effect, be mobilized under some circumstances. Mark Granovetter, "The Strength of Weak Ties," *American Journal of Sociology* 78, no. 6 (1973): 1360.

52. Ibid., 1373–75.

CHAPTER 8

1. The process was called "districting" rather than "redistricting" because the council was a totally new institution.

2. This theme is further developed in Robert W. Bailey, "The City of Greater New York, 1898—1998: Balancing Organizational Capacity and Political Legitimacy," in Sarah Leibschutz, ed., *Government and Politics in New York State: Conflict and Compassion* (Lincoln: University of Nebraska Press, 1998); and Joseph P. Viteritti and Robert W. Bailey, "Capacity Building and Big-City Governance," in Beth Walter Honadle and Arnold Howitt, eds., *Perspectives on Management Capacity Building* (Albany: State University of New York Press, 1986). See also Joseph P. Viteritti, "The City and the Constitution: A Historical Analysis of Institutional Evolution and Adaption," *Journal of Urban Affairs* 12 (1990): 221.

3. See J. David Greenstone and Paul Peterson, *Race and Authority in Urban Politics* (Chicago: University of Chicago Press, 1974).

4. For a review of the impact of the reform movement on New York City's public schools, see Diane Ravitch, *The Great School Wars* (New York: Basic Books, 1974). For the specific inability to deal with changes in the schools, particularly in regard to race, see Marilyn Gittell, *Participants and Participation: A Study of School Policy in New York City* (New York: Praeger, 1967); David Rogers, *110 Livingston Street* (Mew York: Random House, 1969); and Mario Fantani and Marilyn Gittell, *Decentralization: Achieving Reform* (New York: Praeger, 1973).

5. For the impact of school decentralization on policy in New York City's schools, see David Rogers and Norman H. Chung, *110 Livingston Street Revisited: Decentralization in Action* (New York: New York University Press, 1983); and Joseph P. Viteritti, *Across the River: Politics and Education in the City* (New York: Holmes & Meier, 1984).

6. See Robert W. Bailey, *The Crisis Regime: The M.A.C., the E.F.C.B. and the Political Impact of the New York City Financial Crisis* (Albany: State University of New York Press, 1985).

7. Whereas most major American cities are in urban counties and some cities are coterminous with counties, New York is the only city in the United States that is composed of counties.

8. *Andrews v. Koch*, 688 F.2d 815 (2d Cir. 1982).

9. *Morris et al. v. Board of Estimate of the City of New York*, 831 F.2d 384 (1987).

10. By 1989, more than two-thirds of all debt issued in the New York region by New York City and State bonding authorities were outside the city's institutional control. The region as an integrated economic unit now stretched over thirty-two counties as defined by the Port Authority of New York and New Jersey, roughly from the Princeton corridor to halfway through the Hudson Valley to Albany and well into southwest Connecticut. See Rosemary Scanlon, chief economist, Office of the Chief Economist, Port Authority of New York and New Jersey, *Annual Economic Report*, 1992.

11. The Board of Estimate grew out of an older institution established by the state of New York in 1855. When the Metropolitan Police Force was created, combining the New York and Brooklyn police forces into one regional and professional force, a state "Board of Estimate and Appropriations" was established to assess, tax, and appropriate funds to finance the new metropolitan police.

12. Randy Shilts, *The Mayor of Castro Street: The Life and Times of Harvey Milk* (New York: St. Martin's Press, 1982), 152, 162, 165.

13. Interview with Timothy O. Mains, member of the City Council, Rochester, New York, 1993.

14. *City of Mobile v. Bolden*, 446 U.S. 55 (1980).

15. *Thornburg v. Gingles*, 478 U.S. 30 (1986).

16. Pamela S. Karlan, "Maps and Misreadings: The Role of Geographic Compactness in Racial Vote Dilution Litigation," *Harvard Civil Rights—Civil Liberties Law Review* 24 (1989): 200–1.

17. See Bernard Grofman, "Single-Member Districts: Random Is Not Equal" and "The Role of the Expert Witness in Districting Cases," both in Bernard Grofman et al., eds., *Representation and Redistricting Issues* (Lexington, Mass.: Lexington Books, 1982).

18. "Voting Rights Act Overview," memo from Lani Guinier, professor, University of Pennsylvania Law School, to Alan Gartner, executive director, New York City Districting Commission, August 20, 1990.

19. Bruce Cain, "Voting Rights and Democratic Theory: Toward a Color-Blind Society" (paper presented at the Conference on the Twenty-fifth Anniversary of the Voting Rights Act of 1965, Brookings Institution, Washington, D.C., October 15, 1990.

20. *United Jewish Organizations of Williamsburgh v. Carey*, 430 U.S. 144 (1977).

21. Interview with Frank Mauro, director of research, Charter Revision Commission.

22. This concession to the gay community predated the final passage of a "gay rights" ordinance.

23. Draft charter, sec. 52, b.

24. The chief counsel to both the Schwarz Commission and the Districting Commission, as well as the chair of the Districting Commission, read into the record this intended meaning of the word *other*. To activists, the issue had become a matter of some humor. At one public hearing before the commission, Thomas Duane, later elected to the seat created by the district, announced to the commission members that he was "openly *other*." Only one additional group was given this designation: the city's registered Republicans.

25. *New York Daily News*/WABC-TV Democratic primary exit poll, September 1989.

26. For an early review of the issues, see Douglas W. Rae, *The Political Consequences of Electoral Laws* (UMI reprint, New Haven, Conn.: Yale University Press, 1967). Also see Gary King and Robert Browning, "Democratic Representation and Partisan Bias in Congressional Election," *American Political Science Review* 81 (1987); Gary King, "Representation Through Legislative Redistricting: A Stochastic Model," *American Journal of Political Science* 33, no. 4 (1989); and Bruce Cain, "Assessing the Partisan Effects of Districting" *American Political Science Review* 79 (1985): 320.

27. This was the perspective of Alan Gartner, executive director of the New York City Districting Commission, in his "Drawing the Line: Redistricting and the Politics of Racial Succession in New York," a personal report, January 1993.

28. For an overview, see Gary David Comstack, *Violence Against Lesbians and Gay Men* (New York: Columbia University Press, 1991).

29. Strub-Dawson's mailing list as of Fall 1989. More than 43,000 names in the five counties of New York City were on the list.

30. Janet I. Abu-Lughod, "The Battle for Tompkins Square Park," in Janet I. Abu-Lughod, ed., *From Urban Village to East Village: The Battle for New York's Lower East Side* (Oxford: Blackwell, 1994), 233.

31. After the districting process, this area elected an openly gay member to the City Council after a fierce primary with the incumbent liberal standard bearer Miri-

am Friedlander. Friedlander lost in a five-way race to Anthony Pagan, who was both gay and Latino.

32. See Judith Reed, "Of Boroughs, Boundaries and Bullwinkles: The Limitations of Single-Member Districts in a Multiracial Context," *Fordham Urban Law Journal* 19 (1992): 759.

33. Bernard Wong, "The Chinese: New Immigrants in New York's Chinatown," in Nancy Foner, ed., *New Immigrants in New York* (New York: Columbia University Press, 1987).

34. See Jack Newfield, "Hidden Agenda Ruled, Council Gerrymandered," *New York Observer*, June 24, 1991.

35. Elaine Chan and Chino Garcia, cochairs, Lower East District for a Multi-Racial District, "Redistricting: Community Empowerment in Action: A Plan for Redistricting of the Lower East Side/Chinatown Area," March 1991. The proposed district included all of Chinatown down to City Hall Park on the south, the East River on the east, Center Street through Little Italy to East Houston Street, and then north again to East Fourteenth Street. It bordered on Tompkins Square Park.

36. Asians in New York voted more conservatively than Latinos. In the 1993 Giuliani–Dinkins election, Latinos voted 59 percent to 37 percent for Dinkins, whereas Asians voted 56 percent to 35 percent for Giuliani.

37. The incumbent, Carol Greitzer, submitted her recommendations for the district boundaries in May 1991. It contained a multiethnic, Asian/Latino district centered in the Lower East Side and Chinatown and a predominantly white Lower West Side district stretching from Battery Park on the south to Forty-fourth Street on the north. In the end, Greitzer moved into another district and sought reelection there. She was defeated.

38. In a sense, creating two council districts, one to be dominated by gays and the other by Asians, by splitting Thompson Street, the center of older Little Italy, signaled the end of Italian American power in Manhattan, almost thirty years after the defeat of Carmine DeSapio, the Democratic Leader, by a young Ed Koch.

39. The district was 39 percent Asian American when measured by voter age population (VAP). Overall, it could be termed a "majority-minority" district: 60 percent minority—Asian, Latino, and a black middle class in the high risers adjacent to the financial district. Unfortunately, however, the actual number of registered Asian voters in the district was only about 19 percent, since so many were not citizens and others did not have a long tradition of activism in local politics.

40. Norimitso Onishi, "Jackson Heights: In a Gay Haven, a Sense of Community Builds," *New York Times*, Sunday, December 4, 1994, *The City* section, p. 9.

41. John Mollenkopf, "The Wagner Atlas: New York City Politics, 1989" (Ph.D. program in political science, CUNY Graduate Center, June 1989, mimeographed).

42. Onishi, "Jackson Heights."

43. In a breakfast meeting with influential lesbian and gay advocates and representa-

tives of service organizations, Lisa was widely criticized. His opinions were generally disregarded by those who had spend several years in HIV prevention and service programs.

44. Mollenkopf, "The Wagner Atlas."

45. Interview with George Waffle, Lambda Independent Democrats, December 6, 1994, New York City.

46. Ibid.

47. New York City Districting Commission, *Final Plan*, June 3, 1991.

48. Reed, "Of Boroughs, Boundaries and Bullwinkles," 767.

49. Lani Guinier, "The Representation of Minority Interest: The Question of Single-Member Districts," *Cardozo Law Review* 14 (1993): 1169. She cites *Holt Civic Club v. City of Tuscaloosa*, 439 U.S. 60 (1978) to support the statement.

50. Susan MacManus, "City Council Election Procedures and Minority Representation: Are They Related?" *Social Science Quarterly* 59 (1978): 153.

51. Karlan, "Maps and Misreadings."

52. See Susan Welch, "The Impact of At-Large Elections on the Representation of Blacks and Hispanics," *Journal of Politics* 52 (1990): 1050.

53. *Shaw v. Reno*, 113 S. Ct., 2816 (1993); *Johnson v. Miller*, 115 S. Ct., 2475, 2504 (1995); *Shaw v. Hunt*, 116 S. Ct., 1894 (1996).

54. *Butts v. City of New York*, 779, F.2d at 144–45.

55. Pamela Karlan, "Undoing the Right Thing: Single Member Offices and the Voting Rights Act," *Virginia Law Review* 77 (1991): 23.

56. *Johnson v. DeGrandy*, 114 S. Ct., 2647 (1994).

57. Joseph P. Viteritti, "Unapportioned Justice: Local Elections, Social Science and the Evolution of the Voting Rights Act," *Cornell Journal of Law and Public Policy* 4 (1994): 244–47.

58. *Vega v. City of Alamogordo*, D.C. N.Mex. (1987).

59. *Cane v. Worcester County*, 847 F. Supp. 396.

60. Viteritti, "Unapportioned Justice," 260–64.

61. Cain, "Voting Rights and Democratic Theory: Toward a Color-Blind Society."

62. Lani Guinier, *The Tyranny of the Majority: Fundamental Fairness in Representative Democracy* (New York: Free Press, 1994), 152.

63. Bernard Grofman, "Would Vince Lombardi Have Been Right If He Had Said: 'When It Comes to Redistricting, Race Isn't Everything, It's the Only Thing'?" *Cardozo Law Review*, April 1993, 1271.

64. For the economic model of voting, the issue is simpler: Voting outcomes are conceived as the solution to a set of simultaneous equations describing an array of differential preference scales in which the variables include the full set of preferences and the full set of voters. In this case, geography becomes the boundary of the game in two ways. First, its boundaries limit the number of participants in the game, and second, some overriding characteristic(s) can be associated with the "political space" in the geographic boundary. In this view of representative systems, the singularity of the individ-

ual is purely atomistic and mechanical and leaves no notion of community except mathematical associations—at best—in the geographical bounds. The problematization of space is not a direct challenge to the model, since neither community nor identity is the basis of its understanding of the vote.

65. Richard Briffault, consultant to the Districting Commission, to Alan Gartner, executive director, New York City Districting Commission, "A Short History of the Reapportionment of the City Council," June 27, 1990, p. 1. The election of two Communists was a major influence on eliminating proportional representation. See Wallace Sayre and Herbert Kaufman, *Governing New York City: Politics in the Metropolis* (New York: Russell Sage Foundation, 1960).

CHAPTER 9

1. See Leonard I. Ruchelman, *Police Politics: A Comparative Study of Three Cities* (Cambridge, Mass.: Ballinger, 1974); and Leonard I. Ruchelman, ed., *Who Rules the Police?* (New York: New York University Press, 1973). In his concluding essay in the second book, Ruchelman specifically refers to the strength of what he refers to as the (Mayor William) Tate–(Commissioner Frank) Rizzo–Fraternal Order of Police (FOP) coalition. Regarding mayoral-commissioner relations in Philadelphia in the 1970s, Ruchelman concluded: "Contrary to the New York City experience . . . the Mayor of Philadelphia has felt no need to promulgate a chief-executive theory of police supervision" (261).

2. Pennsylvania Crime Commission, *Report on Police Corruption and the Quality of Law Enforcement in Philadelphia* (Philadelphia: Pennsylvania Crime Commission, March 1974); President's Commission on Law Enforcement and Administration of Justice/University of California, School of Criminology, *The Police and the Community: The Dynamics of Their Relationship in a Changing Society* (Washington, D.C.: U.S. Government Printing Office, 1966), field surveys 4.

3. John Anderson, *Burning down the House: MOVE and the Tragedy of Philadelphia* (New York: Norton, 1987); Philadelphia Special Investigation Commission, *The Findings, Conclusions and Recommendations of the Philadelphia Special Investigation Commission* (Philadelphia: City of Philadelphia/Philadelphia Special Investigation Commission, March 6, 1986); and Hizkias Assefa and Paul Wahrhaftig, *The MOVE Crisis in Philadelphia: Extremist Groups and Conflict Resolution* (Pittsburgh: University of Pittsburgh Press, 1990).

4. City of Philadelphia, Commission on Human Relations, "Public Hearing on Unconventional Sexual Orientation, June 3 and 5, 1974," City Hall Annex, Philadelphia.

5. Jane Fischer, "In 1974, Furor over Homosexuals; Now, Hardly a Ripple in Council," *Philadelphia Inquirer*, August 1, 1982, F1.

6. S. A. Paolantonio, *Frank Rizzo: The Last Big Man in Big City America* (Philadelphia: Camino Books, 1993), 66–67; and Mark Stein, "City of Brotherly and Sisterly

Loves: The Making of Lesbian and Gay Movements in Greater Philadelphia: 1948–1972" (UMI reprint, Ph.D. diss., University of Pennsylvania, 1994), 154–208.

7. Stein, "City of Brotherly and Sisterly Loves," 292–93.

8. Interview with Tommi Avicolla-Mecca, August 1996, San Francisco.

9. Harold Jacobs, "Decoy Enforcement of Homosexual Laws," *University of Pennsylvania Law Review* 112 (1963): 259.

10. Note, "Pennsylvania's New Sex Crime Law," *University of Pennsylvania Law Review* 100 (1952): 728–34. The *Review* cites the penalties associated with sodomy and solicitation to commit sodomy as $5,000 or ten years, and $1,000 or five years, respectively. Both were categorized as felonies. The law legislated the sanction for rape, a felony, as only $2,000 or five years, less than the maximum sentence for conviction on a sodomy charge.

11. John A. DeMay, "The Pennsylvania Sex Crimes Act," *University of Pittsburgh Law Review* 13 (1952): 740.

12. Jacobs, "Decoy Enforcement of Homosexual Laws," 259–70.

13. Interview with Thomas Gibbons Jr., police reporter, *Philadelphia Inquirer,* the Roundhouse (Philadelphia Police Department headquarters), Philadelphia, August 14, 1996. Gibbons worked for the *Evening Bulletin* in the 1970s.

14. See Gregory M. Herek and Kevin T. Berrill, *Hate Crimes: Confronting Violence Against Lesbians and Gay Men* (Newbury Park, Calif.: Sage, 1992); Gary David Comstock, *Violence Against Lesbians and Gay Men* (New York: Columbia University Press, 1991); and Gregory M. Herek, J. Roy Gillis, and Jeannie C. Cogan, "Hate Crime Victimization Among Lesbian, Gay, and Bisexual Adults: Prevalence, Psychological Correlates, and Methodological Issues," *Journal of Interpersonal Violence,* April 1997, 195–215.

15. Pennsylvania Crime Commission, *Report on Police Corruption,* 1.

16. Ibid., 20.

17. Ibid., 17.

18. Ibid., 445.

19. Paolantonio, *Frank Rizzo,* 136.

20. Pennsylvania Crime Commission, *Report on Police Corruption,* 216–19.

21. Ibid., 398.

22. Ibid., 729–30.

23. W. Wilson Goode with Joann Stevens, *In Goode Faith* (Valley Forge, Pa.: Judson Press, 1992), 149.

24. An example of these insulting police procedures was the routine intervention of a mental health professional if a gay person was arrested for a crime and stated that he or she were homosexual. Many saw this as an affront.

25. Minutes, Police-Gay Community Relations Committee, August 14, 1980. The minutes of these meetings were taken by Tommi Avicolla-Mecca, a reporter for the *Philadelphia Gay News.* They are on file at the Gay, Lesbian, Bisexual & Transgendered

Library/Archives of Philadelphia's William Way Community Center, 201 South Camac Street, Philadelphia.

26. Ibid.

27. Minutes, Police-Gay Community Relations Committee, September 9, 1980.

28. *Philadelphia Daily News*, August 7, 1980, 4. This made Solomon something of a hero in the lesbian and gay community.

29. Scott Giordano, "Out in Blue," *Philadelphia Gay News*, July 26–August 1, 1996, 1.

30. Interview with Lieutenant Don Jirak, New York Police Department, and an officer in GOAL, the Gay Officers Action League of New York City. June 1996, New York.

31. "Neighborhoods in Brief Profile," *Philadelphia Inquirer*, December 18, 1983, L1.

32. November 15–21, 1983, 16.

33. Mark Bowden, "Part I–A Whorehouse Owner Seeks Revenge," *Philadelphia Inquirer Magazine*, Sunday, July 1, 1984, 16.

34. Tim Weiner, *Philadelphia Inquirer*, April 9, 1985, p. B8.

35. Pennsylvania Crime Commission, *Report on Police Corruption*.

36. MOVE was an African American–identified, antiurban, proenvironment movement that had had serious confrontations with police since the beginning of the 1970s. It should be noted that MOVE's "all-natural" philosophy made it virulently homophobic. In 1975, John Africa, who died in the 1985 fire, testified before the city's Commission on Human Rights, in very strong language, against establishing a gay rights ordinance.

37. There had been another serious incident before the 1985 attack on the MOVE headquarters. In 1979, a police officer was killed and half-dozen residents and officers were injured in a shoot-out on MOVE's headquarters. One lasting effect of the 1979 incident was acute suspicion between the police and MOVE. See Assefa and Wahrhaftig, *The MOVE Crisis in Philadelphia*, 9–18.

38. Goode, *In Goode Faith*, 202–6.

39. Ibid., 257–58.

40. Marc Kaufman, "Harassment Persist, Gay Task Force Reports," *Philadelphia Inquirer*, January 28, 1986, B1. The survey techniques resulted in a heavily white, educated, and middle-class sample and thus is not representative of Philadelphia's population in general.

41. Rita Addessa, "Summary of Policy and Program Recommendations: Status Report for Evaluation Purposes: 1986–1995" (Philadelphia: Philadelphia Lesbian and Gay Task Force, January 1996).

42. Rita Addessa, "Summary of Meetings and Correspondence with the Police Department," Philadelphia Lesbian and Gay Task Force, August 22, 1992.

43. Larry Gross and Steven Aurand, with Rita Addessa, Kathryn Furano, Andrew London, and Judith Porter, "Discrimination and Violence Against Lesbian Women and Gay Men in Philadelphia and the Commonwealth of Pennsylvania," report of the Philadelphia Lesbian and Gay Task Force (Philadelphia: PLGTF, September 1992, mimeographed).

44. Christopher Hepp, "A Sign of Hope for Police Reform: Proposals in Scathing Report Gain Widespread Support," *Philadelphia Inquirer*, March 15, 1997, A1.

45. Christopher Hepp, "Police Hire Professor as a Consultant," *Philadelphia Inquirer*, September 3, 1987, B4.

46. Edward Colimore, "Tucker: Focus on Crimes Aimed at Minority Victims," *Philadelphia Inquirer*, June 18, 1987, B1.

47. Dick Pothier, "Officer Is Charged in Anti-Gay Attack," *Philadelphia Inquirer*, May 19, 1987, B3.

48. *Philadelphia Daily News*, September 2, 1988, 17.

49. Dave Racher, "Cleared Ex-Policeman Wants Job Back," *Philadelphia Daily News*, March 29, 1989, 8.

50. Mark Bowden, Mark Fazlollah, Richard Jones, and Daniel Rubin, "Major Offenses by Philadelphia Cops Often Bring Minor Punishments," *Philadelphia Inquirer*, November 25, 1995.

51. "Report of the Advisory Group to Police Commissioner Willie L. Williams on the September 12, 1991, Confrontation Between Police and Demonstrators," 5–6.

52. Ibid., 28–29.

53. "Executive Summary of the Philadelphia Police Departments's Internal Affairs Division's Investigation into the Presidential Visit of September 12, 1991," March 16, 1993, 10.

54. Ibid., 6.

55. Settlement and Consent Decree, *ACT-UP et al. v. City of Philadelphia et al.* (Eastern District, Pa., February 25, 1992).

56. Interview with Stephen Presser, American Civil Liberties Union of Pennsylvania, August 24, 1996, Philadelphia.

57. The coalition was founded in 1985, after the MOVE confrontation, but faded when Tucker was appointed in 1986. Now it has been revitalized and expanded to include twenty-four neighborhood, community, legal, and religious groups. See Jeff Gammage, "Civic Coalition Urging Permanent Police Review Board," *Philadelphia Inquirer*, July 29, 1992, B1.

58. Jeff Gammage, "Rendell Says No to Police Oversight," *Philadelphia Inquirer*, July 31, 1992.

59. Doreen Carvajal and Jeff Gammage, "Council Backs Civilian Review of Police," *Philadelphia Inquirer*, May 21, 1993, A1.

60. John W. Meyer and W. Richard Scott, "Centralization and Legitimacy Problems of Local Government," in John W. Meyer and W. Richard Scott, eds., *Organizational Environments: Ritual and Rationality* (Newbury Park, Calif.: Sage, 1992), 201.

61. Stephen Leinin, *Gay Cops* (New Brunswick, N.J.: Rutgers University Press, 1993); Angelique C. Praat and Keith F. Tuffin, "Police Discourses of Homosexual Men in New Zealand," *Journal of Homosexuality* 31, no. 4 (1996), 57–73.

62. Interview, Kevin Vaughn, Chair, Philadelphia Human Rights Commission, 1996.

CHAPTER 10

1. See Stephen Elkin, *City and Regime in the American Republic* (Chicago: University of Chicago Press, 1987).

2. J. David Greenstone and Paul E. Peterson, *Race and Authority in Urban Politics* (Chicago: University of Chicago Press, 1974).

3. Adolph Reed, "The Black Urban Regime: Structural Origin and Constraints," in M. Smith, ed., *Power, Community and the City* (New Brunswick, N.J.: Rutgers University Press, 1988).

4. Lynn M. Appleton, "Gender Regimes of American Cities," in Judith A. Garber and Robyne S. Turner, eds., *Gender in Urban Research* (Thousand Oaks, Calif.: Sage, 1995).

5. Harrison White, *Identity and Control: A Structural Theory of Action* (Princeton, N.J.: Princeton University Press, 1993), 293.

6. Chester Hartman, *The Transformation of San Francisco* (Towtowa, N.J.: Rowan and Allanshield, 1984), 11–34.

7. Susan I. Fainstein, Norman Fainstein, and P. Jefferson Armistead, "San Francisco: Urban Transformation and the Local State," in Susan I. Fainstein et al., eds., *Restructuring the City: Political Economy of Urban Redevelopment* (New York: Longman, 1984).

8. Ibid.

9. Frederick Wirt, *Power in the City: Decision Making in San Francisco* (Berkeley and Los Angeles: University of California Press, 1974).

10. Manuel Castells and Karen Murphy, "Cultural Identity and Urban Structure: The Spatial Organization of San Francisco's Gay Community," in Susan I. Fainstein and Norman Fainstein, eds., *Urban Policy Under Capitalism* (Beverly Hills, Calif.: Sage, 1982).

11. Randy Shilts, *The Mayor of Castro Street* (New York: St. Martin's Press, 1982), 58–59.

12. Castells and Murphy, "Cultural Identity and Urban Structure," 153–54.

13. See Shilts, *The Mayor of Castro Street.*

14. Richard DeLeon, *Left Coast City: Progressive Politics in San Francisco, 1975–1991* (Lawrence: University of Kansas Press, 1992).

15. Institute for Labor and Economic Growth, *Grassroots Politics in the 1980s: A Case Study* (San Francisco: Synthesis, 1982), 79.

16. Paul H. Sedgway, "San Francisco Downtown Plan: Office Boom Brings Housing Boom," in Dwight Merriam, David Brower, and Philip Tegeler, eds., *Inclusionary Zoning Moves Downtown* (Washington, D.C.: Planners Press, 1985), 163.

17. DeLeon, *Left Coast City*, 78–82. His definition of socioeconomic status is in both the text and the technical addenda.

18. To DeLeon, gay precincts are those with a large number of single-male or male-male households between the ages of twenty-five and forty (ibid., 178).

19. David Binder, telephone poll conducted August 9–22, 1989.

20. Displaying a chi square of 13.29 (minimum expected frequency of 47.28) significance at <.001.

21. No other demographic group demonstrated sufficient coherence or numbers to meet a test of significance at greater than .05. Income, a dummy variable for single heterosexual men, and housing tenancy came closest.

22. Interview with Melinda Paras, May 1994, San Francisco.

23. The poll of four hundred likely voters was conducted by Moore Methods of Sacramento, on behalf of the prostadium campaign and reported by the *San Francisco Chronicle*, November 2, 1989.

24. Interview with T. J. Anthony, May 1994, San Francisco.

25. Catellus (the new name for Sante Fe development) also agreed to yet another downsizing of the office space projections thus requiring a small exemption, and to build the amend market the space in competition with suburban "back office" type of projects rather then competing with downtown "prestige office space." San Francisco *Chronicle*, December 6, 1990.

26. A weak economy in banking and finance along with the credit crunch again left a glut of office space in San Francisco in the Spring of 1993. Ironically, the rejection of the larger commercial project saved Catellus money and made the entire project more viable financially. San Francisco *Chronicle*, March 22, 1993.

27. San Francisco *Chronicle*, February 26, 1991.

28. DeLeon, *Left Coast City*, 34–37.

29. San Francisco Unified School District, *District and School Profiles: 1991–1992*, February 1992.

30. San Francisco Unified School District, Department of Integration, May 1992.

31. *Lau v. Nichols*, 414 U.S. 565 (1974), filed in March 1970 in U.S. District Court for Northern California.

32. Rosemary Salomone, *Equal Education Under Law: Legal Rights and Federal Policy* (New York: St. Martin's Press, 1986), 98–102.

33. David Kirp, *Just Schools op.cit.* p.114.

34. David Kirp, *op.cit.*, pp.115. Initial cite, "Report of the Citizens Task Force on Bi-Lingual Education," San Francisco United School District, January 21, 1975.

35. Dorothy Waggoner, "School Holding Power in the United States," in *Theory, Research and Applications: Selected Papers from the Annual Meeting of the National Association for Bilingual Education*, vol. 16 (Denver: NABE, 1987).

36. Los Angeles County Commission on Human Relations, "Intergroup Conflict in Los Angeles County Schools," report on a survey of hate crimes (October 1989, mimeographed).

37. See Scott L. Hershberger and Anthony R. D'Angelli, "The Impact of Victimization on the Mental Health and Suicidality of Lesbian, Gay, and Bisexual Youth," *Developmental Psychology*, January 1995, 65–74.

38. Gilbert Herdt, "Gay and Lesbian Youths: Emergent Identities and Culture

Scene at Home and Abroad," in Gilbert Herdt, ed., *Gay and Lesbian Youth* (Bingham-ton, N.Y.: Harrington Park Press, 1989).

39. In some cases, adolescents could not even turn to school staff for assistance, since many lesbian and gay teachers and staff were torn between a professional obligation to state their sexuality and the equally professional concern about appearing to politicize their professions. See John Sears, "Educators, Homosexuality, and Homosexual Stu-dents: Are Personal Feelings Related to Personal Beliefs?" in Karen Harbeck, ed., *Com-ing Out of the Classroom Closet: Gay and Lesbian Students, Teachers and Curricula* (Bing-hamton, N.Y.: Harrington Park Press, 1992), 29.

40. Janet H. Fontaine and Nancy L. Hammond, "Counseling Issues with Gay and Lesbian Adolescents," *Adolescence* 31 (Winter 1996):817–30.

41. The San Francisco *Independent,* April 1990.

42. Their aggressiveness put off devotees of the older, coalition politics that Milk and Britt had pursued. Myna Kopf, for example, who was the senior person on the Board and who had supported gay issues through most of her career was suddenly being cast as indifferent to gay issues: "I knew Harvey Milk. He wanted to build coalitions with people . . . and fought for privacy. The new gay leaders seem to be interested only in their agenda." Personal Interview, January 1994, San Francisco.

43. Telephone interview with Tom Ammiano, April 1994, San Francisco.

44. He also was a professional stand-up comedian in the comedy club circuit in California.

45. See John Chubb and Terence Moe, *Politics, Markets and America's Schools* (Wash-ington, D.C.: Brookings Institution, 1990). One of this book's central points is the lack of accountability to families, politics, or even elected school boards. Also see Joseph P. Viteretti, *Across the River* (New York: Holmes & Meier, 1983).

46. Paul E. Peterson, *The Politics of School Reform: 1870–1940* (Chicago: University of Chicago Press, 1985); and David Tyack, *Managers of Virtue: Public School Leadership in America, 1820–1980* (New York: Basic Books, 1982), and *The One Best System: A His-tory of American Urban Education* (Cambridge, Mass.: Harvard University Press, 1974).

47. Twentieth Century Report, *Facing the Challenge: Twentieth Century Report on School Governance* (New York: Twentieth Century Fund Press, 1992).

48. G. Hess, *School Restructuring Chicago Style* (Newbury Park, Calif.: Corwin/ Sage, 1991).

49. DeLeon used a multivariate analysis based on an inferential approach to cate-gorically defined precincts.

50. DeLeon, *Left Coast City,* 92–93.

51. Ibid., 193, n. 83.

52. David Binder, August 1989.

53. Ibid.

54. *San Francisco Chronicle,* January 1, 1991.

55. *San Francisco Chronicle,* August 30, 1991.

56. David Binder Associates, preelection telephone poll.

57. David Binder Associates, exit poll, November 1991.

CHAPTER 11

1. J. David Greenstone and Paul E. Peterson, *Race and Authority in Urban Politics* (Chicago: University of Chicago Press, 1974), 100.

2. When analyzing the impact of the Community Action Program, Greenstone and Peterson write: "The question can best be clarified by distinguishing between the vesting and institutionalization of interests. Although black inclusive regimes existed in Detroit and New York in the late 1960s, they were still very poorly institutionalized. And the capacity of such regimes to survive changes in leadership remained doubtful even as late as 1971" (ibid., 292).

3. Mark Granovetter, "Economic Action and Social Structure: The Problem of Embeddedness," *American Journal of Sociology* 91, no. 3 (1985): 48.

4. Ibid., 481.

5. Walter Powell, "Neither Market or Hierarchy: Network Forms of Organization," *Research in Organizational Behavior* 12 (1990): 295–336.

6. See Brian Uzzi, "The Sources and Consequences of Embeddedness for the Economic Performance of Organizations: The Network Effect," *American Sociological Review*, August 1996, 674–98.

7. See Werner Raub and Jeron Weesie, "Reputation and Efficiency in Social Interaction: An Example of Network Effects," *American Journal of Sociology* 96, no. 3 (1990): 626; Brian Uzzi, "Interfirm Networks and the Paradox of Embeddedness: Social Structure and Economic Action in New York's Apparel Industry," *Administrative Science Quarterly*, March 1997, 35–67; and Roger Waldinger, "The 'Other Side' of Embeddedness: A Case-Study of the Inter-play of Economy and Ethnicity," *Ethnic and Racial Studies* 18, no. 3 (1995).

8. Mark Granovetter, "The Importance of Weak Ties," *American Journal of Sociology* 78, no. 6 (1973): 1360–80.

9. Uzzi, "The Sources and Consequences of Embeddedness."

10. Sharon Zukin and Paul DiMaggio, eds., introduction to *Structures of Capital: The Social Organization of the Economy* (Cambridge: Cambridge University Press, 1990), 17–18.

11. John Echeverri-Gent, "Between Autonomy and Capture: Embedding Government Agencies in the Societal Environment," *Policy Studies Journal* 20, no. 3 (1992): 343.

12. Ibid., 359.

13. Charles Taylor, The Politics of Recognition," in Amy Gutman, ed., *Multiculturalism* (Princeton, N.J.: Princeton University Press, 1994), 25–73.

14. Harrison White, *Identity and Control: A Structural Theory of Action* (Princeton, N.J.: Princeton University Press, 1993), 226–29.

15. See Albert Karnig and Susan Welch, *Black Representation and Urban Policy* (Chicago: University of Chicago Press, 1980), 150–52; and Dona Cooper Hamilton and Charles V. Hamilton, *The Dual Agenda: The African-American Struggle for Civil and Economic Equality* (New York: Columbia University Press, 1997).

16. Clarence Stone, *Regime Politics: Governing Atlanta, 1946–1988* (Lawrence: University of Kansas Press, 1989), 4.

17. Ibid., 230–31.

18. Stephen Elkin, *City and Regime in the American Republic* (Chicago: University of Chicago Press, 1987), 105–7.

CHAPTER 12

1. See Harrison White, *Identity and Control: A Structural Theory of Action* (Princeton, N.J.: Princeton University Press, 1993), 196–207.

2. See Mark Schneider, *The Competitive City: The Political Economy of Suburbia* (Pittsburgh: University of Pittsburgh Press, 1989).

3. This is the essence of Martin Shefter's book on New York City, *Political Crisis/Fiscal Crisis: The Collapse and Revival of New York City* (New York: Columbia University Press, 1993).

4. Richard A. Musgrave and Peggy Musgrave, *Public Finance in Theory and Practice* (New York: McGraw-Hill, 1984).

5. Mark Granovetter, "Economic Action and Social Structure: The Problem of Embeddedness," *American Journal of Sociology* 91, no. 3 (1985): 506.

6. Akbar Ahmed, *Postmodernism and Islam: Predicament and Promise* (London: Routledge, 1992), 13–123, quote on p. 21.

7. Douglas Yates, The Ungovernable City (Cambridge, MA: MIT Press, 1975).

8. Todd Gitlin, *The Twilight of Common Dreams: Why America Is Racked by Culture Wars* (New York: Holt, 1995).

9. John Dewey, *The Public and Its Purpose* (Chicago: Swallow Press, 1954).

INDEX

⋮⋮⋮